CROSSING BOUNDARIES

A Theory and History of Essay Writing in German, 1680–1815

CROSSING BOUNDARIES

A Theory and History of
Essay Writing in German, 1680–1815

JOHN A. McCARTHY

UNIVERSITY OF PENNSYLVANIA PRESS

Philadelphia

Library of Congress Cataloging-in-Publication Data

McCarthy, John A. (John Aloysius), 1942-
    Crossing boundaries : a theory and history of essay writing in
German, 1680–1815 / John A. McCarthy.
        p.   cm.
    Bibliography: p.
    Includes index.
    ISBN 0-8122-8148-9
    1. German essays—History and criticism.   2. Essay.   3. German
prose literature—Early modern, 1500–1700—History and criticism.
4. German prose literature—18th century—History and criticism.
5. German prose literature—19th century—History and criticism.
6. Enlightenment.   7. Germany—Intellectual life—18th century.
I. Title.
PT717.M39   1989
834'.5'09—dc19   88-26834
                                                                      CIP

The theory of books is noble. The scholar of the first age received into him the world around; brooded thereon; gave it the new arrangement of his own mind, and uttered it again. It came into him life; it went out from him truth. It came to him short-lived actions; it went out from him immortal thoughts. It came to him business; it went from him poetry. It was dead fact; now it is quick thought. It can stand, and it can go. It now endures, it now flies, it now inspires. Precisely in proportion to the depth of mind from which it issued, so high does it soar, so long does it sing.

Undoubtedly there is a right way of reading.

There is then creative reading as well as creative writing.

> Ralph Waldo Emerson,
> "The American Scholar" (1837)

CONTENTS

Preface

The objective of this study is to examine the interrelationship of eighteenth-century Enlightenment and the kind of writing commonly known as the essay. Each topic by itself is perplexingly multifaceted and fascinatingly elusive. In conjunction they pose a challenge to traditional modes of thinking about the nature of literature and its many extra-literary dimensions. *Crossing Boundaries* is designed as an original contribution to the theory and history of the so-called essay from its birth to its first full flowering in the German language.

My approach is informed by two dominant sources of inspiration. The first derives from the twentieth-century debate among literary theorists on the nature of reading and writing. That first impulse has enhanced our general awareness of the dynamic character of *écriture* as a literary event, while underscoring the need to expand the traditional canon on the one hand and to revise genre theory on the other. The second source of inspiration is the current reevaluation among intellectual historians of the true nature of the eighteenth-century Enlightenment. Those efforts have demonstrated to what degree the twentieth century has misinterpreted the original phenomenon. Thus my study straddles at least two disciplinary boundaries and extends perhaps even further.

The thesis of this study, simply put, is that the essay—that enigmatic and elusive genre which seems to defy definition—is best understood or grasped in terms of literature as event and enlightenment as process. In order to illustrate this thesis, I focus on those new intellectual and social factors between 1680 and 1815 that led to the emergence and first flowering of the innovative mode of writing commonly referred to as the essay. Consequently, I am equally concerned with literary history. Finally, we must consider the rise of the essay in the Age of Reason as equally contingent upon the rapidly changing social conditions of the eighteenth century which made possible a new class of professional writer. In effect, this investigation draws upon recent developments in four fields of inquiry: literary theory, intellectual history, literary history, and social history.

In an effort to do justice to these many claims on the literary historian's attention, I am guided in my query by several questions. For instance, what distinguishes the essay from other literary forms? Is it appropriate to speak of this difference in formalistic or descriptive terms? Does the essay constitute a separate genre? What is essayism and how does it differ from the essay? Might it be advisable to revise and expand the canonical triad of the epic, dramatic, and lyric by establishing a fourth category of writing that would account for the essay and its related forms? What is the nature of Enlightenment? What are its characteristics, and how does it relate to essayistic writing? In short, by raising these questions I add my voice to the ongoing debate regarding the notion of a fixed canon and of a triadic generic scheme.

Essential to this undertaking is the framework of eighteenth-century thought which occasioned a critical reexamination of the categories of knowledge and of the means for disseminating information. In the realm of literature it saw the emergence of a number of new modes of writing (e.g., autobiography, journalism, satire, diary novel, and nature poetry). One of the most experimental was essayistic writing. As such it is the clearest reflection of the dialectic interplay among thinking, writing, and reading, all of which are executed in a creative way. Unlike those new writing styles discussed by Jürgen Jacobs (*Prosa der Aufklärung*, 1976), the essayistic mode is most closely related to the *method* of Enlightenment philosophy.

What, my reader can legitimately ask, are the expected benefits of my undertaking? Literature is essentially an expression of the human drive for communication. The objective of communication is to explain, persuade, and ultimately to move the other (i.e., an interlocutor) to action. Just as life is in a state of constant flux, so too is the literary process. Motion begets motion, which in turn begets more motion. By highlighting the interactive nature of literature, I expect to clarify the intimate relationship between the innovative philosophical thinking of the Enlightenment and the rise of a new literary mode in Germany to a position of dominance within the field of literature. On the other hand, I expect to relate the emergence of essayistic writing to the material conditions that helped shape the quality of literary life in the eighteenth century, e.g., the revolution of print, various kinds of publishing activities, the greater incidence of journalism and aesthetic criticism, and the rapid expansion of the reading public. Jürgen Habermas's *Theorie des kommunikativen Handelns* (*Theory of Communicative Action*, 1985) provides a salient theoretical framework for these considerations.

In delving into the nature and interrelationship of Enlightenment and essay writing, I found it fruitful to investigate several related issues. One was the need to depict the role of classical rhetoric as midwife in the creation of the new writing stance (which I designate as essayism or essayistic writing). Another was the relevance of the current literary debate for defining essayism. Aspects of that continuing debate include reader-response theory, genre criticism, the notion of boundary genres, the value of literature, affective stylistics, and a communicative theory of literature.

A third issue was dictated by a common, yet erroneous assumption in essay research: the perception that the German essay did not evolve until after 1750 and then only in response to contemporary eighteenth-century French and British models. That view requires revision. The misperception is understandable given Friedrich Schlegel's high praise of Lessing's critical writings as marking the beginning of a new "combinatory method" of proceeding. That method is informed not only by logic but also by poetic imagination. I argue that there was a native tradition derived from Enlightened skepticism. Fourthly, I have long felt that literary theory and textual analysis should be joined together and not kept separate, as is the norm in essay research. The two realms of inquiry are combined here.

Finally, I sensed the need to free my investigation from the strictures of the usual periodization of German literary history. Thus I argue for historical continuity and against the strict categorization of literary trends. As a result my field of vision was expanded to allow for the tracing of essayistic writing as it evolved between the antipodes of Baroque and Romanticism. While I endeavor to include writers normally passed over in our literary chronicles as belletristic writers (e.g., Thomasius, Pitschel, Kant, Engel, Garve, and von der Recke), I do not intend my survey to be comprehensive or exhaustive. Thus, I expect criticism for not including clearly major writers such as Georg Lichtenberg, Georg Forster, Josef von Sonnenfels, or Jean Paul Friedrich Richter who rightfully deserve a place here. Nor will I satisfy the expectations of those who justifiably wish to enhance our consciousness of the role women writers played in the literary life of the period under investigation (e.g., Adelgunde Culmus Gottsched, Johanne Charlotte Unzer, Ernestine Hofmann, Charlotte Hezel, Sophie La Roche, Elisa von der Recke, Marianne Ehrmann, Emilia von Berlepsch, Caroline Pichler). Even in the case of those writers examined as essayists, I could not be all that detailed. Lessing, Herder, Wieland, and Goethe scholars, for example, will lament the scant attention accorded their voluminous contributions to the genre. If my work accomplishes nothing else, it should at least draw attention to the richness of a largely unexplored field of literary production.

Yet, I must stress that my objective in *Crossing Boundaries* is not to be all-encompassing or to write the definitive study of the essayistic mode in the Age of Enlightenment. I had originally planned the study as a two-volume undertaking. The first volume would have concentrated on the history of a mentality and its impact on society; the second would have offered textual analyses of a greater number of writers. I ultimately rejected that plan for methodological and practical reasons. Regardless of how excellent the end product might have been, the practical problems of finding a publisher for a two-volume manuscript would have been insurmountable. More importantly, I felt my objectives would best be served if I could encourage debate on the whole issue of essayistic writing and its genesis in the Age of Enlightenment and beyond. Rather than presenting a fully detailed portrait of the mode, I felt it to be more productive to develop a new theory of the "essay" against the backdrop of Enlightenment as process and the discussion of literature as event. With the methodology in place, I then wished to offer only a sampling of its applicability to essayistic pieces extending through several literary schools and generations. I wanted to show that the theory was equally valid for the late seventeenth as well as for the early nineteenth century. Thus, I opted for breadth. If my study is successful, others might extend my method to authors (and periods) not included in *Crossing Boundaries* or at least be moved to reconsider received notions of the essay. The book's subtitle is designed to underscore the open, exploratory nature of my approach: *A Theory and History of Essay Writing*. I wished neither to write the definitive history of early essay writing in German nor to insist dogmatically upon my theory of essayistic writing. To do so would be to contradict the manner of thinking that lies at the heart of essayism. In any event, it is clear that much work remains to be done, and it cannot all be done at once.

The complexity of my topic required a complex approach. Consequently, simple derivative thinking within an essentially diachronic framework was insufficient. We need to think in more complex relations that take into account the synchronic dimension of a given historical period as well as the development of writing modes and attitudes over a more extended period of time. The perspective must be an interdisciplinary one that does not heed the artificial boundaries separating social, literary, and intellectual historians from one another. The task was most challenging; it had to be if I were to challenge our conventional thinking on the nature of Enlightenment, essayism, and genre theory.

The dominant vectors of influence contributing to the theory and practice of writing and reading in the eighteenth century are presented in separate chapters. The introductory chapter offers a general understanding of literature as event and of the reading methodology underlying *Crossing Boundaries*. Chapter II addresses the question of attitude as a distinguishing factor in establishing generic designations and discusses pertinent aspects of the critical debate on the concepts of canon and genre in general. The chapter is designed to highlight the dynamic nature of essayistic literature from the vantage point of literary theory. Chapter III discusses the essay and related forms in light of the newly emerged importance of authorial attitude for poetic form. Chapter IV shifts the focus to Enlightenment philosophy in order to provide a different basis by which to judge the newly emerged essay as the touchstone of an innovative mode of writing and reading in the 1700 s. In Chapter V we move squarely into the realm of eighteenth-century literary life, questioning the impact of the institutionalization of the production, distribution, and reception of literature on the new way of thinking, writing, and reading.

Having traced the necessity for close active cooperation between writer and reader as seen through the eyes of the theorist, philosopher, and practitioner, I raise in Chapter VI the logical question of a philosophy of prose style in the eighteenth century appropriate to engaging writer and reader in discourse. Against the backdrop of these theoretical and historical considerations, I then analyze in Chapters VII, VIII, and IX a relatively broad sampling of essayistic writing from Baroque to Romanticism as a means of illustrating the premise of the dialectical interplay informing *Crossing Boundaries*. The Conclusion highlights my most important findings while drawing attention to some chronological problems, and tasks yet to be accomplished. The reader may, of course, read these chapters in any way s/he chooses. But their particular alignment does reflect my endeavor to orchestrate the rich modality of my topic in a logical and progressive fashion.

In pursuing this multifaceted goal, I do not have just the literary historian of German literature in mind. I also endeavor to address the legitimate expectations of the literary theorist and comparatist as well. Moreover, in order to be useful to the student as well as the specialist, the findings of this investigation should be accessible to all. Thus I strive throughout for a lucid style relatively free of jargon.

In an effort to streamline the acknowledgment of informational and inspirational sources, the first mention of a source is cited in a note, thereafter in the text itself in the most economical fashion. A selection of secondary sources informing more than one chapter are listed in a bibliography concluding the study.

One final note on the spelling of recurring terms. Whenever Enlightenment and Enlighteners are capitalized, they always refer to the historical Age of Reason. Otherwise the terms connote a metahistorical process. All translations from the German are my own unless otherwise indicated. The original German is provided only in the case of especially noteworthy passages where the reader might wish to have the original formulation. In Chapters VII through IX where I am concerned with the special qualities of German prose, I take exception to this practice. There I tend to cite the original German more frequently in the text, providing an English translation immediately in the text or in the notes when the passage becomes awkwardly long. I consistently cite the German when I wish to preserve the impact of affective stylistics in the original.

A number of people have left their mark on these pages. I would like in particular to express my gratitude to my colleagues, Frank Trommler and Albert L. Lloyd. In the early stages of this project, Trommler's critical response to my ideas and arguments helped clarify the true dimensions of *Crossing Boundaries*. Himself in great demand for writing and speaking engagements, Frank Trommler nevertheless always found the time to read the evolving chapters closely and to offer encouragement when the task seemed particularly frustrating. Equally unstinting and productive in his assistance was Albert ("Larry") Lloyd whose keen eye and finely tuned editorial skills helped remove many a blemish. Finally, I would like to acknowledge the valuable assistance of Zachary Simpson and Alison Anderson of the University of Pennsylvania Press who worked closely with me on the manuscript. If blemishes remain, the fault lies with me, not with them. To all of the above, but most especially to Mecki, Brian, Monk, and Kristin whose patience with an irritable dad and spouse assumed, at times, biblical proportions, I say, "Thank you!"

Philadelphia   JAM
August 1988

CHAPTER 1

Risk Taking:
On Reading and Enlightment

This book is about a number of boundary crossings. It endeavors to be interdisciplinary, theoretical yet practical, appreciative of the writer as well as reader roles in the "construction" of literature, receptive to the contextualities of a given work, informative for the specialist yet accessible to the novice, and—last but not least—responsive to the need for a social history of literary classifications and genres. It is, in the best sense of the word, heuristic in nature, substituting "thinking in complex relations" for "simple derivative thinking"[1] and does not seek to avoid the difficult questions involved in the systematic correlation of history and literature. The latter asks, for example, what the relationship between semiotic change and social transformation is, inquiring after the micro- and macrosociological dimensions of the correlation. Because this study wants to do a number of things, it runs the risk of losing a clear-cut focus. But the promised gain via its interdisciplinary approach in understanding the multiform diachronic and synchronic relationships between a system of writing and reading and its concomitant social system(s) is such that it is worth the risk-taking.[2]

Ralph Waldo Emerson's (1803–82) famous lecture on "The American Scholar" delivered at Harvard University in 1837 is a most suitable introduction to my present purposes. A classic essay in its own right, "The American Scholar" also addresses itself to the essential quality of essayistic writing regardless of national heritage. The passage cited from that lecture serves as the motto for my investigation because it is a succinct definition of the nature and purpose of the kind of writing that figures predominantly in the following pages. The essay—or rather the *nature and purpose of essayistic writing*—is used to illustrate the quality of truly innovative writing in the eighteenth century.

Drawing on the intellectual advances of the eighteenth century, Emerson highlights the primary duty of humankind: *to think*. He envisions thinking as a dynamic and continuing process that—resultant from an external act—leads inevitably to further action. Against the perceived tendency of his own era toward the "gradual domestication of the idea of Culture" with its incumbent professional compartmentalization and erection of disciplinary boundaries, he speaks of the scholar as the individual delegated by society to be the intellect.[3] In his proper function, we read, the scholar is "*Man Thinking*"; but in the degenerated state the scholar is only a truncated part of the whole and is reduced to the status of "a mere thinker," or still worse, he becomes "the parrot of other men's thinking" (46).

In order to keep in touch with the whole of society, in order to remain a complete human being, thinking man must cultivate the capacity for critical thought. S/he must guard against the temptation of passivity. Books represent the activity of thinking, Emerson argues, and must therefore be viewed as vital action and not as a torpid body of knowledge. If we abstract books from the living world and enshrine them in bookcases treating them as venerable objects for admiration, we miss their point (49). In other words, we misunderstand the nature of writing and reading as creative processes, as boundary crossings.

For at least the past forty years the intense debate on the nature and function of literature has given rise to a plethora of schools and methodologies, each vying with the other for dominance in the Academy. In some instances the language of criticism has evolved into an arcane metalanguage understood only by the select few. Frequently the complaint is heard that literature and literary history have been rejected as inferior to theorizing *about* literature, that there is no interest in reading the primary literature itself, only in studying the metaliterature. The present analysis is intended as a contribution to the ongoing debate regarding literature and metaliterature.

My focus in *Crossing Boundaries* is neither the (literary) text by itself, nor the reader by him or herself. Neither the artifact by itself nor the recipient alone nor even both in conjunction can account wholly for the literary event. Those two components of the literary act must be augmented by others; for example, the writer, the tradition of the writing mode selected, the historical circumstances surrounding the writing. The writer is central because s/he encodes the text with historical circumstances and with authorial intent. The history of genres and types is important because it raises certain expectations on the part of both writer and reader as to the *modus operandi* of any given genre or type in a given age. The object of scrutiny in *Crossing Boundaries* is, therefore, the multifaceted *nexus* of writer, reader, and text in the (re-)production of a literary work.

Additionally, the special relationship between creative writing, creative reading, and the process of enlightenment in the Age of Reason figures centrally in the various stages of this study. The reason for concentrating on the eighteenth century has to do with that age's special emphasis on the need to cultivate the human mind and heart to perfection. In pursuit of that objective the Enlightenment recognized no limits to critical inquiry. Boundaries between theory and practice, science and poetry, anthropology and theology, private and public life, convention and innovation, morality and politics were dismantled. Moreover, to the twentieth-century observer the Enlightenment represents a cultural and intellectual watershed from which the present flows.

To illustrate the integration of all these elements in the most propitious and economical manner, the genesis of the early modern German essay is used as a paradigm of the new strategies. The essay seems best suited to this purpose because it bridges the gap between the systematization of scientific information, the searching inquisitiveness of philosophy, and the innovative expression of the aesthetic experience. Since science and art form the two energizing poles of intellectual movement in life, the choice of the essay for study seems optimal. Ralph Waldo Emerson hints at this binary structure of science and art in "The American Scholar" when he writes: "[Life] came to him business; it went from him poetry. It was dead fact; now it is quick thought" (48). A particular kind of writing and a particular kind of reading is required to transform life into enduring truth, poetry, and inspiration. Thus, Emerson's words stand at the masthead of this undertaking. German writers as diverse as Christian Thomasius, Gotthold Ephraim Lessing, and Elisa von der Recke succeeded in transforming dead fact into quick thought.

Methods of reading and writing have long occupied the Academy's attention. First formalistic elements of literary artifacts and then the discursive dimension of literature were scrutinized. Typical is George Steiner's "In a Post-Culture" (1970). There Steiner insists that new "radical" forms of writing, which are marked by "vital permeations between the exact sciences and deeply imaginative statement" be accorded greater weight in the Academy's discussions.[4] These "innovative" modes of creative writing place new demands on the reader who must now learn to read differently than is the case with the "more permanent" book. The common bond uniting these diverse writing styles is the act of writing itself (*l'écriture*). Steiner asks provocatively: "What are the relations of the act of writing with other types of action, in what ways does *l'écriture* limit or falsify the ontological freedom of language, what are the relations between the writer and the individual psyche—his own, the reader's—in the social and semantic ensemble? In what way must the new art of reading, as Heidegger would have it, be a 'hearing of that which is not in the lines?'" (170).

Signs are everywhere evident that the awareness of the complicated nature of reading and writing has begun to extend beyond the narrow confines of the Academy. That is as it should be. The widening circle of interest in the encoding and decoding activities that constitute the literary act is reflected in an incisive essay published in the *New York Times Book Review* by the novelist and critic Harold Brodkey. Brodkey's views are worthy of special mention precisely because they do reflect basic issues within the academic debate on such questions as the phenomenology of reading, structuralism, semiotics, and deconstruction. Yet he neither uses any of the jargon nor cites any of the recognized authorities. Apparently, the issue of reading and writing is too important to remain purely academic.

The opening paragraph of Brodkey's article, "Reading, the Most Dangerous Game," expresses succinctly an understanding of the reading act which informs the essential thesis of my inquiry into a theory of reading and writing in the eighteenth century. Furthermore, his ideas seem to be an elucidation of Emersonian concepts. He writes, for example: "Reading is an intimate act, perhaps more intimate than any other human act. I say that because of the prolonged (or intense) exposure of one mind to another that is involved in it, and because it is the level of mind at which feelings and hopes are dealt with by consciousness and words."[5] The implicit comparison with a love bond becomes explicit in his following lines. Yet the union and exchange of minds is far more rewarding because the intimate act of intellectual intercourse is an intense and self-reflective one which thus has the propensity to change the way the reader makes judgments. Precisely for that reason, he remarks, writing and reading are dangerous activities. Writer and reader become partners in an activity; they assume a responsibility in entering the bond that affects not just the one but also the other. Reading and writing, therefore, are—or at least should be—serious business.

Writing that has the forcefulness to alter perspectives and attitudes abides by the principle of exteriority, as the process has come to be known in Foucaultian terms. It leads the reader into the text and back out again. Such writing has an inner truth and logic bearing on human concerns; it thus betrays a moral stance. It must be approached by the reader in a spirit similar to the one that guided the author's pen. Such an encounter is an adventure, an experiment whose outcome cannot be wholly foreseen, although the writer hopes by his/her prose and cogency to convert. In the intimate act of reading, the text engages the "practiced and educated" writer and reader in a process of argument, and the outcome of those individual dialogues with the word leaves both different for, at the very least, their consciousness of the other has been enhanced. This kind of reading act involves the risk that one's reality will be altered. Precisely this risk-taking makes the exercise valuable. We can concur when Brodkey avers regarding serious reading and writing: "If the reader is not at risk, he is not reading. And if the writer is not at risk, he is not writing" (45). To be any good the writing and reading acts must have an ethical purpose, that is, evoke change. To write and read in this manner is not easy, for it means that the writer must endeavor to write well while the reader must be willing to learn and to feel. Ultimately, the act requires conscious thought. And that is not easy.

Brodkey's essay clearly summarizes essential concepts of the reader-response school of criticism, which has risen to dominance in the Academy. While he nowhere makes specific reference to the academic debate, he does agree implicitly with Jonathan Culler's assessment that "reading is not an innocent activity" ("Literary Competence," 116), he does echo Wolfgang Iser's notion that "reading is only a pleasure when it is active and creative" ("The Reading Process," 51), does concur with George Poulet's conviction that the reader's "consciousness behaves as though it were the consciousness of another" ("Criticism and the Experience of Interiority," 44), and does indirectly pay tribute to Stanley Fish's belief that the reading operation "is interior and its greatest success is not the organizing of materials, but the transforming of minds."[6] Moreover, we do sense the influence of Sartre's *Qu'est-ce que la littérature?* (1947) with its view of literature as process which takes into account the "freedom" of both writer and reader in the construction or re-construction of the text. We do sense the impact of Iser's psychoanalytical interpretation of the reading act as the transformation of "textual [deep] structures" into the reader's world with the result that the reader experiences a "consciousness raising" (*Bewußtmachen*) of something deep within himself or herself. Reading is thus seen as a series of "acts of understanding" (*Erfassungsakte*) by both Iser and Brodkey.[7] Yet Brodkey does not reiterate merely intuitively professorial views. He goes a step beyond the Academy.

His consciousness is not Poulet's consciousness which is tantamount to the absorbtion of the self in the writer. Poulet leads us into the text but not back out. Brodkey's conception of reading as a most dangerous and

intimate game is not directly equivalent to Culler's or Fish's perceptions
of the reader's lack of innocence in approaching the text or Iser's designation of uninterrupted illusion-building as a "suspect, if not downright
dangerous, process" (Iser, "The Reading Process," 59; similarly Fish,
"Literature," 82). In Culler's (or Fish's) system the reader approaches the
text with certain expectations and preconceived notions that s/he im-
prints upon the printed word. While Iser fears that the reader would
succumb to the appeal of escapism, Brodkey grows anxious at the idea
that there is no escape from serious reading. Finally, Brodkey rightfully
emphasizes that only the practiced and astute reader is capable of playing
the "most dangerous game" as envisioned. (By contrast, Fish's
"informed" reader is not actually seen as a risk taker ["Literature,"
86f.].) The risk involved is, after all, the possibility of permanently altering one's identity through the loss of pet notions, the acquisition of
knowledge, or the dismantling of outright prejudice.

The notion that writing and reading are *complementary* activities is not
new. However, the kind of writing and reading addressed by Brodkey and
to which I shall subsequently refer in Emersonian terms as *creative writing and creative reading* deserves special attention. While I shall draw
upon concepts of the reader-response school of literary thought to illuminate my subject, I do not see my work as part of that debate. Consequently, I am not chiefly concerned with the grounding of "a literary
taxonomy" in a theory of reading.[8] The reason is simple: I see the reading
act as *a posteriori* to the writing act. Therefore, the *act* of writing (as
opposed to the completed act of writing, that is, to the text) will balance
the *re*-action of reading occasioned by it.

My purpose is to argue for a theory of the writing and reading acts as
they evolved in "modern" fashion in conjunction with the rise of Enlightenment thought during the 1700s. I do not propose to view the
eighteenth century through a twentieth-century critical lens but rather to
examine the Age of Enlightenment and its prose writing on its own terms.
Its own perceptions of the theory, function, and process of literature as
formulated by Klopstock, Wieland, Goethe, Schiller, Friedrich Schlegel,
and others stand at the center of this study. Yet there are numerous
parallels between the eighteenth and twentieth centuries because the latter is the direct heir to the concepts, beliefs, and methods of the former.
Where appropriate these similarities are explored. In general it is safe to
say that the exercise of "literary competence" (i.e., the discernment of
literary meaning) was as complex and multilateral in the eighteenth century as it is in our own era.

The Age of Enlightenment is widely recognized as a period of great intellectual and literary foment. Significant changes and innovations occurred in the arts, literature, philosophy, social theory, and law. Moreover, it was an age that did not separate thought into distinct disciplines as strictly as does our own era and lamented already by Emerson in the 1830s. In fact, literature and literary theory had not even evolved into independent categories of esoteric aloofness. Free exchange of information and methods among the various schools of thought and intellectual orientations was the rule rather than the exception. The dominant attitude of the entire Enlightenment world was one of critical skepticism and creative experimentation in an attempt to free humankind from the religious and philosophical conventions of the past. It perceived the need to avoid signification in advance in order to achieve the ideal of self-determination. True liberation for the Enlighteners meant the freeing of thought and feeling from prescribed patterns of response. Liberation meant the crossing of boundaries and the merging of disciplines. We find philosophers engaged in belletristic activities, novelists writing philosophy, and poets merging natural science with literature.

Consequently, the progressive writers (e.g., Pitschel, Herder, and Heinrich von Kleist) rejected the restriction of inherited genres and forms in favor of new writing strategies. In their efforts to remap the terrain of human experience and knowledge, they opted for new ways of assessing and presenting evidence—a move favored by the relative openness of genre theory in the eighteenth century. When they did use inherited forms, they filled them with new content and reshaped them with unaccustomed styles, frequently incorporating into them "sub-genres" as a matter of principle. Writing without genre was as much a liberating prospect for the eighteenth as it is for the twentieth century. Charles Newman notes in his *The Post-Modern Aura* (1985) that "the fragmentation of language and the destruction of genre are Modernism's official clichés."[9] This process of experimentation was an essential trait of the Age of Enlightenment and represents a link between the past and the present.

Related to the desire for self-determination in the 1700s was the attempt to spread the word, to incorporate an ever widening circle of adherents into the movement. The Enlighteners developed fresh writing strategies in order to reach and (re)train a larger, more diverse audience. One of the most successful strategies is what we now label imprecisely the essay (essayistic writing would be more precise). In a very real sense, the searing inquisitiveness characteristic of essayistic style is akin to the method of philosophical skepticism prevalent in the Enlightenment. That

8 RISK TAKING

dialectical method was employed to cultivate the mind in the promotion of the art of critical reflection and personal enlightenment in all areas of life and culture ranging from Shakespeare's art to the social causes of penury, from subtle philosophical problems to equal rights for women.

Even the earliest European Enlighteners advocated the notion of culture "as a series of unexpected alternatives" (Newman, 161), e.g., Leibniz, Thomasius, Bayle, Locke, Montesquieu, and d'Alembert. Later writers (Kant, Garve, and Emilia von Berlepsch) followed that early lead. Furthermore, they knew that if they hoped to alter the way their contemporaries thought and acted, they must forcefully challenge the communications structure. One of their most powerful tools in this struggle was essayistic writing.[10] It would not be inappropriate to speak of the "force of circumstances" (*Sachzwang*) in this regard much as Werner Heisenberg explains the gradual yet ineluctable alteration in the way we think about our world in scientific terms.[11]

The focus on the writing strategies of the emergent German essay is designed to illuminate a fundamental aspect of literature which goes beyond the "mere" question of a literary form and its history. Examination of this new mode of writing will serve to focus my questioning of the nature of writing and reading in its most innovative form between 1680 and 1815. Incidentally, I also intend to meet a need in essay research to trace the continuous development of the essay through its critical first phase from Gottfried Wilhelm Leibniz (1646–1716) to Adam Müller (1779–1829). By beginning in the late phase of the Baroque and concluding in the heyday of Romanticism I also hope to contribute to the reevaluation of the continuity of the historical epoch from the Enlightenment to Romanticism, as reflected in the important relationship between the art of creative writing and the art of creative reading. While agreeing that significant changes in literary life occurred during the 1770s,[12] I do not wish to be blinded by that enhanced activity to earlier innovations. Thus, here too I transgress the traditional boundaries of literary history by calling for a rereading of literary developments during the entire period in which Enlightenment thought held sway in an inspiring manner. Traditional literary historians will find my approach particularly challenging. But then again, reading that does not involve risk is probably not worth the effort.

The role of literature in the dialectics of enlightenment is indisputably central. In fact, it is possible to speak of the age as one of "literary learning." In his attempt to utilize the concept of literary value in assessing the nature of the belletristic canon, Hans-Georg Herrlitz remarked most saliently on the importance of defining goals as a prerequisite to establishing the means to the ends: "Literature, we are accustomed to say, 'cultivates' [*bildet*]. However, this 'cultivation' [*Bildung*] can be adequately described only when we see it as a bundle of functions that produces a literary product in relation to specified learning goals."[13] The eighteenth century had very definite goals in a literary and educational as well as a political sense, be it with the stress on reason or on sensibility. It makes sense, therefore, to foreground authorial intentionality in my consideration of creative writing and reading.

Literature, then, is examined here as the product of a "bundle of functions" (*Bündel von Funktionen*), as Herrlitz formulates the phenomenon. Thus I chose to concentrate on the intimate nexus between the writing and the reading acts in the rise of a novel hybrid literary form in Germany that draws its energy from these interconnected acts in a more concentrated and intense manner than does, say, either the drama or the epic. On the other hand, I do not agree with the contention that a break occurred in the theory of literature during the eighteenth century occasioned by an alleged shift in critical concern from the social effects of literature to a psychology of reading.[14] Enlightenment writing and aesthetics never abandoned its original calling to promote social change through the literary act. That engagement helps to explain the rapid rise in the writing and reading habits in the eighteenth century, on the one hand, and the pervasiveness of rhetoric, on the other.

My multiple thrust in questioning the theory of creative writing and creative reading in the eighteenth century thus takes into account recent theoretical thinking on the questions of canonical texts, literary value, reader response, the essay, social conditions of literary life, and the nature of "true" enlightenment with its distinctive mode of thinking. Only through an analysis of these literary and non-literary vectors of interchange can we hope to do justice to the dynamic quality of literary evolution and strike to the heart of the literary acts of writing and reading.[15]

My presentation of the innovative mode of thinking involved in the production and/or reconstruction of essayistic writing 1680–1815 is itself indebted to the interactive character of the modus scrutinized. In other words, the reader of *Crossing Boundaries* is invited on a journey of discovery that allows one to draw her/his own conclusions. S/he will not simply be confronted with a *fait accompli*. My task as guide is to locate the sign posts clearly so that one does not wander astray from the main path. It seemed paradoxical to me to trivialize the intellectual risk taking

explored in these pages by arresting its heuristic verve in descriptive
stasis. I endeavor to present my findings as if they were in the process of
being found. The undertaking is designed to be hazardous to conventional thinking.

Notes

1. Klaus R. Scherpe, "'Beziehung' und nicht 'Ableitung.' Methodische Über-
legungen zu einer Literaturgeschichte im sozialen Zusammenhang (am
Beispiel der Nachkriegsliteratur)," in *Literatur und Sprache im historischen
Prozeß. Vorträge des deutschen Germanistentages Aachen 1982*, vol. 1:
Literatur, ed. Thomas Cramer (Tübingen: Niemeyer, 1983), 77–90; here
80.
2. On these and related matters of the social history of (German) literature see
Jorg Schönert, "The Social History of German Literature: On the Present
State of Distress in the Social History of German Literature," *Poetics* 14
(1985), 303–319; also Claus-Michael Ort, "Problems of Interdisciplinary
Theory-Formation in the Social History of Literature," *Poetics* 14 (1985),
321–344.
3. Ralph Waldo Emerson, "The American Scholar," *The Selected Writings of
Ralph Waldo Emerson*, introduction by Brooks Atkinson, foreword by
Tremaine McDowell (New York: Random House, 1950), 59.
4. George Steiner, "In a Post-Culture," in *Extraterritorial: Papers on Literature and the Language of Revolution* (New York: Atheneum, 1976),
155–171; here 169. William Ray, *Literary Meaning: From Phenomenology
to Deconstruction* (Oxford: Basil Blackwell, 1984), provides a highly engaging summary of major contributions to the reevaluation of literature as
event. Influential on the German side in advocating the notion of literature
as the process of communication is Siegfried J. Schmidt, *Grundriß der
Empirischen Literaturwissenschaft*, vol. 1: *Der gesellschaftliche Hand-
lungsbereich Literatur*, and vol. 2: *Zur Rekonstruktion literaturwissen-
schaftlicher Fragestellungen in einer empirischen Theorie der Literatur*
(Braunschweig & Wiesbaden: Vieweg, 1980, 1982). Most relevant are his
exhaustive chapters on "Theorie Literarischen kommunikativen Handelns"
(1:130–198) and "Theorie der kommunikativen Handlungsrollen in Literarischer Kommunikation" (1:199–316).
5. Harold Brodkey, "Reading, the Most Dangerous Game," *New York Times
Book Review* (Nov. 24, 1985), 44.
6. Jonathan Culler, "Literary Competence," in *Reader-Response Criticism:
From Formalism to Post-Structuralism*, ed. Jane P. Tompkins (Baltimore
and London: The Johns Hopkins University Press, 1980), 116); Wolfgang
Iser, "The Reading Process: A Phenomenological Approach," in *Reader-
Response Criticism*, 51; George Poulet, "Criticism and the Experience of
Interiority," in *Reader-Response Criticism*, 44; Stanley Fish, "Literature in
the Reader: Affective Stylistics," in *Reader-Response Criticism*, 99.
7. Jean-Paul Sartre, "Qu'est-ce que la littérature" (1947), in *Collection Idées*
(1948; rprt. Paris: Gallimard, 1967), 155–171; Wolfgang Iser, *Der Akt des
Lesens. Theorie ästhetischer Wirkung*. UTB 636 (Munich: Fink, 1976), 177.

8. On the concept of literary taxonomy see Culler, "Literary Competence," 108, and Fish, "Literature," 73.
9. Charles Newman, *The Post-Modern Aura: The Act of Fiction in an Age of Inflation* (Evanston, IL: Northwestern University Press, 1985), 113.
10. In his assessment of the uneasy relationship of literary culture to the general culture in America, Newman misjudges the innovativeness of the situation when he claims that "the most powerful idea to come out of the 20th-century American experiment was the transfer of an Enlightenment view of political life to culture itself. . . . Against the European notion of culture as *standards* enforced by an elite, we have come to see culture as a series of unexpected alternatives, and the greatest legacy of the otherwise dissipated radical politics of the sixties (as well as the greatest oversight of the liberal mind) was the realization that the communications structure must be challenged before you can hope to alter, much less bind, thought and action" (161). It is misleading to imply that the transfer of the political views of the Enlightenment to the general cultural sphere occurred only in twentieth-century America.
11. Werner Heisenberg, "Änderungen der Denkstruktur im Fortschritt der Wissenschaft," in *Schritte über Grenzen. Gesammelte Reden und Aufsätze,* second expanded edition (Munich: Piper, 1973), 275–287; here 286f.
12. See, e.g., Schönert, "The Social History of German Literature" (1985), 314.
13. Hans-Georg Herrlitz, "Lektüre-Kanon und literarische Wertung. Bemerkungen zu einer didaktischen Leitvorstellung und deren wissenschaftlicher Begründung," in *Literarische Bildung und Erziehung,* ed. Harro Müller-Michaelis (Darmstadt: Wissenschaftliche Buchgesellschaft, 1976), 259. Previously published in *Der Deutschunterricht* 19 (1967), 79–92.
14. Tompkins, "The Reader in History: The Changing Shape of Literary Response," in *Reader-Response Criticism,* 214f.
15. Hans Robert Jauss, *Literaturgeschichte als Provokation der Literaturwissenschaft* (Konstanz: Universitätsverlag, 1967), 61: "Prinzipiell wäre eine solche Darstellung der Literatur in der geschichtlichen Abfolge ihrer Systeme an einer Reihe von beliebigen Schnittpunkten möglich. Sie kann indes der eigentlichen Aufgabe aller Historiographie erst dann gerecht werden, wenn sie Schnittpunkte auffindet und ins Licht rückt, die den Prozeßcharakter der 'literarischen Evolution' in ihren epochalen Zäsuren historisch artikulieren."

CHAPTER 2

Attitude and Form

Expanding the Canon: A Fourth Genre?

In his summary of the twentieth-century debate on the nature of the literary act, *Literary Meaning: From Phenomenology to Deconstruction* (1984), William Ray cogently argues for a revision of our traditional thinking about the nature of the relationship between the literary text and literary criticism, between the function of history and of theory. He concludes his historical survey by remarking that the dominant tendency in post-structuralism is to highlight the "most traditional distinction of the canon, namely the difference between the original work and the critical work" since the text as literature requires the aid of criticism to clarify its historical or universal "truth." A prime function of criticism is to "expose the belief systems of a former age" as a means of helping us to fathom our own which is, to a very high degree, the product of bygone eras. Ultimately, Ray suggests, the main by-product of post-structuralism will be to bring about "a form of literary study less obsessed with controlling truth than (perhaps) with its ability to provoke the pleasure of new ideas." Even deconstruction—not as an open, questioning attitude but rather as a paradigm with predictable results— will be insufficient to provoke new ideas or incite pleasure at them let alone change.[1] Literature and criticism, in effect, lose much of their vigor and attraction when reduced to categorical systems. Rigor mortis begins to set into what once used to be a true living event. Whether as critics or as belletristic writers, we must strive to live in a continual present.

The logical extension of these developments is to reassess the traditional literary canon and its triadic scheme of epic/dramatic/lyric on the basis of a self-questioning critical stance. The received canon and its triadic scheme can be viewed as the products of the dogmatic belief or thought systems of their period of gestation. The new critical scheme, whose necessity has been made clear by the shift from phenomenology to deconstruction, must consciously acknowledge the impact of authorial attitude on the shaping of aesthetic form. That move would appear to necessitate augmenting the triadic scheme with a fourth mode which accounts in a special way for the skeptical stance. While critics ranging from George Steiner to Wolfgang Iser and Barbara Herrnstein Smith point to the need for a revitalized canon[2], it was perhaps Friedrich Sengle and Hans Robert Jauss who attracted the most attention, especially in German circles. Of greatest significance in this regard is Sengle's *Vorschläge zur Reform der literarischen Formenlehre (Suggestions for the Reform of Literary Morphology,* 1967) and Jauss's *Literaturgeschichte als Provokation der Literaturwissenschaft (Literary History as Provocation,* 1967), both of which appeared at a time of acute upheaval in the Academy.

Jauss's call to examine the truly complex nature of literary history as a synchronic event as well as a diachronic process which takes full account of past expectations and contingencies while not neglecting present contexts was extremely influential. It ultimately led to a far-ranging review in the 1970s of how best to write literary history in a new sociological mold. He was one of the first, moreover, to emphasize the central role of the recipient as a constitutive agent in the literary process (26, 63ff.). As important as Jauss is in the recent history and theory of literature, we need first to focus on the question of genre since inquiry into the nature and history of literary genres and classifications have proved to be "the most productive area of literary-historical innovations" and hold the most promise for understanding the communicative acts of literature (Schönert, 310f.). The specific question of where to locate the essay, moreover, and how to define it is intrinsically caught up with generic considerations.

The matter of generic divisions is no longer clear cut, if ever it was. While everyone agrees that Plato, Aristotle, and Horace gave rise to classical genre theory with a focus on three major kinds distinguished according to the manner of imitation, not everyone agrees that the triadic scheme is still applicable. At least we should distinguish with Wellek and Warren (1956) between classical and modern theory; the former designates a prescriptive approach while the latter signals a descriptive one which does not recognize a limit to the number of possible kinds of literature.[3] Even with that demarcation we encounter problems. Above all we run the risk of becoming so thoroughly confused by the ambiguous use of the term genre to designate just about anything that we could easily

conclude with critics like Tzvetan Todorov (who, incidentally, decon-
structs Northrup Frye's generic categories) and Lorna Martens (who
takes her cue from Todorov) that the modern study of genre theory has
reached a "methodological impasse."[4]

Impasse or not, it has proved beneficial to group literary works into
categories so that we can speak about them in a manner other than as
unrelated works. To be productive the study of genres must be simultaneously inductive and deductive, historical and abstract, descriptive and
theoretical. Description is to be understood as a purely empirical act
without any organizing principle external to the text analyzed. Theory,
by contrast, is teleological, that is, the text does not give rise to a pattern
but fits one.

In the following I adhere to Todorov's belief that the definition of a
genre is best achieved via "a continual oscillation between the description
of phenomena and abstract theory" (Todorov, 21). It is the oscillation
between the empirical phenomena and the ideal norm that is important
here, not the mental construct by itself. In tracing the history of a writing
mode we are, of course, interested in the concretizations of thought or
sentiment in aesthetically pleasing form. Thus, to dwell on speculative
theory would make little sense for us. I am interested in the concept of
genre as it relates to the genesis of a real, honest-to-goodness *modus
scribendi*. Thus I strive to conjoin description and theory.

On the other hand, I share Martens's skepticism when she asks whether
the idea of genre might be the wrong question, especially in the post
Romantic period. It is and it isn't. While formal expectations and repetitive structural patterns are much more in evidence in the eighteenth than
in the nineteenth century, we must guard against a too rigid notion of
generic classification even in the earlier epochs. It behooves us to consider
definition not as the ultimate objective of genre criticism, but rather as "a
beginning, a working hypothesis" since new evidence might cause us later
to alter our description (Martens, 11).

Nevertheless, the idea of gathering evidence implies that genre study
must be historical. The textual resemblances discerned are arguably not
fortuitous and might, in fact, be traceable to a highly influential book or
author.[5] However, I cannot agree with Martens when she posits an ir-
reconcilability between a generic code and a contextualization, at least
not with regards to essayistic writing. Her conclusion that "describing the
code principle . . . has little to do with actual texts" (16f.) does not apply
to the essay. In the realm of essayistic writing, the generic code and the
contextualization are one and the same.

Sengle's reassessment of the literary canon (contemporaneous with Todorov's concept of genre!) is an endeavor to pay tribute to the all important oscillation between generic theory and literary practice. His *Formenlehre* is also much more to the point for our purposes because of its broad impact on the German situation and explicit concern with nonfictional kinds of writing. Essentially, Sengle recommends expanding the parameters of traditional poetics by including the functional forms of written communication. Among these he numbers biography, autobiography, dialogue, public address, sermon, diary, epistle, aphorism, essay, and the various forms of journalistic writing.[6] However, he does note that the diversity of these *écritures* (as George Steiner would label them) is so rich that "an exact systematizing of all the possible forms is not feasible (24).[7] Nor does it seem fruitful to him to raise a literary type such as the essay to the rank of a fourth genre as advocated by such critics as Hans Hennecke.[8] The elevation of an individual type to a universal norm merely muddies the water further.

Because of the proliferation of types and the potential for endless genres, Sengle concludes that genre theory and literary history would be better served with a more encompassing quadratic rather than triadic generic scheme. This fourth general category would include all the functional, nontraditional poetic forms and would constitute for all practical purposes a fourth genre (*eine vierte Gattung*), but of course not in the same sense as some speak of the essay, the political novel, or the sonnet as genres.

The labels proposed by Sengle are "Zweckform" and "Gebrauchsform" (= functional form and utility form). They are intended to convey a sense of the historical and social roles played by the *écritures* in any given age. Sengle avers: "The notion of a fourth genre of this type is rather appealing" (*Formenlehre*, 15). In order to avoid confusion he explains that "the basic question is not whether we distinguish nondidactic and didactic forms (*zwecklose und zweckhafte Formen*), but whether we will, in principle, open our literary system to all forms" (15). The distinction drawn here between nondidactic and didactic is equivalent to that between nonliterary and literary.

Sengle's reform suggestion is based on the conviction that classical rhetoric is much more important for the production of *belles-lettres* than has been generally acknowledged in modern criticism. The rise of poetic prose over the past two centuries to a position of dominance in critical inquiry has obscured the roots of prose in rhetorical technique. He reminds us that rhetoric and poetics were very closely linked in the pre-Romantic era and therefore urges us to reorient our critical thinking according to the diversified world of letters in the eighteenth century (25). The rhetorical principles of the "manifold" and the "unified" are cited for specific mention, for their "collaborative" effort assures the unity of a work despite the external diversity of its elements and forms. "Unity in Diversification" (*Einheit in der Mannigfaltigkeit*), therefore, should be the overriding guiding principle in the reevaluation of the inherited literary morphology (the phrase derives from J. Chr. Adelung: Sengle, 36f.)

Despite his insistence on the importance of the humanistic tradition of rhetoric (especially the doctrine of modulation (*Töne*) for a revised theory of literature, Sengle does not imply that the new theory should be essentially rhetorical. The distinction between rhetorical and poetic practice must be maintained, for they *are* different in spite of their overlapping. He culminates his argument with a wise admonition: "Since a return to humanistic taxonomy is not possible, we would be well advised to formulate an essentially new literary doctrine of forms which goes beyond traditional rhetoric and poetics. This new literary theory would, on the one hand, have to dispense with the naive classification of verse and prose and would have to overcome the classical ban against mixing genres and styles. On the other hand, however, it would have to allow for the necessary classifications in a new manner."[9]

The response to Sengle's original suggestion of 1967 for reform was broad and persistent. Most productive has been the call to reexamine the nexus of literature and rhetoric as well as the exhortation to liberalize the concept of genre. Our focus on the essay is especially relevant in this regard since it occupies a realm midway between rhetoric and poetics. Not merely utilitarian in the sense of scholarly or journalistic writing yet not aesthetically preoccupied with itself like a Dada poem, the essay maintains an equilibrium between two opposing poles. But more of this tenuous state in the ensuing chapter where we can go into greater depth.

Even as Sengle worked on the revision of his lecture for publication other critics were attempting to revise the triadic model promulgated most notably by Emil Staiger (1946). Of greatest significance for our purposes is the 1968 study by Wolfgang Ruttkowski, *Die literarischen Gattungen. Reflexionen über eine modifizierte Fundamentalpoetik (Literary Genres: Reflections on a Modified Fundamental Poetics).*[10] In an appended footnote to the published version of his lecture (1969), Sengle refers to Ruttkowski's assault on the canonical triad of lyric, epic, and dramatic. Unfortunately, Ruttkowski's recommendation for remapping the generic landscape has found little resonance . . . perhaps because Sengle's brief reference to the work was unwarrantedly snide (see 48f., n.39). A brief review of Ruttkowski's concepts is a fruitful prelude to a specific examination of essay theory and the conditions of its early genesis; that is, the nature of the *Aufklärung*, of literary life in the eighteenth century, and of the intermingling of rhetoric and poetry.

Ruttkowski is important to our consideration of the essay because of his proposal to group texts in terms of authorial posture or attitude (*Haltung*) rather than categories of texts, that is, genres (*Gattungen*).[11] That decision is noteworthy because I propose to speak not about a genre of essayistic writing but rather of a mode or posture evident in the writing. Using Staiger's model of three essential attitudes (lyric, epic, dramatic) as a point of departure, Ruttkowski argues adroitly for an emphatic modification and refinement of Staiger's terminology and conceptions. It is a discussion useful to my present purposes.

Specifically, Ruttkowski contends that Staiger's use of the terms *Gattung* and *Haltung* is fuzzy (16–25, 88–92). Perceiving the need for a more sophisticated differentiation between the two designations, he introduces the speech-act theory developed by Drach and Marie Hed Kaulhausen in *Das gesprochene Gedicht und seine Gestalt* (*The Recited Poem and its Form*, 1953/59). That concept is labeled a "speaker's attitude" (*Sprechhaltung*) and is defined as "the psycho-physical act of reciting by the declaimer of poetry and, by extension, of the poet himself" (Ruttkowski, 17). Moreover, the speaker's attitude (*Sprechhaltung*) is dependent upon the reason for voicing a thought (*Sprechsituation*). Together the reason for speaking and the attitude assumed by the speaker in the act of speaking "determine all those factors which influence the spoken [*Schallform*] or written [*Stil*] text/utterance [*Sprachkunstwerk*]." These various factors are: the speaker's natural character, his/her mood during the speech act, his/her purpose vis-à-vis the audience, and the manner of contact with that audience as well as such purely external considerations as the acoustical characteristics of the space and the physical constitution of the speaker. To these criteria Ruttkowski adds two of his own: the duration of the speech act and the audience's ability and/or willingness to concentrate on what is being said (Ruttkowski, 17). The speaker is not necessarily aware of the impact that the *Sprechsituation* has on the speech act.

Since all literature is the consequence of a speech act either in oral or written form, Ruttkowski proposes that the traditional triad of lyric, epic, and dramatic be subsumed under this original *Sprechhaltung*. Consequently, the concept of genre as a static ideal form must give way to an understanding of lyric, epic, and dramatic as basic human attitudes (*Grundhaltungen*) expressed in oral or written form (19, et passim). In this regard Ruttkowski is still in agreement with Staiger. What we have here, then, is yet another formulation of the notion of literature as process and the reception of a literary work as event. Ruttkowski participates, therefore, in the line of development from Sartre to Steiner, Iser, and Fish. But in describing literature he sets the accents somewhat differently.

A dynamic conception of literature allows Ruttkowski to avoid the pitfalls of a more conventional poetics which seeks to limit the boundaries of genre and helps him to circumvent the impasse of methodology that plagues modern genre theory. Realizing that form is the result of various kinds of interaction, he subscribes to the notion that a literary genre is marked by *accents of meaning* rather than formal or structural elements (16). For him, the speaker's situation and attitude—by analogy we can speak of "authorial attitude"—is more basic than the generic assignment. Moreover, the intermingling of genres and types, noted even by Staiger, is easily explained by Ruttkowski's model: the alteration of authorial mood and attitude within a particular text can lead to lyric and/or dramatic elements in an "epic" context.

Authorial attitude, or *Haltung*, describes for Ruttkowski the relationship of the writer to the text and, via the text, to a potential or intended audience. *Haltung* is thus not to be confused with either the traditional concept of genre or with narrative perspective. The literary work for him is essentially intentional. And yet the determination of the existence of authorial stances in literature rather than types or genres is, in a very real sense, a mere precondition for Ruttkowski's actual purpose which is to argue for the expansion of Staiger's three categories to include a fourth possibility (Ruttkowski, 8f., 86ff.). Thus Ruttkowski's proposal corresponds to Sengle's call for a fourth basic category. Neither Ruttkowski nor Sengle proposes a *Gattung*; both wish to distinguish a fourth "universal, fundamental attitude" (*allgemeinmenschliche Grundhaltung*).[12] Let us now look more closely at the difference between Ruttkowski and Staiger, since both Sengle and Ruttkowski are reacting to the Swiss.

The distancing of the writer (*Distanzhaltung*) from his or her subject matter is the distinguishing trait of literary categories for both Staiger and Ruttkowski. Yet Ruttkowski differs from Staiger in a significant aspect: whereas Staiger conceives of the relationship as between the poet and the text (lyric = emotional identification; epic = descriptive objectification; dramatic = logical conceptualization), Ruttkowski allows for a connection between the writer and the public as well. Such a move corresponds to his fourth attitudinal stance (*vierte menschliche Grundeinstellung*; Ruttkowski, 89–95; see also the chart on 103f.). This fourth stance which is characteristic of the practiced orator (*Vortragskünstler*, 87) Ruttkowski labels "artistic" (*artistisch*) and remarks: "Under this heading we subsume all variants of the contact with the audience which a poet or orator can utilize. And there are many" (94). Consequently, terms synonymous with or related to artistic include: "mimetic," "split," "sophisticated," "audience oriented" (*publikumsbezogen*) "comical," and "didactic."[13] The attitude toward the audience is further defined as *inclusive of* the public not just performed *in front of* it (*zum Publikum dargeboten . . . nicht vor dem Publikum*, 98). Moreover, Ruttkowski refers to the *artistische Haltung* as a "dialectic transcending of the stage" (*eine Dialektik 'über die Rampe,'* 99).

To these traits we should add those qualities derivative of the time element. They are: a conciseness of form, a personal tone, active involvement of the reader which requires some strenuous effort on his/her part, and a dramatic note. On the length of the piece, Ruttkowski remarks: "the shorter and more intense, the better." Regarding reader/listener participation he writes that the recipient must be prepared to think along with the writer/speaker. And on the question of dramatic tension, he observes that there is not one dramatic highpoint as in the drama but rather several tense moments that arise and are resolved. The effect of all of these elements is to maintain a high level of reader/listener interest (see 100).

We can accept Ruttkowski's statement that the categories lyric, epic, dramatic, artistic represent an ascending order of abstractness. That order is describable as a movement from the simple to the complex, from the naive to the self-conscious, from the aimless to the purposeful, and from introverted feeling to effective action (95). The fourth category is thus the most reflective, complicated, and didactic possible stance for a writer to assume. In it we perceive the greatest distance between the author and the text. In fact, the accent is no longer on the author-text relationship, but now on the author-audience connection, obviously still via the text. This shift in accent (focus) places Ruttkowski in the proximity of Iser and Fish. Yet, while the latter zero in on the role of the reader, Ruttkowski is concerned with the role of the author/speaker. It also places him close to Steiner and Sartre with their emphasis on the act of writing. The writer's stance translates into Ruttkowski's "speaker's stance" (*Sprechhaltung*). Finally, Sengle's suggestion for a fourth poetic category to accommodate the didactic forms (*Zweckformen*) corresponds to Ruttkowski's artistic attitude which is the typical posture for the didactic forms cited by Sengle. It accounts for the not infrequent mixing of genres and styles Sengle identified as requiring specific explanation. That mixing is everywhere evident in the essayistic writing discussed in Chapters VII–IX of this study.

Ruttkowski does not attempt to codify fully the types of literary expression that would fall under the rubric "artistic," and in his conclusion he specifically states that his intent is not closure. He does not wish to present us with a closed system but instead to stimulate further thought. It is an easy matter to locate the essay form within Ruttkowski's *artistischer Grundhaltung* and to make clear the relevance of classical rhetoric for his concept of attitudinal stance. In fact, I will argue that the term essayistic is more suitable than either of the designations "didactic" (Sengle) or "artistic" because it is free of the negative connotations of the first and not ambivalent like the second.[14] Because of the relevance of rhetorical strategies to both Sengle's and Ruttkowski's models of classification, we must examine that connection in Chapter VI.

Boundary Literature

The revolution in twentieth-century criticism has not only led to attempts to reform the traditional canon and to expand the number of literary classifications; it has led as well to a radical questioning of the ultimate usefulness of genre designations as noted with regards to Todorov and Martens. The disintegration of genre and the concomitant emergence of multiple modes of writing (and reading) seems to be a general phenomenon in the post-modern era.[15] Writing without genre is the result not of the fragmentation of language but of the enhanced awareness of the audience's participatory role. Writers have come to realize that "enlightened" readers are no longer content to accept signification of meaning in advance. By their active participation in the literary event, they reconstruct the meaning of the text according to their particular situation. It is perhaps the reader more than the writer who has liberated writing from genre. Gary Saul Morson turns to this issue in his *The Boundaries of Genre* (1981).[16] It is yet another way of looking at writing and reading as risk taking in Brodkey's meaning.

Like Sengle and Ruttkowski, Morson examines the question of literary systems and the variability of genre, but he adds a new facet essential to our inquiry. Drawing upon Russian (Bakhtin, Sklovskij, Tynyanov) and North American (J. M. Ellis, Herrnstein Smith) critical inquiry into literary value and literary classifications, Morson identifies writing modes of special interest to us. He calls them "boundary works" or "threshold literature." They are marked by generic ambivalence since they participate simultaneously in more than one writing mode (48–51). These compositions are distinguished by the qualities of Ruttkowski's fourth essential writing posture which calls for an endless interrogation of its own artifice. Morson cites for special attention the essay (or sketch) and the feuilleton (15–17). A brief explanation of Morson's definition of literature and of his category of "threshold art" will prove fruitful in assessing the nature of the essay, for Morson addresses himself to the vital question of whether "documentary" literature can be considered belletristic.

"Boundary works" and "boundary genres" are typical of "threshold art." They may take the form of a preface, an afterword, a diary, interjected commentaries, notes, fragments, a letter, autobiography, utopia, the feuilleton, the essay, etc. The latter five could be considered genres, the others works. They all tend to be didactic; they are definitely problematic in a literary sense. The characteristic trait in each case is an ambivalence of classification. It is not clear to the reader, e.g., which set of mutually exclusive and discontinuous reading conventions should be applied to the text. *Threshold* literature differs from boundary literature in that the author intentionally misleads the reader to decode the text in one way only to reverse himself at the end as if to say: "no, this is fact, not fiction" (or vice versa). *Boundary* works, on the other hand, *become* ambiguous because the conventions of reading change, literary values shift, or the original authorial intent becomes blurred. Here Morson moves close to Fish's (or Ruttkowski's) notion of reading as a series of reversals.

These works and genres are problematic because they lie "somewhere between research and story" (15) and admit of "hermeneutic perplexity" (49). They can, in short, be read according to the conventions of "research" or those of "story."[17] In order to assess their literariness and to distinguish between hermeneutic *perplexity* and hermeneutic *indeterminacy*, Morson argues that we must be able to differentiate clearly between literary and non-literary texts.

Morson's definition of literature reflects major facets of the postmodern debate. His is a definition of literature which is directly applicable to the nature of essayistic writing, for he weights the roles of writer, reader, and text equally. In the following we will refer to essayistic writing as boundary literature, since it is widely acknowledged to be a hybrid of science and literature. Central to the understanding of literature in our context is Morson's insistence that authorial intent, that is, his/her posture—and not any formalistic properties—constitutes the line of demarcation between literature and non-literature. To classify a work as literature rather than non-literature is to open up its semiotic possibilities by not restricting them to its original context of communication. According to Morson non-literary texts are "documentary"; literary texts *may* be "documentary" but are never exhausted as such. Literature, moreover, is inclusive of fiction, but not limited to it (39f., 44ff.).

Decisive, in other words, are not the stylistic qualities in *themselves* but in the way they are treated by the reader. And that manner of treatment, or application of convention, can change synchronically as well as diachronically. The recontextualization of the work may be by authorial design or by reader discovery. In any event, the "gaps" or "blockage" *in* or the inconclusiveness or ambiguity *of* the text force the reader to become coauthor of its literariness (cf. 42). What is at stake in boundary works is the classification of a text, not its meaning or meanings which can, in fact, be diametrically opposed. The reader is forced to make an explicit choice of how to approach the work. That choice is tantamount to an "act of intertextuality" (48).

The effect of that choice in Morson's system is also of relevance in our context. Since boundary works are didactic forms of literature, the entertainment they provide is more than just ephemeral. The author of didactic literature places greater demands on the reader than the author of pure fiction. The reader must be willing to think in unfamiliar ways for the duration of the reading act. And the author takes advantage of that readiness in order to exploit fully the particular pleasure imparted by that kind of literature. Instead of taking us away from reality into a fictional world to be charmed, the author of a boundary work takes us deeper into the real world to be mystified (cf. 94f.). The reader is invited on an open-ended journey of discovery in which the reader repeats the writer's heuristic process (96). That which is discovered is not just the other but also the self. The purpose of the "reading journey" is conversion, is change. Boundary literature, in other words, is especially designed to convert the reading experience into permanent private and social change. The claim is reminiscent of Harold Brodkey's designation of reading as "the most dangerous game" while meeting Schönert's call for a closer "coordination of social history and literature" (Schönert, 312).

These views on literature and specifically on boundary works and genres are typical of recent deliberations on revisionary poetics and offer a way around the impasses of genre criticism posited by Martens.[18] The canon has been expanded to include new classifications and types. A restrictive view of literature as something static and perfected has yielded to one that admits of dynamism in the subsequent recontextualizations of a work as well as in its original conceptualization. The traditional view of the creative act of writing has been augmented by an awareness of the

equally creative act of reading which takes into account both the hermeneutic perplexity and the hermeneutic indeterminacy of literature and its
contexts. The reading act has thus become crucial. We can conclude with
Morson:

> The hermeneutic *perplexity* that characterizes boundary genres
> must be carefully distinguished from the hermeneutic *indetermi-*
> *nacy* of literature itself, that is, the fact that literature may func-
> tion in unforeseen contexts and therefore be emblematic of
> changing concerns and exemplificative of quite different propo-
> sitions to different sets of readers. The disagreements engendered
> by boundary works are of a different order. Strictly speaking, it
> is not meanings but appropriate procedures for discovering
> meaning[s] that are disputable—not particular readings, but
> how to read. The authors' intentions are unclear—not, it should
> be stressed, their intentions about what the works mean, but
> about the sorts of work they would be read *as* (49).

Thus, in recognition of Herrnstein Smith's insight that critics have been
asking the wrong questions—what does the text mean instead of what is
its *value*—we must augment Fish's query "What does the text do?" by
now asking with Morson (and Gerald Graff) "How should it be read?"

The question of *how* is one of attitude and approach in the pursuit of
aesthetic pleasure and personal growth. In the realm of boundary
literature—and now we can speak specifically of essayistic writing—the
aesthetic quality of the text is generated most emphatically in and
through the reading act itself. The pleasure experienced is of a cerebral
kind; it is a delight in illuminating perspectives, in shimmering movement, in a curious roundness of the whole despite an ever manifest openness. The lasting value encountered in an essay results from the creative
reading called into play by the creative writing imbued in the text. The
impact of such writing on the reader is equally central, for it is designed
to alter her/his thoughts and feelings while enticing her/him by its intellectual sparkle and eloquence ever deeper into the text. Although these
critical insights are widely associated with the post-modern aura as described by Newman, they were first proposed by the Age of
Enlightenment.[19]

Aware now of the radical questioning of genre thinking in recent years
and equipped with such innovative notions as boundary literature,
threshold works, and of reading/writing as risk taking, I wish in the
ensuing chapter to apply these insights to the theoretical traditions of the

German essay. After briefly reviewing traditional attempts to define the mode, I will formulate my specific theory of the communicative nature of essayism against the backdrop of the foregoing discussions.

Notes

1. William Ray, *Literary Meaning: From Phenomenology to Deconstruction* (Oxford: Basil Blackwell, 1984), 209–212.
2. Cf., e.g., Hans-Georg Herrlitz, "Lektüre-Kanon und literarische Wertung. Bemerkungen zu einer didaktischen Leitvorstellung und deren wissenschaftlicher Begründung" (1967), rprt. in *Wege der Forschung*, 301, ed. Harro Müller-Michaelis (Darmstadt: Wissenschaftliche Buchgesellschaft, 1976), 243–261; Barbara Herrnstein Smith, "Contingencies of Value," *Critical Inquiry* 10/1 (Sept. 1983), 1–35; Günter Buck, "Literarischer Kanon und Geschichtlichkeit (Zur Logik des literarischen Paradigmenwandels)," *Deutsche Vierteljahresschrift für Literaturwissenschaft und Geistesgeschichte*, 57/3 (1983), 351–365; John A. McCarthy, "'Plan im Lesen': On the Beginnings of a Literary Canon in the 18th Century (1730–1805)," *Komparatistische Hefte* 13 (1986), 29–45. See Monika Schrader, *Theorie und Praxis literarischer Wertung. Literaturwissenschaftliche und -didaktische Theorien und Verfahren* (Berlin and New York: de Gruyter, 1987), for a thorough assessment of the critical debate on literary value since the 1960s from the German perspective. Her focus is on the nexus of aesthetic, social, philosophical, and pedagogical factors in determining literary value. Her thrust is a dual one like my own in *Crossing Boundaries*, for she is interested in both theory and practice. Unfortunately, Schrader's book became available to me only after my manuscript was completed, so it was not possible to incorporate her findings in my study.
3. René Wellek and Austin Warren, *Theory of Literature* (New York: Harcourt, Brace & Co., 1956), 223f.
4. Tzvetan Todorov, "Literary Genres," in *The Fantastic: A Structural Approach to a Literary Genre*, trans. Richard Howard (Ithaca: Cornell University Press, 1975), 3–23, here 22 (originally published in 1970 under the title *Introduction à la littérature fantastique*). See the second chapter of Lorna Martens, *The Diary Novel* (Cambridge: Cambridge University Press, 1985), which she titles "The Impasses of Genre Criticism" (9–21).
5. Wellek and Warren, *Theory of Literature*, 225; Martens, 21.
6. Friedrich Sengle, *Vorschläge zur Reform der literarischen Formenlehre*. Dichtung und Erkenntnis, vol. 1. 2nd revised ed. (Stuttgart: Metzler, 1969), 12.
7. This observation is echoed by Ray in regard to Culler's *Structural Poetics*. Ray suggests that the attempt to codify the proliferating classes of and distinctions between the *écritures* is self-defeating since the proliferation of those classes and distinctions in the historical process is without end (Ray, 122). Nonetheless, Klaus Weissenberg does attempt a partial classification in the volume edited by him, *Prosakunst ohne Erzählen. Die Gattungen der nicht-fiktionalen Kunstprosa* (Tübingen: Niemeyer, 1985).

8. Hans Hennecke, "Die vierte literarische Gattung. Reflexionen über den Essay," in *Kritik* (1958); Sengle, *Formenlehre*, 13.

9. *Formenlehre*, 44. Warren and Wellek argue in similar fashion (*Theory of Literature*, 216ff.).

10. Wolfgang Ruttkowski, *Die literarischen Gattungen. Reflexionen über eine modifizierte Fundamentalpoetik* (Berne and Munich: Francke, 1968). See also Wolfgang Ruttkowski and Eberhard Reichmann, eds., *Das Studium der deutschen Literatur. Eine Einführung für amerikanische Studierende* (Philadelphia: National Carl Schurz Association, 1974), esp. Chapter 1: "Gattungs- und Grundbegriffe" (1–59).

11. The proposal echoes the view of Wellek and Warren who think that "genre should be conceived . . . as a grouping of literary works based, theoretically, upon both outer form (specific meter or structure) and also upon *inner form (attitude, tone, purpose—more crudely, subject and audience)*" (*Theory of Literature*, 221; my emphasis).

12. Haas, "Zur Geschichte und Kunstform des Essays," *Jahrbuch für internationale Germanistik*, 7/1 (1975), 22f., misunderstands Ruttkowski's intent. Ruttkowski does not wish to designate the essay a genre.

13. "Anders ausgedrückt: ich sehe die Satire als eine [komische] Möglichkeit der Didaktik, die Didaktik wiederum als eine [lehrhafte] Möglichkeit der 'Artistik'" (*Die literarischen Gattungen*, 87; see also 88).

14. Despite the suitability of his fourth attitude of writing for describing the essay, Ruttkowski only once mentions the type and does not specifically relegate it to his category of the artistic. On page 16 of *Die literarischen Gattungen*, he uses the indeterminate definition of the essay form as an example of the insufficiency of traditional poetic concepts. Secondly, he only once clearly draws a parallel between his adapted concepts of the *Sprechsituation* and *Sprechhaltung* to rhetorical practice, and that brief mention occurs in a footnote (134, n.19).

15. Charles Newman, *The Post-Modern Aura: The Act of Fiction in an Age of Inflation* (Evanston, IL: Northwestern University Press, 1985). See his chapter on "Writing Without Genre," 113–115.

16. Gary Saul Morson, *The Boundaries of Genre: Dostoevsky's "Diary of a Writer" and the Traditions of Literary Utopia* (Austin: University of Texas Press, 1981).

17. On the paradigm of "research" versus story, see Peter B. Mosenthal, "Defining the Expository Discourse Continuum: Towards a Taxonomy of Expository Text Types," *Poetics* 14 (1985), 387–414.

18. Martens, *The Diary Novel*, 14f., creates an impasse for herself by rejecting the notion that generic codes can be productively foregrounded, preferring to believe that "codes cannot be equated with groups of texts." She fails to see the active reader role as possibly intended by the author as in Morson's scheme of boundary literature. On the widespread interest in genre study, see, e.g., the special issue of *Poetics* 14 (1985), and *Textsortenlehre— Gattungsgeschichte*, ed. Walter Hinck (Heidelberg: Quelle und Meyer, 1977).

19. Newman writes, e.g.: "if we are prepared to accept meaning which is 'immanent' in history *or* language, and hence not strictly discoverable, but the

fruit of an ongoing if finally inexplicable collaboration between the mind and the world, then we can project upon human history the only meaning it can possibly have—which is precisely what literature aims for in its extra-historical, extra-cultural, and extra-psychological assertiveness" (*Aura*, 84).

CHAPTER 3

Essay or Essayism?

Problems Defining the Essay

The essay is perhaps the most indeterminate and elusive mode of writing to confront the literary historian and theorist. In his useful and concise introduction to the history and theory of the type, Gerhard Haas remarks that "scarcely any other literary form is traceable with as much precision back to its beginnings, yet scarcely any other form defies as obstinately as the essay definition or even description."[1] In a more recent commentary on the essay, Klaus Weissenberger states that it reveals "absolutely no normative criteria" in comparison with the epic, dramatic, and lyric and that it is "an indefinite, thereby self-confirming creative poetology."[2] As the genre par excellence whose method is its form, it attracts repeated attempts to pin down its slithery nature.[3] The effort is analogous to trying to catch a wriggling fish in the open hand. That indeterminacy holds great fascination for the critic as well as the writer who are charmed by its individual intelligence and sparkle.[4]

In the widely used *A Handbook to Literature* (1960) by Holman, Thrall, and Hibbard, for example, the unsuspecting reader is confronted by the resigned assessment concerning the Sisyphcan task of naming the essay: "Because of the wide application of the term, no satisfactory definition can be arrived at. . . . Nor can a wholly acceptable 'classification' of *essay* types be made. Among the terms that have been used in attempting classifications of the *essay* are: moralizing, critical, character, anecdotal, letter, narrative, aphoristic, descriptive, reflective, biographical, historical, periodical, didactive, editorial, whimsical, psychological, outdoor, nature, cosmical, and personal. Such a list, although depressingly long, is incomplete; obviously the task of classifying the *essay* like that of defining it, has eluded human skill."[5] The sigh of frustration is almost audible in these lines. Wellek and Warren did not even attempt such a classification. While granting that works should be organized into groups based on both outer form (meter, structure) and inner form (attitude, audience, purpose), they write that, in their opinion, the concept of genre should be formalistic rather than topical. Subject-matter classifications seem little fruitful.[6]

Holman's assessment points to the major difficulties encountered in defining the writing mode known as the essay. There is a tendency to apply the label indiscriminately to all kinds of shorter prose pieces so that critics are forced to speak in terms of "genuine" or "true" essays. There is the further tendency to apply generic (e.g., "letter"), thematic ("nature"), and attitudinal ("whimsical") categories without paying much attention to differences among them. Thirdly, the essay is not generically pure. It shares certain features with other literary forms. For example, it can be descriptive like the narrative, intense like the drama, or magical like the lyric poem. Adorno's assessment of 1958 is still largely true thirty years later despite the revolution in literary thinking: "the German essay stands in ill repute as a mixed genre (*Mischprodukt*); its form lacks a convincing tradition" (1:61).

The specific *German* situation within the European tradition of the mode is complicated even further by the fact that the term essay is a loan word. The Germans did not have a term to designate the kind of writing, reading, and thinking that goes into the making of the essay. In fact, it has been argued that the essay is alien to the German mentality and experiences only sporadic periods of popularity.[7] In any event, the term essay did not gain wide acceptance until the second half of the nineteenth century after it was introduced by Herman Grimm (1828–1901) in 1865. While it is disputed whether the *concept* of the essay existed in the minds of writers as a specific mode of writing before the nineteenth century, critics grant that *essayistic writing* did exist in Germany before the label was applied to designate a specific genre (Haas, 1969, 20). Between 1680 and 1815 essays appeared under the guise of the *Abhandlung* (scholarly article), *Bemühung* (endeavor), *Brief* (letter), *Denkwürdigkeiten* (memoirs), *Einfälle* (inspirations), *Fragment* (fragment), *Gespräch* (discourse), *Gedanken und Meinungen* (ideas and opinions), *Probe* (test), *Rede* (oration, speech), *Versuch* (attempt), *Vorrede* (preface), and *Wäldchen* ("little woods" = fragment). It is not surprising then that Rohner, who penned the most extensive study of the essay, requires more than 360 pages to summarize the various attempts to define and classify the mode. Moreover, his finely tuned definition of the form, distilled from all previous characterizations, runs to seven and one half pages and still does not avoid ambiguity (672–679). No wonder then that the claim can be heard that the essay does not exist as an abstract idea, but only as individual productions.[8]

It is clearly a difficult task to pin down a mode of thinking and writing that is filled with movement. Yet there is common agreement that the essay represents a hybrid form of literature, partaking as it does of both poetry and science. In his seminal article on the topic in the *Deutsche Philologie im Aufriß* (*An Overview of German Philology*), Klaus Günther Just describes the literary category as "a small, yet significant space *between* pure literature and strict science; in a certain sense it is the marketplace where all intellectual achievements are to be freely exchanged."[9] Max Bense, for his part, speaks of the essay as "a strange frontier between poetry and prose" and he defines it as "an autonomous part of reality in prose, but interested in poetry, frequently cloaked in pathos and rhetoric" (Bense, 1:51). Lukács revives Friedrich Schlegel's term of *intellektuelles Gedicht* (intellectual poem) to describe its ambivalent nature and the epithet has stuck.[10]

Clearly, the literary form exists on the margins of two apparently irreconcilable areas. Yet, paradoxically, it draws its very energy and life from the polarization of poetry and prose, literature and science. It is not a matter of vacillating between the opposing fields of attraction; rather it is a question of an equilibrium achieved and maintained between poetic inspiration and scientific rigor in the expression of ideas and feelings. Consequently, we cannot speak of a mere contrast between sober science and affective aesthetics. The appropriateness of Morson's concept of *boundary genres* in this regard is incontestable. It should alert us to the need to focus not on what any particular essay means, but instead on what sort of work it should be read as.

Critics of the form have seemed preoccupied with its classification into types, which in turn, has led to a dilution of the focus on the genre, or as I prefer to say, the mode (cf., e.g., Bachman, 8–11). All considerations of the mode and its history include a discussion of its distinguishing traits. But somehow the essential difference between the general category and the canonical triad (epic, dramatic, lyric) has receded into the shadows. Even Wardell fails to avoid this Charybdis in his 1986 dissertation which explicitly sets out to formulate a specific definition of the essay. Wardell isolates four qualities that he feels are indispensible. Yet none of them is

really *essay*-specific. In keeping with the major thrust of literary theory to
reappraise the canon and redefine the nature of literature, we should
concentrate on the essentials that are truly distinctive of a *modus
scribendi*.

Etymologically, the term *essai* is quite revealing. Herman Grimm, a
nineteenth-century theoretician of the essay, suggested a connection with
the Italian word, *saggio*, which is derived from the Latin term, *exagium*.
However, that connection is etymologically dubious, although the connotation of both the Italian and Latin words is similar. While *saggio*
means a sampling or a testing, *exagium* connotes the process of weighing
something.[11] Michel Eyquem de Montaigne (1533–1592), the initiator of
essayistic writing as a literary form, had a similar connotation in mind
when he labeled the individual chapters of his autobiographical musings
essais.[12] The connotations of *essai* in seventeenth-century France, moreover, were richly nuanced, running the gamut from touch to test, taste,
experience, tempt, attempt, risk, endanger, weigh, deliberate, and begin
(Haas, 1969, 1).

Similarly Sir Francis Bacon of Verulam (1561–1626), the other inaugurator of the literary type, referred to his *Essays* as only fragments of the
whole, calling them "contemplations and studies," "dispersed meditations," and "deliberations." In both cases, moreover, the writer wanted
to give a sampling of his private self, of his manner of thinking and
feeling, and was not interested in a public display of talent. In sum, *essai*
designates a methodology rather than literariness.

The tell-tale signs of essayistic writing tend to be of a stylistic nature.
For instance, Michael Hamburger rejects the notion that it must fit a
prescribed form. The literary modus is really a matter of a *style* of
writing.[13] Hamburger's differentiation between form and style points
toward the *essentials* of essayistic writing not readily discernible in the
linguistic or rhetorical qualities of a piece and which imprint upon an
individual instance of essayism its outward "visage." Accordingly, we
should ask ourselves, what idea, concept, or authorial attitude predeter-
mines the formalistic qualities of the mode.

Since a writer always assumes an attitude toward the idea or feeling
s/he endeavors to express literarily, the particular idea or concept is
always subservient to the essayist's *purpose* for writing. That purpose is
framed consistently by an awareness that the writer writes in order to be
read, if even only by him/herself. As Bruno Berger notes, there is a "high
degree of accordance between essayist and reader" (190). Our focus,
therefore, should be on the author's stance or attitude toward a potential
reader via the text created rather than on canonical qualities of the

supposed perfect form of a readily identifiable genre. With this statement we have arrived back at Ruttkowski's suggestion for a fourth, encompassing category characterized by its *Publikumsbezogenheit* (audience awareness). However, we must guard against assuming with Haas that Ruttkowski (and Sengle) call for designating the essay a fourth genre. It is decidedly not their purpose to assign the so-called essay a value parallel to the epic, the drama, and the lyric poem. Rather they clearly argue for recognizing a fourth *mode of thinking and writing* analogous to the epic, the dramatic, and the lyric.[14] Ruttkowski's label *artistisch* will, however, be replaced in the following by essayistic.

The relevance of Ruttkowski's theory for our present examination of the essay is underscored by Friedrich Schlegel in his assessment of Lessing's prose style as a new mode of writing. Schlegel praises Lessing's "genial energy" and "combinatory" method which, drawing upon a wealth of information, imparts to his style an "original stamp"; it is characterized, namely, by "daring associations" and "surprising twists."[15] In a more recent, small but important contribution to the debate on the nature of the essay entitled "Audience and the Tradition of the German Essay in the Eighteenth Century," Vincent J. Dell' Orto forcefully moves the question of audience into the foreground of the discussion.[16] Regrettably, that article has not been accorded its deserved attention and could not be included in Haas's reassessment of the history and theory of the essay which appeared in the same year as Dell' Orto's piece (1975). Dell' Orto's discussion of the history of the German essay in the eighteenth century will be engaged in a later chapter. Of note here is his insistence on the importance of the author-reader relationship for defining the classification. Dell' Orto argues that "varying interpretations of the bond between author and audience result in different kinds of essays" and concludes with the admonition to isolate those features "which, like the author-reader relationship, account for the essay's manifestation in many diverse forms" (123 et passim). That call echoes Haas's almost simultaneous recognition that the underlying attitude on the part of the essayist is decisive, not the particular manifestation (1975, 21). Despite the astuteness of the observation scholars are still inclined to continue the effort of isolating the multifarious features that make up essayistic writing as Berger (1964), Rohner (1966), Haas (1969), Auer (1974), and Wardell (1986) have done.

Rather than labelling constitutive parts, we should now seek the common basis. That common denominator is the writer's invitation to the reader to enter into a collaborative relationship in the method of thinking that lies at the heart of the literary form. That method has been seductively characterized as "methodically unmethodical" (Adorno, 1:72), but we would err to assume that essayistic writing lacked a method. In the following I will endeavor to specify its peculiar methodology with greater precision by having recourse to the triadic model of writer–text–reader especially as defined by Ruttkowski and Morson.

Before we examine the nature of that collaborative relationship between author and reader via the essayistic text in detail, it will be helpful for purposes of common understanding to review the dominant *traits* of the mode. I will argue for retaining some of the descriptive features as being to the point, while rejecting others as being imprecise. My purpose is to show that the *non*-ambivalent traits can all be related back to the nature of the author-reader nexus. By focusing on the question of ambiguity, I hope to clear up some of the theoretical fuzziness that makes comprehension of the method of essayistic writing more difficult. Ultimately, I wish to take issue with Ludwig Rohner's authoritative judgment that the essay cannot be defined in terms of its method, that such efforts have led to chaos in the scholarly debate (1966, 788).

Topography of the Essay

The various attempts to sketch a topography of the essay can be organized according to four general criteria (Haas, 1969, 60):

> the subject matter,
> the essayist's stance,
> the "interference" from other genres, and
> the nature of the relationship between author and reader

These criteria for distinguishing the groups do not, however, appear to be discrete enough. First of all, the thematic approach (#1) seems to be of little value, for essayistic writing is open to all topics. If there is no way to restrict the themes treated, topic is not a reliable discriminator. Nor does the admixture of dramatic, epic, or lyric elements (#3) qualify as a legitimate indicator of types within the specific genre. From the beginning of essayistic writing, "interference" from other literary forms has been part and parcel of the writing mode. Almost thirty years ago Just argued that the hybrid nature (*Mischcharakter*) of the individual essay is an essential discriminator of all essayistic writing (col. 1900). Haas himself echoes this view when he concludes that future poetological discussions must recognize the mixing of genres as a tell-tale sign of the essay mode.[17]

We must ask ourselves, therefore, whether generic impurity is an appropriate discriminator for a type *within* as well as *for* a classification. Double application of generic codes tends to confound the issue.

Finally, the boundary between #2 and #3 is shaded. Is it not possible that the author's stance toward her/his purpose could determine whether the tone of the essay is predominantly epic, dramatic, or lyric? What really distinguishes an instance of essayism from other major forms? Ruttkowski's speech-act based theory provides some answers here. Furthermore, the difference between #2 and #4 is not sharp enough; the author's attitude toward his/her writing or motivation *for* writing could very well be determined by the thought that someone might (should?) read what has been written. In recent years we have seen a proliferation of the view of literature as event. Accordingly, literature is not literature *until* it is received, until the text is reconstructed, whether it be in Sartre's, Iser's, or Fish's manner. Consequently, Haas' groupings #2 and #4 could easily be merged into one. And that is exactly what I propose to do.

Since its publication in 1954 Klaus Günther Just's history and topography of the essay has been pivotal in the subsequent scholarly debate.[18] Of greatest significance in our present context is Just's clustering of the types into six broad categories. (It is regrettable that Haas did not examine them closely.) Five of them are determined on the basis of topic, the sixth is characterized by the writer's stance toward the subject matter. The six classifications are labeled:

> the conceptual essay (*der begriffliche Essay*)
> the culturally critical essay (*der kulturkritische Essay*)
> the biographical essay (*der biographische Essay*)
> the literary critique (*der literaturkritische Essay*)
> the graphic essay (*der gegenständliche Essay*)
> the ironic essay (*der ironische Essay*) (cols. 1902–06).

These six categories could be further refined into innumerable subcategories, but we are here interested in the essential qualities of the broad classifications as perceived by Just.

The "conceptual essay" is anything but an abstract, philosophical piece of writing, for it is capable of translating abstract ideas into concrete form and hard action. This type of composition does not present the reader with a systematic ordering of rational syllogisms; it expresses the realization that the thinking process is a natural phenomenon of life itself.[19] Humanity is not the topic of this kind of writing, but rather humankind's ability to think. Typical of this group is Schiller's *Über Anmut und Würde* and W. Heisenberg's *Veränderungen der Denkstruktur*.

The "culturally critical essay" is related to the conceptual one. The difference between these two content-oriented types is the enhanced degree of liveliness in the manner of depiction that draws heavily on historical facts of a political, military, or intellectual nature to make its point. Whereas mankind is not an object of interest in the "conceptual essay," it is definitely part of the content of the "culturally critical" one, since cultural history is the direct result of human endeavor. Man as creative subject is a focal point. An example of this type of writing would be Möser's *Harlequin* or Schiller's *Die Schlacht bei Lützen.*

The "biographical essay" differs from the previous type in that the individual personality of one or more persons rather than the historical event is of primary concern. Moreover, the individual is viewed as a mirror of the era. In order to convey a vivid impression of the particular biography as a rendition of the times, an intensity of experience is called for. In personal terms this intensity appears as intimate knowledge of the person or persons. When viewed together the intensity and intimacy of depiction can produce a miniature portrait of the age's literary atmosphere. Examples of this kind of writing are Goethe's *Zum Shakespeares-Tag,* Wieland's *Erasmus,* Friedrich Schlegel's *Georg Forster,* or Herman Grimm's *Emerson.*

The "literary critique" is a refined form of the biographical essay. While both the biographical essay and the literary critique focus on a renowned personality—in the case of the latter, a poet or writer—the literary critique examines the literary work itself rather than the writer. Because literature is a preferred topic of essayistic writing in any age, a history of the mode frequently proves to be a history of this particular type of book reviewing. Of special interest of any literary essay would appear to be the progressive qualities revealed by the work examined. Thus the avant-garde is a characteristic of the literary critique. As Just writes: "The great essayist is a staff officer in the struggle for new forms and content in literature" (1905). We would do well to remember the connection between avant-garde tendencies and essayistic writing, for it seems to be critical to the nature of the mode. Lessing's *Hamburgische Dramaturgie* and Herder's *Kritische Wälder* contain many such book reviews.

Just considers the "graphic essay" to be opposed to the conceptual one while simultaneously complementing it. A characteristic of both types is the tendency to focus on the subjective nature of perception and the diverse interpretations resultant of it. Despite the predominant concern with the possibilities, however, priority is really given to the what of the matter rather than the how of it. In any event, the composition does not degenerate into a merely realistic, sober depiction of a thing. Like the celebrated *Dinggedichte* of a Meyer or a Rilke, the "graphic essay" achieves a felicitous harmony of realistic description and deeper symbolic meaning. As an example Just offers Goethe's *Granit*.

Just's final category, the "ironic essay," differs from the foregoing in that its nature is determined by considerations other than those of content and can therefore include literary, biographical, and cultural critiques. The ironic type is marked by precision and nimbleness of perspective and by the propensity for experimentation with ideas and concepts. Seemingly indisputable truths are sometimes developed ad absurdum by the author who appears simultaneously as court jester and sage until inherent contradictions become evident and one is no longer sure what is certain and what is tentative. The designation ironic derives from this playful inventiveness which is far from being mere play. The ultimate purpose of the ironic method is to make clear the nature of the thought process itself. Although Just cites no examples, we could locate here Christian L. Liscow's "Die Vortrefflichkeit und Notwendigkeit der elenden Skribenten" (1734), Lichtenberg's "Über die Physiognomik; wider die Physiognomen" (1778–80), Wieland's "Worin der Autor eine tiefe Einsicht in die Geheimnisse der Ontologie an den Tag legt" (= chapter 1, Book 4 of *Die Abenteuer des Don Sylvio von Rosalva*, 1764), or Friedrich Schlegel's "Über die Unverständichkeit" (1800).

Of Just's six categories of essayistic writing, the last one holds the most promise as a valid discriminator of the entire writing mode. I propose to accord the ironic version a higher status than just a sub-classification, raising it to the status of designator for all forms of essayistic writing regardless of the topic treated. This move is somewhat justified by Just himself who cites the interest in the *process* of thought as a mark of the conceptual, the culturally critical, and the graphic styles. Moreover, the stimulant to creative thinking seems to occasion the focus on modernist tendencies in the fourth category, the literary critique or book review. If, furthermore, we consider that the difference between Just's biographical essay and literary critique can be slight (i.e., emphasis on the writer versus his/her work), the content-oriented categories could all be viewed as variations on a theme.

Strangely enough, Weissenberger makes no mention of Just's ironic category although he speaks of "absolute subjectivity" (*Absolutsetzung des Ichs*) and its related "play character" characteristic of essayism. Weissenberger mistakenly claims that the deeper, ontological dimensions of this *Spielcharakter* have gone unrecognized in essay research (107). On the other hand, he rightly points out the importance of "conscious rhythmic structuring" as the bonding principle in essayism (*Prinzip eines 'ganz-heitlichen' Rhythmus*," 108) and as a major contributing factor to its function as event or discourse. Yet Weissenberger fails to note that this *ganzheitlicher Rhythmus* is rooted in the principles of classical rhetoric, especially that of *numerus oratorius* and the related impression of "verve," *tour*, or *Schwung* (see Chapter VI).

Theorists of essayistic writing have oft noted that the mode is open to *all* topics so that even Just's suggestion for a division into the categories *begrifflich, kulturkritisch, biographisch, literaturkritisch,* and *gegen ständlich* neither avoids ambivalence nor does it cut to the heart of the matter. The content-oriented classifications with their individual characteristics will be more useful in later discussions of the history of the genre than such nebulous epithets as "formal" versus "informal" (Holman), "aesthetic versus perceptive" (Bense, 1:57), or "early, classic, modern" (Rohner, 301–312). Yet the content seems incidental, whereas formalistic characteristics figure prominently because they reveal the writer's attitude toward her/his subject matter *and* toward the audience. As Rohner himself notes: "Neither the topic, nor the substance, nor even the formalistic elements make a more precise classification possible; decisive is the function which the author imparts to the essay. The peculiar intellectual quality of the essay depends on the attitude, way of thinking, and intention of the writer toward his topic" (645). Consequently, Just's sixth category will serve as the focus for determining the essential qualities of the writing mode per se.

Three aspects of the twentieth-century debate on the nature of literature merit reiteration here, for they have a bearing on the interrelationship between modern literary theory and the practice of essayistic writing from its inception. The first is Steiner's perception that the "permanent" book form (= product) is rapidly being replaced by "ephemeral" forms of writing (= *écriture*) so that more attention must be paid to the quality of shorter prose forms ("In a Post-Culture," 169f.). The eighteenth century had a similar sense of shift from the "weighty" book to the facile article. The second aspect is the notion of creative reading promulgated by such critics as Iser and Fish. The enhanced role the reader plays in the literary event provides the counterweight to the writer's role. The third aspect is best summed up by Morson's notion of "boundary genres." The boundary genre presumes the reader's active participation in reconstituting the text and is distinguished from other kinds of literature by its mixing of science and fiction. We will have occasion to return to these implications in our ensuing discussions.

The Topoi and Their Origins

The exact nature of the influence on the genesis of essayism has been the frequent object of investigation. Despite these efforts, however, the genesis of essayistic writing and its relationship to similar kinds of writing is still rather murky (Haas, 1969, 6–9).[20] While I will argue that the mode of thinking which lies behind essayistic writing is different from the method of related short forms, I must grant that the *modus scribendi* of essayism shares some formalistic traits with those other kinds of composition. In this section, therefore, I would like to draw attention to the differences between the essay and related prose forms before I delve more deeply into the reason for that difference. (By concentrating on prose writing in *Crossing Boundaries*, I do not mean to imply that verse is an inappropriate vehicle for essayistic expression. The wide impact, for example, of Alexander Pope's didactic poem, *An Essay on Man*, attests to the frequent use of verse in essayistic writing. For spatial reasons I chose, perhaps wrongly, not to include verse compositions.)

The intermingling of method and style is, of course, traceable to the interaction of dialectics and rhetoric which all humans employ more or less in the discussion of ideas and positions. While dialectics refers to the art of logical reasoning, rhetoric has to do with the art of persuasive argument.[21] Thus we can accept Annemarie Auer's verdict that essayistic writing originates in the chronicling of the history and philosophy of a given culture but develops from there its own distinctive quality (Auer, 133). In examining the reasons for the rise of essayistic writing in the eighteenth century, furthermore, we must reconsider Rohner's assertion that the German essay reveals a strong monologic tendency. He claims, namely, that the style derives from "the scholarly article, from the scientific tract—less from the diary, aphorism, epistle, and dialogue" (Rohner, 677).

Native sources of inspiration for the essay in Germany appear to be twofold. The first is writing of a scholarly nature on historical and philosophical topics; the other includes the social forms of communication. Both involve forms of dialectical reasoning and rhetorical argument. These latter aspects will be examined in Chapters IV and VI respectively. For the moment we are interested in differentiating essayistic writing from other forms that seem to have influenced it formalistically.

Vehicles of Scholarly Communication

1.   *Die Abhandlung* (scholarly article). The *Abhandlung* represents one means of depicting the product of one's thinking. It is marked by a

strictly logical movement toward a predetermined goal and has no artistic aspirations. As such the *Abhandlung* is the suitable manner of communication on scientific, philosophical, and scholarly matters aimed at a closed and restricted audience. Primary for the author of the *Abhandlung* is the content, not his/her audience. Haas feels that the *Abhandlung* can hardly be considered a source of essayistic writing because of its strictly logical manner of proceeding (Haas, 1969, 65).

2.   *Der Traktat* (scholarly tract). Similar to the *Abhandlung,* the tractate usually signifies a piece of religious edification of biblical exegesis which lays no claim to literariness. In a wider sense, the *Traktat* designates writing of a theoretical and ponderous nature. Its purpose is to communicate the results of an investigation in a sometimes aggressive, but always didactic manner to a rather limited audience. A sign of the tract is a clear doctrinal stance.

3.   *Der Aphorismus* (aphorism). The aphorism is a close relative of essayistic writing. Fritz Martini argues that the essay in its early stages was hardly distinguishable from the aphorism (1:408). Essentially, there are two kinds of aphorism: the sudden inspiration (*Einfall*) and the clarification (*Klärung*). The first is a sudden vision of the total conceptual context of an individual phenomenon or a symbol, while the clarification presents the solution found at the conclusion of the reflective process.[22] Although the aphorism and the essay draw equally upon the simultaneity of logic and poetic intuition in their manner of proceeding, the essayistic piece displays this connection much more graphically than does the aphorism. Relatively speaking, it can be stated that the essay represents an open, the aphorism a closed manner of arguing. Nevertheless, some aphorisms can still be considered essayistic, especially those that hark back to Bacon's style (e.g., Lichtenberg).

4.   *Der Aufsatz* (composition). The term *Aufsatz* is somewhat indeterminate because of its broad applicability. It is used to designate school compositions, but also *Abhandlung, Traktat,* and *Essay.* In this regard, *Aufsatz* is analogous to the breadth of meaning in the English designation essay. In German, essayistic writing is not uncommonly called *Aufsatz.* Yet the difference between *Aufsatz* and *Essay* is rooted in the teleological orientation of the former as opposed to the open-ended, experimental character of essayism.

5.   *Der Brief* (the epistle, letter). Etymologically *Brief* refers to a short piece of writing and is one of the oldest literary forms, traceable back to antiquity. The letter is characterized by a personal, familiar, often even rambling tone but is not without an inner organizing principle. Originally aimed at a distant interlocutor, the letter is frequently used to address a

larger and anonymous audience in an engaging fashion on a large number of issues. The eighteenth century provided an especially fertile climate for the personal as well as literary letter which frequently masked essayistic compositions. Thus we can safely say that the letter has literary aspirations, but the distinction between an epistle and an essay is not always clear. In fact, as we shall see in Chapter VI, theorizing on the form and style of the letter acted as a stimulus for essayistic writing.[23] Lessing's *Literaturbridefe* or the Goethe-Schiller, Schiller-Körner correspondence could be considered here.

Vehicles of Social Communication

1. *Die Predigt* (sermon). In the hands of gifted clergymen and mystics since the Middle Ages (Berthold von Regensburg, Johannes Tauler, Heinrich Seuse, Martin Luther, Abraham à Sancta Clara), the sermon was raised to the level of an aesthetically pleasing prose form. It shares many features in common with classical oratory, the dialogue, discourse, and the later feuilleton. In its perfected form, the (written) sermon approximates the appearance of the so-called essay (see, e.g., Luther, Herder, and Emerson). For purposes of distinction, however, we must stress that the sermon is directed at a specific, known audience and seeks to lead the listener to a predetermined conclusion. I list the sermon first in category 2 because it straddles the boundary between the doctrinaire and the social.

2. *Der Dialog* (dialogue). While all essayistic writing is marked by an essentially dialogic structure, the essay differs from the dialogue with regard to the author's attitude toward his/her subject. Like essayistic writing the dialogue is used to reflect upon philosophical issues, but in the dialogue there is a strong tendency to lend the questioning an air of objectivity in the pursuit of absolute truth. By contrast, the essay is subjective and associational in tone. Nevertheless, like its sister literary type the dialogue also aspires to literary excellence, and the line separating the two ways of engaging a wider audience in collaborative discussion is not all that distinct, especially in the Socratic dialogue which was so popular in the eighteenth century. Thus many dialogues can be considered essayistic (e.g., Lessing's *Ernst und Falk*).

3. *Das Gespräch* (discourse). For most critics the conversational tone with its sense of spontaneity, familiarity, and immediacy is the cardinal distinguishing feature of all essayistic writing. Thus, like the dialogue, the conversation would appear to be a very close relative of the essayistic mode. The discourse has much in common with the dialogue. The main

difference between the *Gespräch* and the *Dialog* seems to reside in the perception that the former is an actual social occurrence, such as Goethe's conversations with Eckermann, while the dialogue is literary and less spontaneous. However, the distinction is slight, for the discourse or conversation was frequently used in the eighteenth century in the same sense as dialogue. An example of this interchangeability is Wieland's collection *Göttergespräche* (*Discourses of the Gods*). Their tone is similarly casual and familiar. Nonetheless, we must differentiate between the *Gespräch* as the (supposed) chronicle of an actual conversation and the essay as the representation of an individual's inner mode of thought.

4.   *Die Rede* (lecture, speech). The lecture has qualities in common with the discourse and the sermon. It is intended for oral delivery to an audience present before the speaker. Although the dialogic and rhetorical features of the speech are undoubtedly applicable to the essay, there is a decided difference. Essayistic writing is not intended for oral delivery, but instead requires close reading, perhaps even rereading in order to savor its aesthetic brilliance. The speech tends to contain more direct and more forceful appeals to the listener in order to win over a diversified audience, while the essay is subtler, more playful in manner, seeking to seduce the reader into a participatory act by the dazzling interplay of fine nuance, half tones, and probing forays into unexplored realms. Goethe's *Rede zum Shakespeares-Tag* (1773) or Schiller's *Rede über die Frage: Gehört allzuviel Güte, Leutseeligkeit und große Freygebigkeit im engsten Verstande zur Tugend?* (1779) and *Was kann eine gute stehende Schaubühne eigentlich wirken?* (1784) could be considered essayistic compositions even though they are ostensibly speeches.

5.   *Das Vorwort* (preface). Especially in the eighteenth century the preface was frequently used in the manner of an independent literary type so that it should be listed here. Its purpose was to gain the attention of an anonymous reading public and prepare it for the style and content of the novel, journal number, or document to follow without revealing too much of the matter at hand. Consequently, prefaces are often light and cordial in tone and can even be experimental in character as they attempt to engage the reader's personality so that they are scarcely indistinguishable from essayistic writing. The kind of preface I have in mind is represented by Gottsched's introduction to his *Der Biedermann* (1. Blatt, 1727), the *Vorbericht* to the first edition of Wieland's *Geschichte des Agathon* (1766/67), Lichtenberg's lead-in to his *Patriotischer Beitrag zur Methyologie der Deutschen* (1773), the introduction to Schiller's *Der Verbrecher aus verlorener Ehre* (1786), or the *Vorrede* to Johann Adam Bergk's *Die Kunst, Bücher zu lesen* (1799).

6. *Das Feuilleton* (feuilleton). The word feuilleton was introduced in 1800 by Julien Louis Geoffroy to designate a new supplement of a single page (*feuille*) in the *Journal des Débats*. His intent was to apprise the reader of a change in journalistic stance. The feuilleton presented personal or subjective views on burning issues of the day and aspired to a certain literary quality in discussing them. The proximity of the feuilleton to the essay is attested to by the polarity of views among critics. Some say that they are diametrically opposed; others claim that they are interchangeable. Critical in separating the two modes of writing despite the similarities between them seems to be the writer's conception of his/her audience. While the journalist must win over an anonymous audience very quickly and cannot expect the reader to be amenable to great intellectual exertion, the essayist relies upon the willingness of the anonymous reader to become an active participant in the reading event. As a result, the essayistic piece tends to be longer than the feuilletonistic article. Nevertheless, the boundary between the feuilleton and the essay is not very clear especially when the feuilleton rises above polemics and momentary fashion to engage the reader in experimental, entertaining discourse as happens in the better, literary newspapers and journals. The line of demarcation is further blurred by the frequent appearance of poets as journalists (e.g., Klopstock, Wieland, Schiller, Heine, Fontane, Hofmannsthal, Grass).

From the foregoing it is easy to see that the essay shares many features in common with other kinds of shorter, nonfictional writing. The above alignment of forms is designed to highlight a progression from the more logically structured and less personal brand of writing to the more associative, rhetorical, and familiar kinds. However, it should not be misconstrued to be a value judgment; the ordering is merely descriptive. As a hybrid form, essayistic writing shares equally in both the rational and the personal. Evident, in any event, is the difficulty of citing any one source of inspiration for the essay. Thus it is wise to seek the distinguishing trait not in formalistic qualities as has been the general practice, but rather to locate the distinctive trait in the non-directive attitude of the writer toward her/his subject and audience. The freedom of both writer and reader, then, as envisioned by Sartre in *Qu'est-ce que la littérature?* (1947) is an indispensible quality. By way of summary I list here those essayistic traits and topoi derived from the corpus of previous essay research which have survived the test of essentiality. I cite them as a means of succinctly highlighting the fundamentally experimental, inquisitive attitude of the essayist toward her/his subject.

1. thought association (topos of the leisurely walk)
2. dialogic structure and/or tone
3. a weighing of the possibilities (*Prozessualität*)
4. the open form (encourages productive interaction, stimulates thought)
5. a dialectical view of reality (polyperspectivity)
6. a tentativeness of approach (subjectivity, point of view)
7. experimental character, play on variation
8. freedom from dogmatic systems of thought or belief
9. skeptical attitude
10. playfulness of tone (designed to prepare the reader for the experiment in thinking)
11. a critical note (invitation to co-judge)
12. the tendency to refashion culturally what has already been given cultural form (*Gestaltung von Gestaltetem*) (see Haas, 1969, 47–57).

These isolated features of essayistic writing are traceable back to the two modern originators of the European essay, Michel Eyquem de Montaigne and Sir Francis Bacon of Verulam. Strictly speaking, Montaigne and Bacon were not the originators of the mode; they merely reintroduced it as a literary form. Both freely acknowledged their indebtedness to such ancients as Socrates, Seneca, Plutarch, and Cicero.[24]

Derived from Montaigne's informal manner in his *Essais* (1580) are the topos of the leisurely walk, the skeptical stance, the personal tone, the carefree treatment of profound topics, an easy elegance and spontaneity, and an undogmatic, digressive manner of arguing a point (cf., e.g., Rohner, 30–45; Schon, 8–13). From Bacon's formal manner in his *Essays* (1597) comes didactic practicality, precision of thought, clarity of structure, and an aphoristic style (see, e.g., Rohner, 45–56; Just, col.1911; Hass, 1969, 14–17). While Montaigne laid no claim to certitude, conceiving his work as *un registre des essais de ma vie* for the use of relatives and close friends so that they might be able to form a picture of his personality as a reflection of the times, Bacon wrote his "deliberations," his "contemplations and studies," as practical and moral recommendations for his contemporaries. He was confident of his views and presented them in a straightforward, closed style, drawing liberally upon rhetorical technique (Rohner, 68–76).

The anchoring of all essayistic writing in the postures of Montaigne and Bacon seems to support Wellek and Warren's opinion that genres should be based on the reception of influential writings. "Books are influenced by books," they write; "books imitate, parody, transform other books" (*Theory*, 225).

It has been the custom in essay scholarship to emphasize the differences between the two styles, evaluating the one or the other (informal versus formal) as more appropriate. We know better now. Just as Goethe and Schiller serve as complements to one another in their roles as "naive" and "sentimental" poets, Montaigne and Bacon can be viewed as integral perspectives. The one proceeds intuitively, deductively, the other rationally and inductively toward the same goal: a tentative, holistic apprehension of humankind and its world.

The commonality of Montaigne and Bacon lies in their use of the printed word to promote critical and independent thought. Both were skeptics, both sought free expression of their personal views, both rejected rigid rationalistic systems. Both endeavored to instill in their audiences a willingness to be open to other views. What Montaigne and Bacon strove for in their writing was an enhanced sensitivity to the social and intellectual environment. Both did so by presenting themselves and their personal views. This thrust toward cultural and intellectual consciousness raising (to borrow a popular term from reader-response theory) is a quintessential feature of all subsequent essayistic writing. For this reason Bense can speak of the history of the mode as a kind of "sociology of the human spirit" (Bense, 1:60).

The proximity of this stance to Iser's theoretical concept of *Bewußtmachen* is transparent and will be examined in subsequent chapters of this treatise. Moreover, in his historical overview of the German oration (*Rede*), Walter Hinderer concludes that its primary function in bygone ages was to raise the level of public awareness.[25] Since the oration draws heavily upon rhetorical strategies to achieve its public end, we are safe in assuming the relevance of rhetoric to the essayist's method of consciousness raising. The essayist's ultimate purpose is to link up with another's mind in order to teach critical thinking, but to do it in an aesthetically pleasing manner. It seems obvious that the quality of *purposeful* consciousness raising must be viewed as a major mark of all essayistic writing.

Although recent theorists and historians of the essay have cited the constitutive characteristics of essayistic writing as shaped by the peculiar nature of the author-reader bond and the writer's desire to promote "right" thinking, the exact alignment which I wish to suggest has not been made. Some of the most frequently cited theorists (Bense, Adorno) come very close to making the connections, but subsequent research has not picked up on the cue and gone the extra step. Even Dell' Orto does not draw upon the insights of Bense and Adorno. Yet solely on the basis of eighteenth-century historical evidence, he still arrives at the same conclusion about the structure of the author-reader bond.

We can use Bense and Adorno to begin constructing a philosophical foundation upon which to erect an aesthetic theory of the essay inclusive of all types and topoi discussed in this chapter. The attempt can be viewed as an extension of the scholarly thrust of the essayistic stance. I will then draw upon Habermas's communicative theory of action in order to augment the scholarly element with the social one.

Yet I must point out that neither Bense nor Adorno discusses the method of Enlightenment thought or poetics in connection with essayism. And Habermas is not concerned with the quality of essayistic writing at all. These facts deserve special citation because, as I endeavor to show in chapters IV and V, their theories are anticipated *in nuce* by eighteenth-century thinkers.

Toward a Communicatiive Theory of the Essay

Bense and Adorno

In "On the Essay and Its Prose" ("Über den Essay und seine Prosa," 1952), Bense identifies essayistic writing as the expression of an experimental method of thinking and composing and elaborates upon the contention as follows: "He writes essayistically who composes in an experimental manner, who not only scrutinizes his object from various vantage points, but also—*during the act of writing itself, during the formulation and communication of his thoughts*—discovers his topic or invents, questions, examines, tests, and thinks it through showing what is discernible at all under the aesthetic, ethical, practical, and intellectual conditions set by the author" (1:52, my emphasis). Bense's use of synonyms to clarify the connotations of essayistic recalls the popular connotations of the original French word *essaier* in the sixteenth century.

Continuing in the same vein Bense further explains that the ability to experiment with one's thoughts is a skill that must be learned. The so-called essay is no mere stringing together of ideas and words; it is like a poem that demonstrates an inner wholeness and harmony. As a result, he contends, the essayistic piece ceases to be contingent upon the subject matter discussed. Instead it takes on a life of its own; "it is the result of the combination, of the contours, of the contrasting of the objects treated" (1:53).

Moreover, this modus of experimental communication can draw upon the vast array of logical arguments and affective strategies necessary to realize its purpose. Among these strategies are numbered reflection, meditation, deduction, description, metaphor, abstract signs, doubt, demonstration, provocation, destruction, concealment, radical formulation, concretization, optical perspectives, and mechanical montage. These strategies, he concludes, "are the armory of this general art of experimenting" (1:54f.). Such an explicit portrayal of essayism as the art of critical thinking is rare in essay research. With his notion of the essay as an *ars combinatoria* (1:58) Bense harkens back to Friedrich Schlegel's description of Lessing's critical method. It describes not only the rhetorical manner of proceeding, but also explains the mode's inner dialectical *raison d'être*. This characteristic is manifest in such essayistic samples as Johann Michael von Loen's "Die Schweitz im Jahre 1719 und 1724" (1749), Christian Garve's "Das Weihnachtsgeschenk" (1775) or Herder's "Shakespeare" (1771) analyzed in later chapters.

Lukács for his part, underscores in his "On the Essence and Form of the Essay" ("Über Wesen und Form des Essays," 1910) the dynamic aspect of essayistic writing as critique (1:28) which is concerned with the essence of life (1:37f.). In fact, he refers to it as the "category of the possibilities of experience" (*Kategorie der Erlebnismöglichkeiten,* 1:46) and concludes with the notation that the essay is a "judgmental process" (*Prozeß des Richtens,* 1:47). However, Lukács fails to establish a connection between the writer's intent and the reader's response.

Adorno, like Bense, recognizes in his "The Essay as Form" ("Der Essay als Form," 1958) the abhorrence of the essayist to any kind of dogmatic system because of its tendency to limit the free flight of thought. The philosophical principle at work in an essayistic piece is genuine skepticism. Thus Adorno considers the inner principle of form in essayistic writing to be that of "heresy" (*Ketzerei,* 1:83). Heresy, or the critique of systems, is a fuller elaboration of Lukács's notion of essayism as literary criticism (Lukács, 1:28) and is much closer to Bense's understanding of it as a dialectical methodology.

Adorno intuitively recognizes that Lukács's attempt to define the literary type was colored by the immediate reason for his writing, namely, to provide a foreword to his collection of articles, *Die Seele und die*

Formen (*Soul and Form*, Berlin, 1911). Cast as an open letter to Leo Popper, the preface seeks (perhaps unconsciously) to justify the form of the collection it accompanies. Adorno's use of such terms as *Kulturbetrieb von Prominenz* (cultural business of prominent persons), *konformistisch* (conforming), and *Kulturgeschwätz* (cultural gossip) (1:64f.) in connection with his criticism of Lukács makes the difference between their interpretations of aesthetic form clear.

In contrast to traditional notions of form as expression of wholeness or completeness, Adorno contends that the essayistic form does the opposite. The ambivalent form essayism assumes suggests instead that any attempt to give form to ultimate truths must remain fragmentary, for it is not possible to sketch the whole. The impossibility of expressing the whole is the truth that fascinates the essayist. Thus Adorno can claim that essayistic "totality . . . is that of being not total" and its particular identity as a literary form lies precisely in the "awareness of lacking any particular identity."[26] Like Nietzsche, Adorno considers any formalistic attempt to give specific shape to the totality of existence a distortion of that totality, in effect, a lie. Placed in this light, the essayist's (and Adorno's) aversion to dogmatic systems is readily understandable.

The essay is bound, Adorno argues further, by no preconceived notion, philosophical or literary. Its ultimate purpose is not to seek out the expression of eternal ideas in our transitory world but to lend that transitoriness itself permanence.[27] In short, it seeks to expose the quintessence of reality (*Urgegenbenheit*, 1:70). In order to do so it must engage in a new kind of criticism that eschews traditional ordering and evaluative principles designed to bring about a stoppage of motion and embrace the dynamism of life itself with its momentary impermanence as life's (biological *and* intellectual) essence. The truth expressed in essayistic writing is its negation of traditional notions of absolute, permanent truth. As a writing mode essayism assumes the critical stance par excellence; it is *Ideologiekritik* (1:77ff.); it constitutes a forum for the ultimate skeptic. It encourages boundary crossings. Leibniz in "Ermahnung an die Teutschen, ihre Sprache und Verstand besser zu üben" ("Admonition to the Germans to Use Their Language and Understanding in a Better Manner," (1683), Theodor Lebrecht Pitschel in "Schreiben von der Stärke der einmal angenommenen Meynungen" ("Discourse on the Tenacity of Opinions Once Acquired," 1743), Wieland in "Unmaßgebliche Gedanken des Autors" ("The Author's Humble Opinions," in *Don Sylvio von Rosalva*, 1764), Lessing in "Ernst und Falk" (1778), and Kant in "Was ist Aufklärung?" (1784) all reflect this mode of thinking.

Habermas

Apart from its epistemic-analytical thrust the so-called essay has another "scientific" dimension; it functions as a vehicle of (social)
communication.[28] The roles of discourse and dialogue in this regard are
obviously central. Jürgen Habermas examined the pivotal function of
private and public discourse as vehicles of change in his seminal study on
the rise of bourgois society and mentality in the eighteenth century,
*Strukturwandel der Öffentlichkeit (Transformations in the Structure of
the Public Sphere*, 1962). Whether via conversations in the coffee houses
and reading clubs or via the periodic press—which, as he notes, contains
"periodical essays"—dialogue and discourse were instrumental in
prompting "the process of reciprocal enlightenment."[29] In his *Theorie
des kommunikativen Handelns (Theory of Communicative Action*,
1981), he pursues the question of "reciprocal enlightenment" with
greater intensity and in greater theoretical depth.

Habermas takes as his point of departure the concepts of rationality
and argument, positing an integral connection between analytic philosophy and a theory of communication. That connection is obviously central to our current undertaking, so it warrants some elucidation here. We
will be most interested in his judgment that "analytic philosophy with its
core discipline of the theory of meaning offers great promise for a theory
of communicative action."[30]

Habermas begins his exegesis by noting that rationality traditionally
has to do with knowledge. Yet it is not concerned with the nature or
possibility of knowledge; instead it aims at acquiring and applying it.
Previous theorists, he suggests, seemed preoccupied with the grounding of
rationality in logical proofs. Habermas proposes to broaden that focus as
rationality relates to a theory of communication. In so doing he distinguishes between "communicative rationality" and the traditional "cognitive, instrumental rationality" popularized by such thinkers as
Horkheimer and Adorno in the twentieth century. The main purpose of
instrumental rationality is to ensure the survival and dominance of the
individual agent (1:25–28). In order to explain what he means by "communicative rationality," Habermas must first explain the theory of argument that underlies it.

One can distinguish three aspects of argumentative discourse. It can be
seen as *process*, as *method*, or as *product*. Of these three uses of argument
the first has the greatest relevance for our purposes. It alone is unrestricted and free from external duress and is aimed at a universal audience. Habermas readily grants that the "processual" aspect is the most

idealistic of the three, for it presupposes the interlocutors' desire to arrive at a true understanding of the other. As soon as the manner of argument becomes controlled by a normative procedure not determined by the interlocutors or obsessed with "proving a point," it is no longer argument as process in Habermas's meaning. Instead, it concentrates on disproving via rational argument the claims of one's opponent. Finally, when discursive interaction is designed to test the truth of axiomatic assertions, it is seen to concentrate on the product it wishes to produce or maintain. In the latter two cases, the arguments are directed at a rather limited audience (1:44–51). Nevertheless, Habermas concedes, the three levels of analytical discourse usually interact. He concludes this little digression by noting that they can be subsumed under the triadic scheme of Aristotelian thought: "rhetoric is concerned with argumentation as *process*, dialectics informs the pragmatic *procedures* of argument, and logic focuses on its *products*" (1:49).

Habermas's next step is to show that communication involves both an internal and external component. The internal component has to do with the internalized social, moral, religious, and other kinds of values that inform any society or social group. The external component might be paraphrased as the formalistic systems that structure argumentative discourse. However, the traditional meaning of rationality is not broad enough to include both these constitutive components, for it abides only by the external perspective. An inner connection between the internal and external perspective is required. Habermas finds the bridge in the notion of "a plurality of claims" (1:55f.). The term implies that no one claim (or interpretation) can rightfully be raised to the level of a categorical imperative.

Following these propaedeutical sections of his *Theorie des kommunikativen Handelns*, Habermas then turns his attention to a close examination of our notion of action, drawing distinctions between four essential kinds. The first, dominant since Aristotle, is termed *teleological*. Its distinguishing mark is the goal-orientation of the single actor in the encounter with the world. In fact, teleological action is premised on the existence of an objective world; values such as absolute truth and effectual behavior are central. The actor utilizes those means promising greatest success. A subcategory of the teleological mode is *strategic* action. Whereas only one actor is involved in teleological action, strategic action entails the collaboration of at least one other person in achieving a commonly agreed upon goal. Operative here is the notion that there is but one objective world (*Ein-Welt-Begriff*).

Normative action, the second category, refers to value-centered group action. It is not the individual who stands at the center of the decision-making process, but rather the group (identity). The individual is reduced to following rules and role playing within the group. In other words, the objective world of existent facts is now augmented by a second, more decisive sphere of influence: the world of social values. The latter become internalized and they inform the individual's own sense of worth while motivating his/her decisions. While each person participates in both the factual and social realm, their actions are largely determined by the social context.

The third notion is that of *dramaturgic* action. Of those discussed thus far, this one, Habermas concedes, is the least theoretically evolved notion in the social sciences. The term refers to neither the single actor nor to the group member, but specifies instead participatory agents (*Interaktions-steilnehmer*) who compete with one another to win over an audience. Their self-representation is not spontaneous by any means, for they engage in role playing. They stylize the expression of their individual experiences in order to elicit those feelings and desires from an audience that best serve their own solipsistic ends. The key principles here seem to be encounter and performance.

Related to, yet decidedly different from, the foregoing is the concept of *communicative* action. According to this notion two self-determining actors engage in an interpersonal dialogue in either verbal or non-verbal fashion. Their purpose is to devise a mutually agreeable plan in an effort to *coordinate* their actions. Their purpose is not to dominate or to subordinate an other. Accordingly the communicative mode of action is marked by a clear sense of impartiality, unlike the other forms of communication. Their cooperation is based on a consensus of perceived sensible coordinates of action dictated by a given situation, not on absolute truth. Obviously, in this scheme of genuine collaboration, the act of interpretation assumes a central role. Consequently, Habermas accords language a prominent position within this concept of communicative action (1:126–138).

Language, of course, plays a role in the other modes of communication as well. But, Habermas argues, in the other three concepts the use of language is one-sided and monopolistic. Only in the communicative paradigm of action is language freed from the usual deterministic fetters for the task of unencumbered, penetrating interpretation. Thus, for example, the teleological model of action applies language as only one of several means to achieve a predetermined, self-centered goal. In this context language is deeply indebted to intentional semantics. Language for the

normative mode of action is used to transmit cultural values and information; language does not *create* those values, it merely reproduces them.
Its connection with cultural anthropology is, Habermas opines, manifest.
Finally, the dramaturgic model of human action utilizes language in an
aesthetic or stylistic manner in order to project the speaker in the best
possible light. "Only the communicative model of behavior," Habermas
concludes, "posits language as a vehicle of uncurtailed understanding
whereby the interlocutors establish reference points from the framework
of their predetermined, commonly shared world simultaneously to something in the objective, social, and subjective spheres in order to negotiate
common definitions of situations."[31]

In the communicative paradigm, the speech act is seen as a highly
complex process; it stands in contrast to the teleologic, normative, and
dramaturgic models which Habermas labels "boundary cases of communicative action" (*Grenzfälle kommunikativen Handelns*). They are
"boundary cases" because of their unilateral implementation of the in-
terpretive function of language. The speech act is used namely (1) to
realize the speaker's own solipsistic ends, (2) merely to reproduce an
already existent normative value system, and (3) for purposes of self-
aggrandizement in front of an audience. In each case only one function of
language is utilized. By contrast the communicative behavior model
draws equally upon the concept of symbolic interactionism (Mead), the
notion of language as game (Wittgenstein), speech-act theory (Austin),
and the principles of hermeneutics (Gadamer) (1:143).

At this point in his argument Habermas pauses to define his notion of
action. For him an act is a symbolic expression that establishes a connection between the actor and at least one of the spheres of reality (social,
objective, or subjective) but is always inclusive of the objective realm.
Moreover, an external act has two components: physical movement and
mental operations. The physical movement of the body can, in turn, be
either "instrumental" or "communicative." In the first instance, the subject intervenes directly in the world; in the second s/he expresses an idea
or interpretation. Both kinds of act, however, do impact upon the world
either in a causally or semantically relevant manner. Examples of causally
relevant actions include stretching one's body, raising one's arms, and
crossing one's legs. Semantically relevant movements include movements
of the tongue and lips in speech, nodding one's head, and moving one's
hand while writing. Yet it would be wrong to think of these movements

as action (*Handlung*), for they are only a constituent *part* of action in the true sense. The other constituent part derives from mental or speech processes (1:145f.). Habermas calls them "operations" and sees them as the "infrastructure of other actions" (1:147).

It is important to note that Habermas's concept of communicative action is based on the interlocutors' full awareness of the subjective nature of factual interpretation. They are constantly aware that any conclusion is only preliminary and that contradictory opinions are always possible and always worthy of closer examination. Thus they tend to relativize their statements and claims. In brief, their claims for validity are based on an essential intersubjectivity (1:148). The purpose of communication for them is to raise, defend, attack, and ultimately accept a series of validity claims that fit into a commonly agreed upon interpretation of an act or phenomenon. However, the process never ceases, for the interlocutors must continually reevaluate previous conclusions drawn. As a result the important element is not the agreement reached, but rather the process of reaching an agreement. In this model of communicative action the perspective is provided by the interacting individuals themselves rather than by a pre-ordained system of values or a universally valid objective world (1:149).

Each communicative act occurs against the backdrop of a cultural horizon in which the actor is placed. The framework of cultural knowledge is not in and of itself problematic. Parts of it, however, can become problematical when the interacting individuals thematize it in order to consider how it might or does fit into the ordering system under debate. In any event neither of the interlocutors has a greater right to make claims than the other; nor is the stability and clarity of maintaining one's position the ultimate goal. Both participants know that their views will require constant revision. Yet "communicative action" does not degenerate into mere hermeneutical game playing. The participatory subjects are working toward a goal, Habermas explains, for each wishes to understand the other better and via the process to understand oneself more fully. The focus is equally on the listener's reaction as well as on the speaker's action (1:150f). While Habermas does not wish to equate action with communication, his emphasis on the listener's role as simultaneous *reactor and actor* indicates that the distance between communication and action is not all that great. He later investigates that nexus in greater detail (1:397ff.).

The purpose of the communicative act in this context is to engage the interlocutors in a "process of understanding" that is different from "strategic action." The latter is designed to manipulate the readers/listeners by depriving them of their freedom to think critically (1:383ff.). In the speech act as communicative act the reader is not forced to give up her/his role as self-directing agent (1:387). Communicative action occurs in a commonly shared world that is in a state of flux and builds upon the pre-existent deep structures of the common culture backgrounding the speech act. "The concept of action which is oriented toward mutual understanding," Habermas states further, "has the additional and quite different advantage of illuminating this [common] basis of implicit knowledge" (1:449).

At the same time the act of communication is not totally dependent upon this "background of implicit knowledge." Using Wittgenstein's "On Certitude" ("Über Gewißheit," 1970), Habermas concludes that the literal meanings of words in a text or utterance always exist in a broader if unstated context. They are relative to a deeply rooted, implicit knowledge base of which we are normally unaware because that background remains unproblematic. We accept the essential assumptions of our intellectual and cultural framework as correct (1:451f.). Consequently, I might add, the modern reader must expend extra effort to comprehend the eighteenth-century writer's socio-, ethno-, and psycholinguistic horizons before s/he can enter into a communicative relationship with that writer as envisioned by Habermas.

For Habermas the communicative act is further complicated by the layered meanings of written or oral expression. We cannot merely assume that author-intentionality is sufficient to instigate and complete the speech act as a process of understanding. The structure of the speech act itself is most instructive and can be used to balance the concept of intentionality. Drawing upon semiotics Habermas explains that the linguistic use of signs (*Zeichenverwendung*) is threefold: as symbol, symptom, and signal (1:372). As symbol language serves a "cognitive function" by describing the content (*Sachverhalt*); as symptom it assumes an "expressive function" by relating the speaker's or writer's personal experiences; and as signal it fulfills an "exhortative function" aimed at manipulating the audience.

I have argued earlier that essayistic writing (Ruttkowski's "artistic" mode) is thoroughly informed by audience awareness and the desire for consciousness raising. In view of Habermas's notion of "understanding . . . as a process of reaching an agreement among subjects equally capable of speech and action" (386), we can now see essayistic style as an especially apt form of communicative discourse which transcends prefixed boundaries. Its openness of form and its habitual questioning posture constitute a major facet of essayistic writing as a true vehicle of mutual understanding. It is conducive to the deconstruction of belief systems without either inducing chaos or usurping the individual's right to self-determination. It engages the audience in critical discourse without recourse to manipulation or browbeating. In fact the essayist, like Habermas's interlocutor and in keeping with Sartre's model of the literary act, encourages her/his participatory partner to maintain as much freedom as possible from all those varied vertices of influence that work to restrict individual action and thought. The reader must constantly cross various kinds of boundary lines in order to maintain an independent stance. This stance and attitude informs the essays by Gellert, Wieland, Lessing, Kant, Berlepsch, Schiller, Schlegel, Kleist, and Müller analyzed in *Crossing Boundaries.*

Reading "into" or "out of" the Text?

Let us now return to Adorno and the specific theorizing on the aesthetic quality of essayistic writing. We can use the social ingredient in Habermas's theory of communication to complement the "scientific" quality identified by Bense and Adorno as distinctive of essayistic writing. Adorno clearly recognizes that the essay is designed to engage the reader in a dialogue with the writer. Through the act of writing, authors "pour" themselves into the object which has captured their attention and which they treat via the word. An author's personality may indeed disappear in the object examined, but her/his intent in concentrating on that particular object is encoded—or, to speak with Sartre, frozen—in the text. To read the text "appropriately," Adorno suggests, the reader must learn to decode the message transmitted by the invisible progenitor of the text. The problem, of course, is to know whether one is decoding according to the encoder's intent. In the case of extremely dry texts, where there is no obvious trace of the writer's personality, we have no guarantee of ever knowing with certitude whether the author's intention has been correctly recognized. Reassurance of "proper" decoding is possible through identification of the author's essential *attitude* toward his/her work by any means available and then adopting it.

In order to complete the theoretical framework of essayistic writing we need to augment Adorno's view of authorial attitude with a differentiated view of the extra-textual influences that serve as the "infrastructure" of the writing and reading acts. Our examination of Habermas's theory of communicative action has revealed some fundamental characteristics of "dialectical" discourse. We must, however, be careful to keep the term "dialectic" free of the negative connotations associated with the notion of

"instrumental rationality." Habermas is at pain to show that "instrumental rationality" à la Horkheimer and Adorno is not marked by open
discourse but rather characterized by a teleological drive to maintain or
strengthen one's own position (1:489–534).

We can identify at least four fundamental traits of communicative
action: *intersubjectivity, principle of flux, perspective of the listener, and
discourse as interpretation.* All four qualities underscore the need to
establish a common, mutually determined basis of interaction. Habermas's shift from a single focus on the speaker's purpose to a double focus
that includes the listener's intention makes it less incumbent upon us to
zero in on the *actor's* intention in speaking or writing. As important for
Habermas is the *re*-actor's effort to understand the actor's purpose. Habermas's kind of communicative discourse, therefore, is open-ended and
digressive; it posits the possibility that the speaker/writer can alter his/her
views in the process of participatory descant as easily as the discussant.
Such were the clear expectations of the progressive essayist in the Age of
Enlightenment.

We must guard against merely adopting Habermas's categories, however, as a way of defining the essayistic mode. Although that communicative action is not devoid of a teleological purpose (1:150f.), it describes
primarily oral discussion. As written discourse, the essay does not allow
the precise juxtaposition of two interlocutors in a session of give and take.
This problem has been noted above. What Habermas's theory does allow
us to do, nevertheless, is to perceive the communicative action as acts of
interpretation similar to Iser's notion of the reading act. Since the world
of the speaker and listener is in a state of flux, any attempt to bring about
a prolonged state of stasis is bound to fail.

We can use Habermas's notions of communicative discourse to enhance our appreciation of essayistic writing as the conscious interpretation of the world of motion. It is an interpretation in constant need of
revision because of the natural, evolutionary flow of things. In this regard
Habermas neatly augments and supplements Bense's and Adorno's theories of the essay.

Translated into the realm of literature, Habermas's theory is not without merit. The distance between the communicative act and the literary
event is not large. When the text is *re*-infused with life by a decoder who
responds with the *same imaginative creativity* as originally brought to the
task by the encoder, we have a process not unlike the conversational
descant. In other words the text with its cultural framework must become
the basis of a dialogue between author and reader, even when the author
is a silent interlocutor. Using Habermas's meaning of the communicative

act, we could then state that the essayist's message or intention is identical to the dynamic shape the ideas take. Unlike the more established generic categories, the style of essayistic thinking is the lesson to be learned by the reader; or put more objectively: the encoded text is "properly" understood if it causes self-reflective motion and reassessment in the decoder.

We can now understand Sartre's notion of the author's intention as being "frozen" in the text in a fuller manner. We can even go a step further. In speaking of boundary literature, Morson indicated that "it is not meaning(s) but appropriate procedures for discovering meaning(s) that are disputable," adding that the reader's purpose is not to determine what the individual work means, but rather what sort of work it should be read *as* (49). When the decoder's imaginative creativity parallels the imaginative creativity of the encoder (past or present), the decoder or reader has determined *how* the boundary work is to be read. And that procedure is primary in essayistic writing, not the determination of a specific meaning.

My reading of Adorno's intent in "Der Essay als Form" against the backdrop of Habermas's *Theorie des kommunikativen Handelns* is justified, I think, by Adorno's insistence on analytical skepticism on the one hand, and by his views on interpreting the text on the other. The reader and writer are not unrelated interpreters, for the author of "objective" prose wishes to be interpreted in a certain way, i.e., understood. Adorno asserts emphatically:

> Understanding, then, is nothing but the unravelling of that which the author intended to say at any given moment or at least of his individual psychological impulses inadvertently imparted to the text ("Phänomen"). However, since it can scarcely be determined what an author thought here or there—or what he felt—we really do not gain much by that kind of insight. A writer's impulses are obscured by the objective content to which he subordinates them. Nevertheless, the objective wealth of signifiers encapsulated in every intellectual phenomenon demands—if it is to be appreciated—the same subjective imagination on the part of the decoder as was rejected by the writer to ensure the objectivity of the discipline. Nothing can be interpreted "out of" a text which was not interpreted "into it.[32]

At the conclusion of his article, Adorno returns to this concept of purposeful, directed interpretation by noting the important function in the essay not only of logic, but also of rhetoric. In combination they provide the stimuli for following the text as designed. The logic employed is "more dialectical than dialectics itself" (1:78) while the rhetorical techniques embedded in the fabric of the text are "traces of the communicative act" originally imparted to the text by the writer (1:80). The logic is a discursive type that does not predetermine the relationship of ideas by subordinating the one to the other, but rather by coordinating them so that the reader will not be prejudiced to view them in a prescribed fashion. The rhetorical techniques cajole and prompt; they do not dictate. This kind of literature is definitely designed to be read in a certain way. As a boundary genre the essay not only utilizes formalistic qualities of the traditional genres; it also straddles the line between mere pragmatic rationality and seductive literariness. The author's intentions about how threshold literature should be read is not always clear to contemporary or later audiences.

But essayistic writing is not intended by its author to be solely cognitive or documentary, that is, meant merely as a vehicle for the transmission of ideas. Its design is equally "expressive" and "exhortative." In other words it is part document and part literary text; its function as document suggests certitude, while its function as literary text presupposes indeterminacy and hermeneutic complexity. When a reader discovers the text's suitability for interpretation apart from its merely "scientific" dimension, that reader becomes together with the author a codesigner of the work as literature.[33]

Obviously, a novice reader would have difficulty in deciphering the hermeneutically complex text as delineated here. Rather a "fit" (Fish) or an "ideal" (Iser) reader would be required. The creative act of reading must be learned just as one must learn to write creatively or to think experimentally. Moreover, a reader must be disposed to intellectual exertion, and the times are not always favorable to that disposition. Obviously, an age that cultivates participatory interaction would serve as a hotbed of essayistic style. In the next chapter we will look at the intellectual climate of the Enlightenment as it favored the new mode of thinking and writing.[34]

Habermas, Bense, and Adorno provide us with a fitting conclusion to our review of pertinent aspects of the debate regarding the nature of discourse. They point to its dialectical nature and its role as stimulator of creative participation. If we add the distinction between the essay as a contextualization of an epistemic, aesthetic principle and essayism or essayistic stance (*Essayismus* or *essayistische Haltung*) as that underlying principle—as advocated by such critics as Peter M. Schon (1954), Richard Exner (1962), Dieter Bachmann (1969), and Gerhard Haas (1975) —we have a working definition of essayistic writing as used in this study.

The distinction is between an aesthetic *form* and a fundamental *mode* of conceiving. It is, in a very real sense, a paradox because form posits some kind of containment or stasis, while the mode of conceiving implies incessant movement and change.

Essayism Versus the Essay

Traditionally scholars have endeavored to define the essay as a genre whereby the meaning of genre remained ambiguous. It could imply that the essay is a mere subcategory or a classification essentially equal to the canonic triad. In any event critics focused on the qualities of writing that distinguish an essayistic composition from the poem, the epic, or the drama as well as from other subtypes. Rohner's synthetic definition of the generic category essay is thoroughly informed by this desire to specify the essay's generic location. As an analogue to the canonic system of lyric, dramatic, and epic, the attempt is understandable. But its inherent ambivalence as both genus and species points to the ultimate failure to grasp firmly the elusive idea of the essay.

The debate within the literary Academy over the past few decades regarding the nature of literary and generic studies has taught us to be wary of thinking too strictly in terms of traditional or finely profiled genres. Within each so-called genre there are possibilities for wide divergence from the ideal norm. Poems do not have to be lyrical or rhymed, dramas do not have to be tragic or in five acts, epics do not have to be in verse or heroic. Even if a work is judged "bad" according to the given paradigm, it can nevertheless be subsumed under the rubrics lyric, dramatic, or epic without causing alarm. Why should it not be possible to incorporate in similar fashion widely differing forms in appearance under the heading essayistic writing be they so-called essays, epistles, dialogues, tractates, sermons, and so on as long as the underlying paradigm is discernible? If a poorly executed drama can retain its claim to the generic classification dramatic, it must surely be feasible for a poorly executed essayistic piece to retain its model classification. It may indeed be a bad essay, but if the essential paradigm is intact, it still remains essayistic. Because of this diversity we should be wary of using the terms, *Essay* and *essayistische Haltung*, interchangeably as Rohner does while formulating his definition (cf.678). An essay does not necessarily have to appear in the form of a rigidly construed essay.

Arguing that the form is secondary while the creative impulses are primary, critics such as Sengle, Steiner, and Ruttkowski have urged us to speak in terms of *modes* of writing rather than of *genres*. Of course, the distinction between form and idea has always been acknowledged. Bense, for example, found the relationship between the idea and the form in essayistic writing to be especially troublesome. Yet the stress should not be on the idea as such, but rather on the circumstances which determine how that idea is conceived and transmitted. That approach would enable us to sidestep the ambiguity which plagues the use of such terms as genre and essay.

The poet's choice of form for the expression of his/her idea is prede-termined by the nature of the idea. It is well known that creative writers intuitively recognize whether the idea is best cast as a play, poem, nar-rative, or essay. What works as a poem is not likely to work well as a play. The choice of generic mode is dependent partially on the author's pur-pose, but primarily on the particular way of *thinking* about the idea and of presenting it to an audience. The suitability of a generic classification is determined by those two concerns. We must endeavor to distinguish more carefully the relationship between the fundamental *modus cog-itandi*, its *modus significandi*, and its desired effect upon an audience.

True essayism reflects a multiplicity of perspectives presented in an engaging form designed to awaken and maintain reader interest even after the piece of writing has been "completed." In this latter sense, even when the essay is finished, it is not complete. If a so-called essay is not marked by a discursive, open-ended quality, if it is not a living event as genuine literature should be,[35] we should think twice about labelling it essayistic. On the other hand, if the learned treatise, aphorism, feuilleton, book review, letter, journal entry, and so on are marked by such enduring qualities, perhaps they should be subsumed under the same general head-ing as essayistic writing. The *genus*, therefore, should be essayism and not essay; the latter would be a possible *species* within the larger category even as comedy, tragedy, and melodrama are subclassifications of the dramatic.

In light of the twentieth-century reassessment of the nature of literature and of Habermas's theory of communicative action, I must reject Rohner's view that Lukács, Adorno, and Bense "define less the literary form of the essay than the spirit of the essay" (786). He is led to this false conclusion by misunderstanding the implication of Adorno's phrase *methodisch unmethodisch*. The method of essayism as described by Adorno is, in fact, not whimsical; it only appears to be so. The "spirit of the essay" (*Geist des Essays*) *is* the mode's one genuinely essential quality. Because that spirit of skeptical inquiry, daring experimentation, and ironic play can be maintained at a level of brilliance for only brief periods of time, the essayistic compositions tend to be short.[36] Similarly, Rohner's verdict that Adorno's and Bense's insights are applicable only to the modern German essay must be rejected as false (787). Not only do the essayistic samplings from Thomasius to Müller belie the assertion, our foregoing considerations of reader-response theory and Habermas's theory of communicative action underscore the universal relevance of Adorno's and Bense's ideas on the nature of essayistic writing. Finally, why should the canonical barriers remain so rigid? Dieter Bachmann tells us that "essayism in literature signifies the transgression of the canonical boundaries; this is an ambivalence which is itself characteristic of the actual essay."[37]

Our point of comparison should thus be the "generic" way of thinking not the incidentals of a supposedly perfect form. I must note, moreover, that essayism is not the same thing as the "conversational style" (*Gesprächscharakter*) ascribed to the essayistic mode. While the discursive style is descriptive, essayism is epistemological and involves deep structures.

In sum the criteria used in this study to define essay and essayistic are rooted in the dialectical nature of the manner of conceiving and proceeding (see Haas, 1969, 21). While we can retain as essential characteristics of essayistic Rohner's statement that the essay is basically art rather than science, that it is concerned with form as well as with ideas, that language is its medium, and aesthetic pleasure its ambition (674), we dare not conclude that the aesthetic form is rigidly prescribed. The initial impulse of the essayist as a *poeta ductus* can and does lead to great diversity in appearance.

Because of the poet's attitude the essayistic piece galvanizes writer and reader in a dialectical exchange of ideas and emotions, which is different from the dramatic, epic, or lyric paradigms. Its purpose is to promote intellectual agility by imitating the natural dynamics of systole and diastole. This essential characteristic was fully recognized by Friedrich Schlegel, one of the first and most important theorists of the German essayistic manner: "The essay is like a mutual galvanism of the author and reader; it is also an inner arousal for each independently. It is a systematic alteration between rest and motion. Its purpose is to cause motion, to combat intellectual arthritis, to promote agility."[38] Rohner comes close to saying this himself, but somehow it gets lost in the verbiage of his 900-page opus (cf. 645).

It is now appropriate to sketch the intellectual atmosphere and the social conditions of literature in the eighteenth century, for they gave birth in Germany to the kind of thinking encoded in essayistic style. We can now view that method as "communicative action" in Habermas's meaning of the word rather than as "methodically unmethodically" as is the usual wont.

Notes

1. Gerhard Haas, *Essay* (Stuttgart: Metzler, 1969), 30.
2. Klaus Weissenberger, "Der Essay," in *Prosakunst ohne Erzählen*, ed. Klaus Weissenberger (Tübingen: Niemeyer, 1985), 105, 124 (Schöpfungspoetologie). Apparently Weissenberger intends to pursue the aspect of "creative poetology" further, for the subscription announcement for *Sinn und Symbol*, ed. Karl Konrad Polheim (Berne and New York: P. Lang) lists a contribution by him under the title: "Der Essay als Schöpfungspoetologie—Zur Typologie einer literarischen Gattung."
3. See, e.g., Richard Exner, "Zum Problem einer Definition und einer Methodik des Essays als dichterische Kunstform," *Neophilologus* 46 (1962), 169; Max Bense, "Über den Essay und seine Prosa," *Deutsche Essays. Prosa aus zwei Jahrhunderten*, ed. Ludwig Rohner (Munich: dtv, 1972), 1:58 (first published in *Merkur* 1 [1947], 414–424); Georg (von) Lukács, "Über Wesen und Form des Essays. Ein Brief an Leo Popper (1910)," *Deutsche Essays*, 1:42); Theodor W. Adorno, "Der Essay als Form" (1958), *Deutsche Essays*, 1:71; Peter M. Schon, *Vorformen des Essays in Antike und Humanismus. Ein Beitrag zur Entstehungsgeschichte des Essais von Montaigne* (Wiesbaden: Steiner, 1954), 3; Ludwig Rohner, *Der deutsche Essay. Materialien zur Geschichte und Ästhetik einer literarischen Gattung* (Neuwied and Berlin: Luchterhand, 1966), 115, 628–638; Annamarie Auer, *Die kritischen Wälder. Ein Essay über den Essay* (Halle/Saale: Mitteldeutscher Verlag, 1974); Bruno Berger, *Der Essay. Form und Geschichte* (Munich and Berne: Francke, 1964); James Raymond Wardell, "The Essays of Christoph Martin Wieland: A Contribution to the Definition and History of the Genre in its European Context," Dissertation, University of Michigan 1986; James Van Der Laan, "The German *essay* of the Eighteenth Century: An Ecology," Dissertation, University of Illinois at Urbana/Champaign 1984; Robert Victor Smythe, "Christoph Martin Wieland as Essayist," Dissertation University of Texas at Austin 1980. These are only a few of the more important attempts to define and classify the protean form of the essay in German.
4. See Elizabeth Hardwick, "Its Only Defense: Intelligence and Sparkle," *New York Times Book Review* (Sept. 14, 1986), 1, 44–45.
5. William F. Thrall and Addison Hibbard, *Handbook to Literature*, revised and enlarged by C. Hugh Holman (New York: The Odyssey Press, 1960), 183.
6. René Wellek and Austin Warren, *Theory of Literature* (New York: Harcourt, Brace & Co., 1956), 221–223.
7. See Rohner's discussion of *Essayfremdheit* in Germany: *Essay*, 116–131; Haas, 1969, 18.
8. Dieter Bachmann, *Essay und Essayismus* (Stuttgart: Kohlhammer, 1969), 9. James Wardell swims against the current in his dissertation (see note 2).

2

2

Wardell premises his investigation on the view that essay studies have been hampered by vague definitions of the genre and he presents his work as the first attempt to examine the history of the early European essay on the basis of a precise definition ("Introduction," xx). He devotes his first chapter ("Defining the Essay," 33–127) to isolating the essential traits of the essay which differentiate it from other short prose forms. Wardell's conservatively formalistic, perhaps even atavistic approach, is obviously counterposed to my belief that we must broaden not narrow, the perspective—combine what is mutually attracted rather than artificially separate what belongs together.

Wardell isolates four qualities of an "exploratory epistemological stance" (86): (1) it is reality oriented and non mimetic, (2) its conclusions are preliminary and its statements not verifiable, (3) by nature it is of a small format, and (4) it is a conscious work of art (39, 128). The problem with these concepts are that they are not all that precisely defined (is anything except nature itself non-mimetic?), nor are they all restricted to designating the so-called essay. For example, it can be argued that as works of art all belletristic writing is self-conscious. And the conclusions of a scientific research project are frequently preliminary and non-verifiable. What happens when the essay appears as an epistle or a discourse? Must the "short format" exist separately from a larger context (e.g., a novel) in order to be considered a "true" essay? (Wardell himself includes an excursus on essayistic passages in Wieland's novels of the 1760s [293–317].) Why is he inconsistent in his use of the term *genre*? Sometimes it refers to groupings of writing, at other times to individual types within a group.

His own methodology is based on the "building blocks" of stylistics: *form, macrostructure, microstructure,* and *genre structure* (xxv) which, he explains, are not indebted to any one particular school of literary theory. They do, however, draw heavily upon classical rhetorical strategies (xxviiif.; cf. 94–103). Nevertheless, the line between rhetoric and artistic expression (as well as between genre and form) is not all that clearly drawn. Despite his laudable diligence in trying to restict the definition of what an essay really is, Wardell's endeavor ultimately fails to formulate a definition that accounts for its countless countenances. In effect, the wriggling fish flips out of his hands. Nevertheless, Wardell is right to remind us of the long recognized truth that the essay is both practical function and aesthetic experience (92ff.).

9. Klaus Günther Just, "Der Essay," *Deutsche Philologie im Aufriß*, ed. Wolfgang Stammler (Berlin and Bielefeld: E. Schmidt, 1957–62), 2:1897.
10. Lukács, 1:47. See also Walter Mannzen, "Die Stunde G. Benns," *Frankfurter Hefte* 5 (1950), 550, and Rohner, *Essay*, 305.
11. My thanks goes to my colleague Albert Lloyd who was most helpful in determining the etymological relationships between *exagium, saggio,* and *essai.*
12. Herman Grimm, "Zur Geschichte des Begriffs Essay" (1890), in *Deutsche Essays*, 1:25.
13. Michael Hamburger, "Essay über den Essay," *Akzente*, 12/4 (1965), 290–292: "Der Essay ist keine Form, sondern vor allem ein Stil." Bruno Berger, *Der Essay*, seems preoccupied with the form of the "ideal" essay.

This focus on formalistic qualities prevents him from seeing the further implications of his own statements such as the following: "The essential factor in the genesis of a typical, relatively short size of the essay form is . . . the artistic feeling for the form; *the inner form, as the result of the formulation of ideas and their expression, determines the outer shell*" (my emphasis, 114). Even though he recognizes the intimate relationship between the manner of thinking and the expression of that manner, he restricts its validity to only one kind of essay. This same prejudice later leads him to denigrate the significance of experimentation as a critical factor of any essay (115–127).

14. Gerhard Haas, "Zur Geschichte und Kunstform des Essays," *Jahrbuch für internationale Germanistik* 7/1 (1975), 23.

15. Friedrich Schlegel, "Lessing. Vom Wesen der Kritik," *Schriften und Fragmente* (Stuttgart: A. Kröner, 1956), 57.

16. Vincent J. Dell' Orto, "Audience and the Tradition of the German Essay in the Eighteenth Century," *Germanic Review*, 50 (1975), 111–123. Wardell (1986) also recognizes audience participation as an essential ingredient in essayistic writing (cf. 88ff.).

17. Haas (1969), 36. See also Theodor W. Adorno, "Der Essay als Form" (1958), in Rohner, *Deutsche Essays*, 1:61. Wardell (1986) is adamant in rejecting the plea.

18. Almost as influential has been Fritz Martini's article on the essay in *Reallexikon der deutschen Literaturgeschichte*, 2nd Ed., ed. Klaus Kanzog (Berlin: de Gruyter, 1955ff.), 1:408–410. See Rohner's summary of the attempts to classify the essay according to types in *Essay*, 639–645.

19. Such is the premise of the anthology of essays and excerpts edited by Horst Günther: *Wie Man Lebt und Denkt. Ein Lesebuch zum Denken*, 2nd ed. (Frankfurt a.M.: Insel, 1981). The volume is comprised primarily of eighteenth-century texts.

20. See Berger, 29–48, Rohner (1966), 481–626, and Haas (1969), 61–68, for attempts to distinguish the essay from related short forms.

21. The interaction of method and style has long been part and parcel of Western thought. Aristotle noted in the opening paragraph of his treatise on rhetoric, for example, that rhetoric is the counterpart of dialectic: "Both alike are concerned with such things as come, more or less, within the general ken of all men and belong to no definite science. Accordingly all men make use, more or less, of both; for to a certain extent all men attempt to discuss statements and to maintain them, to defend themselves and to attack others." *Rhetoric*, trans. W. Rhys Roberts (New York: Random House, 1954), 19.

22. Franz Mautner, "Der Aphorismus als literarische Gattung," *Zeitschrift für Ästhetik und allgemeine Kunstwissenschaft* 27 (1933), 154f.

23. The proximity of the epistle to the essay is evident in the description of the former as "maintaining an air of casualness, effortlessness, and naturalness," as being "an harmonious balance of art and nature," and as having no limitation of subject matter. Moreover, particularly in the informal epistle "it is the personality of the writer and his relationship to the recipient

that controls the tone of the epistle." See Markus F. Motsch, "The Forgotten Genre: The Poetic Epistle in Eighteenth-Century German Literature," *Studies in Eighteenth-Century Culture* 4 (1975), 119–124; here 123.

24. See Schon's informative study on the history of the essay to the seventeenth century: *Vorformen des Essays in Antike und Humanismus* (Wiesbaden: Steiner, 1954). Friedrich Hiebel, *Biographik und Essayistik. Zur Geschichte der Schönen Wissenschaften* (Berne: Francke, 1970), pays particular attention to the biographical element in essay writing, tracing it from Aristotle and Cicero to the classical period of the modern essay in the nineteenth century.

25. Walter Hinderer, "Kurze Geschichte der deutschen Rede," *Über deutsche Literatur und Rede. Historische Interpretationen* (Munich: W. Fink, 1981), 246: "nicht umsonst ist die Rede das wichtigste *Produktionsmittel* des öffentlichen *Bewußtseins*" (my emphasis).

26. Adorno, 1:76f; "Seine Totalität ist die des nicht Totalen," "das Bewußtsein der Nichtidentität von Darstellung und Sache." Similarly Eva Acquistapace, *Person und Weltdeutung. Zur Form des Essayistischen im Blick auf das literarische Selbstverständnis Rudolf Kassners* (Bern: H. Lang, 1971), 9–24: "Die Nicht-Identität als Wesen essayistischer Welterfassung."

27. Adorno, 1:70: "Der Essay aber will nicht das Ewige im Vergänglichen aufsuchen und abdestillieren, sondern eher das Vergängliche verewigen."

28. Wilbur Samuel Howell, *Poetics, Rhetoric, and Logic: Studies in the Basic Disciplines of Criticism* (Ithaca and London: Cornell University Press, 1976) argues forcibly for an understanding of the "artistic enterprise" as part of the "enterprise of communication" (215). His method is to expose points of juncture between poetry, rhetoric, and logic. While I agree with his insistence on the communicative nature of literature, I cannot accept his strict division of poetic utterance into "the literature of symbol" and expository prose, journalistic writing, and oratory into "the literature of statement" (223f.). The elimination of the symbolic use of language in expository prose makes no allowance for the essayistic writing. To be sure, Howell is unconcerned with essayistic writing and is therefore unaware of its aesthetic/scientific bifurcation. I think Walter Pater's classification of all verbal literature into "literature of fact" and "literature of the imaginative sense of fact" is more appropriate for my purposes of examining the communicative as well as literary qualities of essayistic writing. The essay is easily subsumable under Pater's second category (cf. 231f.).

29. Jürgen Habermas, *Strukturwandel der Öffentlichkeit. Untersuchungen zu einer Kategorie der bürgerlichen Gesellschaft* 16th Ed. (Darmstadt and Neuwied: Luchterhand, 1986), 59.

30. Jürgen Habermas, *Theorie des kommunikativen Handelns*. Vol. 1: *Handlungsrationalität und gesellschaftliche Rationalisierung*, third ed. (Frankfurt a. M.: Suhrkamp, 1985), 370.

31. Habermas, *Theorie des kommunikativen Handelns*, 1:142: "Allein das kommunikative Handlungsmodell setzt Sprache als ein Medium unverkürzter

Verständigung voraus, wobei sich Sprecher und Hörer aus dem Horizont ihrer vorinterpretierten Lebenswelt gleichzeitig auf etwas in der objektiven, sozialen und subjektiven Welt beziehen, um gemeinsame Situationsdefinitionen auszuhandeln."

32. Adorno, "Der Essay als Form," 1:63. Because of the specific nature of his formulations I cite the original here: "Verstehen ist dann nichts als das Herausschälen dessen, was der Autor jeweils habe sagen wollen, oder allenfalls der einzelmenschlichen psychologischen Regungen, die das Phänomen indiziert. Aber wie kaum sich ausmachen läßt was einer sich da und dort gedacht, was er gefühlt hat, so wäre durch derlei Einsicht nichts Wesentliches zu gewinnen. Die Regungen der Autoren erlöschen in dem objektiven Gehalt, den sie ergreifen. Die objektive Fülle von Bedeutungen jedoch, die in jedem geistigen Phänomen verkapselt sind, verlangt vom Empfangenden, um sich zu enthüllen, eben jene Spontaneität subjektiver Phantasie, die im Namen objektiver Disziplin geahndet wird. Nichts läßt sich herausinterpretieren, was nicht zugleich hineininterpretiert wäre."

33. On the nature of literature as being either designed or discovered, see Gary S. Morson, *The Boundaries of Genre* (Austin: University of Texas Press, 1981), 15, 39–49. He specifically names the essay [in Russian: "sketch"] as a boundary genre and demonstrates its proximity to the feuilleton in Russian literature (26–30).

34. Adorno grants that the twentieth-century reader (he writes "German reader" but we can universalize the statement) is languishing in a period of "insipid enlightenment" (*nur laue Aufklärung*, 1:62) and is consequently not disposed to intellectual exertion. The eighteenth century, on the other hand, was disposed to such mental activity and social intercourse.

35. Iser, "The Reading Process," states for example: "Any living event must remain open" (56). The underlying premise of Newman's *Post-Modern Aura* is the notion that his work is "a brief account of an incomplete idea" (5). He concludes with a consideration of "the permanent crisis unsprung" (170ff.). Similarly, Ray summarizes the significance of his own effort to sort out the most recent theories of literary meaning by affirming the open-ended quality of his analysis: "It would be an exercise in self-contradiction to argue the permanent truth of a dialectical model of meaning. . . . Thus if my account of meaning is correct, it must disqualify its own closure: analytic discourse is as self-differing, its truths as slippery, as any literary work" (206).

36. According to Rohner the ideal length is sixteen pages, but he does allow for variations between a low of 400–500 lines to a maximum of 4000–5000 lines, indicating that most essays contain less than fifty pages (347–349). Berger speaks in terms of reading time; three to four hours of slow reading strikes him as being maximal (189).

37. "Essayismus in der Literatur meint eben gerade das Überspringen der kanonischen Grenzen. Das wiederum ist ein Charakteristikum auch des eigentlichen Essays" (Bachmann, 10).

38. "Der Essay ist wie ein wechselseitiger Galvanism des Autors und des Lesers und auch ein innrer für jeden allein; systematischer Wechsel zwischen

Lähmung und Zuckung.—Er soll Motion machen, gegen die geistige Gicht ankämpfen, die Agilität befördern" (Friedrich Schlegel, *Kritische Werkausgabe*, Vol. 18: *Philosophische Lehrjahre I. Fragmente zur Philosophie*, ed. Ernst Behler [Paderborn: F. Schöningh, 1963], 18/2:221).

CHAPTER 4

The World of Eighteenth-Century Thought

Prolegomenon: Adorno's Enlightenment

While in exile in Southern California during the Nazi period, Max Horkheimer and Theodor W. Adorno joined forces to write *Dialektik der Aufklärung*. In it they continued the line of reasoning exemplified by Hegel and Nietzsche in a sweeping interpretation of the Enlightenment. Completed in May 1944, the book was published in June 1947 and reissued twenty-two years later in 1969. Their "philosophical fragments," as the work was subtitled, had a greater impact than the authors had envisioned, for it became something of a cult work among young academics trained during the fifties, sixties, and early seventies. As a result it provided an understanding of the *Aufklärung* which came to be widely held in the Academy.

Horkheimer and Adorno, however, were not that concerned with the actual quality of the eighteenth-century Enlightenment despite their references to Bacon, Descartes, Leibniz, Kant, de l'Ambert, and Sade. Their chief concern was with the dialectical interplay between myth and knowledge since the beginning of Western civilization as initially expressed in Homer's *Odyssey*. Their purpose was to argue that the dehumanization of humankind (= *Verdinglichung*) in modern industrialized society is directly traceable to the Enlightenment's penchant for developing rational systems. They took from the aforementioned writers of the European Enlightenment ideas and concepts useful to their main purpose of theorizing on the modern consequences of cultural anthropology through the ages (see their preface). Thus their work was not intended as an inventory of actual eighteenth-century Enlightenment thought in all its complexity. They were guided in their interpretation of the dialectics of enlightenment by perversions of such Enlightenment notions as methodical analysis, universality, perfectibility, and felicity so that their musings constitute in fact a frontal assault on fascism and the underlying principles of capitalism (= *Warengesellschaft* or *Kulturindustrie*). While overplaying the characteristics of the scientific Enlightenment, they tended to downplay that movement's views on moral values such as self-direction (= *Mündigkeit* and *Selbstdenken*) and autonomy.

As critics of our age they have been very effective in promoting debate. Unfortunately, they have unwittingly contributed to a one-sided and therefore distorted picture of the European Enlightenment in general and of the German *Aufklärung* in particular because their work lends itself to a misreading as a focused critique of *eighteenth-century* thought. They were, to be sure, largely responsible for the currently fashionable notion of the "wretchedness" (*Elend* or *Misere*) of the *Aufklärung*—that is, its impotence in promoting utopian ideals—as its legacy to the twentieth century.[1]

Critical to a judicial understanding of early essayistic writing is a proper understanding of the diversified intellectual climate that nurtured its development. There is no need to go into a detailed discussion of Enlightenment philosophical anthropology in its dizzying configuration from Thomasius to Rousseau, Kant, and Herder, but we do need to correct some essential misperceptions inadvertently promulgated by *Dialektik der Aufklärung*. The misperceptions tend to gravitate to three major foci of Enlightenment thought: the meaning of *Aufklärung*, the role of critical thinking, and the nature of the human being.

Horkheimer's and Adorno's assessment is based on two cardinal assumptions. The first of these is that knowledge translates into power. Citing Bacon's formulation (they could have begun with the story of Adam's and Eve's fall from paradise), they apply it to the entire European Enlightenment, assigning it a crassly political connotation.[2] Secondly, they hold that the primary tenet of "enlightened social behavior was that of self-preservation" which they apparently derived from the Enlightenment's concept of utility (*Nützlichkeitsbegriff*) (36, 90 et passim).

As a consequence of these assumptions, they are led to make seemingly definitive statements about the nature of the Enlightenment in their chapter on the concept of enlightenment:

- "Enlightenment is totalitarian" (12);
- "its ideal is that of the system from which each and everything ensues" (13, cf. 92);

- "the Enlightenment acts toward things the way the dictator behaves toward people. He will acknowledge them only in as far as he can manipulate them" (15);
- "the quintessence of the Enlightenment is choice, which inevitably leads to domination. Humankind had always to choose between its submission to nature and nature's subjection to the self" (38).

Not only in this conceptual chapter but everywhere in their study the reader encounters the notion of restrictive choice, domination, the need to control or be controlled in turn. In vain do we search for the eighteenth-century's belief in individual emancipation through self-determination (*Mündigkeit* or *Selbstdenken*), the necessity of freedom of thought (Kant: *der Hang und Beruf zum freien Denken*), and human compassion (=*humanitas*). It is clear that the example of a totalitarian regime which claimed to be the heir of German Classical traditions was squarely in view as Horkheimer and Adorno proceeded with their cultural reassessment.

Their simplification of the Enlightenment as rational reductionism in the pursuit of happiness led Horkheimer and Adorno to conclude that the Age of Enlightenment did not truly value autonomous, experimental thought, but was interested only in its applicability for devising a well ordered, prosperous world. Fascinated by Bacon's formulation of knowledge as power, they failed to see that the Age of Enlightenment, while far from disdaining the "redemptive" quality of knowledge, valued the release from dogmatic sectarianism much more than the mere accumulation of clear and distinct ideas. Consequently, they depicted the fundamental Enlightenment concept of thinking in one-sided fashion. To be sure, the *Aufklärung* initially relished the freedom of intellectual inquiry from dogmatic strictures, they contend, but thinking rapidly declined from philosophical innovation designed to liberate human potential into mere sciential studies intended to regulate human intercourse (42).

In other words, they saw the critical process of thinking as "strictly goal oriented"; that is, as *instrumentale Vernunft* (36). Thinking as an activity was reduced for them to a mere "tool" and "object" (*Werkzeug* and *Sache*, 32). Its sole function became that of finding ways to dominate others (44, 45), relentlessly applying mathematical principles to all areas of life. In short, the activity of thinking became yet another prison of the spirit, a strait jacket (= *Zwangssystem*, 45f., 88–90, 95) as restrictive and blind as the dogmatic systems it was to have replaced. Not surprisingly then Horkheimer and Adorno conclude that both critical, independent thinking and the Enlightenment itself quickly betrayed their original calling, degenerating into mere mechanical reflection and system-building. They write: "Intellectual activity reduced itself to a self-activated, automatic process much like that of a machine, which it has itself created so that the machine could one day make individual thinking obsolete. Enlightenment reneged on the classic exhortation to think critically and independently."[3] Enlightenment philosophy thus ceased to be philosophy in the true sense. In its presumed pursuit of felicity through unanimity (cf. 42), it lost the element of self-reflection (44). To adopt Harold Brodkey's terminology, it ceased to be risk-taking.

The Enlightenment concept of humankind did not fare any better at Horkheimer's and Adorno's hands. In keeping with the radical positivism of their general emphasis, the two critics speak of the age's new alignment of the human individual with the divinity. The point of comparison resides in the notion of patriarchal rule. Humankind is godlike in its drive to gain mastery over nature and society even as God rules over the universe. Humankind resembles the divinity when it commands and directs: "The divine image of man consists in his sovereignty over the world, in the [ruling] gaze of the Lord, in [the power of] command" (15). In holding this view, Horkheimer and Adorno disregard the Enlightenment's hostility to paternalism on moral grounds.[4]

The social contract is interpreted to signify a loss of individuality and identity to the faceless crowd. The social structure is intended to ensure the demise of the individual through the all-pervasive manipulation of the collective. Individual happiness is sacrificed to the harmonious sameness of regulated social intercourse. The allegedly logical, ideal subject in successive ages is the slave owner, the free entrepreneur, and finally the administrator. Nor is felicity achieved through virtue, which Horkheimer and Adorno portray in Nietzschean fashion as the most insidious form of enslavement (88–127).

Repeatedly in their chapters on "the Concept of Enlightenment," "Myth and Enlightenment," and "Enlightenment and Morality," Horkheimer and Adorno return to Kant's writings to prove that the purpose of all Enlightenment thinking was to develop an all encompassing philosophical system which would answer all human questions by reducing philosophy to definite principles and categorical imperatives. Such a system would enable humans to order and control both nature and human action in their pursuit of self-preservation. The central Kantian insistence upon the need for intellectual self-responsibility and independence as the cornerstone of any worthwhile human and social reform is willfully reduced to petty self-preservation (e.g., 90). The problem with *Dialektik der Aufklärung* and its offspring is that only the opening passage of Kant's famous essay is cited where he attempts to offer a definition of *Aufklärung*. Rarely does an analysis of Kant's position reflect a careful reading of the entire piece which is, in effect, an explanation of the opening definition.

True Enlightenment

Truly, one does not recognize the eighteenth-century German Enlightenment in Horkheimer's and Adorno's *Dialektik der Aufklärung*. The Enlighteners did not speak with one voice. Yet *Dialektik der Aufklärung* singled out the natural-science orientation and manner of applied thinking satirized by Goethe in Faust's gifted but pedantic assistant, Wagner, as representative of the entire movement. They overlooked the fact that Faust himself embodied the best principles of the *Aufklärung*. Kant surely took the proverbial turn in the grave when the book appeared. If the essence of the Enlightenment were as Horkheimer and Adorno depict it, the literary mode of essayism would have been still-born. It is shocking to think that there are others who, like Horkheimer and Adorno in their trend-setting book, fail to differentiate between the real thing and its perversion. In literary and intellectual histories well into our century, for example, appreciation for the accomplishments of the Age of Reason suffered from a generally bad press. The bias toward Classicism and Romanticism prevented an objective evaluation of the intellectual climate from which both later movements drew inspiration. Even Ernst Cassirer's judicious assessment in his celebrated *The Philosophy of the Enlightenment* (1932; English trans. 1955) was not enough to stem the tide.

There was obviously a need to explain what *true* Enlightenment was and is. A concerted effort to amend the inherited, simplified view of the Enlightenment movement began in the late 1960s and has continued into the 1980s. The major impetus for the renewed interest was imparted by Horkheimer and Adorno themselves. A turning point toward a more positive attitude vis-à-vis the significance of the European Enlightenment is reached in the work of such intellectual and cultural historians as Peter Gay, Klaus Epstein, Norman Hampson, Reinhart Koselleck and Jürgen Habermas during the 1960s.[5] They tended to stress the complexity of the European phenomenon in social, political, and philosophical terms without losing sight of its deeper roots reaching back to the Renaissance and Greek and Roman antiquity. During the 1970s the focus was narrowed to the specific situation in Austria and Germany between approximately 1680 and 1800 (e.g., Vierhaus, Pütz, and Schneiders). Of pivotal importance in our context is the study by Werner Schneiders, *Die wahre Aufklärung* (*True Enlightenment*, 1974).[6]

The study is seminal for at least two reasons. First, it was conceived as a direct response to wide-spread misconceptions about the nature of the Enlightenment as well as about its historical configurations. Secondly, through its solid scholarship, objective tone, and clear writing, *Die wahre Aufklärung* became the new source of inspiration for subsequent inquiries. The continuing deliberations in the 1980s on the meaning and possibility of enlightenment cannot afford to bypass Schneiders's exegesis. The newest work, either *expressis verbis* or tacitly, draws upon his insights and the material he discusses.[7]

Schneiders's point of departure is the belief that an interpretation of *Aufklärung* as commonly used in the twentieth century cannot disregard the historical movement's interpretation of itself. A more complete understanding of the eighteenth-century school offers a better footing for twentieth-century thinking on the nature and purpose of enlightenment in general and of the German Enlightenment in particular (19). Thus he devotes the bulk of his 250 pages to a retelling of the long-forgotten, intense debate on the nature of Enlightenment waged by theologians, politicians, writers, and educators during the final quarter of the eighteenth century.

The discussion which had begun with Christian Thomasius in the late seventeenth century heated up significantly with the announcement by the Prussian Academy of Sciences in 1777 of the topic for a new composition contest. The question posed was: "Est-il utile au peuple d'être trompé soit qu'on l'induise dans de nouvelles erreurs, où qu'on l'entretienne dans celles où il est?" (Is it advantageous for the people to be deceived either by leading them into new errors or by preserving them in the old ones?) The selection committee received forty-two submissions, an astonishing number for the time (28). The responses were by no means unanimous, with opinions ranging from unqualified affirmation to absolute rejection of the implication that people can and should be deceived if it is for their own good. The debate on the nature of Enlightenment continued long after the competition itself had been concluded. Schneiders's findings on the diversified nature of the Enlightenment (e.g., 189) affirm Ernst Troeltsch's forgotten assessment of 1897 that it is "not possible to reduce [its] infinitely varied content to a simple formula," an insight that now runs like a leitmotif through the secondary literature.[8]

Critical for our purposes is the definition of *true* Enlightenment which Schneiders culls from the approximately seventy more or less obscure essays on the essence, value, possibility, necessity, basis, and/or limits of enlightenment published between 1779 and 1802. Few were penned by so-called classical writers (Kant, Lessing, Wieland); most were by obscure men of letters (Stuve, Riem, Bentzel); twenty were published anonymously. Cautious as he is in attempting a formulation of true Enlightenment, Schneiders is braver than Pütz who declines to offer a "definitive answer to the question: 'What is Enlightenment?'" in his assessment of recent research on the age.[9]

In order to decide what true Enlightenment is, one must first decide what the goal of enlightenment in general is. Is its intended goal self-enlightenment or the enlightenment of others (*Selbstaufklärung* or *Fremdaufklärung*)? The difference is critical, for it is a matter of self-directed versus other-directed inquiry and impacts directly upon essayistic writing with particular forcefulness. Does one seek to understand the reasons why or is one only interested in promoting unanimous opinion in others? Is one interested in *truth per se* or only in the *power* knowledge makes possible? In other words, the difference between *Selbst-* and *Fremdaufklärung* is the distinction between cultivation of critical thinking (*Selbstdenken*) and the accumulation of information (Schneiders, 195). (I translate *Selbstdenken* as "critical thinking" because the German term connoted for the Enlighteners more than just the ability to understand, i.e., *Verstandesdenken*. See Schneiders, 200.)

His analysis of the eighteenth-century controversy leads Schneiders to conclude that true (also *richtig, echt, gut*) Enlightenment is equated with self-enlightenment. The distinguishing attributes of *Selbstaufklärung* are the freedom and ability to think for oneself in clear and distinct terms (= *Selbstdenken, Freidenken, Helldenken*, and *Richtigdenken*). The objective of such thought is not the accumulation of information, but rather the recognition of and emancipation from prejudice. The emphasis is not on the use of knowledge to achieve progress in the technical realm but rather on the enhanced awareness of the tentativeness of all knowledge. It is an ongoing, self-determined activity with a very strong moral component. In fact, the process is primarily a moral one, for the goal of *Selbstaufklärung* via the process of *Selbstdenken* is ultimately the achievement of *Mündigkeit*. The individual's calling according to eighteenth-century philosophical anthropology is to become an autonomous, self-directing, and more perfect human being (191–194, 201–203, 210). Schneiders concludes: "Self-enlightenment is self-determination through informing oneself. Emancipation in the sense of self-emancipation requires therefore a special effort, which is moral in kind. It is dependent on a revolution in the way one thinks and feels, that is, emancipation requires a radical change in the will to act, it is posited on an initiation of one's own initiative."[10]

The big question nevertheless remains: how is one to achieve genuine enlightenment? How does the individual come to desire freedom through truth as expressed in terms of *Selbstaufklärung*? One is not free, Schneiders notes, without really wanting to be free nor can one take the initiative if one has no idea of where to begin. The paradox is that self-enlightenment is apparently not possible without an external stimulus, that is, without one mind working upon another. But how does the other achieve the necessary illumination to teach the learner the "right" ideas and method of proceeding? The dilemma is an existential one. The way out of this dilemma would seem to lie in the principle of negation. One must question everything in order to learn which ideas, which actions advance an individual toward perfection as a moral being (210f.). Yet how does one avoid the danger of becoming so self-critical that one is consumed with self-doubt? How does one attain objectivity without losing one's self? Schneiders poses all these questions, but he does not venture an answer. He writes: "We cannot here address the question of how . . . self-enlightenment is to be initiated from outside or is to be promoted by the actions of others [= *Fremdaufklärung*], that is, how the openness of an individual to suggestions can be exploited pedagogically."[11] Instead he begs the question by pointing to the nature of enlightenment as an ongoing *struggle.*

It is my intent to offer with this present study a plausible response to the unanswered question of the *possibility* of enlightenment emphasized by Schneiders. Moreover, I will use the phenomenon of innovative essayistic writing as it evolved in conjunction with the experimental mode of the *Aufklärung* to explain how that possibility functioned. To achieve this end, however, we must make a distinction not drawn by Schneiders or other critics who have recognized the problem. Perhaps their reluctance to make the connection is due to the general aversion to any notion of elitism. My solution could be misconstrued as elitist. Yet it is based on suggestions, ideas, and assumptions of eighteenth-century *Aufklärer* from Thomasius to Schiller who were, for the most part, privileged in comparison to the general populace but who had the interests of all human beings at heart.

The stumbling block for Schneiders is the paradox of self-initiated self-enlightenment. He argues that to assume an enlightened teacher as the initiator of self-enlightenment in others is to beg the question of how that enlightened teacher became enlightened. This paradox becomes less problematical, I suggest, if we assume that certain individual circumstances (e.g., freedom to travel, "benign neglect" by authority figures, benefits of social class, and availability of books and learned tutors) can combine with native ability (inquisitiveness, intelligence, industry) to provide the spark necessary to ignite the desire for liberation from false assumptions and prejudice. Moreover, that combination could easily lead to the recognition that one must take responsibility not only for one's socio-economic life but—more importantly—for one's moral existence. There are any number of examples of individuals throughout history who had at least begun the process of *Selbstaufklärung* without having achieved its perfection (e.g., Aristotle, Montaigne, Descartes, Kant). The Enlightenment world view was rooted in Hellenic and Judeo-Christian idealism which posited a perfect form or being of which reality and the individuals populating it are imperfect reflections but which are destined to evolve toward the perfect state. According to Enlightenment theory, furthermore, the doctrine of perfectibility assumes that the process of perfection would take a very long time, perhaps millennia. This is a notion repeatedly encountered in writings of the eighteenth century beginning with Leibniz's *The Theory of Monads* (*Monadologie*, 1714), continuing through Wieland's *The History of Agathon* (*Geschichte des Agathon*, 1766/67), Lessing's "Erziehung des Menschengeschlechts" ("The Education of the Human Race," 1780), Kant's "Was heißt: Sich im Denken orientieren?" ("What Does It Mean to Orient Oneself in Thinking?" 1786), and achieving consummate literary expression in Goethe's *Wilhelm Meister's Apprenticeship* (*Wilhelm Meisters Lehrjahre*, 1795/ 96). Modern would-be enlighteners make the mistake of expecting enlightenment to lead *immediately* to improved social and political conditions. The true Enlighteners in the Age of Reason realized how vain that hope is. Individual moral perfection must precede any political utopia.

We *can* assume, even as Kant argues in his pivotal response to the nature of enlightenment, "Beantwortung der Frage: Was ist Aufklärung," that the impulse to self-enlightenment can and does come from within as well as from without.[12] That presumed paradox should not be a stumbling block. The real problem lies in the implicit assumption that the general populace must be educated, persuaded, cajoled, or whatever within a generation or two to accept and appreciate the call to self-direction. Modern thinkers generally seem much more impatient than Kant, or Herder, or Lessing, or Wieland were. The latter realized, e.g., that enduring socio-political reform could be achieved only through "a genuine reform of the way we think" (Kant, AA, 8:36; Zehbe, 56). Modern thinkers—Horkheimer, Adorno, Chargaff, etc.—accord too little attention to the full import of gradual evolution envisioned by such thinkers as Leibniz and Kant. Consequently, the twentieth-century critic often appears less optimistic even when recognizing that the essential ingredient of *Aufklärung* is a radical change in the way we think.[13]

Thus we should distinguish between isolated instances of self-enlightenment and universal self-enlightenment. The goal is obviously the universal kind, but it will be long in coming. The seed for it, however, is contained in the isolated instance. Kant represented the general view of his age when he wrote (with a few lightly veiled ironic barbs aimed at governmental officials of his day): "It is more likely, however, that a people [*ein Publikum*] would enlighten itself. Indeed, it is almost unavoidable, if they are only given the chance, since a few independent thinkers can always be found, even among those charged with responsibility for the common people. After these few individuals have cast off the yoke of tutelage from themselves, they will begin to popularize the spirit of individual self-worth and the notion that every person think for him/herself."[14] Moreover, to achieve the ultimate goal, one must recognize the difference between false, or illegitimate, and true, or legitimate, enlightenment.

It is to this issue that Kant turned in his "Was heißt: sich im Denken orientieren?" ("What Does It Mean to Orient Oneself in Thinking?") two years after his famous response on the nature of Enlightenment. While stressing the need for open, uninhibited critical discussion in the development of reason in the true sense of Enlightenment, Kant defines *Aufklärung* as "the maxim always to think for oneself," commenting that it is not such a difficult task. He states: "Beginning [the process of] enlightenment in *individual subjects* via education is, therefore, rather easy. All you have to do is begin early to accustom young people to reflect critically upon ideas. To enlighten *an entire epoch* is much more tedious since there are so many external hinderances which either limit or make that kind of education later in life impossible" (Kant, AA, 8:146f.). If the *Aufklärung* has failed, it is because its nature has been misunderstood. Adorno, Horkheimer, Chargaff, and others speak of the false kind; Schneiders exposes the genuine article that Kant formulated so clearly.

Adorno makes amends somewhat for his one-sided view of the Enlightenment in later writings by calling attention to the need for critical thinking. Of special note is Hellmut Becker's interview with him aired on the Hessian radio network one week after Adorno's death on August 6, 1969. That interview was entitled: "Erziehung zur Mündigkeit" ("Education for Intellectual Independence"). (The topic also provided the title for the collection of essays and discussions written between 1959 and 1969 and published in 1970.) In a certain sense, therefore, Adorno's comments on the need for educating people to intellectual maturity are his last words on the subject. Like so many others, he takes his cue from Kant's famous formulation: "Enlightenment is the emergence of human-kind from its self-incurred tutelage." Here, more than thirty years after the first publication of *Dialektik der Aufklärung*, Adorno is judicious in his appraisal of Kant's true intent. The prerequisite for true enlighten-ment is the courage of each individual to use his/her critical abilities fully and independently. Genuine democracy cannot occur without that indi-vidual element. The critical use of reason must be taught and nurtured if intellectual activity is not to degenerate into a rote, mechanical process. Adorno clearly equates here "thinking and indeed resolute and insistent thinking" with the Kantian challenge to mankind to be truly free.[15]

Adorno's revised assessment of the true nature of the Enlightenment places him in line with the view formulated by Ernst Cassirer in his *The Philosophy of the Enlightenment* (1932), but which is frequently ignored by contemporary critics. Cassirer's approach to eighteenth-century thought is premised on the belief that the age was highly diverse, so a static, historical chronology of major theorems or systems would hardly gain access to the true nature of its intellectual climate. Not the breadth or length of view is the proper method in the case of the Enlightenment but rather the depth of perspective. In his introduction (ix) Cassirer states:

> The true nature of Enlightenment thinking cannot be seen in its purest and clearest form where it is formulated into particular doctrines, axioms, and theorems; but rather where it is process, where it is doubting and seeking, tearing down and building up. All this constantly fluctuating activity cannot be resolved into a mere summation of individual teachings. The real philosophy of the Enlightenment is not simply the total of what its leading thinkers—Voltaire and Montesquieu, Hume or Condillac, d'Alembert or Diderot, Wolff or Lambert—thought and taught.

The conviction that the inner intellectual life of the Enlightenment and its concept of reason is best captured by such formulations as "pro-cess," "pulsation," "original intellectual force," "energy," "concept of agency," "irreducible manifold," "unity in multiplicity," "creative activ-ity," and "the constant renewal of the spirit" recurs throughout his study.

While the preponderance of these designations occur in the chapter on the method of the Enlightenment ("The Mind of the Enlightenment," 3–36), they are found everywhere.[16]

With their emphasis on the dynamism of the intellectual life of the eighteenth-century and insistence that its unity lies in its diversity, critics such as Schneiders and Barnard ultimately arrive at Cassirer's original standpoint which had been forgotten with time. They would all agree with Cassirer's summarizing statement that "the whole eighteenth century understands reason . . . not as a sound body of knowledge, principles, and truths, but as a kind of energy, a force which is fully comprehensible only in its agency and effects" (13). Yet, as noted, Cassirer's pioneering efforts are rarely mentioned.

Drawing the Consequences

The ideas exposed by Schneiders in his *Die wahre Aufklärung* of 1974 have been elaborated upon by others in the 1980s.[17] The tendency has been to concentrate on the one or the other characteristic of "true" enlightenment. Thus, for example, Gerhard Sauder in "Kritik des Vorurteils—Vorurteile der Aufklärung" ("The Critique of Prejudices— The Prejudices of Enlightenment," 1983) singles out the "critique of prejudice" as the distinctive trait of *Selbstdenken*, suggesting that it constituted *the* program of the Enlightenment.[18] In arguing, however, that the *Aufklärung* failed to recognize that prejudice and myth are part and parcel of the *conditio humana* and that they could therefore not be easily eradicated (277), Sauder momentarily relapses into a depiction of the "false" Enlightenment which he had otherwise endeavored to keep separate from the "true" version. From Crusius, Brockes, and Gellert right through to Wieland and Kleist, the genuine *Selbstdenker* were aware of the limits of reason and said so in their esssayistic compositions. For that reason Hamlet's famous comment to Horatio about the limits of reason became somewhat of a topos among the *Aufklärer* and their successors in the Storm and Stress and Romantic schools. In paraphrased form that idea is: "There are more things on earth and in heaven than philosophers have ever dreamed of." The topos can be taken as a sign of the Enlightenment's awareness of the permanence of prejudiced views. Schneiders himself has contributed to a more complete understanding of the role of prejudice in Enlightenment thought in his thorough study, *Enlightenment and the Critique of Prejudice: Essays on the History of Prejudice Theory* (1983).[19]

The central role and essential meaning of *Mündigkeit* in Enlightenment thinking as it evolved from Christian Thomasius to Kant and Herder is the topic of a cogent study by the intellectual historian, Frederick M. Barnard (1983).[20] Barnard argues that *Mündigkeit* assumed the status of a moral category in the eighteenth century and that it is analogous to the modern concept of "giving reasons" as the dominant form of account-ability in acting or asking others to behave in a certain way. He concludes that this "capacity for reflective awareness" (293) is "the quintessential legacy of the Enlightenment" (296f., cf. 288). It is important to note, however, that the freedom, which is a condition as well as a derivative of self-direction, is not absolute. All three philosophers examined here speak of the limitations to personal freedom imposed from within (e.g., preju-dice and misperception) as well as from without (e.g. physical hinderance and censorship). Absolute freedom would be contrary to the human condition. Moreover, it is not something that is given, but a state that must be constantly practiced (286).

While Barnard is to be commended for his insights into the actual nature of an important Enlightenment concept, a slight correction of his views seems in order, at least for our purposes in laying the theoretical groundwork for an appreciation of early German essayism. Barnard con-tends, namely, that Herder, in realizing that there are limitations to human autonomy and "that maximizing knowledge or rationality did not *mean* maximizing freedom as the realm of choice," departed profoundly from the philosophical view of his day (287f.). Barnard's interpretation does not give Kant his just due. Kant *was* aware of the limitations to individual autonomy, relegating essential freedom to the moral sphere.[21] Thomasius, and especially Christian Wolff, coming at the onset of the movement, were perhaps more optimistic than the later Kant could be about humanity's ability to free itself from prejudice and thus achieve absolute freedom. Be that as it may, the significance of Barnard's study for us lies in his differentiated view of self-direction as well as in his realization that few of the "true" Enlighteners were "sanguine optimists or naive progressivists" (297). While steadfastly working toward the lofty goals of humanism, they were fully aware that humanity might not achieve those objectives during a single lifetime. These Enlighteners shared Lessing's conviction that the *search* for truth (perfection), not its final possession, is the human lot. These insights are significant for us because that salient dynamism of the *Aufklärung* informs the attitude of the eighteenth-century essayists, as will become evident in the later chap-ters of this inquiry.

Finally, I have tried to show elsewhere that arguments in the Age of Reason for freedom of speech and of the press were based on the concept of inalienable human rights.[22] The deep conviction of these writers (e.g. Lessing, Schiller, and Wieland) was that humankind is by nature destined to be a free and self-directing *agent*. All attempts to treat the individual as an *object* of manipulation amounts to a perversion of human nature and must be protested vigorously. The only allowable restriction of free speech comes from within. The logic of this restriction is clear: destined by human nature to be a self-directing and free agent, only the individual has the right to curtail his or her own inalienable right. External attempts to control that right are nothing more than censorship. Important in our present context is the anchoring of free expression in a *moral, inalienable right* of which all humans partake as a necessary precondition to the full realization of each individual's humanity.

To argue for a separation of enlightenment and humanism, as Michel Foucault does, is to confuse the nature of false enlightenment with that of true enlightenment.[23] For the *Aufklärer* true Enlightenment and the ideals of humanism are intimately linked. Although, strictly speaking, enlightenment is the *means* of perfecting humanity (= goal of humanism) and not identical to humanism itself, the ideals of humanism cannot be realized without true enlightenment. That is the underlying premise of Herder's *Letters on the Advancement of Humanity* (1793–97). In the twenty-fifth letter Herder emphatically asserts: "Perfectibility is thus no illusion. It is the means and ultimate purpose for cultivating everything which our essential nature, *humanitas*, demands and grants."[24] Thus the leading German exponents of *wahrer Aufklärung* speak of Enlightenment as the "destiny of humankind" (*Bestimmung der Menschheit*.[25] The destiny of humanity, like human nature itself, is essentially unchanging and independent of any particular historical, ethnic, or cultural circumstances that might tend to favor or obstruct its fulfillment in the individual. The precepts of metahistorical humanism are anchored in these anthropological constants. Christian Thomasius, Christian Wolff, Johann Gottfried Herder, and Immanuel Kant, among others, expressed the conviction that "our whole philosophy" would one day become "anthropology."[26] Kant's formulation in his lectures on pedagogy can stand for them all: "The human race has the [moral] obligation to develop little by little its essential nature through its own effort. One generation educates the next" (Weischedel, 12:697).

Enlightenment as Active Thought Process

The means by which the ultimate goal of humanity can be attained is the faculty for conscious reflection. Obviously that faculty requires cultivation. Thus, before we leave the topic of eighteenth-century thought, we need to hear some specifically eighteenth-century voices on the seminal role of critical thinking in perfecting human nature. These voices will serve as a balance to the jaundiced view presented by Horkheimer and Adorno in their *Dialektik der Aufklärung*. The purpose of the ensuing overview is to demonstrate that critical, independent thinking was a *constant* hallmark of the *Aufklärung* from its inception; it did not first emerge with Kant, nor did it quickly expire after Thomasius. Moreover—and this is of great significance for *Crossing Boundaries*—a startling number of the theorists of the art of thinking in the time frame 1680—1815 turned to essayistic writing to express their ideas in particularly salient fashion.

First of all, it must be understood that "critical" thinking in our context has nothing to do with metaphysics, although it is concerned with an ultimate "discourse on method." Beginning with Thomasius and Leibniz, a major thrust of the Enlightenment was moral and practical. This major emphasis is evident in the titles of works from Thomasius's *Ausübung der Vernunftlehre* (*The Practice of Rational Doctrine*, 1691) to Kant's *Anthropologie in pragmatischer Hinsicht* (*Anthropology in a Pragmatic Light*, 1798). The explanation for the continuing interest in the practical application of knowledge is clear: the focus of these true Enlighteners was consistently trained on humankind itself. The human race, as Pope had put it, is the proper study of mankind. All other kinds of knowledge are extraneous to this gravitational point.

Thus it is that Thomasius' philosophy is designed as an assault on metaphysics despite his indebtedness to Descartes's manner of proceeding in the *Discours sur la méthode* (1637). Having come of age, he argues, people are inherently capable of forming their own judgments.[27] In fact, they have a moral obligation to test the validity of inherited truths against their own experiences through the use of their five senses. Thomasius exhorts his reader: "Learn from the natural order of things external to yourself and by means of your outer senses more and more about previously unrecognized, indisputable truths."[28] But he is not interested in knowledge for its own sake. Its suitability for advancing human perfection and felicity is primary. This kind of knowledge is different from speculative philosophy; the former he regards as genuine *Gelarheit* and opposes it to the metaphysical twaddle fashionable among his fellow intellectuals. Of this practical knowledge Thomasius writes: "Practical knowledge is a recognition by means of which a person is empowered to distinguish the true from the false, the good from evil. It makes him/her capable of understanding the essence of the true or, as the case may be, of proffering probable causes [of it] in order to advance his/her own temporal and eternal welfare as well as that of others in the flux of social life."[29] We encounter here a first expression of the modern concept of accountability, that is, that reasons must be given for holding certain ideas to be true or actions to be beneficial. Additionally, the insights gained from practical experience are clearly aimed at improving the quality of human existence, individually and collectively, here in this world.

Twelve years earlier Gottfried Wilhelm Leibniz had composed a short piece on the art of thinking entitled: "Of an Organum or Ars Magna of Thinking."[30] In it he first presented his binary system of thought arrived at independently from Thomas Harriot. Leibniz returns to the topic in later writings, most notably in "Of Universal Synthesis and Analysis; or, of the Art of Discovery and of Judgement" (c. 1683). Of interest to us is not so much the binary system itself, which is widely used in digital computers, but rather Leibniz's attitude toward the human *capacity* for thought. The philosopher considers the ability to think to be "the most powerful of human faculties." As the most potent of human abilities, the power of thinking is the surest guarantee of progress toward the fulfillment of human destiny, for "the supreme happiness of man consists in the greatest possible increase in his perfection" ("Ars Magna," 1).

These essential ideas are taken up and popularized by Leibniz's most productive disciple, Christian Wolff (1679–1754), who saw his task to lie in the schooling of men's minds. For him the capacity for thought was the surest path to improvement. Yet Wolff's significance as the most respected and widely known German philosopher in the eighteenth century prior to Kant resides not simply in his successful efforts to systematize Leibnizian thought. While indebted to Leibniz in many respects, Wolff was no blind imitator, blazing his own critical path. His major contribution to the Enlightenment school (after the creation of a philosophical language in German) may, in fact, be the different emphasis he gave to the notion of "practical knowledge" (*nützliches Wissen*). By redefining philosophy as the science of all possible things and how they can be known, Wolff opened up the concept of practical knowledge to all ideas that are even only *potentially* useful. The previous tendency was to limit practical knowledge to those insights of immediate benefit to one's professional or personal life. In contrast to that dominant view, Wolff declared: "Whoever is serious about acquiring beneficial insights will prefer to choose the safe approach as long as he is undecided and will not lose the opportunity to learn something [potentially] useful if it can be done without neglecting one's responsibilities."[31] In other words, Wolff took the next logical step down the path of self-determination. If one is supposed to be skeptical about the validity of facts until one has measured them against personal experience, it stands to reason that one can never know what experiences or bits of information might hold the answer to some future question. Thus Wolff would allow the study of subjects not directly related to one's immediate needs. The path to truth is not always straight, since one does not know for certain where to look for it.

Wolff's stress on potentially useful knowledge is central to the attitude underlying the mode of essayistic thinking. It is reminiscent of the spiral path traced by the method of "weighing the possibilities," cited as a mark of the essay. Moreover, it gave birth to the celebrated notion of *Bildung* as it gained expression in the literature of the latter eighteenth century (*Geschichte des Agathon, Wilhelm Meisters Lehrjahre*). A major goal of essayism is the promotion of the individual's sense of value through the cultivation of reason and sensibility (elements of *Bildung*). This goal is achievable only in a "civil society" that values the increase in knowledge and awareness. When we enter the world we are pure potential. In order to realize that potential, we must evolve through a process of cultivation and refinement. In other words, as Wieland tells us in 1770, "humankind must be its own second creator."[32]

Contemporaneous with Wieland, Herder also states his conviction that the capacity for thought (and sentiment) is mankind's most powerful faculty, which, however, must be perfected. It is a capacity, not a full-fledged ability. Although mankind must be freed from deception, the release from prejudice and deceit is only the beginning of the emancipatory act. People must be taught to act individually. In the *Letters for the Advancement of Humanity* (1793), he writes: "It is not sufficient to free mankind from deception; the human race must also be imbued with a sense of its own strength of spirit."[33] Even as creation evolves toward perfection—that is, the realization of inborn potential—each individual creature is also destined to strive for perfection. In fact the whole phenomenon of evolution is inherent in the concept of *Bildung* advocated by Herder and others. In a very definite sense all of Herder's as well as Wieland's, Lessing's, and Schiller's works are examples of such advancement toward full realization of one's potential. Like his contemporaries Herder realized that moral, aesthetic, and intellectual progress required prodding. Consequently his writings, as one leading Herder critic puts it, "do not simply talk about a process of formation, they make the reader undergo the process" itself.[34] To achieve this objective the reader must be engaged intellectually and emotionally via the written and spoken text. Since truth for these Enlighteners does not consist simply in pure concept but has a sensual or emotional component as well, writing which desires to promote progress must be multivalent. These ideas on growth and cultural reform are, to be sure, ultimately derivative of the thinking that went into Leibniz's *Monadologie* (1714) and "Ermahnung an die Teutschen" (1683).

But, of course, Kant is still the most widely acknowledged major source of Enlightenment ideas regarding the need for critical thinking as the means of realizing human destiny. Side-stepping his well-known essay on the nature of Enlightenment, we shall turn to his less famous *Anthropology From a Pragmatic Perspective* (*Anthropologie in pragmatischer Sicht*, 1798) published just five years before his death. It represents his last word on the significance of Enlightenment. The work also represents the culmination of practical philosophy since Thomasius.

In the preface to the *Anthropologie*, Kant clarifies his use of the term pragmatic, separating it from physiological. "Physiological anthropology" refers to the study of nature's formative influence on the development of the human race, while "pragmatic anthropology" connotes the study of mankind as a "free-acting agent." It is the investigation of that which mankind has made of itself or could and should make of itself. Kant is interested in pragmatic anthropology because *"man is his own ultimate purpose"* (Weischedel, 12:399; Kant's emphasis).

The first insight that we gain through the practical study of man, Kant tells us, is that every individual is by birth egoistic. Like Rousseau in *Emile* (Book IV), Kant argues that love of self is the original innate passion prior to all the others. Accordingly, each human being is first concerned only with him/herself. Each of us is prejudiced to place trust in our own experiences and the views we develop from them. We are prepared by our very nature to expect the other person to be in error if there is a conflict of opinion. Our implicit trust in the accuracy of our convictions accords them the force of fact. In order to overcome this "philosophical" idealism, it is necessary to be exposed to a pluralistic society. The antidote to egoism is, thus, pluralism. Kant contends: "Egoism can be countered only by pluralism, i.e., the manner of thinking which conceives of and treats the individual not as encompassing the whole world in his/her own person, but as a 'mere' citizen of the world."[35] When we become aware that every other individual is as egoistic as we ourselves, we will begin to understand how subjective our views possibly are. We will then begin to see ourselves as a "mere" part of the whole rather than as the whole itself.

But how does one gain this awareness? Not everyone will. At least Kant speaks only of the "class of thinkers" who—by one means or another, in the manner of development described by Descartes or Leibniz—have achieved enough self-detachment to be able to observe the operations of this world. They quickly determine that the propensity for differing opinions on the same point is very great indeed. On the basis of these observations, the "class of thinkers" has formulated three immutable maxims:

1. to think for oneself ("*Selbst*denken");
2. to try to follow the other person's argument ("Sich in der Mitteilung mit Menschen] in die Stelle jedes *anderen* zu denken");
3. to be always consistent in one's own thinking ("Jederzeit mit *sich selbst einstimmig* zu denken") (Weischedel, 12:549; Kant's emphasis).

These maxims correspond to three fundamental modes of thinking. The first is "negative," that is, a skeptical attitude. Kant elaborates by adding: "nullius addictus iurare in verba magistri" (charged not to judge by the authority of another). The second is "positive" or "liberal" because it entails accommodating another way of thinking. The third is "consistent" (*konsequent*) within itself. Of these three modes of thinking, Kant continues, the history of pragmatic anthropology provides many examples; yet they are still outnumbered by examples of their opposite stances.

Kant concludes his musings on the modes of reflecting by equating them to "the most important revolution in the soul of man." That momentous alteration is none other than the release of humankind from its self-incurred tutelage (Kant even uses the same formulation as in his essay of 1784). The individual dares to use her/his reason independently in the manner just outlined, rejecting slavish imitation of "foreign masters," following her/his own experience, and being fully aware how tentative every independent step must be: "The most important revolution for mankind occurs within individuals: it is the 'emergence from their self-incurred tutelage.' Instead of allowing others to do their thinking for them or to be led blindly around by the nose, they dare to set foot into the realm of self-directed experience, however trembling their steps might be."[36]

Kant's maxims of responsible thinking are derived from the tradition of humanistic thought since the fifteenth century; they are a salient expression of progressive views in the eighteenth century. His exhortations to think for oneself, to try to understand the opposing (or simply: other) point of view, and to be consistent in one's own logical reasoning provide a major tenet of the process of Enlightenment. When conjoined with sensual and emotional appeal as advocated by more aesthetically oriented writers (Gellert, Garve, Goethe) the principle of critical thinking provides the foundation for the manner of writing and reading essayistic compositions. Essayistic style and the path of true Enlightenment would appear to be inextricably intertwined since each is premised on the active collaboration of the reader/listener. (The question of affective stylistics is addressed in later chapters of *Crossing Boundaries*.)

How broadly disseminated were these ideas on the need for critical thinking is saliently underscored by their use in the work of the prominent Romantic philosopher, Johann Gottlieb Fichte (1762–1814) at the end of the century. For example, in his advocation of copyright laws, "Beweis der Unrechtmäßigkeit des Büchernachdrucks" ("Proof of the Illegality of Book Pirating," 1793), he posits a distinction between physical ownership and "intellectual ownership" (*geistiges Eigentum*) of the written work. Without the Enlightenment notion of intellectual self-determination, the Fichtean distinction could never have been drawn. The mere purchase of a book, Fichte avers, does not mean that the purchaser is automatically in possession of its content. In order to gain intellectual possession, the book owner must diligently study its contents, retracing the author's line of thought and reflecting on its various implications. Only after the purchaser has gone through the same intellectual exercises as the author of the book can the reader claim to be in possession of the book in the fullest possible sense. "This collaborative effort," Fichte concludes, "is the only fitting equivalent for mental training, be it in oral or written form."[37]

Equally significant is Fichte's preface to his *Die Bestimmung des Menschen* (*The Destiny of Humankind*, 1800). After explaining that his treatise on current moral anthropology is aimed at the layman, not at "the professional philosopher," and that it is therefore written in an easy to understand style, Fichte concludes with a clarification of his use of the first-person form in the body of the text. The passage is so important for the theoretical underpinnings of *Crossing Boundaries* that it deserves citation in full: "the I that speaks in this book is by no means the author. Rather the author desires that the reader him/herself become this I. He hopes that the reader will treat the text not simply as an historical artifact but actually engage the text in a real dialogue during the reading act itself, mulling things over, drawing consequences, making decisions just like his/her representative in the text. The author hopes further that the reader, drawing purely upon him/herself through such individual effort and reflection, will cultivate the manner of thinking modelled in this book, adopting it as his/her own."[38] This passage summarizes in succinct fashion the basic premise of *Crossing Boundaries* that enlightenment, creative reading, and critical thinking go hand in hand. Their cultivation is, in fact, the ultimate human destiny.

Conclusion

If we were to try to summarize the foregoing reflections on the nature of the Enlightenment and of enlightenment in general, we might say the following. Each modern critic discussed uses Kant's famous definition as the point of departure in his individual hermeneutic exercise and each gravitates to the conviction that true enlightenment is first of all a dynamic, ongoing, never ending *process* and not a mechanical self-perpetuating movement. As dialectical skepticism, in the best sense of the term, it is uninterested in the mere amassing of information in the manner of a forty megabyte computer. It posits a creed of continual contradiction and questioning, presupposes the freedom to think the unthinkable, prefers to transgress boundaries, and is not timid about merging or even dissolving systems in the single-minded—if somewhat peripatetic— pursuit of truth. *True* Enlightenment sees that humankind's avocation for autonomous self-direction is situated within "a matrix of interaction in which diverse, if not opposite, elements blend with rather than exclude one another, not unlike a field of balanced tensions" (Barnard, 295). Consequently, the binary system of numbers, as developed by Leibniz in which all numbers are "expressed by unity and by nothing" would seem to form the basis of the thought process. The concept of self is contingent on the perception of the other so that the two perceptions form a reciprocal unity. The perceptions of "opposites"—of the self and of the other, of something and of nothing—blend into a unity. As Leibniz writes: "Although there is no hope that men can, in this life, reach this hidden series of things [= binary system] by which it will appear in what way everything comes from pure being [= God] and from nothing, it is sufficient to carry the analysis of ideas as far as the demonstration of truth requires" ("Organum," 3). This manner of dialectical proceeding to the infinite which *in*cludes rather than *ex*cludes is fundamental to essayism.

Truth and self-realization through a continual "balancing act"—not dominance, not self preservation, as Horkheimer and Adorno argue—are Enlightenment's goals. Scholars emphasize now what Horkheimer and Adorno failed to note in their famous study, although Cassirer had placed it at the center of his inquiry, namely, that the Enlightenment was an *attitude of mind* rather than a course in science and philosophy. As such, it is closely linked to Modernity, which Foucault prefers to define as an attitude rather than as a period in the flux of time. Both the Enlightenment and Modernity are marked by "a permanent critique of our historical era" (Foucault, 42). Even the so-called "Post-Modern aura" is typified by "the tendency of all Post-Modern arts to become historical commentaries on whatever genre they adopt" and can, moreover, be seen as a critique of systems (Newman, 182f.). Thus the Enlightenment was far from being a closed philosophical system with a rigidly prescribed method of analysis. Nor was it limited to constructing rational systems— the fabled crystal palace so pungently mocked by Dostoevsky's Underground Man (and so comparable with Adorno's view of twentieth-century society). Thinking is practiced for its own sake, sometimes even without an apparent, definite object and moves in curvilinear fashion. Yet even *das fruchtloseste Denken* ("the most fruitless thinking")—as Erwin Chargaff labels it—often leads to valuable insights (Chargaff, 203). In short, true Enlightenment should not be seen in isolation as "construction," or "deconstruction," or as "reconstruction"; it engages in all three activities, sometimes simultaneously (cf. Cassirer, 234f.). Moreover, as primarily an attitude of mind, the Enlightenment expanded into all areas of life from ethics and pedagogy to capital punishment and hygiene, from theology to agriculture.[39] These topics and this *modus cogitandi* are endemic to essayistic writing.

While the Enlightenment occasioned a radical restructuring of cultural institutions and literary life in the eighteenth century, its essential philosophical and anthropological principles found expression in periodical literature, much of which can be classified as essayistic. When we consider that Enlighteners from Thomasius to Lessing to Kant and Wieland all subscribed to the principle of free intellectual discourse in full view of the public eye as the only sure means of safeguarding against prejudice and as the test of one's own critical thinking, it is easy to understand why the eighteenth century saw the rise of the modern phenomenon of public opinion. Nor is it astonishing that the uninhibited form of essayistic writing rose to the fore in an atmosphere of public debate.[40]

Notes

1. In this regard see the anthology, *Der Traum der Vernunft. Vom Elend der Aufklärung*. Eine Vortragsreihe der Akademie der Künste Berlin (Darmstadt and Neuwied: Luchterhand, 1985).

2. Max Horkheimer and Theodor W. Adorno, *Dialektik der Aufklärung. Philosophische Fragmente* (Frankfurt a. M.: Fischer, 1969), 9f., 49 et passim).

3. Horkheimer and Adorno, 31: "Denken verdinglicht sich zu einem selbsttätig ablaufenden, automatischen Prozeß der Maschine nacheifernd, die er selber hervorbringt, damit sie ihn schließlich ersetzen kann. Aufklärung hat die klassische Forderung, das Denken zu denken beiseitegeschoben."

   In his *Theorie des kommunikativen Handelns* (Frankfurt a. M.: Suhrkamp, 1985) Jürgen Habermas traces this "critique of instrumental reason" and the incumbent reinterpretation of "rationalization as objectification" (*Rationalisierung als Verdinglichung*) from Georg Lukács to Theodor Adorno (1:461–488; 489–534). Habermas notes Horkheimer's and Adorno's view of the paradoxical subjection of the individual in his/her struggle for self-determination labelling it "dialectics of rationalization" (*Dialektik der Rationalisierung*, 1:501). Horkheimer and Adorno tend to strip the concept of *Verdinglichung* of its specific historico-economic context and of any interpersonal dimension (1:508). It was precisely this interpersonal, moral aspect of human existence that was a primary focus of the Enlightenment and Habermas criticizes Horkheimer's and Adorno's emphasis of the "autonomy of the subsystems of goal-oriented action" (*Verselbstständigung der Subsysteme zweckrationalen Handelns*) to the neglect of the interpersonal and communicative component of Enlightenment thought (cf., e.g., 1:472f.). In any event Habermas is concerned with showing the limitations of the Horkheimer/Adorno model of the dialectic process by shifting his focus to communicative theory (1:518ff.). He suggests replacing the concept of "instrumental reason" with that of communicative reason (*kommunikative Vernunft and kommunikative Rationalität*, 1:523, 532). The advantage of communicative reason over instrumental reason is that it does not *blindly* serve the self-preservation of the individual who treats everything else as objects. According to Habermas's model the self sees itself as a subject imbedded in a fluctuating, subjective world and contributing to the reinterpretation of the world as a means of reinterpreting and defining itself. Thus the complete opposite of *Verdinglichung* occurs, for the so-called objectification of the world and society is nothing more than a subjective interpretation (very Nietzschean in thrust!). Habermas says of communicative reason: "Sie erstreckt sich auf eine symbolisch strukturierte Lebenswelt, die sich in den Interpretationsleistungen ihrer Angehörigen konstituiert und nur über kommunikatives Handeln reproduziert. So findet die kommunikative Vernunft nicht einfach den Bestand eines Subjekts oder eines Systems vor, sondern hat Teil on der Strukturierung dessen, was erhalten werden soll" (1:533). With that statement Habermas reintroduces a major tenet of the true Enlightenment which Horkheimer and Adorno had passed over. The notion of communicative reason is surprisingly close to our understanding of the role and function of the essayistic mode of expressing ideas within the Enlightenment tradition.

4. See Frederick M. Barnard, "'Aufklärung' and 'Mündigkeit'": Thomasius, Kant, and Herder," *Deutsche Vierteljahresschrift für Literaturwissenschaft und Geistesgeschichte* 57/2 (1983), 296.

5. Klaus Epstein, *The Genesis of German Conservatism* (Princeton: Princeton Univ. Press, 1966); Norman Hampson, *The Enlightenment* (Baltimore: Penguin Books, 1968); Reinhart Kosellek, *Kritik und Krise. Ein Beitrag zur Pathogenese der bürgerlichen Gesellschaft*, 2nd ed. (Freiburg and Munich: K. Alber, 1969); Jürgen Habermas, *Strukturwandel der Öffentlichkeit. Untersuchungen zu einer Kategorie der bürgerlichen Gesellschaft* (Neuwied and Berlin: Luchterhand, 1966).

6. Werner Schneiders, *Die wahre Aufklärung. Über das Selbstverständnis der deutschen Aufklärung* (Freiburg and Munich: K. Alber, 1974). See also Rudolf Vierhaus, *Deutschland im Zeitalter des Absolutismus* (Göttingen: Vandenhoeck and Ruprecht, 1978); Peter Pütz, *Die deutsche Aufklärung* (Darmstadt: Wissenschaftliche Buchgesellschaft, 1978); *Aufklärung, Absolutismus und Bürgertum in Deutschland*, ed. Franklin Kopitzsch (Munich: Nymphenburger Verlagshandlung, 1976).

7. Cf., e.g., Peter Pütz, *Die deutsche Aufklärung*. Erträge der Forschung 81 (Darmstadt: Wissenschaftliche Buchgesellschaft, 1978); Hugh B. Nisbet, "'Was ist Aufklärung?': The Concept of Enlightenment in Eighteenth-Century Germany," *Journal of European Studies* 12 (1982), 77–95; Gerhard Sauder, "Aufklärung des Vorurteils—Vorurteile der Aufklärung," *Deutsche Vierteljahresschrift für Literaturwissenschaft und Geistesgeschichte* 57/2 (1983), 259–277; John A. McCarthy, "The Art of Reading and the Goals of the German Enlightenment," *Lessing Yearbook* 16 (1984), 79–94. All these efforts have culminated in the founding of a new journal devoted exclusively to the study of the Enlightenment entitled: *Aufklärung. Interdisziplinäre Halbjahresschrift zur Erforschung des 18. Jahrhunderts und seiner Wirkungsgeschichte* (Hamburg: Felix Meiner, 1986ff.). Appropriately, the inaugural volume was devoted to the central concepts of eclecticism, self-directed thinking, and intellectual maturity.

8. Ernst Troeltsch, "Aufklärung," *Realencyklopädie für protestantische Theologie und Kirche* 2 (Leipzig, 1897), 225–241, rpt. in *Aufklärung, Absolutismus und Bürgertum in Deutschland. Zwölf Aufsätze,* ed. Franklin Kopitzsch (Munich: Nymphenburger Verlagsbuchhandlung, 1976), 245.

9. The books by Schneiders (1974) and Pütz (1978) complement one another to a high degree. While Schneiders focuses on the *debate* regarding the nature of the Enlightenment in the latter part of the eighteenth century, Pütz seeks to sort out the *research* on the epoch penned in the last fifty years or so (Schneiders, 18; Pütz, 1)

10. "Selbstaufklärung ist Selbstbestimmung durch Selbstinformation. Emanzipation im Sinne der Selbstemanzipation bedarf also einer eigenen Anstrengung, die eine moralische Leistung ist; sie bedarf einer Revolution der Denkungsart oder Gesinnung, d.h. eines Willensaktes oder einer Initiation

aus eigener Initiative" (Schneiders, 198). This is an echo of Diderot's expressed hope that the *Encyclopédie*, which was on the cutting edge of Enlightenment thought in France at mid-century, would effect a change in the general mode of thinking: *"pour changer la façon commune de penser"* (see Cassirer, 14).

11. "Wie die Selbstaufklärung von außen her in Gang gebracht werden oder durch Fremdaufklärung gefördert werden kann, d.h. wie die Ansprechbarkeit pädagogisch genutzt werden kann, muß hier unerörtert bleiben" (Schneiders, 212).

12. Immanuel Kant, "Beantwortung der Frage: Was ist Aufklärung?" in *Kant's Werke*, vol. 8, ed. Königlich Preußische Akademie der Wissenschaften (Berlin: G. Reimer, 1912), 36. Hereafter cited as "AA." Also in *Was ist Aufklärung? Aufsätze zur Geschichte und Philosophie*, ed. Jürgen Zehbe, 2nd ed. (Göttingen: Vandenhoeck and Ruprecht, 1975), 56. Hereafter cited as "Zehbe."

13. Cf. Erwin Chargaff, "Der Traum der Vernunft erzeugt Ungeheuer," in *Der Traum der Vernunft*, 214. Michel Foucault, by contrast, is reservedly optimistic like the true German Enlighteners of two hundred years ago. Foucault concludes his essay on "What is Enlightenment" with the heartening remark: "I do not know whether it must be said today that the critical task still entails faith in Enlightenment. I continue to think that this task requires work on our limits, that is, a patient labor giving form to our impatience for liberty" (50).

14. "Daß aber ein Publikum sich selbst aufkläre, ist eher möglich; ja es ist, wenn man ihm nur Freiheit läßt beinahe unausbleiblich. Denn da werden sich immer einige Selbstdenkende, sogar unter den eingesetzten Vormündern des großen Haufens finden, welche, nachdem sie das Joch der Unmündigkeit selbst abgeworfen haben, den Geist einer vernünftigen Schützung des eigenen Werts und des Berufs jedes Menschen, selbst zu denken, um sich verbreiten werden" (Kant, AA, 8:36; Zehbe, 56).

15. Theodor W. Adorno, *Erziehung zur Mündigkeit* (Frankfurt a.M.: Suhrkamp, 1970), 137: "Denken, und zwar . . . unbeirrbares und insistentes Denken."

16. Ernst Cassirer, *The Philosophy of the Enlightenment*, trans. Fritz C. A. Koelln and James P. Pettegrove (Boston: Beacon Press, 1955), ix, 13f., 18, 30, 360. Originally: *Die Philosophie der Aufklärung* (Tübingen: J. C. B. Mohr, 1932).

17. Cf., e.g, *Erforschung der deutschen Aufklärung*, ed. Peter Pütz (Königstein/Ts: Athenäum, 1980); *Aufklärung. Ein literaturwissenschaftliches Studienbuch*, ed. Hans-Friedrich Wessels (Königstein/Ts: Athenäum, 1984). The renewed interest in the 1980's in the nature of the German Enlightenment was facilitated by the reprinting of important eighteenth-century essays in various anthologies. Most notable here are *Was ist Aufklärung?*, ed. Norbert Hinske (Darmstadt: Wissenschaftliche Buchgesellschaft, 1973); *Was ist Aufklärung?*, ed. Ehrhard Bahr (Stuttgart: Reclam, 1974); and *Aufklärung und Gedankenfreiheit. Fünfzehn Anregungen, aus der Geschichte zu lernen*, ed. Zwi Batscha (Frankfurt a.M.: Suhrkamp, 1977). A further sign of the

reconsideration of the Age of Enlightenment is the fact that Volume 2, number 2 for 1987 (published 1988) of the interdisciplinary journal *Aufklärung* is devoted to the concept of Enlightenment as process. See esp. Vierhaus's instroduction, "Aufklärung als Prozeß—der Prozeß der Aufklärung," and his contribution, "Aufklärung als Emanzipationsprozeß," (2/2:3–18). Unfortunately, it was no longer possible to incorporate the results of that volume in this study.

18. Gerhart Sauder, "Aufklärung des Vorurteils—Vorurteile der Aufklärung," *Deutsche Vierteljahresschrift für Literaturwissenschaft und Geistesgeschichte* 57/2 (1983), 259–277; here 268,276.

19. Werner Schneiders, *Aufklärung und Vorurteilskritik. Studien zur Geschichte der Vorurteilstheorie. Forschungen und Materialien zur deutschen Aufklärung*, ed. Norbert Hinske (Stuttgart-Bad Cannstatt: frommann-holzboog, 1983).

20. Frederick M. Barnard, "*Aufklärung* und *Mündigkeit*: Thomasius, Kant, and Herder," *Deutsche Vierteljahresschrift für Literaturwissenschaft und Geistesgeschichte* 57/2 (1983), 278–297.

21. Cf. Charles Taylor, "Kant's Theory of Freedom," *Concepts of Liberty in Political Philosophy*, ed. Zbigniew Pelczynski and John Gray (London: Athlone Press, 1984), 100–122.

22. See John A. McCarthy, "Die gefesselte Muse?: Wieland und die Pressefreiheit," *MLN*, 99/3 (1984), 437–460; also my "'Das sicherste Kennzeichen einer gesunden, nervösen Staatsverfassung': Lessing und die Pressefreiheit," *Lessing und die Toleranz*, ed. Peter Freimark, Helga Slessarev und Franklin Kopitzsch. Sonderband zum *Lessing Yearbook* (Munich: edition text + kritik, 1986), 225–244; J. A. McCarthy, "'Morgendämmerung der Wahrheit': Schiller and Censorship," *"Unmoralisch an sich . . . " Zensur im 18. und 19. Jahrhundert*, Wolfenbütteler Schriften zur Geschichte des Buchwesens, vol. 13, ed. Herbert G. Göpfert & Erdmann Weyrauch (Wiesbaden: Harrassowitz, 1988), 231–248. Kant specifically discusses freedom of thought and of the press in his "Was heißt: Sich im Denken orientieren?" (AA, 8:133–147).

23. Michel Foucault, "What is Enlightenment," *The Foucault Reader*, ed. by Paul Rabinow (New York: Random House, 1984), 32–50; here 43–45.

24. Johann Gottfried Herder, "Briefe zu Beförderung der Humanität," *Herders Sämtliche Werke*, 33 vols., ed. Bernhard Suphan (Berlin: Weidmann'sche Buchhandlung, 1877–1913), 17:122 (Letter no.25, para.36; see also letters 27 and 32).

25. Cf., e.g., Mendelssohn, "Über die Frage: was heißt aufklären?" in *Was ist Aufklärung?*, ed. Jürgen Zehbe, 129–132; Kant, "Einleitung zu *Über Pädagogik*," in *Werkausgabe*, ed. W. Weischedel, 12:704 *et passim*; Herder, *Briefe*, Suphan, 17:138f., 152–154; Johann Gottlieb Fichte, *Die Bestimmung des Menschen*, ed. Theodor Ballauff and Ignaz Klein (Stuttgart: Reclam, 1981). See Hans M. Wolff, *Die Weltanschauung der deutschen Aufklärung in geschichtlicher Entwicklung*, 2nd Ed., ed. Karl S. Guthke (Berne and Munich: Francke, 1963) for a detailed treatment of the topic.

26. Herder, "Wie die Philosophie zum besten des Volkes allgemeiner und nütz-licher werden kann" (1763), in *Herder. Ein Lesebuch für unsere Zeit*, ed. Günter Mieth, Ingeborg Schmidt and Walter Dietze (Berlin and Weimar: Aufbau, 1984), 3 (= Suphan, 32:31–33).

27. Christian Thomasius, *Ausübung der Vernunftlehre* (1691), 16–18, 82–88; also *Ausübung der Sittenlehre* (1696), 540f.

28. "Erfahre vermittelst der euserlichen Sinnen in natürlichen Dingen ausser dir immer mehr und mehr die zuvor unbekante unstreitige Wahrheiten (*Einleitung der Vernunftlehre*, 275).

29. "Die Gelarheit ist eine Erkäntniss durch welche ein Mensch geschickt gemacht wird, das wahre von dem falschen, das gute von dem bösen wohl zu unterscheiden, und dessen gegründete wahre, oder nach Gelegenheit wahrscheinliche Ursachen zu geben, um dadurch seine eigene, als auch anderer Menschen im gemeinen Leben und Wandel zeitliche und ewige Wohlfahrt zu befördern" (cited according to H. M. Wolff, *Weltanschauung*, 29).

30. Gottfried Wilhelm Leibniz, "De organo sive ars magna cogitandi" (c.1679), *Philosophical Writings*, ed. G. H. R. Parkinson, trans. Mary Morris and G. H. R. Parkinson (London: J. M. Dent & Sons, 1973), 1–4.

31. "Wem es ernst ist, keine Erkäntniss zu verabsäumen, die ihm nützlich seyn kan, der wird, so lange er zweifelhaft ist, lieber den sicheren Teil erwehlen und daher die Gelegenheit nicht aus den Händen lassen, massen es ihm nicht schadet, wenn er gleich ohne Verabsäumung des Nöthigen etwas unnützes gelernet hat" (cited by H. M. Wolf, *Weltanschauung*, 20). A recent readable assessment of Wolff's importance for eighteenth-century German thought is offered by Thomas P. Saine, "Who's Afraid of Christian Wolff?" in *Anticipations of the Enlightenment in England, France, and Germany*, ed. Alan C. Kors and Paul J. Korshin (Philadelphia: University of Pennsylvania Press, 1987), 102–133. See esp. 102–109 for a discussion of Wolff's innovation.

32. Christoph Martin Wieland, *Beiträge zur Geheimen Geschichte der Menschheit*, in *Werke*, ed Fritz Martini and Hans Werner Seiffert (Munich: Hanser, 1967), 3:231; see also 3:245.

33. "Es ist also nicht genug, Menschen den Trug zu entnehmen, man müßte ihnen auch *eigne* Stärke des Geistes einhauchen können" (rprt. 1971; 1:105).

34. Wulf Koepke, "Herder's Craft of Communication," in *The Philosopher as Writer: The Eighteenth Century*, ed. Robert Ginsberg (Cranbury, NJ: Associated University Presses, Inc., 1987), 94–121, here 113. Koepke offers an excellent appraisal of Herder's writing as communicative act and how it relates to his concept of *Bildung*. I refer my reader to it for a more detailed appreciation of Herder's place within the intellectual and cultural foment of the later eighteenth century, which in point of fact, should rival Kant's significance as a cultural critic of his day.

35. "Dem Egoism kann nur der *Pluralism* entgegengesetzt werden, d.i. die Denkungsart: sich nicht als die ganze Welt in seinem Selbst befassend, sondern als einen bloßen Weltbürger zu betrachten und zu verhalten" (Kant, *Anthropologie*, 12:411) (= AA, 7:130).

36. "Die wichtigste Revolution in dem Innern des Menschen ist: 'der Ausgang desselben aus seiner selbstverschuldeten Unmündigkeit.' Statt dessen, daß bis dahin andere *für* ihn dachten und er bloß nachahmte, oder am Gängelbande sich leiten ließ, wagt er es jetzt, mit eigenen Füßen auf dem Boden der Erfahrung, wenn gleich noch wackelnd, fortzuschreiten" (Kant, *Anthropologie*, 12:549) (= AA, 7:229).

37. Johann Gottfried Fichte, "Beweis der Unrechtmäßigkeit des Büchernachdrucks," in *Sämmtliche Werke* (Berlin, 1846), 8:226: "Dieses Mitdenken ist denn auch . . . das einzig passende Aequivalent für Geistesunterricht, sey er mündlich oder schriftlich."

38. Fichte, *Bestimmung des Menschen*, Reclam, 6.

39. Cf. Hampson, *Enlightenment*, 146; Vierhaus, "Zur historischen Deutung der Aufklärung: Probleme und Perspektiven," in *Aufklärung in Deutschland*, ed. P. Raabe and W. Schmidt-Biggemann (Bonn: Hohwacht, 1979), 27; Nisbett, "Concept of Enlightenment," 93; Schneiders, *Wahre Aufklärung*, 13ff.; Foucault, "Enlightenment," 43.

40. On these questions see Ernst Manheim, *Aufklärung und öffentliche Meinung. Studien zur Soziologie der Öffentlichkeit im 18. Jahrhundert*, ed. Norbert Schindler (1933; rprt. Stuttgart-Bad Cannstatt: frommannholzboog, 1979).

CHAPTER 5

The Ethics of Writing and Reading

Enlightenment Through Print: A Different Kind of Revolution

The development of essayistic writing in Germany concurrent with the rise of the *Aufklärung* was not coincidental. Those individuals in any given generation who have started down the path of self-enlightenment either by chance or design recognize their ethical responsibility to promote the new way of thinking among their fellow human beings. One instrument they employed was the quill. And they cultivated a new way of writing designed to communicate their individual insights to others. That writing was not only clear and accessible, it was also structured to *engage* the entire person who happened to take the printed page in hand to reflect critically upon inherited ideas and concepts. It was, as Friedrich Schlegel remarked at the close of the century, "the tendency . . . to question all rigid disciplines."[1] That questioning attitude has come, in fact, to mark the entire epoch of the Enlightenment. Rudolf Vierhaus states pithily: "The Age of Enlightenment was one of writing, reading, reflecting, reviewing, and critiquing."[2]

The perception that an author had an obligation to cultivate active reader response stood in stark contrast to the dominant tendency of the preceding era. Formerly, a small band of erudite men wrote stilted tracts for mutual consumption. Their purpose was to push back the frontiers of science. Since the scholarly world was homogeneous and straightforward in its reading requirements, there was no need to pay special attention to the style of writing. Moreover, scholarly writing accounted for the lion's share of all publications in the first phase of the Enlightenment. All of that changed in the course of the eighteenth century. The purpose of this chapter is to sketch those conditions of the marketplace which altered the nexus of writers, readers, and texts and which favored the genesis of a new way of writing: essayism. In doing so I hope to shed light on the reciprocal relationship between society and the essayistic stance which Haas cites as a specific *desideratum* in essay research (83).

In the year generally taken to mark the commencement of the classical period in German literature, 1787, Carl August Böttiger (1760–1835), published a treatise on the misuse of German reading material in the schools. An associate editor of popular journals like *The German Mercury* (*Der Teutsche Merkur*, 1797–1809) and *Journal of Luxury and Fashion* (*Journal des Luxus und der Moden*, 1795–1803) as well as educator and author, he stood in contact with leading lights of the age. Because of these contacts and activities, Böttiger was in a favorable position to follow the dominant literary tendencies of his day. He observed a dramatic change in people's attitude toward the printed word, remarking: "A powerful revolution [*eine gewaltige Revolution*] has occurred in the German language and literature. Future generations will be amazed at the number of first-class writers who have appeared on the scene in the last forty years. In many literary genres we have almost achieved perfection; in others we have achieved parity with our neighbors; and even in the realm of truly classical prose we do not lack models worthy of emulation."[3] Böttiger's assessment can serve as a pithy summary of important changes in the literary fare and its reception which occurred during the course of the eighteenth century, changes that warrant further scrutiny. Two particularly intriguing questions are: what is the nature of this "vast revolution" in literary life and what are the marks of this "truly classical prose"?

Germany can lay historical claim to having invented the printing press. Ever since the late fifteenth century, she was a leader in the publication of books. Rolf Engelsing argues persuasively that it was only a matter of time before the revolutionary means of printing books was followed by a revolutionary manner of dealing with books. Thus the reader revolution, as he labels the phenomenon, was a logical consequence of the ready availability of the printed word.[4] That development was delayed by the devastating Thirty Years War fought mainly on German soil. Under the liberating influence of Enlightenment thought, the conditions for the reader revolution ripened. It was set in motion in the early 1700s.

The early decades of the eighteenth century saw a gradual secularization of reading matter and an initial energizing and sensitizing of a small but growing, anonymous reading public. In 1727 Johann Christoph Gottsched (1700–1766) could write in the inaugural number of his Moral Weekly, *The Man of Honor* (*Der Biedermann*, 1727–1729), that this anonymous audience whom he hoped to win over had already formed the habit "of perusing each week several Moral Weeklies and benefiting from the sensible observations made in them." Gottsched labels this habit "a praiseworthy activity" because it reveals the reader's desire for perfection and happiness.[5]

The anonymity of this reading audience is an important factor from Thomasius's *Monats-Gespräche* (1688f.) on because it forced the writer to reconsider his writing posture; he could no longer assume that his reader would be willing to follow his contorted argument. That anonymous audience, namely, had little in common with the traditional, scholarly reader who read for professional reasons and had specialized interests. The ranks of the scholar-reader were gradually being augmented by a growing number of "generalists" drawn from the lower nobility, patrician, and artisan classes, who were motivated by a desire to improve themselves morally and culturally while amusing themselves. They read in their leisure time and by choice. Consequently, those persons who desired to write for this new group of readers were forced to establish a closer, more personal relationship with their counterparts. The adoption of a personal tone on the part of the authors and narrators is a distinguishing mark of the new kind of writing in novel and Moral Weekly before 1750. Thomasius's prefatory remark to his *A Brief Sketch of Political Astuteness* (*Kurtzer Entwurf der Politischen Klugheit*, 1710) is typical of this new attitude toward an unaccustomed, non-academic audience: "These pages are presented to you for your judgment. Peruse them as you would a usual, rambling introduction and take them as you like. I have been moved to this project by the particular thought of how useful this present treatise can be even to those who have not attended a university, but who pursue a different profession either at court, in the military, in commerce, or in the home . . . yes, I have even thought of women" (unpag. #2). The developments in the literary market place in the first half of the century laid the ground work for a phenomenal rise in the incidence of reading and writing in the second half.[6]

In terms of the number of publishers, authors and readers involved and the volume of books and journals published, the character of the change between c. 1740 and c. 1790 (the time span mentioned by Böttiger) was indeed prodigious. Terms to describe the transformation range from "flood of books" (*Bücherflut*), "reading madness" (*Lesewut*), "reading addiction" (*Lesesucht*), and "writing rage" (*Schreibwut*).[7] The effect on traditional attitudes was so radical that Engelsing likens the alteration to the Industrial Revolution in England and the political Revolution in France. Although England and France also experienced rapid growth in the literary marketplace and although Germany too profited somewhat from industrial and economic innovation, those developments do not rival the magnitude of the reading revolution's impact on the intellectual life of the German-speaking territories (Engelsing, "Perioden," 982; McCarthy, "The Art of Reading," 79).

In 1805 Karl Morgenstern, a librarian in Dorpat by profession, summed up the nature of these developments in a lecture revealingly entitled "Plan in Reading" ("Plan im Lesen"):

> The general and widespread reading habit [*Lesegeist*] is right-
> fully counted among the characteristics of the century just past.
> Among the more civilized nations it was primarily Germany
> where the reading habit developed into a mania, and that just
> in recent decades. In Italy, the well-spring of modern literature,
> the reading habit was never universally dominant. In France . . .
> it was widespread even earlier. In England, more than anywhere
> else, because of its system of government, the reading habit was
> directed at politics, especially the politics of the day. But in
> Germany—or rather among the far flung German nations . . .
> the age of reading [*Leseperiode*] only began with Gellert's pop-
> ular works [= from c. 1745], yet since then everyone who has
> hands and eyes is reading and writing and reading.

Morgenstern's judgment of the significance of the reading revolution is echoed everywhere in the second half of the eighteenth century.[8]

Some statistical figures will help exemplify the nature of this different kind of eighteenth-century revolution. Thus, for example, it was not until 1764 that the German book industry with 1200 new titles per year finally achieved the level of production experienced prior to the Thirty Years War (1618–1648). Following the conclusion of the Seven Years War (1757–1763), the growth in publishing activity heated up. In 1765 the book fair catalogues announced 1,517 new titles by 210 publishing houses. Twenty-five years later those figures had risen to 3,222 new titles and 260 different publishers. When compared with the period 1721–1763, book production activity between 1763 and 1805 increased more than tenfold.[9] In the 1770s and 1780s there were almost 250 active publishing houses which each year produced more and more works in the service of the Enlightenment. Moreover, these publishing houses were located all over the German territories—in large and small mercantile centers (Hamburg, Leipzig, Ulm), and in large and small capitals (Vienna, Gotha, Altenburg) as well as in university towns (Halle, Göttingen).

Figuring that each title would have been printed on the average in about one thousand copies, Raabe estimates that fifty million books were printed in the twenty-year span; that amounts to more than two million per annum ("Aufklärung durch Bücher," 93). Even if we were to reduce Raabe's estimates (which do not include either pirated editions or unauthorized reprintings by the lawful publisher) by twenty-five percent to compensate for inaccuracies in the sources used, we would still end up with a conservative figure of more than 1.5 million volumes per year. When we combine this figure with the estimate of 175,000 new German titles published in the course of the eighteenth century, of which about 58,000 were published before 1760, the rate of publishing activity in German is revealed as truly revolutionary.[10]

Estimates place the total German-speaking population of central Europe at the beginning of the century at twenty million persons; by century's end that number had risen to about thirty-seven million.[11] Of these roughly 80,000 could be regarded as potential recipients of literature in the early part of the century; they were predominantly college-educated. Despite the growth in the size of the reading public that certainly occurred between 1700 and 1765 (from the influence of the Moral Weeklies), the writer and philosopher Thomas Abbt (1738–1766) felt in 1765 that scarcely 80,000 persons were capable of appreciating the best writing (*die witzigste Schrift*). The remaining 19,920,000 Germans, he scorned, were not even aware of the existence of the Moral Weeklies.[12] In contrast to Abbt's splenetic opinion, economic and educational statistics suggest a potential reading public of 2.5 million by 1800. However, this figure includes the full range of readers from the marginally literate to the very best.

If we were to eliminate all those persons capable of reading only the Bible and a prayer book, or who did not have the leisure time to spend on reading, or who could not afford the price of a book, or did not have access to a reading circle/society or lending library, the resultant group of "habitual" readers would be much smaller. I have conservatively estimated elsewhere that the realistic size of the potential audience for literary and better journalistic fare in the last third of the century was probably in the neighborhood of 250,000 individuals. This figure compares with Jean Paul's 1799 calculation that the size of the reading public was 300,000 persons. If we accept the figures of about 80,000 elite readers in the first half of the century to about 1765 and approximatey 250,000 by 1800 as geometrically if not arithmetically accurate, we can speak of at least a threefold increase in the size of the reading public in about a forty-year time span. These figures do not represent the literature audience *en gros*, but rather the top-echelon readers. These "practiced readers" would have been the likely recipients of essayistic writing with its greater demands on creative collaboration than that required, for example, by travel literature or novel reading.[13]

Additional contemporary eighteenth-century estimates corroborate these figures more or less. Thus for example, while indicating in his satirical novel, *Sebaldus Nothanker* (1773ff.), that the traditional scholarly audience of professors and students numbered only 20,000 members, Friedrich Nicolai (1733–1811), an important publishing and literary personage in Berlin, implies that the non-scholarly reading public was much larger. He puts the German-speaking population at twenty million. A year later the poet and journalist, Christoph Martin Wieland (1733–1813), assumed that he could easily find 10,000 buyers from among the twenty-four million German speakers for his journal, *Der Teutsche Merkur*, if the Germans were only more interested in improving themselves. Apparently, there were many more citizens capable of reading and purchasing books but who lacked the proper motivation. Of course Wieland's estimate of 10,000 buyers is not intended to reflect the actual size of the journal's potential audience. Because of the general practice of sharing reading material in the Age of Reason (be it via organized reading societies, commercial lending libraries, or more informal reading circles), we can assume that each copy of the *Merkur* would have reached ten to twenty readers, which would translate into 50,000–100,000 readers in 1774.[14]

The increase in book production and consumption was matched by a similarly radical change in the number of persons engaged in writing for those increased numbers of publishers and readers. The number of authors active during the 1760s is placed at 2,000–3,000. By 1776 that group had grown to 4,300 members, topped 5,200 by 1784, reached 7,000 by 1791, and supposedly exceeded 12,000 by 1810. A computation of the authors listed in Christian Gottlob Kayser's *Vollständiges Bücherlexikon* for the years 1750–1832 reveals that there must have been 20,000 active authors during the period—a veritable army of writers given the size of the total population. In 1790, for instance, it has been calculated that there was on the average one author for every 4,000 German-speakers.[15] This formidable group included scholars, educators, lawyers, clerics, and bureaucrats as well as freelance writers who sought to live by their pens alone. It would seem that the needs of the general reading public, as noted by Nicolai in 1773, were quickly met by the influx of young men and women all too eager to establish themselves as journalists, essayists, pedagogues, and enlighteners. They were motivated by the traditional desire to promote the public good as well as by the hope of earning a living.

The continuous rise in the number of self-proclaimed writers is due, at least partially, to the high jobless rate among the university trained during the 1700s. As the century progressed, students in ever greater numbers abandoned the humanities in favor of law and political science in the hope of improving their marketability. Yet a consolidation of political power and a streamlining of the bureaucratic machinery within the over three hundred states comprising Germany reduced the need for skilled cameralists, administrators, lawyers, and clerks. Consequently, many job seekers—traditionally drawn from the burgher classes—found themselves without career opportunities. The university student population at the end of the seventeenth century is placed at 7,000–8,000; estimates place that number at a mere 6000 at the end of the eighteenth century despite the nigh doubling of the overall population. Nevertheless, the decline in the number of graduated students was not enough to compensate for the enlarged influx of job candidates seeking career opportunities in the traditional fields of law and political science.[16] A great many of these academics turned to a literary life, writing for periodicals or composing occasional poems, popular novels and plays. The German territories developed their own version of Grub Street where hack writers were employed by publishing speculators to satisfy the desires of the rich for poetic glorification or of the less discriminating readers for raw entertainment while creating new needs. An anonymous satirist in the 1740s, Wieland in the 1750s, Nicolai in the 1770s, and Goethe around 1800 all describe these conditions with telling irritation.[17]

Thus, the number of new journals founded increased rapidly, rising from 176 new endeavors in the 1730s to 2,191 undertakings between 1766 and 1790. As early as 1767 an anonymous contributor to the *Deutsche Bibliothek der schönen Wissenschaften* lamented: "We are living in an age of the journal; our entire literature is inundated with weekly, monthly, and quarterly publications" (cited by Wilke, 1:78). For this reason we can term the age "the century of the journal" and speak of the "birth of the journalist in the Enlightenment."[18] Of course many of these publications were short-lived, scarcely surviving a year or two, but others were enduring. Furthermore, these numbers include Moral Weeklies, almanacs, scientific and scholarly journals, review journals, and literary periodicals. They also represent a wide diversity in quality of content and writing, ranging from the esoterically challenging *The Muses* (*Die Horen*,

1795) to the popular, low-brow *Olla Potrida* (1778–1797). While the former sought to raise the reader into the thin atmosphere of dizzying cerebral and aesthetic heights, the latter was fully content to cater to the common taste. Nevertheless, these publications, with few exceptions, pursued a didactic course endeavoring to improve their readers' minds, sentiments, and judgment. These various journals were published in editions of between 800 and 2,500 copies.[19]

In addition to journalistic activity, belletristic writing also increased sharply and was not infrequently published in periodical form. In fact, as the century progressed the conditions influencing periodical writing came to infuse various forms of belletristic writing as well. Belletristic writing encompasses theory, music, poetry, narrative, and drama. The number of new titles in this category rose from 44 (about 5.8% of the total book production) in 1740 to 188 in 1770 (about 16.5% of the total book production) and finally to 551 works in 1800 (about 21.5%). Winners as well were the disciplines of pedagogy, mathematics, medicine, the natural sciences, agriculture, and economics. Percentage losers were theology and devotional tracts which went from 19 percent of the total in 1740 to 5.8 percent in 1800 although the absolute numbers of works actually increased (Goldfriedrich, 3:270–280; Ungern-Sternberg, "Schriftsteller," 135; McCarthy, "Lektüre," 45). Goldfriedrich sums up the revolutionary changes in literary life from early to late century, referring to the roles played by publishers, authors, readers, and reading material by commenting metaphorically: "The reading and writing conflagration of the former period was like a slowly and evenly burning fire. The older literary fuel [= scholarly treatises] was like chunky peat. The new flame crackled and flared up and glowed more vigorously. It was fed with wood and coal which burned more rapidly and thus had to be replenished more quickly. The publishing industry warmed itself on this fire and strove to keep it burning to the best of its ability."[20] It is little wonder that there was much talk in the late eighteenth century of a *Bücherflut, Vielschreiberei,* and *Lesewut.*

Reader Typologies, Educational Goals, and Strategies

These revolutionary developments can, of course, be traced to the economic strategies and self-preoccupation of publishers and authors alike who were chiefly interested in competing with one another for public favor and personal gain. Such ignoble ambition produced much writing of very poor quality and of little lasting value. This dark side of the reading and publishing revolution was castigated by many observers.

Representative of them is the noted publicist, Johann Georg Heinzmann (1757–1802), who sharply criticizes these developments in his *Appeal to my Nation on Enlightenment and Enlighteners* (*Appell an meine Nation über Aufklärung und Aufklärer*, 1795). He laments the lack of concern on the part of so many of his fellow authors and publishers for their true calling as teachers and guarantors of all that is noble and beautiful in man. That indifference, he is convinced, had led to a decline in both moral and aesthetic sensitivity.[21] He divides writers and their readers into two general classes: the fashionable authors and their readers who are by far in the majority (*Scheindiener*, 147; *armseliges Publikum*, 146, and *das sogenannte Lesepublikum*, 53) and a much smaller band of sincere authors and their more exclusive public (*das wirklich aufgeklärte Publikum*, 53; *redliche Männer*, 108ff.). In regard to the classification of writers and their readers, we might also refer to Friedrich Gottlieb Klopstock (1724–1803), one of the most celebrated authors of the age, and Johann Carl Wezel (1747–1819), one of its most puzzling.

In one of his contributions to Johann Andreas Cramer's journal, *The Nordic Overseer* (*Der nordischer Aufseher*, 1758–1760), Klopstock addresses himself to the question of the reading public. He classifies the readers into three groups: "judges" (*Richter*), "experts" (*Kenner*), and the "great masses" (*der große Haufen*). Of these he is interested only in the first two categories, which—because the difference between them is really very slight—can be merged together. For Klopstock only these expert readers form the "real" or "actual" reading public because they are the consumers of what he considers to be "real" literature: fine arts, belles-lettres, and scholarly writing (*Arbeiten der schönen Künste, der schönen Wissenschaften, gelehrte Schriften*). With regard to belles-lettres the judges are those few superior readers who immediately, almost intuitively, recognize the value of the content and style of a newly published work, that is, they are so confident in their judgments that they require no guidance from others. A rung below these recipients are the much more numerous experts.

What separates the experts from the judges is the degree of literary sophistication. Having schooled themselves on the classics and in society with the genuinely refined, both classes display a firm grasp of true taste and of the "right way of thinking"; they also adapt themselves easily to changes in the manner of conceiving and presenting ideas. However, the judges are even more flexible and astute, and if they were to take pen in hand, they would write excellent prose. Although Klopstock does not specifically state the connection, the connotation is clear: the judges are on an equal footing with the authors. The experts still make errors in judgment, are not wholly in tune with aesthetic niceties, and are not free of prejudice. In other words, these members of the "true reading public" have stopped short of perfection. Nevertheless, it is clear that these top echelon readers form an elite group, which is not surprising given Klopstock's status as an elitist poet.[22] These notions are later repeated in his *Republic of Letters* (*Gelehrtenrepublik*, 1774).

Coming at mid-century Klopstock's comments on the nature of the German reading public would seem to give weight to Friedrich Maximillian Klinger's (1752–1831) view of the developments within the reading world. Klinger, for example, labels the reading habit "aristocratic" in the Middle Ages, "republican" from 1450 to 1750 and "democratic" beginning around 1750.[23] It is generally accepted that the reading public was very active in late century—the period that Heinzmann and most other contemporary critics have in mind—but the view of significantly increased activity before 1770 is not widely shared.

In his 1781 assessment of the situation, Wezel shifts the focus to the central position of the prose writer in the new scheme of things, for the new audience has been won over almost exclusively to prose writing. Wezel remarks: "The prose writer does not compose merely for academics; he writes for the enlightened portion of the entire nation" (*Kritische Schriften*, 3:150). From this statement we can infer at least two subdivisions of the reading public at large: the scholarly segment and a larger one comprised of citizens subscribing to Enlightenment notions and making greater demands on the author. Unlike Klopstock, Wezel makes no mention of a third group, *der große Haufen*.

The preferred audience singled out by Klopstock, Wezel, and Heinzmann are surely one and the same. We can identify this elite readership with the 250,000 or so readers referred to earlier. It is this group and its kind of preferred writing that holds the greatest interest for us. The reading public at large and its literary fare is of little import in our present context. Of special importance to us is "the method of professional writing" (*Methodik der Schriftstellerei*) that evolved in the pursuit of the Enlightenment's goals (Goldfriedrich, 3:303). Thus the sincere writer's desire (e.g., Nicolai, Wieland, Lessing, Wezel, R. Z. Becker) to educate, cultivate, and refine the public through the printed word is our major concern. It would not be amiss to speak of a plan of education in this regard just as one came to speak of a plan of reading in the eighteenth century to combat the undesirable side-effects of the rapacious reading habit. The terms plan of reading and plan of education should not evoke the negative connotations of a "limited Enlightenment" (*beschränkte Aufklärung*).

Johann Rudolph Gottlieb Beyer, a village pastor in Sömmerda near Erfurt, can serve as an example of these latter endeavors at the provincial level. In his 1795 address to the Society of Sciences in Mainz entitled "On the Reading of Books," he advises against repressive action to contain the spread of the reading habit, for it would also have a negative impact on the general level of Enlightenment. Any form of censorship, he argues, poses a real threat to all writing, be it "frivolous" or not. Censorship is essentially a curtailment of the human right to freedom of expression and must be avoided as much as possible. Thus edicts, the suppressing of books, and the levying of penalties, should be as rare as comets and active volcanos are in nature. Instead, Beyer urges regents and their ministers to influence the public's choice of reading material in a positive manner, that is, like a genuine, inspired teacher of the people (*Volkserzieher*). His recommendation is not without a caveat: "but they dare not take traditional school discipline as their model. Otherwise the censors and book judges will cause the same mischief in the public realm as petty school tyrants and pedants have in the classroom. The latter crippled and paralyzed young people's minds more often than they nurtured or cultivated them. They treated every outburst of youthful exuberance, every expression of independent thought, every candid question or answer as a petulant outrage." In order to avoid the same mistakes, a plan for educating the reader to a "proper" selection of reading matter must be devised.

Beyer bases his reform suggestions on the following two principles: (1) "the authorities must reduce the current state of the reading rage by a certain degree," and (2) "the readers must be lured away from fruitless reading, which only fritters away time while filling the mind with intellectual waste, and become accustomed to reading works which are useful, sound, and nurturing [of their humanity]."[24] The balance of Beyer's address contains suggestions for implementing a plan of action to advance these humanistic principles. They include recommendations for encouraging more intensive study of a limited number of works representative of secular humanism, the establishment of controlled reading societies, and the formation of lending libraries (25–34).

Beyer's stance on the question of reading is typical of that group of writers and educators sincerely interested in the achievement of the Enlightenment's educational goals. Strictly speaking, it is not right to speak of a "limited enlightenment" in their regard because they insisted on the inalienable right to freedom of the press and were therefore ready to tolerate the publication of inflammatory or frivolous and prejudiced views even if they posed a threat to the authority of the ruling classes. At the same time, these guardians of the public interest recognized the need to assist the reader in selecting reading materials from the flood of books which would make him/her a better person and more productive citizen while avoiding the socially undesirable side effects of indiscriminate reading activity. Their motivation was not to preserve the political status quo by preventing the "proletariat" and agricultural worker from acquiring the skills and knowledge necessary to liberate themselves from "bondage," but rather to advance humanity toward perfection. That path led through ethics and practical philosophy. Their primary concerns were humanitarian in character, not political in terms of power brokerage.

Thus we can agree with Schenda when he concludes his assessment of the reading and publishing revolution from 1770 to about 1870 with the statement: "The overwhelming achievement of the Enlightenment occurred in the realm of philosophy, perhaps also in that of economics and practicality, but absolutely not in the political sphere." Yet it seems to me that Schenda becomes a bit extreme when he adds: "What the readers between 1770 and 1870 could learn from their reading materials was to think in a devout manner, to act practically, only to dream about adventures, to be satisfied with their lot, and to execute orders" (Schenda, *Volk*, 141). This final judgment tends to ignore the essential conviction and intent underlying Enlightenment thought as I have tried to detail it in Chapter IV of this inquiry. All the authors and educators considered in this present study share Beyer's views on the dignity and worth of each human being who must be accorded the opportunity to develop her/his potential. Although they might be judged conservative from the twentieth-century point of view, these true Enlighteners were progressive for their times and not obsequious servants of political masters. It is not entirely fair to castigate the Age of Enlightenment for failing to achieve its lofty goals via the printed word as Schenda does when he writes (53): "The image of a nation of readers who could soon be transformed into a nation of thinking readers and because of their capacity for critical thought and steady progress toward a more perfect commonweal would not need a revolution—this image was too good to be true."[25] Our own age would be unthinkable without the humanistic endeavors of our eighteenth-century forerunners. The Age of Enlightenment is not over; it continues in the open debates carried on in the press, the halls of academe, and the parliaments of government in twentieth-century democratic societies.

But to return to the previous point, Mattenklott's argument for a philosophy of reading as a complement to the Academy's studies of the historical reading phenomenon is well taken.[26] His call was fully anticipated by the Enlighteners for their own historical age. They not only noted the radical change, they also asked why it occurred, analyzed how the reader approached the text, and suggested ways of directing and reforming the reading act itself. In view of such self-questioning, we should apply the term "limited Enlightenment" in limited fashion.

The seeds of this reading plan go back to the earliest Enlightenment writers. Leibniz, for example, in his "Call to the Germans to Use Their Reason and Language in Better Fashion" ("Ermahnung an die Teutsche, ihren Verstand und Sprache besser zu üben," 1683) proposed the establishment of a "Pro-German Society" ("Teutschgesinnte Gesellschaft") for the promotion of Enlightenment to all persons with "sensibility and good sense" regardless of their social background (Leibniz, 67). Through the sophisticated use of oral and written language, Leibniz argues, citizens will cultivate insightful thinking, mature judgment, moral sentiment, and aesthetic sensitivity (Leibniz, 68ff.).

These ideas were picked up and popularized by subsequent generations until the concept of Enlightenment and the goal of educating all social classes became synonymous.[27] Each generation of writers repeated the maxim, varying it slightly, but forever adhering to the conviction that the success of the Enlightenment was dependent upon the expression of individual opinion—especially dissenting views—in print. This notion underlies Kant's writings, perhaps the most highly regarded of the German Enlighteners, and is at the heart of his "An Answer to the Question: What is Enlightenment?" The philosopher clearly states that individuals must make use of their reason "in full view of the entire reading public"; they must do it "publicly, that is, through the printed word" (Kant, "Aufklärung," 57–59).[28] This notion recurs in Kant's introduction to his *Anthropologie* of 1798 where he writes about the importance of literature for enhancing our understanding of pragmatic anthropology. He states: "Travel is one of the means of broadening our knowledge of anthropology in the larger sense, even if it is only the reading of travel descriptions." As other kinds of reading material useful to the armchair traveler the philosopher further cites works on world history, biographies, even plays and novels (Kant, *Anthropologie*, 12:400f.; cf. also Goldfriedrich, 3:279f.).

Writing in 1797, Friedrich Schlegel (1772–1829), one of the initiators of the Romantic movement, paid tribute to the vast influence of books and journals in influencing a revolutionary change in the way the middle classes perceived themselves and their potential.[29] He contended that anything of cultural value (*Bildung*) was the product of the writing revolution. Two years later, Johann Adam Bergk (1769–1834), a prolific popularizer of Enlightenment ideas, added significantly to the notion of human perfection through print when he explained in his *The Art of Reading Books* (*Die Kunst, Bücher zu lesen*, 1799): "The reason why we read books must be, therefore, to perfect our mental powers and increase their level of activity; the purpose must be to cultivate all our potential, liberating it so that we might become self-directing in all things" (Bergk, *Kunst*, 80f.).

By 1800, then, printed matter had become a kind of *Erziehungsanstalt*, that is, an educational institution, continuing the function of the Moral Weeklies as a "school of reading" (Martens, *Botschaft*, 404ff., 432ff; Raabe, "Aufklärung durch Bücher," 101). The continuity of the comments on the value of reading from Leibniz to Kant, Schlegel, and Bergk is demonstrated by the opinions of writers at mid-century (e.g., Johann Georg Schnabel, Gottsched, Breitinger). Representative of such statements is the following drawn from the Moral Weekly, *The Sincere Person* (*Der Redliche*, 1751): "Education, society, travel: these are the means of making us sociable beings. However, to all of these means I prefer the reading of books. Books provide a threefold advantage: (1) we increase our knowledge and sharpen our intellect [*Nachdenken*]; (2) we entertain ourselves in a most sensible manner; and (3) we become sociable, useful, and well liked in society."[30] It should be noted that this view was expressed a good ten years before the revolution in reading habits commenced in earnest. From beginning to end, then, the German Enlightenment placed a premium on the formative value of literature.

The Enlighteners clearly envisioned what harvest they hoped to reap from their writing. But what of the *manner* of writing and reading? How were they envisioned? And what are the marks of a truly classical prose that is worthy of emulation? Let us turn now to this second part of Böttiger's assessment quoted at the beginning of this chapter.

The Art of Reading, Writing, and Thinking

The emergence of an anonymous reading public and the attendant ascendancy of journalism and belletristic writing between about 1680 and 1815 affected not only *how much* was written, but also *how it was read* and *how it was composed*. Let us first look at the emergent art of reading, although it is not possible to separate entirely the reading act from the style of presentation. The specific traits of the new prose will be examined in a later context.

Engelsing has described the transition in reading habits occasioned by the Enlightenment as an evolution from "intensive" to "extensive" reading. In his terminology intensive implies a repeated studying of a limited

number of select works over and over again to the point that portions of
the text are memorized. Normally such works experienced multiple reprintings. An example of this approach to reading is the use of the Bible
or popular devotional works like Johannes Arndt's (1555–1621) *True
Christianity* (*Wahres Christentum*, 1605ff.) or Benjamin Schmolcke's
Prayerbook (*Gebetbuch*) among vast segments of the populace well into
the nineteenth century. The extensive approach, on the other hand, is
characterized by a one-time perusal of a great variety of written material.
The new kind of reader was interested in many different topics and
devoured whatever s/he could find for its informational and entertainment value. Works that presented familiar settings and situations were
most preferred (Engelsing, "Perioden," 973 et passim; Schenda, *Volk*,
59–62, 473–477). We must, however, guard against the easy assumption
that repetitive, intensive reading is inherently more rewarding than the
singular, extensive type which some might be prone to identify with
"trivial" literature.[31] Thus we must take care to stress a specific connotation implicit in Engelsing's terms.

   "Extensive" can be taken to connote "broad reading interests" rather
than merely "one-time, cursory reading." For example, the new kind of
rapacious reader was encouraged to become addicted by the many Moral
Weeklies that sprang up everywhere and were intent upon the continued
moral improvement mostly of the patrician and artisan classes through
the introduction of "secularized devotional literature." In this light the
reading process was seen as the "practice of virtue" (*Tugendübung*).[32]
Attracted initially to the Moral Weeklies for spiritual edification, readers
gradually became accustomed to reading something other than the Bible
or collections of sermons on a regular basis. Enticed by articles on practical and literary matters published side by side with the moralizing
pieces, a growing number of these readers simultaneously developed an
appetite for ever more varied pieces. Such readers, weaned from predominantly devotional literature were joined by the traditional audience for
the various kinds of novels published since the late seventeenth century
for students and other members of the heterogeneous bourgeois classes
(not to be confused with the modern middle class). Moreover, contemporary eighteenth-century journalists specifically cited the efficacious effect of periodic literature in prodding the reader's inquisitiveness so that
s/he would be moved to study a piece more carefully. Gottsched before
1730 and Heinrich Wilhelm von Archenholtz (1743–1812) after 1780,
for instance, both refer to the value of rereading essays in the journals.
Gottsched reports that it is being done, while Archenholtz laments its
absence.[33] Engelsing himself grants that the difference between intensive

and extensive is one of degree and not necessarily one of quality. Extensive readers can still read intensively. Finally, contrary to the common assumption in reading research, Engelsing notes not only the role of the journals in effecting the transition from the intensive to the extensive approach because of the regularity of its publication and technique of publishing articles in installments, he also draws special attention to the discursive nature of this reading method ("Perioden," 973, 946–956). With that remark we have found a catchword for the technique of essay writing.

In his essay on eighteenth-century reading societies, Otto Dann identifies even more clearly this discursive aspect of the new approach to reading. Dann argues, namely, that the avid reader's passive attitude of mere reception can easily lead to active communication, that is, to a discussion with others of the material read. In fact, that is exactly what frequently happened in the age. One of the most celebrated examples of the private discourse turned public is Lessing's own life, especially his controversy with the Hamburg pastor Melchior Goeze, but by no means limited to that episode.[34] Jürgen Habermas and others have documented the rise of public debate exceedingly well. Dann thus refers to the reading act as the "medium of social communication" (*Medium sozialer Kommunikation*, Dann: "Lesegesellschaften," 161). If we accept this discursive element of the writing and reading styles of the eighteenth-century as the essential feature of the "powerful revolution" which occurred between 1680 and 1815, then we can agree with Wolfgang Langenbucher's modification of Engelsing's designation, *Leserevolution*. Placed within the history of social communication, the German contribution to the spate of revolutions in the eighteenth century would appear as a *Kommunikationsrevolution*.[35] (The appropriateness of Habermas's theory of communicative action to the literary situation of the eighteenth century is therefore readily apparent.)

Strikingly, Kant cites the "*discursive* manner of putting things" (*diskursive Vorstellungsart*) as the most propitious form of communication for the moral and aesthetic education of humanity. Aesthetic taste, he says, is a matter of communicating one's feeling of pleasure or displeasure to another. The act of communication itself, moreover, occasions in the communicator a sense of community with the recipients and, consequently, a sense of pleasure. While music and the plastic arts—which Kant labels the "intuitive rendition of an object"—give rise only to a sense of form by affecting our capacity for sight or sound (he overlooks the tactile sense), the *diskursive Vorstellungsart* is more involved. Defining discursive communication as either the spoken or the written word,

Kant concludes that it involves two of the arts (*Künste*): rhetoric and poetry (*Anthropologie*, 12:569–571). Without going into a discussion of how accurate Kant's assessments of the various arts are or whether his explanation of the sense of aesthetic pleasure is valid, we can adopt his definition of the *diskursive Vorstellungsart* as useful to our consideration of essayistic writing and reading. We can do this because essayistic writing is marked more so than any other literary mode by the harmonious integration of rhetorical technique and literary style.

Schenda argues in *A People Without Books* (*Volk ohne Buch*, 1977) that educators in the late eighteenth century were preoccupied with teaching practical and useful matters. A secondary concern was the moral and spiritual edification of their charges. He is very insistent, however, in asserting that these same pedagogues paid no attention to developing the students' minds, that is, to teaching them how to think, or how to understand a book and enjoy reading. Indeed, the training of teachers and the quality of instruction left much to be desired. Yet the admittedly poor situation in the schools does not fully justify Schenda's ensuing generalization that "the bourgeois Enlightenment did not formulate a common, transregional, and progressive theory of reading and learning" (Schenda, *Volk*, 87; see also 50, 88, 181). His meaning is that the Enlightenment failed to develop a theory of reading that involved the ability to reflect upon what has been read. In order to appreciate the efforts of the Enlighteners it is necessary, I think, to recall the distinction between true and false Enlightenment. The perception that the *Aufklärung* expected to achieve its goals within a generation or two has led to confusion and disillusionment among many modern observers. True Enlighteners were not so naive as to think that they could reform humanity and society overnight. Nor did they place the emphasis on the accumulation of knowledge. They realized that critical reflection had to precede any kind of genuine change. That is why they *did* stress critical thinking in their writing. They even developed a theory that intimately related the art of reading and writing to the ability to think independently. In fact, the art of writing for eighteenth-century stylists was dependent on the art of thinking.

All true Enlighteners agreed that one could not write well (i.e., persuasively, clearly) without first having mastered the art of thinking "correctly." The art of thinking is like any other skill: it must be learned through much practice. It is not a facility that comes easily. For that reason Kant argued against a violent political revolution from below; without a reform in the way the people think, political reform through revolution could not succeed in the long run. Early in the century it was widely held that the philosophy of Christian Wolff was instrumental in introducing "a more careful [*gründlicher*] manner of thinking and writing in Germany." As early as 1728 Gottsched prophesied that this more solid technique "would soon spread everywhere" (*Biedermann*, 2:22).

Three years before Gottsched's remark an anonymous contributor to the Moral Weekly, *The Patriot* (*Der Patriot*, 1724–1726), drew a clear connection between writing and thinking. He contended: "The art of writing well is based primarily on the ability to think clearly and well. This facility is innate, to be sure, but it must be cultivated" (*Patriot*, 2:16). The adjectives used to describe this "right" thinking are *wohl und ordentlich* which have the connotation of being clearly ordered and logical. We are reminded of the qualities of *Richtigdenken* and *Helldenken* which Schneiders identified as constitutive elements of true enlightenment.

The anonymous writer in *Der Patriot* of 1725 elaborates upon his/her statement by arguing that whoever thinks "unnaturally" must of necessity write in an obtuse and bombastic manner. Nevertheless, he does grant that clarity of thought does not automatically lead to clarity of expression. Clarity can be achieved, we are told, through a clean, lively, and pleasant presentation of the ideas. In fact, he continues, every writer has the duty to write in an easily comprehensible fashion. The Moral Weeklies were effective in disseminating this straightforward style. In their efforts they were supported by such popular authors as Gellert who was convinced that "whoever wants to write well, must be able to think clearly about a thing."[36]

The "proper" way of thinking was equated by and large to these attributes of clarity and distinctness. The interconnection between independent thinking and "proper" thinking and their relationship to the ultimate moral improvement of the individual evolved into a cardinal characteristic of the writer-reformer. Writers of the late Enlightenment repeatedly cited Horace's dictum, "scribendi recte sapere est et principium, et fons" (to know how to write well is both the source and wellspring [of everything else]). For example, Adolph Freiherr von Knigge (1752–1796) argued in his assessment of the literary marketplace, *On Writers and Writing* (*Über Schriftsteller und Schriftstellerei*, 1793), with the full conviction of his age, that "only he can speak and write well, who *thinks correctly and clearly*." Neither great erudition nor great oratory skill are a substitute for "sound" and "unmuddled reasoning."[37]

But nowhere was the nexus of thinking, writing (and reading) more clearly defined than by Wieland in an essay from the year 1799 entitled "Something on Prejudice" ("Etwas über Vorurtheile überhaupt"): "Humanity cannot be helped if people do not become *better* human beings. They cannot become better human beings if they do not become wiser, if they do not *think properly* [*richtig denken*] on *all* matters which affect their well being. And they will never think properly as long as they are not allowed to *think freely*—or to put it differently: *as long as reason is not accorded its full rights.* Everything which cannot stand up to its illuminating gaze must be discarded [*verschwinden*]."[38] The act of thinking freely is not just "free thinking." An unlimited field of vision, the innate right to examine all objects and ideas is, to be sure, the major connotation of *frei denken.* However, there is another implicit side to the connotation for the true Enlighteners. That other side is resultant of the demand to liberate thinking from all traditional, especially dogmatic *systems* of thought. Consequently, the freedom to think also implied freedom from doctrinal schools and tended to allow the free association of ideas. The rebellious attitude of the young Storm and Stress generation to the pedantic, insipid syllogisms of the older generation was shared by the *true* Enlighteners from that older group.

Writers had long known that readers did not always approach a piece of writing in the manner envisioned by its creator. But with the rise of a "large" anonymous reading public, the "proper" reception of a work became a major concern of the writers. From Wieland's essay collection *Sympathies* (*Sympathien*, 1756) to Friedrich J. Riedel's (1742–1785) *Letters on the Reading Audience* (*Briefe über das Publikum*, 1768), Joachim Christoph Friedrich Schulz's (1762–1798) *Literary Travels Through Germany* (*Litterarische Reisen durch Deutschland*, 1786), and Heinzmann's *Appeal to my Nation* (*Appell an meine Nation*, 1795), the nature of the anonymous public was a hotly debated issue. Typical of the age is Schulz's assessment:

> The German public is a real treasure, but for the life of me, I could not give a proper definition of it. You cannot imagine a more inconsistent, insatiable, fickle, and ungrateful beast. Its constituent parts are contradictory to one another, yet it is a whole. Its appetite for the new is rapacious and it has no use for the old. . . . It thinks its views infallible, but bends most willingly in the prevailing winds of opinion and conviction. . . . It complains loudly about the growing heap of new books, but goes out and buys them anyway. It complains that thoroughness and order are sorely lacking in the new kind of writing, yet it enthusiastically celebrates every cheap exhibitionist [*Seiltänzer*]. . . . This reading public is an incessantly devouring and regurgitating monster.[39]

Schulz's mentor as a professional writer, Wieland, had similarly grown aware of the complex nature of the anonymous public. If in his early work he had targeted a small, select group of like-minded, "sympathetic" readers from the larger anonymous reading public which he had already identified in the 1750s, his ambition by the 1770s was to increase his share of the public's attention as much as possible. Since his rise as a "professional" author was concurrent with the dramatic changes in the literary marketplace, he knew how important the reader had become as an integral, if silent, partner in the discursive process of writing and publishing. Additionally, as the editor-in-chief of the highly successful journal, *The German Mercury* (*Der Teutsche Merkur*, 1773– 1810), he had to have his fingers on the pulse of literary life in Germany and Austria. Thus, scattered throughout his writings published in his journal are comments that tend to profile the relationship between writer, reader, and the text. Wieland played such a dominant role in the literary life of the eighteenth century in shaping the taste and opinions of the top-echelon readers that we can take his reflections upon the reading public as symptomatic of the age. "The manner in which most people read," he averred in 1781, "is the key to all these occurrences grown so common place in the literary world."[40] Although he knew a successful writer could not ignore the demands of that larger audience, he—like so many of his fellow poets—was unwilling to compromise his aesthetic ideals and perceived, moreover, a moral obligation to contribute to the improvement of his fellow beings.

A revealing document in this regard is the preface to his collection of essays and narratives, *Essays on the Secret History of the Human Heart and Understanding* (*Beiträge zur Geheimen Geschichte des Menschlichen Verstandes und Herzens*, 1770). There the author reflects upon the kind of reader he hopes to appeal to. In doing so Wieland delineates the respective obligations of writer and reader. On the one hand, he acknowledges the reading public's right to expect a writer to put forth his best effort in composing a work because the reader, after all, must pay for it. Thus the work must be entertaining as well as instructive. On the other hand, Wieland makes clear that the author also has certain expectations of his potential reader. If the reader does not meet the writer's requirements, no amount of good intention on the author's part will ensure the success of the book (Wieland, *Beiträge* 3:198). No author, he explains, can ever be sure how the reader would respond. For instance maybe the reader bought the book out of "curiosity or a love of learning or out of boredom or a passion for reading or a desire to find fault or out of any other conceited purpose." Or maybe the reader didn't buy the book at all but rather borrowed it from a friend "in order to read it, or just page through it, or review it, or criticize it" (Wieland, *Beiträge*, 3:198).

In any event, an author can have at least certain expectations of a reader. The expectation shared by all serious authors during the Age of Reason is that potential readers *have the capacity to think*. Wieland writes: "I know, dear readers, all that you are justified in demanding of me. But permit me to say that I have a reciprocal requirement of you which is equally justified. If I am to amuse your wits and entertain your hearts, then I have every right to expect that you already possess wit and sentiment before you begin to read, for I am no Prometheus" (3:200). The remark that he is not Prometheus emphasizes the nature of the intended reader. Any person with *Witz* and *Herz*—that is, the ability to discern differences and to appreciate sentiment—is the writer's intended recipient. Unlike the demigod Prometheus, no mere human author can impart new qualities to the reader. Through his writing an author can only cultivate what is already present in another. Elsewhere the poet speaks of the writer's inability to make the blind see or to influence those who willfully reject all views except the ones they already hold (see McCarthy, "Poet as Journalist. Part Two," 87). Thus the *capacity to think* and the *willingness to listen* are the central demands that an author can legitimately make of a reader. Even though they themselves might only be "relatively enlightened" (*mäßig aufgeklärt*) and accustomed to only "moderate reflection" (*einiges Nachdenkens fähig*), these readers make up the enlightened readership cited by Klopstock, Heinzmann, and others.[41] The rest is up to the writer.

A contribution to the *Merkur* in July 1796 by Joseph Rückert (1771–1813), a philosophy professor in Würzburg, contains a theoretical section on the "appropriate" selection of and approach to reading materials. Because Rückert's treatise, "On Reading" ("Über Lektüre") summarizes so many of the ideas and expectations regarding the necessary attitude toward reading in a changed literary world, we would do well to look at his argument a little more closely. Phrased as a fictive, personal letter to a lady friend reminiscent of the style of the Moral Weeklies earlier in the century, "On Reading" aims to formulate guidelines for "right reading."

Rückert begins by lamenting the passive approach of most readers in search of mere entertainment and excitement. The result is that the authors are in total control of the reading act. Because readers do not understand the true art of reading, writers are at liberty to manipulate the reader at will. One-dimensional, passive reading, Rückert loudly asserts, is the single greatest cause of emotional abuse in the literary marketplace

(*NTM*, 62:244). He reminds his reader that "reading is an intellectual need and is harmful if it does not energize the mind" (*NTM*, 62:240). Consequently, readers should not restrict their requirements to sentiment or fantasy alone; they should seek intellectual stimulation as well. They should endeavor to enhance their knowledge, clarify their ideas, and refine their opinions on moral and social matters. They should never read only with their hearts, for that is tantamount to reading with only half a personality, and an author cannot perfect half a person. Nor should they expect the author to plant the seeds for development in them, the readers. That is a false expectation and a misperception of the writer's role. The germ of moral and aesthetic perfectibility exists in each human individual. All the writer can do, Rückert opines, is stimulate growth (*NTM*, 62:245f.). Thus, it is imperative that readers think while they read, making judgments about the correctness of the author's point of view as they move along. The conclusion (*das Urteil*) one reaches is not the important thing; instead, the *act of reaching a judgment* (*das Urteilen*), of coming to a conclusion, is the crucial factor in the true reading process (*NTM*, 62:253). If the reader fails to read critically, s/he falls easy prey to the writer's skills of manipulation. Such passivity would thwart the ultimate purpose of the reading act and would provide scant satisfaction. Rückert explains: "Only one's own animation and the increase in energy represent the true pleasure of reading."[42]

Finally, in order to practice the art of reading in the "correct" fashion, readers must approach the page with an open mind and with a sincere interest in profiting from the printed word. The reader's aim should not be to acquire some ephemeral information or obscure fact, but rather to plumb the nature of moral and aesthetic sentiment. The reader's goal, in other words, should be to ennoble and cultivate her/his own human nature (*NTM*, 62:247). The influence of Enlightenment anthropology and the exhortation to think for oneself is readily discernable in this little essay. Moreover, Rückert is clearly addressing the top-echelon readers, the "judges" and "experts," within the reading public at large.

This more specific audience and the qualities demanded of it are essentially the same ones identified by Leibniz a hundred years earlier. Leibniz had defined the intended reader of his "Ermahnung an die Teutsche," for example, as those "who are willing to nurture their minds with good books and good company." This group is composed of scholars and students, bureaucrats, men of the world, and also women. The members of this group are not distinguished by wealth, power, or birth—the normal criteria for distinction in society—but rather by their level of general education and sophistication (*gebildet*). These readers do not live blindly day by day with no thought of the future and are not slaves to their baser drives. Rather they are inquisitive, flexible, sociable, and willing to learn. Their actions are based on common sense, and their treatment of others is marked by sensitivity (Leibniz, "Ermahnung," 66f.). We are reminded, of course, of Klopstock's characterization of the reading public around 1760.

The Dynamism of the Reading Bond

There exists between the enlightened authors and their intended readership a "sympathetic bond" (cf. Wieland, *Beiträge*, 3:235) that initially attracts a potential reader to her/his work. The writer has the task of tightening this bond in order to advance the reader toward the goal of perfection. Writers throughout the eighteenth century repeatedly referred to the special relationship authors sought to establish with their intended audience. The relationship was not envisioned as that of the preacher to the parishioner or of the schoolmaster to the pupil. Because of the recipient's capacity for thought and desire for (moral) improvement, the author sought a positive discourse with him/her. If the reading act remained one of passive reception, it would amount to nothing more than surrogate thinking. No, the writer sought in the ideal reader an alter ego. Friedrich von Hardenberg (1772–1801), the esoteric Romantic writing at century's end, saw the "true reader" as "the extended author."[43] The connotation is of equality rather than of subservience. Already in 1762 Johann Georg Hamann (1730–1788), the "Mage of the North" and mediator between Enlightenment and Storm and Stress, clearly conceived of the reader and author roles as constitutive factors not just in the act of reading, but already in the act of writing. In his essay on "Readers and Critics" ("Leser und Kunstrichter," 1762), for example, he states that "the concept of the reader is an aid to the author," for the consciousness of an audience contributes significantly to a clear yet rich orchestration of a work with simultaneous appeals to intellect and sentiment. Appropriately, Hamann defines the relationship between writers and readers as complementary halves. Despite their disparate natures they have common needs and pursue "the same goal of unity" (*gemeinschaftliches Ziel ihrer Vereinigung*).[44]

A few years after Hamann's remarks, David Schirach went a step further by combining the notions of the author's consciousness of his reader and that of the reading act as process designed to elicit intellectual, ethical, and ultimately social progress. Against a reader typology reflecting general approaches to reading material, Schirach formulates a view of the ideal reader widely subscribed to in his age. He designates the ideal type as poetic (*dichterisch*) or critical (*kritisch*). He writes: "The poetic reader applies feeling and discriminating taste to his perusal of prose and verse writers in order to stimulate his imagination, refine his understanding, or to sharpen his wit" (Schirach, 55). However, as soon as the poetic reader begins to judge works for others, he slips into the role of critical reader. The critical reader, we are told, is the only one who does not read for his own benefit; he reads for others (58). In that ultimate reading capacity the recipient endeavors to enter into the mind of the writer in order to interpret his meaning as faithfully as possible. In doing so, the critical reader assumes the function of author by identifying her/his individual consciousness with that of the author. In current reader-response criticism this union of consciousness—this thinking the writer's thoughts as if they were one's own and yet not one's own—is designated "the point at which author and reader converge" (Iser, "The Reading Process," 66). It is also a hallmark of reading as "the most dangerous game" as outlined by Harold Brodkey and which can be labelled "the ethics of reading."[45]

Although the progressive writers of the age looked upon reading and writing as serious business, that is, as an exercise in creative or critical thinking, they did not restrict their appeals to the intellect alone. If they were to achieve their ultimate goal of perfecting their readers, of trans-forming these "unpracticed" readers into "practiced" ones—in short, if they were to create of the reader an alter ego—then their appeal must be broader.[46] It must include the heart as well as the head. Human perfec-tion, after all, entails more than just intellectual refinement. An anony-mous contributor to the Moral Weekly *Der Mensch* argued in 1751 that "whoever did not read with feeling had not yet learned how to read correctly" (205). The reference to "feeling" underscores another aspect of the Enlightenment not yet dealt with specifically: the cultivation of sen-timent.

The epistemological concern with clarity and distinctness of thought characterized the philosophical objectives of the eighteenth century. Sen-sibility (*Empfindsamkeit*), a tendency within the Enlightenment, had its own objectives that merged at times indistinguishably with the philo-sophical goals of the *Aufklärung*. Sensibility focused on the intuitive and empathetic powers of the human soul and sought to nurture them to perfection. Less intellectually inclined, *sensibilité* devoted its energies to cultivating and perfecting sentiment, not the maudlin or incapacitating kind to which the extremes of the movement led, but the noble and sublime impulses capable of lifting the human creature to the heights of benevolence. The convergence of the intellectual and sentimental strains of the age produced a more balanced reading objective. This goal went beyond the desire for logical clarity to include ethical development by engaging one's entire personality. The ideas presented had to be intensely felt as well as comprehended. Only then could they be considered useful or, we might add, purposeful. Animation of the head or heart alone would miss the mark. When the cognitive faculties work in concert with the emotional response, then the twofold goal of distinctness and involvement can be attained. Such is the meaning of the anonymous writer's summarizing remark in the article on the art of reading in *Der Mensch*: "We endeavor to write in accordance with human dignity" (208). His wish is that the reader, for his/her part, accept and judge the written word in the manner intended, that is, as contributing to human perfection. The response he envisions (*menschlich*) is essentially a moral one with an emotional as well as an intellectual component designed to motivate the practical implementation of newly acquired or confirmed insights in the fulfillment of the collective human destiny.

This theme of cooperation between reason and sentiment in the appreciation of literature as an aesthetic and ethical event became a standard feature of poetics in the second half of the century. It could of course draw upon a tradition since Thomasius's reappraisal of the gallant attitude and the early Enlighteners' advocation of a new way of writing. But a significant variation of the theme was introduced in the 1770s by such authors as Herder and Wieland. In *Of the Cognition and Sensation of the Human Mind* (*Vom Erkennen und Empfinden der menschlichen Seele*, 1780) Herder accorded priority to sense impression over ratiocination, arguing that human sensations are transformed into knowledge through verbalization. Truth cannot exist without this cooperative effort. In his political novel, *The Golden Mirror* (*Der goldne Spiegel*, 1772), Wieland is emphatic in reversing the relationship between reason and sentiment, ascribing a more decisive function to sentiment than to reason in attaining human perfection and happiness: "But to achieve happiness via *nature* one must have retained its most generous gift unspoiled: *sentiment*, for sentiment is the instrument of all her other benefactions. Indispensable to *right sentiment* is *right thinking* (*Spiegel*, Part I, chapter 4; Wieland's emphasis).

In the 1790s Enlighteners frequently returned to the notion that sentiment must take precedence or that the reading act involved both the lower and higher faculties of cognition. For example, Christian Ernst Karl Graf von Benzel-Sternau (1767–1849) cites the need to energize man's thoughts and feelings as a prime responsibility of writers in his essay on

"Recommendations for Writers of our Age" ("Gesichtspunkte für den Schriftsteller unsers Zeitalters," 1796) published in the *Neuer Teutscher Merkur*. He insists that "the energy of the soul extend to the intellect, the heart, and the will; that critical thought is the result of mental vigor; and that one can achieve independence of sentiment only if the heart is fully animated." And he concludes: "Independent action derives from the faculty for independent volition."[47]

The notion of involving both the lower and higher faculties of cognition through the reading act was also cited by Karl L. von Knebel in 1792 as a sine qua non for aesthetic pleasure. Knebel uses a reading of Goethe's *Iphigenie* to explain how the reader must respond to the poet's appeal to the emotions as well as to reason, if he is to appreciate fully the achievement of Goethe's play. Knebel's purpose is to demonstrate to his reader that a mere rational comprehension of the content of the drama is an inadequate response to Goethe's intention. In addition to understanding the ideas correctly, the viewer/reader must also correctly apprehend the nuances. In pursuing his argument, Knebel points out the paradoxical nature of language itself: on the one hand it is an agent of reason ("Die *Sprache* ist eigentlich ein bloßes *Vernunftorgan*"), on the other it is called upon to express the passions ("Sie wird aber auch zum Ausdruck der *Leidenschaften*"). Consequently, language seeks to express simultaneously both rational clarity and emotional vigor. The only realm of language exempt from this dual demand is that of "the abstract sciences." In all other cases the appeal of written or oral speech is always inextricably intellectual and sensuous.[48] Thus the "literary" reader must be able to respond to the word on two distinct levels.

From the foregoing it is clear that the Enlightenment dictum of *Richtigdenken* had an emotional counterpart that we might call *Richtigempfinden* (right feeling). The style of writing best designed to engage the reader in "right sentiment and thinking" was obviously an important goal of these writers, for they wished to use it to promote perfection in their readers. It is safe to say that neither the ideal nor the route to it was static. The path to it leads through psychological animation, which is really nothing other than a prelude to physical action. The stimulator in this process for the Enlighteners was language, specifically: literary language. In his essay on poetics in the late 1750s Klopstock elucidated this connection in a fashion that strikingly foreshadows an important part of Habermas's definition of communicative action: "A poem without action is like a body without a soul. Action consists in the exertion of the will in the attainment of a goal. Action is falsely perceived, if it is seen first and foremost as external movement. Action begins with a firm resolution and progresses . . . through various steps and turns until the goal is reached. Action in its earliest form is paired with passion" ("Zur Poetik," 269). Elsewhere in *Der nordische Aufseher* Klopstock defines the essence of poetry as the total and simultaneous impact of language on the mind, imagination, and emotional life of the reader.

On the connection between poetic pleasure and activity, Klopstock notes that "the deepest mysteries of poetry reside in activity which it causes in our souls. Activity is, in fact, essential to our sense of pleasure. Less gifted poets seek to lure us into a life of inactivity with them (*Pflanzenleben*) ("Gedanken über die Natur der Poesie," 258f.). In his *Gelehrtenrepublik* (1774) Klopstock returns to these ideas, stating unequivocally that writing in this sense is, in fact, by far preferable to action in the traditional sense. His reasoning is clear: the individual action tends to be a one-time occurrence, whereas the written word can evoke a response long after the writer's death. Moreover, he concludes, more than one reader can react to the text and each of those readers can, in turn, act upon other persons so that the impact of the written word is potentially much further reaching than any individual act in time (*Gelehrtenrepublik*, 193). The poet obviously envisions the readers' responses in this chain reaction as reflecting the writer's intention encoded in the text.

Now, we might ask, what do these musings on the dynamism of the writer-reader bond have to do with essayism? The answer is: a lot. We need only recall how large Gottfried Ephraim Lessing (1728–1781) looms in the literary life of the eighteenth century, the modern aesthetics of the interactive audience, and in the history of essayistic writing itself. He is widely regarded as "the glorious father of German prose" on the one hand and, on the other, as the "inaugurator" of a specific essay genre (Rohner, 611). Because of his important double role, I have saved Lessing for last.

Bruno Berger sees a first definition of the essay in a remark of Lessing's contained in the preface to his *Sogenannte Briefe an verschiedene Gottesgelehrte* (*So-called Letters to Various Theologians*, c. 1780), which were found among the poet's unpublished papers after his death (Berger, 198). Although Lessing specifically speaks of the letter form, we know that essayistic writing is not restricted to a certain form, especially in the eighteenth century. Lessing's formulation is so striking that it deserves to be quoted in full:

> So-called letters are a kind of literary composition whose
> makeup is not all that clear. It is seldom necessary to put them
> in the mail. Occasionally there is some usefulness in printing

them and sending them out into the world as books. They might be called one-sided dialogues, because the writer really does carry on a conversation with an absent partner, who, however, is not allowed to speak himself even though the letters contain numerous exhortations such as: 'What do you think, sir? Will you answer me, sir?'

Figuratively, letter writing is the most accommodating manner of book writing, although—for that reason—not necessarily the worst kind. What it loses in terms of clear structuring, it gains by its light touch. On the other hand, it is easier to introduce order into a letter than it is to impart a sense of liveliness to a didactic treatise which is aimed at no one in particular and is so impersonal in tone that it seems written by old, sedate truth herself (cited according to Berger, 198f.).

The qualities ascribed by Lessing to letter writing—the casual organization of the writer's thoughts, a lively tone, a warm and personal style in engaging an imagined reader in conversation on a general kind of topic, and the indeterminate nature of the writing mode itself (is it designed for publication? does another have to read it in order for it to have a purpose?)—have all been absorbed into the canon of essayistic style. They are, of course, part and parcel of the Enlightener's ideal of engaged intellectual discourse as a means of realizing the Enlightenment's goal of general education via pleasant dialogue.

In his eulogy of Lessing, Herder characterized the former's prose style as conveying the impression that the reader is not presented with the results of his thinking but instead actually experiences the writer's thought processes as they evolve. His writing is like a "running poem with interjections and digressions, but always in movement, always working, progressing, developing."[49] This quality has to do, to be sure, with Lessing's manner of thinking, but it also evolves from his sense of obligation to engage his reader as fully as possible in the process. For example, Lessing himself tell us that he seeks to animate the reader's rational and imaginative powers through the act of writing. In fact he considers it necessary, not just useful, to clothe rational arguments in metaphorical language and to elucidate secondary concepts via allusions (LM, Hanser, 8:251). Lessing obviously shared the conviction of the progressive writers that writing and reading should be serious, yet enjoyable business.

The connection between essayistic writing and the ethical view of writing and reading in the eighteenth century as formulated in this chapter is also underscored by Friedrich Schlegel in his evaluation of Georg Forster

(1754–1794), "Fragment of a Characterization of the German Classical Writers" ("Fragment einer Karakteristik der deutschen Klassiker," 1797). In essay research Schlegel is widely considered the first theorist of essay style, and Forster is regarded as a classic example of an essayist.

Schlegel prizes as progressive features of Forster's prose writing its ability to stimulate active reflection, to widen our horizons, and expand our feelings. Far removed from the musty air of the scholar's littered room, Forster's writing exudes the freshness of a sun-filled spring morning in the countryside. Surrounded by vibrant and pulsating life, the reader feels him/herself pulled along to higher planes. Schlegel writes that the reader is scarcely ever left untouched by Forster's work because Forster makes simultaneous appeals to the reader's powers of reason, imagination, and emotion (*DE*, 6:221ff.). This forward, pulsating movement and broad appeal have become cardinal traits of the essayistic attitude. They seem to go hand in glove with the dynamic interaction between writer and reader.

The intellectual and literary life of the eighteenth century everywhere reflects this notion of activity and motion toward the perfection of humanity prompted by affective stylistics.[50] It would not be inappropriate to speak of a vitalistic psychology of reading or a philosophy of essayistic writing analogous to Friedrich Schlegel's phrase *Philosophie des Essays* which is both experimental philosophy and realistic philosophy (*Realphilosophie*; *Werke*, 18:202). The essentially dialectical nature of this phenomenon can be explained appropriately in terms of Habermas's theory of communicative behavior and it is definitely ethical in purpose. Let us turn now to an examination of the chief criteria of that new, essayistic style of prose composition which is discursive, affective, and—yes—rhetorical.

Notes

1. Friedrich Schlegel, *Kritische Werkausgabe*, ed. E. Behler, J.J. Anstett, and H. Eichner, Vol. 18, *Philosophische Lehrjahre 1796–1806* (Paderborn: F. Schöningh, 1963), 220: "Tendenz unsres Zeitalters, alle Wissenschaften zu essayiren." Schlegel's remark recalls Kant's characterization of the age in philosophical terms as "das eigentliche Zeitalter der Kritik, der sich alles unterwerfen muß" (I. Kant, preface to *Kritik der reinen Vernunft*, 1781).
2. Rudolf Vierhaus, *Deutschland im Zeitalter des Absolutismus (1648–1763)* (Göttingen: Vandenhoeck and Ruprecht, 1978), 109.
3. Carl August Böttiger, *Ueber den Mißbrauch der Deutschen Literatur auf Schulen und einigen Mitteln dagegen* (Leipzig, 1787), rprt. in *Der Deutschunterricht auf dem Gymnasium der Goethezeit. Eine Anthologie*, ed. Georg Jäger (Hildesheim: Gerstenberg, 1977), 14. See also Johann Carl Wezel, *Ueber Sprache, Wissenschaften und Geschmack der Teutschen* (1781),

which is designed to correct the distorted view of German literary life as promulgated by Frederick II, King of Prussia, in his *De la Littérature allemande* (1780), in *Kritische Schriften*, ed. Albert R. Schmitt (Stuttgart: Metzler, 1975), 3:1–6.

Two other informative works by contemporaries of the era to which I refer the interested reader are: (1) Johann Rudolph Gottlieb Beyer, "Ueber das Bücherlesen, in so fern es zum Luxus unsrer Zeiten gehört. Vorgelesen in der churfürstl. mainz. Academie nützlicher Wissenschaften zu Erfurt, am 2ten Febr. 1795," in *Quellen zur Geschichte des Buchwesens*, Vol.10: *Die Leserevolution*, ed. Reinhard Wittmann (Munich: Kraus-Thomson, 1981), 185–216; and (2) Friedrich Christoph Perthes, *Der deutsche Buchhandel als Bedingung des Daseins einer deutschen Literatur* (Leipzig, 1816; rprt. Stuttgart: Reclam, 1967). Beyer's lecture depicts the situation from the reader's point of view, while Perthes's essay reflects the events from the publisher's standpoint.

4. Rolf Engelsing, "Die Perioden der Lesergeschichte in der Neuzeit. Das statistische Ausmaß und die soziokulturelle Bedeutung der Lektüre" *Archiv für Geschichte des Buchwesens* 10 (1970), col.982. On the question of popular culture and the expanding book market see also Peter Weber, "Die Anfänge einer Massenliteratur," *Geschichte der Deutschen Literatur 1789–1830*, ed. Hans-Dietrich Dahnke et al. (Berlin: Volk and Wissen, 1978), 7:72–92.

5. Johann Christoph Gottsched, *Der Biedermann*, facsimile of the 1727–29 Leipzig edition with an afterword and commentary by Wolfgang Martens (Stuttgart: Metzler, 1975), 1:1.

6. For a detailed discussion of these developments see my articles "The Gallant Novel and the German Enlightenment 1670–1750," *Deutsche Vierteljahresschrift für Literaturwissenschaft und Geistesgeschichte* 59/1 (1985), 47–78, and "Lektüre und Lesertypologie im 18.Jahrhundert (1730–1770). Ein Beitrag zur Lesergeschichte am Beispiel Wolfenbüttels," *Internationales Archiv für Sozialgeschichte der deutschen Literatur* 8 (1983), 35–82, as well as Albert Ward, *Book Production, Fiction, and the German Reading Public: 1740–1800* (Oxford: Clarendon Press, 1974).

7. See Paul Raabe, "Aufklärung durch Bücher. Der Anteil des Buchhandels an der kulturellen Entfaltung in Deutschland 1764 bis 1790," in *Aufklärung durch Bücher*, ed. P.Raabe und W. Schmidt-Biggemann (Bonn: Hochwacht, 1979), 93; Dominik von König, "Lesesucht und Lesewut," in *Buch und Leser*, ed. Herbert G. Göpfert (Hamburg: Hauswedell, 1977), 91–93.

8. Karl S. Morgenstern, "Plan im Lesen. Rede bey Bekanntmachung der Preisaufgaben für die Studirenden der kaiserlichen Universität zu Dorpat, gehalten den 12. Dec. 1805," in K. S. Morgenstern, *Johann Müller oder Plan im Lesen* (n.p., 1808), 55–90, here 65. Cf. also Christian Ernst Karl Graf zu Benzel-Sternau, "Gesichtspunkte für den Schriftsteller," *Neuer Teutscher Merkur* (May 1796), 62:34–74, especially 34–44, and the examples in Rudolf Schenda, *Volk ohne Buch. Studien zur Sozialgeschichte der populären Lesestoffe 1770–1910* (Munich: dtv, 1977), 59–63.

9. Wolfgang von Ungern-Sternberg, "Schriftsteller und literarischer Markt," in *Hansers Sozialgeschichte der deutschen Literatur*, Vol. 3: *Deutsche Aufklärung bis zur Französischen Revolution 1680–1789*, ed. Rolf Grimminger

(Munich: dtv, 1980), 3/1:134. See also Paul Raabe, "Der Buchhändler im achtzehnten Jahrhundert in Deutschland," in *Buch und Buchhandel im achtzehnten Jahrhundert*, ed. Giles Barber and Bernhard Fabian (Hamburg: Hauswedell, 1981), 271–291, especially 282–288.

10. Johann Goldfriedrich, *Geschichte des deutschen Buchhandels*, Vol. 3: *Geschichte des deutschen Buchhandels vom Beginn der klassischen Literaturepoche bis zum Beginn der Fremdherrschaft (1740–1804)* (Leipzig: Börsenverein, 1909), 3:248; Ungern-Sternberg, "Schriftsteller," 134 (see fn. 6); McCarthy, "Lektüre und Lesertypologie," 45 (see fn. 6). Reinhard Wittmann, "Der gerechtfertigte Nachdrucker? Nachdruck und literarisches Leben im achtzehnten Jahrhundert," in *Buch und Buchhandel* (1981), 293–320 (see fn. 9), provides a concise evaluation of the positive contributions of pirate publishers to the expansion of the publishing and reading revolution in eighteenth-century Germany.

11. Helmuth Kiesel and Paul Münch, *Gesellschaft und Literatur im 18. Jahrhundert. Voraussetzungen und Entstehung des literarischen Markts in Deutschland* (Munich: Beck, 1977), 14.

12. See McCarthy, "Lektüre und Lesertypologie," 45 (see fn. 6).

13. For a discussion of these questions see McCarthy, "The Poet as Journalist and Essayist. Part Two," *Jahrbuch für Internationale Germanistik* 13/1 (1982), 77ff.; Engelsing, "Perioden," 984 (see fn. 4); Ungern-Sternberg, "Schriftsteller," 136 (see fn. 6); Rudolf Schenda estimates the potential literacy rate at higher levels: 15% of the population in 1770, 25% in 1800, and 40% by 1830. See *Die Lesestoffe der kleinen Leute. Studien zur populären Literatur im 19. und 20. Jahrhundert* (Munich: Beck, 1976), 38. In his generally useful introduction to the "business" of the Enlightenment Klaus Berghahn speaks of the figures 20,000 and 300,000 as "die Eckzahlen für die gebildete Schicht," but does not differentiate between early and late century nor between degrees of literary competence. See Berghahn, "Das schwierige Geschäft der Aufklärung," in *Aufklärung. Ein literaturwissenschaftliches Studienbuch*, ed. Hans-Friedrich Wessels (Königstein/Ts: Athenäum, 1984), 32–65.

14. Friedrich Nicolai, *Das Leben und die Meinungen des Herrn Magisters Sebaldus Nothanker* (Berlin: Nicolai, 1773–76.; rprt. Darmstadt: Wissenschaftliche Buchgesellschaft, 1967), 72. Friedrich H. Jacobi, *Auserlesener Briefwechsel* (Leipzig: Fleischer, 1825–1827; rprt. Berne: H. Lang, 1969), 1:68. Jürgen Wilke, *Literarische Zeitschriften des 18. Jahrhunderts (1688–1789), Part I: Grundlegung* (Stuttgart: Metzler, 1978), 1:107. On the important role of various kinds of reading institutions in the dissemination of ideas and development of reading, strategies see Marlies Prüsener, *Lesegesellschaften im achtzehnten Jahrhundert* (Frankfurt a.M.: Buchhändler-Vereinigung, 1972); Otto Dann, "Die Lesegesellschaften des 18. Jahrhunderts und der gesellschaftliche Aufbruch des deutschen Bürgertums," in *Buch und Leser*, ed. Herbert G. Göpfert (Hamburg: Hauswedell, 1977), 160–193; and *Die Leihbibliothek als Institution des literarischen Lebens im 18. und 19. Jahrhundert*, ed. Georg Jäger and Jörg Schönert (Hamburg: Hauswedell, 1980).

15. The foregoing statistics are based on Goldfriedrich, 3:249f. (see fn. 10); Ungern-Sternberg, "Schriftsteller," 135 (see fn. 6); and Raabe, "Aufklärung durch Bücher," 97ff. (see fn. 7).

16. See Alberto Martino, "Barockpoesie, Publikum und Verbürgerlichung der literarischen Intelligenz," *Internationales Archiv für Sozialgeschichte der deutschen Literatur* 1 (1976), 141ff.; Pamela Currie, "Moral Weeklies and the Reading Public in Germany, 1711–1750," *Oxford German Studies* (1968), 81ff.; Wilke, *Literarische Zeitschriften*, 1:72–79; Goldfriedrich, 3:299f. (see fn. 10).

17. Anon., "Der Autor," *Belustigungen des Verstandes und des Witzes* (Leipzig: Breitkopf, 1743–1744); Wieland, "Sympathien" (1756); Nicolai, *Sebaldus Nothanker* (1773ff.); Goethe, *Faust*: "Vorspiel auf dem Theater" (verses 1796ff)

18. Wilke, *Literarische Zeitschriften*, 1:64; Wolfgang Martens, "Die Geburt des Journalisten in der Aufklärung," *Wolfenbütteler Studien zur Aufklärung* 1 (1974), 84–98. Berghahn, "Geschäft," rightfully speaks of the periodical as the "actual vehicle of Enlightenment" (34), but it is no longer true that periodical literature is still a neglected aspect of literary life in the eighteenth century as he claims in his opening sentence (32).

19. Cf. Wilke, *Literarische Zeitschriften*, 1:64ff.; Goldfriedrich, 3:312–329; Ungern-Sternberg, "Schriftsteller," 135; Margot Lindemann, *Deutsche Presse bis 1815* (Berlin: Colloquium Verlag, 1969), 201, 237. For a discussion of the nature, popularity, and function of the belletristic almanacs in the Age of Goethe see *Kalender? Ey, wie viel Kalender! Literarische Almanache zwischen Rokoko und Klassizismus*. ed. York-Gotthart Mix. Ausstellungskatalog der Herzog August Bibliothek No. 50 (Wolfenbüttel: Herzog August Bibliothek, 1986), and York-Gotthart Mix, *Die deutschen Musen-Almanache des 18. Jahrhunderts* (Munich: Beck, 1987).

20. Goldfriedrich, 3:297. In 1792 Friedrich Justin Bertuch (1747–1822) published an anonymous article entitled "Ueber Mode-Epoken in der Teutschen Lektüre" in his popular *Journal des Luxus und der Moden* (1786–1795; partial rprt.: Leipzig, 1967), 365–73. In it we find a succinct characterization of the rapid changes in popular literary fashions at the end of the century. I include a longer excerpt here for the curious reader: "Darin werden alle Mode-Leser mit mir einstimmig seyn, daß vor etwa 18 Jahren nichts so sehr intereßirte als Werthers Leiden . . . Vom Siegwart an sorgte eine ganze Fluth von Romanen . . . dafür, daß die Tränen nicht versiegten; . . . Karl von Karlsberg gab bald einen neuen Ton an. Er sprach auch viel von Elend, er wollte aber bey dem Elende nicht gewinselt, sondern räsonnirt haben und ihm abgeholfen wissen . . . . Alles sprach jetzt von Reformiren der Welt, von Verbesserung einzelner Einrichtungen, von zweckmäßigerer Erziehung, u[nd] dergl[eichen] . . . . Ich weiß nicht, waren sechs Bände voll menschlichen Elends zu viel auf einmal; . . . kurz, die Epoche des Karl von Karlsberg dauerte nicht lange. Man schweifte nun in verschiednen kleinen Abwegen umher, bis man sich auf dem Tournierplatze der Ritter wiederfand. Die Rittergeschichte hat etwas eignes Anziehendes. Sie war daher bald allgemein die neue Lieblingslektüre . . . . Ich weiß nicht, welchen Stoß die Ideen der Lesewelt von innen oder außen her erhalten mußten, daß sie sich

auf einmal auf eine Sache fixirten, von der man sonst gar nichts wissen
wolte. Ich meyne die Geisterseherey und alles, was dazu gehört . . . Seitdem
liest man nichts mehr gern, wobey's natürlich zugeht, und fühlt wenig
Interesse bey Dingen, die nicht durch verborgene Kräfte bewirkt werden.
. . . Die schwarzen Brüder, den Genius und a[nderes] hat wahrscheinlich das
Bedürfniß der Lesewelt herausgepreßt. Sie sind mehr verschlungen als
gelesen, und wahrscheinlich ist von ihnen in der schönen Welt mehr
gesprochen worden, als in der gelehrten von Kant's sämmtlichen Schriften."

21. Johann Georg Heinzmann, *Appell an meine Nation über Aufklärung und Aufklärer* (Berne: n. p., 1795; rprt. Hildesheim: Gerstenberg, 1977), 88, 137, 145, 282f., 291).

22. See Friedrich Gottlieb Klopstock, "Von dem Publico," *Werke in einem Band* (Berlin and Weimar: Aufbau, 1979), 254–258.

23. Friedrich Maximillian Klinger, "Betrachtungen und Gedanken," *Werke*, 2 vols., ed. Hans Jürgen Geerdts (Weimar: Volksverlag, 1958), 2:505.

24. Johann Rudolph Gottlieb Beyer, "Ueber das Bücherlesen, in so fern es zum Luxus unsrer Zeiten gehört. Vorgelesen in der churfürstl[ichen] main-z[erischen] Academie nützlicher Wissenschaften zu Erfurt, am 2ten Febr. 1795," in *Quellen zur Geschichte des Buchwesens*, Vol. 10: *Die Leserre-volution*, ed. Reinhard Wittmann (Munich: Kraus-Thomson, 1981), 24f.: "Regenten und Minister müssen zwar als Volkserzieher auch auf die Gei-stesnahrung und Bildung des Volks ihr Augenmerk richten, und die Lektüre mit in ihren Plan ziehen, aber sie müssen sich darinnen auch nicht die alte Schuldisciplin zum Muster nehmen, sonst treiben die Censoren und Bücherrichter mit dem Publiko eben den Unfug, den ehemals Schulmonar-chen und Schulpedanten mit der lieben Jugend trieben, deren Geist oft mehr gelähmt und verkrüppelt, als entwickelt und ausgebildet, und wo jeder Ausbruch der jugendlichen Lebhaftigkeit und Thätigkeit, jede Aeusserung des eignen Nachdenkens, jede freymüthige Frage oder Antwort, als muth-williger Frevel mit dem Stocke, oder Cariren, oder Einstecken bestraft wurde . . . . (1) Man muß die Lesesucht unsrer Zeitgenossen in etwas ver-mindern. (2) Man muß sie von der unfruchtbaren Zeit- und Geistverder-benden Lektüre ab- und auf nützliche, gesunde und stärkende Geistesnahrung zu lenken suchen." See also McCarthy, "Plan im Lesen" (1986); D. von König, "Lesesucht und Lesewut" (1977); Martens, *Botschaft* (1968); Raabe, "Aufklärung durch Bücher" (1979).

25. On the question of "limited Enlightenment" (*beschränkte Aufklärung*) see R. Schenda, *Volk ohne Buch*, 107–141 et passim; Gerhard Sauder, "'Verhältnismäßig Aufklärung.' Zur bürgerlichen Ideologie am Ende des 18. Jahrhunderts," *Jahrbuch der Jean-Paul-Gesellschaft* (1974), 102–126. There are problems, I think, with the concept of *beschränkte Aufklärung* within the framework of true Enlightenment. For example, Schenda rightly points out that "only a very thin layer of highly educated people were engaged in reading 'classical' authors during the entire epoch" (458) or were interested in reading for ideas (477). Moreover, the spread of the reading habit was mostly confined to bourgeois classes. In fact, he argues, the "common reader" (*der gemeine Leser* or *der große Haufen*) cannot be identified with the working classes; instead the term designates uneducated

members of the aristocracy and bourgeoisie (456f.). If that is, in fact, true—as it would seem to be—should one even speak about a "limited enlightenment" as the conscious exclusion of the unskilled laborer from exposure to certain ideas if the worker did not take advantage of the available materials or if the "common reader" was not interested in developing critical insights (50, 86)? In other words, was the official strategy repressive or was the intended audience unresponsive? An examination of Lessing's, Schiller's, and Wieland's attitudes toward Enlightenment and freedom of the press demonstrated the reluctance of these classical authors to restrict the free exchange of ideas in any official manner (see my essays of 1984 and 1987). The question of "limited enlightenment" pivots, I suggest, on the question of authorial intent and reader response, so that the writer's and reader's states of mind must figure dominantly in a consideration of the goals and strategies of the Enlightenment. All the same, the notion of relative enlightenment is much too complicated for us to go into it here in any depth. Let it suffice to point out Schenda's predilection for stressing the negative side of the phenomenon to the neglect of its accomplishments (cf., e.g., 53ff.). I focus on Schenda because of his broad impact on the attitude of researchers.

26. Gert Mattenklott, "Lesefieber. Plädoyer für eine historische Philosophie des Lesens," *Neue Sammlung* 21 (1981), 298–309, here 307.

27. The essential principles of Klopstock's eagerly awaited *Gelehrtenrepublik*, for example, revolve around the concepts of education and perfection via the written word. I include here a striking passage from the section "Von den Grundsätzen der Republik" for the curious reader: "Deren haben wir nur drei. Der erste ist: durch Untersuchung, Bestimmung, Entdeckung, Erfindung, Bildung und Beseelung ehemaliger, neuer und würdiger Gegenstände des Denkens und der Empfindung sich recht viele und recht mannigfalte Beschäftigungen und Vergnügungen des Geistes zu machen. Der zweite: das Nützlichste und Schönste von dem, was jene Beschäftigungen und Vergnügungen unterhalten hat, durch Schriften, und das Notwendigste auf Lehrstühlen andern mitzuteilen. Der dritte: Schriften, deren Inhalt einer gewissen Bildung nicht nur fähig, sondern auch würdig ist, denen vorzuziehen, die entweder ohne diesen Inhalt oder ohne diese Bildung sind." In *Dichtungen und Schriften* (Munich: Goldmann, n.d.), 193. On education and Enlightenment see the proceedings of the International Standing Conference for the History of Education, 6th Session, Herzog-August-Bibliothek, Sept. 3–6, 1984, *Informationen zur Erziehungs- und Bildungshistorischen Forschung*, Vols. 23–25: *Education and Enlightenment* (Hannover: Universität Hannover, 1984).

28. Rolf Grimminger broke with the dominant tradition in scholarship of stressing only Kant's insistence on the need for independent, critical thinking in his famous essay when he pointed out that the full impact of "Selbstdenken" can be realized only when individuals engage in open, public debate. R. Grimminger, "Aufklärung, Absolutismus und bürgerliche Individuen," *Hansers Sozialgeschichte der deutschen Literatur* (1980), 3/1:61. On the question of Enlightenment through print see W. Martens, "Journalisten," 90–96 (see fn. 18); Raabe, "Zeitschrift als Medium," *Wolfenbütteler Stu-*

dien zur Aufklärung 1 (1974), 99–112; Raabe, "Aufklärung durch Bücher" (1979) (see fn. 7); McCarthy, "Art of Reading" (1984); Klaus Berghahn, "Das Geschäft der Aufklärung" (1984) (see fn. 13). Reinhart Siegert points out, however, that these efforts to refine the common man were not wholly successful: "Aufklärung und Volkslektüre," *Archiv für Geschichte des Buchwesens* 19 (1978), cols. 565–1348; here 1158.

29. See Friedrich Schlegel, "Georg Forster," *Deutsche Essays. Prosa aus zwei Jahrhunderten,* ed. Ludwig Rohner (Munich: dtv, 1972), 6:219. Karl Biedermann, *Deutschland im 18. Jahrhundert* (1854–1880; rprt. Berlin: Ullstein, 1979) also describes this development (397–410).

30. *Der Redliche,* 1/13 (Nürnberg, 1751), 194; see also the untitled article on the art of reading in *Der Mensch. Eine Wochenschrift* 64.St.,2 (Halle, 1751), 201–208; Benzel-Sternau, "Gesichtspunkte für den Schriftsteller unseres Zeitalters," *Neuer Teutscher Merkur* 62 (May 1796), 34, 38, 43f.; and Martens, *Botschaft,* 404ff.

31. Cf. René König, "Geschichte und Sozialstruktur," *Internationales Archiv für Sozialgeschichte der deutschen Literatur* 2 (1977), 136.

32. See Günter Erning, *Das Lesen und die Lesewut* (Bad Heilbronn/Obb: Klinkhardt, 1974), 45, 55; Martens, *Botschaft,* 408, 426f.,458.

33. Gottsched, *Der Biedermann,* 1:1; Heinrich W. von Archenholtz, "Gedanken über die Journallektüre," *Neue Literatur und Völkerkunde* (1788), 2:3–9; rprt. in P. Raabe, "Die Zeitschrift als Medium der Aufklärung," *Wolfenbütteler Studien zur Aufklärung* 1 (1974), 128–132; here 130.

34. See J. A. McCarthy, "'Das sicherste Kennzeichen einer gesunden, nervösen Staatsverfassung': Lessing und die Pressefreiheit," *Lessing und die Toleranz.* Special Supplement to *Lessing Yearbook,* ed. Peter Freimark, Franklin Kopitzsch, and Helga Slessarev (Detroit: Wayne State University Press; Munich: edition = kritik, 1986), 225–244.

35. Wolfgang R. Langenbucher, "Die Demokratisierung des Lesens in der zweiten Leserevolution," in *Lesen und Leben,* ed. Herbert G. Göpfert et al. (Frankfurt a. M.: Buchhändler-Vereinigung, 1975), 13.

36. Christian Fürchtegott Gellert, *Die epistolographischen Schriften* (1741 and 1751; rprt. Stuttgart: Metzler, 1971), 184.

37. Adolph Freiherr von Knigge, *Über Schriftsteller und Schriftstellerei* (Hannover, 1793; rprt. Hildesheim: Gerstenberg, 1977), 16–19 in original edition; 102–104 in reprint (Knigge's emphasis).

38. Christoph M. Wieland, "Etwas über Vorurtheile überhaupt" (1799); rprt. in Bernd Weyergraf, *Der skeptische Bürger* (Stuttgart: Metzler, 1972), 146–151; here 149 (Wieland's emphasis).

39. Friedrich Schulz, *Litterarische Reisen* (Vienna: Wucherer, 1786), cited by Heinzmann, 145f. See also Riedel's views on the reading public in *Briefe über das Publikum* (Jena, 1768; rprt. Vienna: Bundesverlag, 1973), 113–115, and G. Benedikt Schirach, *Litterarische Briefe an das Publikum,* 3 Vols. (Altenburg: Hennings in Neisse, 1769–1774), 1:50–63 (= third letter, 1769). Schirach classifies the reading public into "simple," "curious," "vain," "sentimental," and "critical" readers.

40. Wieland, "Wie man liest," *Der Teutsche Merkur* (Januar, 1781), 70–74; here HA, 3:430.

41. Cf. Wieland, "Über die Rechte und Pflichten der Schriftsteller," *Der Teutsche Merkur* (1785); here, HA, 3:482.

42. Joseph Rückert, "Über Lektüre," *Neuer Teutscher Merkur*, 62 (1796), 244: "Denke zugleich und urtheile selbst nach aller deiner Kraft. Hierin liegt das Geheimnis des höchsten Genußes und der Kunst, deinem schlauen Autor die geheime Kraft über Dich zu nehmen, wodurch er Dich mißbraucht. Nur eigene Thätigkeit und ihr Gewinn an Kraft ist wahrer Genuß."

43. Friedrich von Hardenberg (Novalis), *Gesammelte Werke,* ed. Carl Seelig (Herrliberg/Zurich: Bühl, 1945), 2:44.

44. Johann Georg Hamann, "Leser und Kunstrichter," *Sturm und Drang. Kritische Schriften,* ed. Lambert Schneider and Waltraut Schleuning (rprt. Heidelberg: L. Schneider, 1963), 164.

45. See J. Hillis Miller, *The Ethics of Reading* (New York: Columbia University Press, 1987). Miller examines the attitudes of Kant, de Man, Eliot, Trollope, James, and Benjamin toward the reading act. See also my article, "The Ethics of Reading," in *Germanistik aus interkultureller Perspektive. Articles réunis et publiés par Adrien Finck et Gertrud Gréciano en hommage à Gonthier-Louis Fink* (Collection Recherches Germaniques, 1) (Strasbourg: Université des Sciences Humaines, 1988), 39–48.

46. See Johann Bernhard Basedow, *Lehrbuch prosaischer und poetischer Wohlredenheit* (Kopenhagen: Brummer, 1756), 420.

47. Benzel-Sternau, "Gesichtspunkte für den Schriftsteller unsers Zeitalters," *Neuer Teutscher Merkur* (May 1796), 62:67f. "Die Energie der Seele erstreckt sich auf Geist, Herz und Wille. Selbstdenken ist das Resultat der Geisteskraft; unabhängig fühlen kann nur ein Herz voll Energie; Selbsthandeln entspringt aus dem Vermögen eines selbstständigen Willens."

48. Karl L. von Knebel, "Ueber die Kunst zu lesen," in *Die deutsche Prosa von Mosheim bis auf unsere Tage. Eine Mustersammlung,* ed. Gustav Schwab, second Ed. in three parts, ed. Karl Klüpfel (Gütersloh and Leipzig: C. Bertelsmann, 1868), 1:258–268; here 258f. Knebel culminates his line of reasoning with the telling remark: "Das Reich der Sprache ist also das Reich der Vernunft und der Sinnlichkeit, beide in einander wirkend; denn selbst bei den abstractesten Vorstellungen nimmt der Ton des Redners etwas Gefälliges, den Sinnen Schmeichelndes, an, und bei den sinnlichsten Aeußerungen muß er auf den Gedanken wirken" (258f.). The essence of the statement and even the use of the term "orator" (*Redner*) reveal how closely associated rhetoric is with artistic expression. That nexus is the topic of chapter VI.

49. Herder, *Kritische Wälder*, Erstes Wäldchen, in Suphan, 3:1-188. For a more complete study of Lessing's significance for Herder see Wulf Koepke, "Herders Totengespräch mit Lessing," *Aufnahme—Weitergabe: Literarische Impulse um Lessing und Goethe,* ed. J. A. McCarthy and A. Kipa (Hamburg: H. Buske Verlag, 1982), 125–142.

50. Mattenklott, "Lesefieber. Plädoyer für eine historische Philosophie des Lesens," *Neue Sammlung* 21 (1981), 298–309, calls for an "historical philosophy of reading" in order to discern the real significance of the nature of the reading act as action (*Handlung*).

CHAPTER 6

The Poetry of Prose

The Theory of Prose

"One side of the seventeenth century had developed a consciously artistic style, striving towards the greatest intensity of expression and as far away as possible from the *volkstümlich*. The same century had also seen the emergence of a counter-current demanding naturalness . . . . It was the achievement of the first half of the eighteenth century to produce a prose style that avoided the excesses of both these tendencies. It lay between the too rhetorical and the too ordinary. It was a plain, lucid style avoiding both flatness and extravagance." In this fashion Eric A. Blackall sums up the major development in literary prose of the early eighteenth century.[1] On the one hand writers esteemed surface brilliance as a way to astound the reader, while on the other they valued the rapid expression and quick comprehension of ideas.

What I wish to stress in our present context is not so much the well-known ideal of Enlightenment prose as being plain and lucid, but rather to elaborate upon that quality of prose writing which leads to what Johann Jakob Bodmer labelled "Poesie in der Prosa" (poetry in prose). In 1728 Bodmer explained: "Poetry is at home not only in verse compositions; prose works can also be rich in poetry. And there is a poetry of prose."[2] Any student of English composition knows that his or her essay must be readable and understandable, yet those qualities do not impart an artistic flair to the work. We would expect the practice of classical rhetoric to inform the Enlightenment's ideal style if only for historical reasons. The Enlightenment was heavily indebted to the philosophical and cultural ideas of Hellenic Greece and Augustan Rome and is generally considered the second surge of humanistic fervor following that of the Renaissance. However, within that tradition of imitation is a specific matter pertinent to our deliberations. Both classical rhetoric since Aristotle, Quintilian, and Cicero and Enlightenment philosophy since Thomasius and Leibniz appealed to the intellect.[3] This intellectual aspect easily explains the age's penchant for lucidity and plainness. But it will not bridge the gap between merely expository and genuinely artistic prose, since the latter appeals to our lower, non-rational faculties of perception (sensibilities, imagination). Moreover, as the century began, prose writing (*ungebundene Rede*) was classified under the rubric of rhetoric and not under poetics, which was reserved for verse compositions (*gebundene Rede*).

It was not until the second half of the era that prose finally gained wide recognition as a vehicle of true literary expression culminating the ideas of such early advocates as Christian Thomasius (1655–1728), Friedrich Andreas Hallbauer (1692–1750), Christian Weise (1642–1708), Johann Jakob Bodmer (1698–1783), Johann Jakob Breitinger (1701–1774), Christian Fürchtegott Gellert (1715–1769), Johann Joachim Winckelmann (1717–1768), and G. E. Lessing (1729–1781). From that era date some early masterpieces of poetic prose such as Wilhelm Ehrenfried Neugebauer's *Der teutsche Don Quichotte* (1753), Moritz A. von Thümmel's *Wilhelmine* (1764), Wieland's *Don Sylvio von Rosalva* (1764), and Goethe's *Werther* (1774). Moreover, contemporaneous with the belletristic production, literary theorists began to accord prose style a more prominent position in their poetics. Here we need only recall such central works as Herder's *Über die neuere deutsche Literatur. Fragmente* (*On Recent German Literature. Fragments*, 1766–67), Johann Georg Sulzer's *Allgemeine Theorie der schönen Künste* (*A General Theory of the Fine Arts*, 1771, 1774), Johann Jakob Engel's *Über Handlung, Gespräch und Erzählung* (*On Action, Dialogue, and Narrative*, 1774), and Johann Joachim Eschenburg's *Entwurf einer Theorie und Literatur der schönen Wissenschaften* (*Plan for a Theory and Literature of the Arts*, 1783, 1789).

Thus the real question for us is not whether rhetorical concepts played a role in the emergence of a new ideal of prose writing. They did. It was generally accepted by the nineteenth century that poetics was the theory of poetry and rhetoric the theory of prose.[4] The real question is whether there was a crossover between the poetry and prose, whether rhetoric was a contributing factor to the evolution of prose as legitimate *artistic* expression. The difference is between mechanical comprehensibility and genuine *literary* verve. The question is pivotal in a consideration of essayistic writing with its hermaphroditic essence of reflection and imagination, science and poetry.

Blackall remarks that critics and writers gave no thought to a "philosophy of style" in the first half of the century. Prose writing was something quite mechanical; there was no understanding of how the various parts of a composition should fit together in order to achieve a full aesthetic impact (161). Is that judgment accurate? What are we to make of Blackall's earlier remark that the new style was neither "too rhetorical nor too extravagant"? Is there not any underlying theory of prose in that golden ideal before the 1760s? These questions will guide our thinking in the following pages.

The view that there was no theory of prose style in the first half of the eighteenth century is supported by Theodor Mundt's social history of *Die Kunst der deutschen Prosa* (*The Art of German Prose*, 1837). The whole purpose of his undertaking is to formulate a theory of prose which had come to dominate the nineteenth-century literary scene.[5] For him as well as for Buffon and the young Herder (whom he cites, as well as Hamann whom he does not mention), language and style were very individualistic matters. Each person had his/her own style which was rooted in the person's language and thought. It is not surprising, then, when he arrives at the insight that "there are no rules to regulate the artful perfection of style because style changes with its object; even external euphony and rhythm must be made dependent on the inner, directing ideas and be modified by them. Each content brings with it a different tone of style, a different music, a different scale (Mundt, 122). Moreover, the rhythm of prose writing is equated to a "dialectic of movement" which, in turn, reflects the "dialectic of thought" (Mundt, 123).

Derivative of Herder's notions, Mundt's evaluation of prose style would appear to be more satisfactory from an aesthetic point of view. His concept of an individualistic style seems more modern and more appropriate to a description of the literary essay than the plain and lucid style identified by Blackall. Yet Mundt's notion that "external euphony and rhythm must be made dependent on the inner, directing ideas and be modified by them" has been encountered before. Blackall, for example, stresses that the linkage of ideas (*connexio realis*) rather than that of words (*connexio verbalis*) is the critical factor in the new prose form (Blackall, 164, 169). Surprising, in any event, is the contradiction inherent in Mundt's thesis. While insisting on the uniqueness of expression, he neglects to explain how that uniqueness is retained despite its anchoring in thought which, because of its origin in logic, is shared. Nor does he explain how the rules of logic are overcome in the act of artistic expression. This point is critical to a theory of creative (or original) prose in the Age of Enlightenment.

Mundt's assessment of the role of rhetoric in the genesis of this new pervasive, literary prose is also of significance to us. He flatly denies that rhetorical technique has had any nurturing effect on this literary prose. On the contrary, he contends, stylistics has traditionally been based on rhetoric and for that reason has been false. Instead of leading to an aesthetic experience, it has achieved just the contrary, degenerating into tastelessness and stilted speech (*Schönrednerei*, 116).

This brief look at the gist of Blackall's and Mundt's ideas on the new form of writing has served to uncover some contradictory statements about its nature. Most glaring is the contrast between the tentative recognition of rhetoric on the one hand as midwife and, on the other, its complete rejection as progenetor of art. Moreover, the dominant traits of ideal prose in the early eighteenth century would seem to be plainness and lucidity, while the later ideal is that of expressive individuality; yet both are linked to rational thought. Can these disparate assessments be reconciled? Or do we fall back on the common assumption of a disruptive transition in the eighteenth century from rationalism to irrationalism supposedly epitomized in the brash revolt of the Storm and Stress writers in Herder's wake and—if one is feeling especially generous—foreshadowed in the clash between the literary schools of Leipzig (Gottsched) and Zurich (Bodmer and Breitinger) over the proper role of the wondrous in belles-lettres?[6] Although it concentrates on the origination of an original German prose *after* mid-century, Heinrich Küntzel's *Essay und Aufklärung* (*Essay and Enlightenment*, 1969) offers a possible solution to the dilemma.[6a]

Küntzel discovers a correspondence between such contrary notions as beauty and exactness, idea and feeling, understanding and imagination, naturalness and precision of expression. He cites this correspondence of contradictory terms as "a fundamental trait of Enlightenment philosophy and criticism" which forms the basis of "a theory of original prose" in the eighteenth century. This thesis underlies Küntzel's entire study and sets him apart from Blackall in two important respects. First, Küntzel is specifically interested in the connection between Enlightenment philosophy and a *theory* of poetic prose; and secondly, he focuses on the development of the essay as the harbinger of new impulses. Blackall suggests that the early Enlightened critics did not have a conscious theory of prose and does not address himself to essayistic writing per se.

Moreover, Küntzel is freer of the usual prejudices incumbent upon a literary historian such as Mundt who is driven by the need to expose the differences between epochs in an effort to portray the "unmistakable" preeminence of a later period over an earlier one. Thus Küntzel is inclined throughout his inquiry to stress the unity of the several literary schools in vogue during the period from 1680–1815. It is misleading to identify *only*

clarity and lucidity as Enlightenment ideals or to want to see a decided
transition from rationalism in the first half of the century to irrationalism
in the second half. With regard to eighteenth-century critical theory,
Küntzel avers: "Deliberations on the fundamental unity or possible mixing of poesy and prose were not foreign to Enlightened critics. Nor, on the
other hand, were their boundaries first drawn by the [German] Classical
writers. Their unity is anchored in a philosophical theory of expression,
of language, and in what has been called reason, ability to think, or
self-reflection. The differences are explained on the basis of classifiable
diversity inherent in human psychology. Rhetorical concepts are interpreted anew and more profoundly in explaining both their unity as well
as the divergences between them" (32). Later Küntzel elaborates upon
this idea by ascertaining "a surprising consistency" throughout the century in the image of the creative prose writer. That image is marked by
"concepts such as inspiration, independent thought, genial individuality
of style and thought; [by] contrasting pairs such as '*prose* of the *poet*,'
conciseness and disconnectedness, logic and fantasy, strangeness and
verisimilitude, casual spontaneity and mathematical precision" (39f.).
These insights have been passed over by subsequent chroniclers of the
early essay.[7] In contrast to Blackall, Küntzel recognizes the obvious importance of rhetoric for the ascendency of modern German prose and
places it squarely at the center of his inquiry.[8]

   In their recent authoritative depiction of the history and impact of
rhetoric on German literature, *Grundriß der Rhetorik* (*An Outline of
Rhetoric*, 1986), Gerd Ueding and Bernd Steinbrink clearly demonstrate
the correctness of Küntzel's view, arguing convincingly that both individuality of expression and a metapersonal harmony of idea and formulation were highly valued by Enlighteners from Hallbauer to Eschenburg.[9]
Regrettably, Ueding and Steinbrink belong to that large number of literary historians who have taken no note of Küntzel's work. Be that as it
may, the authors emphatically state that "rhetoric is the school of German literature in the eighteenth century" and apply that statement
equally to rhetorical theory in both halves of the century (*Grundriß*, 126).
Every page of this exhaustive study provides evidence of the ubiquity of
rhetorical thought in school, university, workplace, and social gathering
so that we are not surprised to hear that the theory and practice of
rhetoric eventually gave rise to the new type of professional writer in the
Age of Enlightenment who engaged an anonymous reader in a dialogue

designed to promote understanding and stimulate action (cf. 127). Moreover, Ueding and Steinbrink make clear that eighteenth-century theorists from Thomasius to Eschenburg distinguished between the true and false practice of rhetoric.[10]

Mundt's view on the perversion of literature through the influence of rhetoric we must therefore reject as inaccurate. Mundt, namely, does not differentiate between its "true" and "false" practices, that is, the difference between artificiality (*connexio verbalis*) and naturalness (*connexio realis*) goes unheeded.

While not expressly interested in essayistic writing per se nor in the nexus of rhetorical and prose theory as it has evolved here, Hans-Otto Rößer's *Bürgerliche Vergesellschaftung und kulturelle Reform* (*Bourgeois Socialization and Cultural Reform*, 1986) is relevant to our line of questioning. His stated purpose is to scrutinize the "social and more or less political" context of the stylistic developments in the writing of Johann Gottfried Herder and Christian Garve within empirical philosophy and the "bourgeois ideology."[11] As such Rößer takes a similarly interdisciplinary and complex view of literary style which also lies at the heart of *Crossing Boundaries*. He is especially interested in developing a theory of prose for the post-1765 period.

The strength of Rößer's inquiry lies in its focus on two major prose writers who had a broad impact. However, like other critics before him, Rößer fails to recognize the roots of a philosophy or theory of prose in the first part of the century. Awareness of that intellectual tradition would have alerted him to the tremendous significance of rhetoric in the evolution of the middle style of writing advocated and practiced by Herder, Garve, and others. Rößer apparently does not know Blackall's and Mundt's treatises at all, passes blithely over Küntzel with hardly a word, and is little interested in the role of rhetoric. Had he placed his investigation within the context of inquiry since Theodor Mundt, Rößer would have enhanced the impact of his work, and we would have been able to situate Herder and Garve as the culmination of our musings on the theory of prose. Nevertheless, Rößer does offer his reader a richly detailed and provocative view of late eighteenth-century popular prose. Anyone interested in the topic will want to consult Rößer's work.

In the following pages we must bear in mind that eighteenth-century writers were fully aware of the history of rhetoric since antiquity and that they differentiated between its appropriate and inappropriate application. Gottsched showed in the foreword to his *Rhetoric* (*Redekunst*, 1728), for example, that the art displayed a tendency to become mechanical and exaggerated when it lost sight of its true function. As soon as it became too conscious of itself as an art form it degenerated into artificiality (cf. Blackall, 154). What then was this true function?

If we are not too strict about the separation, the traditional relegation of poetics to verse and rhetoric to prose is useful. It is useful because the identification of *Beredsamkeit* with prose underscores the nexus of the art of writing and the art of presenting. In fact, Johann Joachim Eschenburg gathers all forms of prose writing under a unifying umbrella which he labels a "theory of prose writing."[12] The move can be seen as an anticipation of Mundt's appeal for a theory of prose almost three generations later. In any event, we must not forget that prose writing rose so rapidly to the fore that verse compositions were soon overshadowed. (On the other hand, we dare not forget that rhetoric also informs the didactic poems of the era just as much as the prose.)[13] With the publication of such diverse works as Gellert's *Briefe* (*Epistles*, 1751), Winckemann's *Gedanken über die Nachahmung der Griechischen Werke in der Mahlerey und Bildhauer-Kunst* (*Reflections on the Imitation of Greek Works in Painting and Sculpture*, 1755) Herder's *Kritische Wälder* (*Critical Forests*, 1769), Georg Forster's *Reise um die Welt* (*Journey Around the World*, 1778–80), and Georg Lichtenberg's *Ausführliche Erklärungen der Hogarthischen Kupferstiche* (*Detailed Commentaries on Hogarth's Copperplate Engravings*, 1794–99), the value of poetic prose was so firmly established that Wilhelm von Humboldt could claim that elevated prose was the "companion of poetry" (*die Gefährtin der Poesie*).[14] The theoretical ground work for their styles was laid early in the century. A few examples will suffice to demonstrate the essential concepts.

The Philosophy of Rhetoric

We know, of course, that the Enlightenment was essentially a philosophical school of thought. It would be somewhat surprising, indeed, if it lacked a philosophy of style as some have argued.[15] We need not look far for evidence of an underlying philosophy. We find it in the 1720s, a decade that saw the first impact on German thinkers of Leibniz and Thomasius but also of such central British works as John Locke's (1632–1704) empirically oriented *An Essay Concerning Human Understanding* (1690), Joseph Addison's (1672–1719) "The Pleasures of the Imagination" (1712), and Shaftesbury's (1671–1713) *Characteristics of*

Men, Manners, Opinions, Times, etc. (1711/1714). As such the 1720s represent a period of intense intellectual agitation which brought a shift from an object-oriented, universalistic manner of thinking to a subject-oriented, individualistic mode (Vietta, 71ff.).

In the fifty-sixth number of *The Man of Honor* (*Der Biedermann*, 1727–29) Gottsched refers to the "more solid manner of thinking and writing in German" popularized by Christian Wolff. He follows up that thought immediately with that notion that rhetoric must be anchored in philosophy in order to be genuine; it must be predicated on a sound rational theory. Moreover, both the orator (including the prose writer) and the poet must fortify themselves with psychological and moral insights if they are to write anything decent.[16] In advancing this argument Gottsched is merely following the lead of Aristotle who saw rhetoric as the counterpart to dialectics (Eisenhut, 3, 29f.).

It is not possible to demarcate for the first part of the century the connotations of *Beredsamkeit* on the one hand, and *Rhetorik* or *Oratorie* on the other, as Hinderer does for the latter part of the era. While the seventeenth century distinquished between *rhetorica* as the theory and *oratoria* (or *eloquentia*) as the practice of rhetoric, the early eighteenth century was not as strict in the use of the terminology. Gottsched, e.g., uses the word *Beredsamkeit* in the passage cited and his meaning is clearly not restricted to the practical side of rhetoric.[17] In general Gottsched does not present us here with any further details on the qualities of this writing, but he did go into very fine points in his *Ausführliche Redekunst* published in 1736 as well as in his *Critische Dichtkunst vor die Deutschen* (1730) which was reprinted many times. Let it suffice for now merely to determine that the notion of a philosophy of rhetoric (= prose writing) was formulated in a popular Moral Weekly early in the century.

In the 1720s and 1730s Gottsched was known to subscribe to the ideal of the gallant which was all the rage in Leipzig ("little Paris") in the early decades of the century, and we might surmise that the ideals of gallantry influenced his poetic theory as well. For example, his definition of *Wohlredenheit* (eloquence) in the *Redekunst* reveals a striking similarity to the tenets of the gallant style. (In the course of the eighteenth century *Wohlredenheit* came to designate a special stylistic quality.) Gottsched writes: "Eloquence merely refers to the sound of the words and to the skill for speaking or writing in a graceful and elegant manner. It consists, therefore, almost wholly in good style or in sensible and well formulated ideas."[18] In any event, we must revise Blackall's judgment that Gottsched rejected the concept of gallantry altogether (*Emergence*, 95). Although he did condemn the excesses of the fashion, Gottsched distinguished between two qualitatively different gallant modes.[19] In contrast to Blackall, Dell' Orto rightfully draws a connection between the emergent style of writing and the gallant mode ("Audience," 113f.). We might also recall that the return of classical rhetoric as a major discipline to the University of Leipzig was due in large part to the efforts of Thomasius. He combined it with the French ideal of the *galant homme* (not *homme galant*!) and popularized a correct understanding of the notion in his lectures and various publications in the late seventeenth century.[20] His ideas contributed significantly to the concept of the *vir bonus* which dominated eighteenth-century anthropological thought, became fused with Shaftesbury's model of the virtuoso, and peaked in the ideal of a European aristocracy marked not by advantages of birth or fortune but rather by moral and aesthetic qualities.[21]

Noting the wide confusion on the true meaning of gallantry, Thomasius undertook to isolate its essential qualities. Among them he numbers cultivated manners, sensibleness, erudition, sound judgment, politeness, and a pleasant manner. He specifically rejects "stiffness, affectation, and coarseness" (*Zwang, affectation, und unanständige Plumpheit*).[22] Thomasius was confident that any individual who was willing and sensible could be educated to this ideal, thereby achieving perfection as a human being.[23] What the young philosopher's recommendation amounts to is a formulation of the goal of *humanitas* to which all humanity aspires. In his introduction on "The Significance of Rhetoric for Literature" to his "Short History of the German Oration" (1981), Walter Hinderer notes the proximity of rhetorical theory to the later notion of *Bildung*, indicating that the so-called *Kunstepoche* benefitted from the earlier concept. He states quite rightfully that "a history of rhetoric will . . . simultaneously be a history of the cultural evaluation of humanity" (215, 217, et passim). In terms of the eighteenth century, a continuous line of development in the ideal of the *vir bonus* can be traced in Leipzig from Thomasius to Christian Wolff to Gottsched and Goethe. This is, in fact, what Ueding accomplishes in his chapter on "The Ideal of the Orator and Bourgeois Education from Thomasius to Knigge" (*Grundriß*, 115–122).

In Thomasius's wake many others ruminated on the question: what is the proper behavior for the gallant? Numerous handbooks were composed with advice on how to write letters, how to converse, how to behave in public and private, even how to dress. Writers like Christian Friedrich Hunold (1680–1721), Christoph Heinrich Amthor 1678–1721), and Erdmann Neumeister (1671–1756) frequently appeared in print. There was, to be sure, much chaff mixed in with the grains. Still the patient reader can discover enough golden shafts to warrant the trouble. Benjamin Neukirch (1665–1729) is a case in point. In his handbooks of the 1720s, he elaborated upon the gallant attitude as reappraised by Thomasius. Of greatest import are those passages in his *Anweisung zu Teutschen Briefen* (*Guide to Writing German Letters*, 1721) which charactize both the *galant homme* as well as the recommended style of gallant writing. "Gallant people," he states, "are those who are not only physical fitness buffs, but who are also of sound and quick mind, have amusing and clever ideas, are of a friendly and pleasant disposition, and always act in a civil yet free and spontaneous manner. They are people who love a good joke and can also take a joke; they judge others not by their station in life but by their abilities."[24] Neukirch's charactization is fully in line with Thomasius's emphasis on a balance of urbane manners, a good sense of humor, and a sensible attitude. The privileges of birth, power, and money are of no particular consequence.

In volume four, chapter 6 of the *Anweisungen*, Neukirch addresses himself to the question of gallant style. He describes it as "a mixture of the astute, witty, and satiric modes" (*eine vermengung der scharffsinnigen, lustigen und satyrischen styli*), yet it is not merely a composite of the three, for it is neither as earnest, as vulgar, nor as caustic as each individually. In the gallant mode of writing, each of the three styles softens the others so that the extremes are avoided. By heeding moderation, the gallant style is capable of "not just pleasantly entertaining the reader, but also of enthralling him" (40). This assessment makes transparent that the would-be gallant writer must have three distinct qualities: native talent (*ein herrliches ingenium*), good powers of discernment (*ein gutes judicium*), and above all a quick mind (*ein hurtiger geist*). Neukirch then briefly mentions the figures of speech, expressions, and phraseology charactristic of true gallant speech.

Even as Thomasius had recommended the tailoring of speech to the intended audience in his reviews and essays published in the *Monatsgespräche*,[25] so too does Neukirch impress upon his reader the requirements of different social situations. One does not address a duke as one would a friend or mistress. The ideal style maintains a balance between natural and cultivated speech. While the rules of rhetoric are beneficial in regulating speech, they should not come to dominate the phrasing and structuring of our ideas. Not oratory but rather nature provides the creative impulse; rhetorical technique should only assist; restraining, enhancing, and structuring where necessary to achieve the profoundest effect dictated by the given situation. In contrast to the centrality of the interlocutor as a determining factor in finding the appropriate tone, the topic is irrelevant. Whether one speaks of lofty or lowly affairs, of learned matters or amorous ones, is all the same. The main thing is that the writer maintain a sense of decorum, as the ancients called it or *tour* and *je ne sai quoi*, as the French titled the phenomenon, because it cannot be defined exactly. It is not clear how the facility is attained. Enough courtiers can be identified, Neukirch continues, who have never studied rhetoric, but who have nevertheless mastered the gallant style. On the other hand, the mastery of rhetoric does not inevitably lead to mastery of the gallant *modus scribendi*. Thus Neukirch insists that natural talent (a creative spark) is a *sine qua non* for the new style of writing.

Finally, Neukirch specifies some of the rhetorical categories indispensable to the proposed manner of writing: the *connexio, numerus,* and *constructio.* Each has more to do with the total effect of the composition than with any of its individual subdivisions or parts. Neukirch contends: "The linkages in the gallant style must be brief and 'real' [i.e., an inner cogency must exist], its rhythm absolutely not oratorical, and its total organization moderate, natural, and clear" (41). These and the foregoing traits of the gallant style are then summed up in six guidelines for the reader. The first three deal with the mixing of the three dominant styles and of the appropriate tone for the envisioned audience. The final three rules treat specific rhetorical techniques. The fourth rule exhorts the reader to avoid pure oratory and hyperbole. If they are used, they should be tempered by irony. The fifth rule urges the gallant to write in a colloquial style, avoiding bombast and introducing a hint of playfulness into the line of reasoning. Neukirch notes: "Gallantry consists in sheer playfulness, while playfulness consists in moderate liberty. This freedom, however, is not just the freedom to choose one's words." Neukirch's meaning here is somewhat clarified in the sixth guideline which admonishes the would-be writer to eliminate from his writing everything that smacks of artiness. The writer should strive for a supine attitude since that is the mark of a true gallant. If the care and the rules which have gone into the making of his composition are evident, his work will miss the intended effect (42).

Four years after the appearance of Neukirch's *Guide to Writing German Letters,* Friedrich Andreas Hallbauer (1692–1750) published his *Anweisung zur Verbesserten Teutschen Oratorie (Guide to Improved German Oratory,* 1725). Hallbauer adds his voice to those of Thomasius, Neukirch, and Gottsched in calling for the rejection of the decorative, stilted, and bombastic style of the preceding era. He too demands clarity, accuracy, and objectivity in the expression of ideas. A distinct echo of previous urgings is audible in his assertion that the necessary ingredients of good style are correctness, purity, clarity, normalcy, consistency, naturalness, balance, and elegance. Moreover, he insists that the tone of a composition be appropriate to the topic, the particular audience, and the author's intent in any given instance.[26] Important above all in our context is Hallbauer's insistence on qualities of elegance (*zierlich*) and natural consistency (*zusammenhängend, ungezwungen*), for he explains that elegance consists in a "pleasant sound" (*angenehmer Klang*), "appropriate harmony" (*rechte Übereinstimmung*), "sound connections" (*gute Verknüpfung*), "suitable shape and order" (*richtiges Maß und Ordnung*), and "sprightliness" (*Lebhaftigkeit*) of rhythm.[27] This elagance of style is related to the decorum or *tour* rated so highly by advocates of the gallant manner and informs Gottsched's definition of *Wohlredenheit*. It cannot be stressed enough that for Hallbauer, as for other contemporary theoreticians on matters of prose style, the successful orator/author never loses sight of her/his intended audience. Awareness of one's audience is a central factor in shaping written expression.

The concept of gallantry and the gallant writing style which Thomasius, Gottsched, Neukirch, and Hallbauer expounded upon were a prelude to Bodmer's indictment of popular aesthetic taste in his critique of the Moral Weeklies *Der Patriot* and *Die Vernünftigen Tadlerinnen* published in 1728.[28] There he addresses himself to the *scharffsinnige Schreib-Art*, listing six principles of good writing. These principles are obviously derivative of the contemporary debate. In order they are: the poetic work must (1) be entertaining, (2) be informed by an underlying symbolism, (3) abide by the concept of verisimilitude, (4) have an inner ordering principle, (5) must relate all metaphors and images to the underlying symbolism, and (6) integrate the constituent subsystems of rhetoric (*Bilder des erdichteten Systematis*) and symbolism (*des Mystischen Systematis*) in the overall structure of the poetic work (Bodmer, 40). When all these elements come together, "there is a poetry in prose" (Bodmer, 38). Poetry has its place, he states, in prose as well as in verse. An adaption of Bodmer's formulation, "Poesie in der Prosa," thus fittingly serves as the title of this present chapter.

The ideas expressed on prose style from Thomasius to Bodmer are not without value for an assessment of essayistic writing throughout the entire century. Blackall is unable to assess the real significance of the gallant style because he fails to note the distinction between the false and true applications of the manner drawn by eighteenth-century writers themselves. Consequently, he equates the meaning of *homme galant* with *galant homme*, arguing that the meaning of gallant "becomes confined to the external forms of courtly behavior" (*Emergence*, 95). His assertion is not borne out by the available evidence. Additionally, scholars have generally failed for some reason to note that the intended audience of the stylistic directives and handbooks were students, educators, public officials, courtiers, and cultivated women. In other words, the same anonymous public addressed by the Moral Weeklies and from which the future generations of writers and critics were drawn. Moreover, it is clear that the traditional audience of the popular gallant novel, which flourished during the first three decades of the eighteenth century, also found pleasure in the Moral Weeklies.[29] The time has come to recognize the continuity of audience and prose style in evaluating the aesthetics and ethical objectives of writing and reading, especially in essayism, throughout the century. An attempt will be made in the following pages.

The Nexus of Early and Late Enlightenment Theory

Two of the most popular and widely celebrated authors of the age, who were products of the philosophical, religious, and aesthetic doctrines of the first half of the eighteenth century as well as major contributors to the continued refinement of language and style in the second half, were Christian Fürchtegott Gellert (1715–1769) and Christoph Martin Wieland (1733–1813). Neither writer figures prominently in Ueding's *Grundriß der Rhetorik* which is astonishing given their prominence in eighteenth-century letters. Gellert was an influential professor in Leipzig (where he was also educated) during the 1740s, 1750s, and 1760s and penned enormously popular fables, narratives, and model epistles. Wieland's star began to rise as Gellert's was setting. The Swabian became the Saxon's heir as *praeceptor germaniae*. Both are widely acknowledged for their impact on the refinement of the German language; each stands with one foot in the first half and one foot in the second half of the century. Of interest to us here are Gellert's concept of style and Wieland's notion of rhetoric.

Despite the claim that Gellert's *Briefe, nebst einer praktischen Abhandlung von dem guten Geschmack in Briefen* (*Letters, Combined with a Practical Treatise on Good Epistolary Style*, 1751) amount to "nothing less than a break with the entire tradition" of letter writing and rhetoric, Gellert's indebtedness to both the ideals and clarity and simplicity of expression of the gallant manner is unmistakable.[30] Like others before him Gellert emphasizes the primacy of inner cogency (*connexio realis*) over the empty shell of external rules (*connexio verbalis*). Thus he rejects the mechanical organization of letter writing into six categories (*salutatio, captatio, benevolentiae, narratio, petitio, conclusio*) or three (*ante-*

cedens, connexio, consequens) in favor of a natural and simple mode of expression. In place of the purely external organization, Gellert advocates a tailoring of style to the ideas being expressed. The idea and its expression should be in harmony. Thus Gellert exhorts his reader not to employ "any artificial order or any tedious apparatus, but to follow instead the natural sequence of one's thoughts, committing them to paper as they arise. In this manner the structure, organization, or form of the letter will be natural."[31]

Whoever writes spontaneously, automatically writes in a middle style, that is, in a loose Senecan fashion. The epistler composes the way s/he speaks. The outcome is to lend the written word the quality of a casual conversation which engages the other in a pleasant discourse (Gellert, 3). Although Honnefelder argues that Gellert specifically rejects any use of artificial or purely rhetorical strategies, the ideal of naturalness advocated by Gellert is shared by Thomasius or Neukirch who recognized the value of genuine rhetoric and thus did not discard an entire tradition because of its excesses.

Gellert's singular contribution to the discussion of appropriate style is the notion that every individual has the right and the ability to think and to express one's thoughts in a manner unrestrained by external rules. The anthropomorphic unity of the species assures the mutual understanding of individual expression. "Good taste" does not evolve only after the application of guidelines; it is inherent in characteristic expression. However, Gellert does grant that this talent is best cultivated in social intercourse where the skills of thinking and speaking can be honed. While he essentially repeats the stylistic and aesthetic maxims of his predecessors at the University of Leipzig (Thomasius and Gottsched), Gellert deemphasizes the role of traditional rhetoric. Yet it is misleading to claim that he introduces a "new rhetoric" or a "new morality" (Honnefelder, 12f.). The aesthetic and ethical components of Gellert's epistolary ideal were already present in early century. Wieland shares many of the same views with Gellert, but shows how the aesthetic expression of naturalness and ease is enhanced by rhetorical strategies.

More emphatically than Gellert, the young Wieland acknowledged the poet's indebtedness to the practice of oratory. At the beginning of his long and successful writing career, Wieland lectured for several years in the 1750s in Zurich on the history of poetry and rhetoric from ancient to modern times. These lectures were published in 1757 and provide greater amplification of the detailed awareness shared by his generation of the pivotal role played by rhetoric in the creation of literature.

In his *Theorie und Geschichte der Red-Kunst und Dicht-Kunst* (*Theory and History of Rhetoric and Poetry*, 1757) Wieland endeavored not only to explain the origins, purpose, and composition of oration but also to clarify the relationship of rhetoric to poetry. This latter intent is of particular significance to us because of the indebtedness of essayistic writing to rhetorical technique. When we intermingle rhetoric and poetry, we have the two essential ingredients of the literary essay (cf., e.g., Adorno, "Der Essay als Form," 1:80f.). Ueding and Steinbrink conclude emphatically that rhetoric was the progenitor of the entire style of essayistic writing and was primarily responsible for its emergence in the eighteenth century (*Grundriß*, 126).

Wieland begins with a definition of rhetoric which I cite here as representative of the age

> Rhetoric is the ability . . . to express oneself well, that is, to convince the listening audience by logical reasoning, to win it over through emotional appeal, and to manipulate it toward a predetermined goal. Oratory ability, then, is granted us by nature for no other purpose than to communicate our thoughts to one another, to influence each other, and to advance our personal ends. Or, to put it differently: by means of rhetoric we impact upon the minds and wills of others. Thus it follows that the mark of the accomplished orator is the ability to persuade others by the power of the word to accept an idea or to take action.[32]

This rather straightforward statement of the rhetorician's purpose of persuading another must be softened by other qualities before it can be useful as an explanation of essayistic compositions. As a way of investigating the literariness of rhetoric, let us hear what this contemporary of the eighteenth century had to say about the intricacies of the art.

The ancients recognized, Wieland remarks, three kinds of oration, each tailored to a specific situation: *demonstrativum, deliberativum,* and *judiciale.* The appropriate use of the first (*genus demonstrativum*) is in arguments of praise or vituperation directed at an individual. The posture of arguing is *ad hominem.* Biased toward a foregone conclusion, this manner of proceeding is little suited for use in essayism. The second category (*genus deliberativum*) encompasses orations that advise a listener to accept or reject a new or differing opinion. This kind of oration was used in the Roman Senate and at public assemblies and is marked by a broader appeal than the other two. Its tone is conciliatory and persuasive, not obviously manipulative or badgering. The third category (*genus judiciale*) designates oratory typical of the legal courts as practiced by professional lawyers. Wieland sums up these distinctions by citing Cicero's definition: "Demonstrativum genus in laude vel vituperatione; deliberativum in consultatione; iudiciale in controversia positum est.[33] It is evident that the second category is most closely related to the deliberative tone of essayistic writing which stresses weighing the possibilities. Future mention of the positive influence of oratory will refer to this kind.

In regard to the relationship between rhetoric and poetry, Wieland again cites Cicero, who noted that rhetoricians and poets were frequently indistinguishable from one another ("Poetis proximam cognationem esse cum oratoribus"). The cardinal difference between the two functions is one of intention: "While the orator seeks to instruct and persuade, the poet wishes to delight and move [*ergötzen und rühren*]." Although principles of rhetoric were undeniably important for the creative writer, s/he had greater freedom in the use of melodic tones and poetic imagery (AA, 4:335).[34]

Wieland's *Theorie und Geschichte der Red-Kunst und Dicht-Kunst* is particularly valuable for its revealing discussion of the various subdivisions of rhetorical principles, their purposes, and intended effects only hinted at by Thomasius, Neukirch, and Hallbauer. In great detail Wieland elaborates upon those elements which contribute to a perfect oration—perfect, that is, in its ability to persuade and move the listener. The chief rhetorical categories are *inventio* (accumulation of evidence), *dispositio* (arrangement of evidence), *elocutio* (linguistic expression, not elocution!), and *executio* (oral delivery). Of these *inventio* and *elocutio* have the greatest bearing on creative writing. *Dispositio* as understood by Wieland was a rather mechanical process that called for a logical ordering of the argument and evidence. The weakest points should always be made first with the strongest ones coming last so that a logical progression and a heightening of tension is created. In essence the *dispositio* refers to the logical alignment of the particular ideas (*ideas partium*) with the central thesis (*idea totali*). The seemingly random association of ideas as they occur in dreams is to be avoided (AA, 4:310).

The structuring of the argument with its encumbant arrangement of evidence would not seem to be a contributing factor to the emergence of essayism since—as we have seen earlier—the infrastructure of essayistic compositions is determined by the active thought process itself rather than by a fully formed, static idea. However, we should guard against any hasty assumption that an essay lacks an internal ordering principle. The apparent random association of ideas in an instance of essayism is deceptive. We should bear in mind that true rhetoric employs the internal principle of *connexio realis*, shunning the merely external one of *connexio verbalis*. The genuine rhetorician values the linkage of ideas much more highly than the coupling of words and phrases. Neukirch's remark that true gallant writing does not betray the sweat of composition is pertinent here. The studied effort that went into creating the impression of casualness, Neukirch stated, must not be discernible. This same principle of feigned spontaneity is operative in essayistic compositions. To be sure, the ordering principle of rhetoric tends to be rationalistic and mechanistic, yet it is not without significance for essayism, especially if its "stiffness" is muted by a sense of whimsicality reinforced by other stylistic techniques.

We can ignore the classification of *executio* as not relevant to our consideration, for it deals with such voice qualities as texture, fullness, and intonation as well as with the accompanying body language (AA, 4:312f.). These qualities are specific to the speech act and are not transferable to the written text.

The categories of *inventio* and *elocutio* on the other hand, require some amplification. *Inventio* is concerned with the six major elements of any oration: the *exordium, expositio, divisio, confirmatio, confutatio,* and *conclusio*. The *exordium* designates the beginning of an argument. It should be formulated in such a way that it catches the audience's attention in a singular way and leads it into the "text." One normally begins with known information, a mention of the specific motivation for the talk or text, a reference to the importance of the topic, or with an evocation of images and preconceived notions central to the orator's purpose. The ensuing *expositio* should provide a pithy, chronological accounting of the pertinent historical facts or of the logical steps in the philosophical argument. Although this section should be short, it must not be so laconic that the listener is unable to grasp the relationship between the individual parts of the argument (*ideas partium*) and the central thesis (*idea totali*). If executed skillfully, the exposition will present the thesis as being thoroughly plausible. The third stage of the *inventio* is even briefer. Its purpose is to define precisely the parameters of the topic under consideration. Thereafter, the kinds of evidence submitted in support of the main argument are to be cited (= *confirmatio*). These might be references to accepted authority, allusions to historical instances, ironic juxtapositions, arguments based on the inherent value of the idea, or appeals to personal experience. In order to convince the audience of the appropriateness of one's own stance, opposing views should be presented and refuted (= *confutatio*). Finally, the *conclusio* should culminate the main argument in a crescendo of graphic images designed to leave the audience with a single, dominant impression. The accomplished orator will show his real mettle in this all-important section (AA, 4:308ff.).

The rhetorical subdivision of *elocutio* must figure prominently in a study of essayistic compositions, for it is concerned with the various means of expressing an idea or emotion. *Elocutio* thus moves us closer to literariness. Like *inventio*, elocution employs the literary principle which Bense calls *ars combinatoria* (Bense, 66). Unlike, *inventio* however, *elocutio* is more emotive, subjective, associative. The ploys available to the speaker/writer include the choice of diction, adages, sentence structure, *tour* or verve (*Schwung*), tropes, and sonorous harmony (*numerus oratorius*). Of diction and adages Wieland states that the speaker/writer should know when something is best expressed colorfully (*voces proprias*) or metaphorically. The importance of sentence structure lies in the pleasing effect caused by alternating length, interruptions (parenthetical comments, anacolutha, prolepses, postscripts), by changing the interrelationship of the sentence sectors (*Vorfeld, Satzfeld, Nachfeld*), and by the similarity or dissimilarity of sequential sentences to each other.[35] By observing these guidelines the author would at the very least avoid the convolutedness and stiltedness of scholarly writing. And that was, of course, an intent of the new style introduced at the beginning of the eighteenth century.

Wieland gives us a definition of that nebulous stylistic quality of writing recognized by the gallant writers as *tour* or *je ne sai quoi*. He uses the German word *Schwung* to translate the French, which is equivalent to English verve, energy, animation, warmth, or ardour. Wieland's description is as follows: "It would not be amiss to speak of *Schwung* as the gradations of light and shade in which an idea is presented. Actually, it consists in that kind of formulation by means of which an idea takes on a lively, unexpected, sublime, elegant, or novel turn. This art of presenting ideas can be achieved only by attentively reading the best writers and only after much practice."[36] Verve is obviously central to poetic writing. Moreover, an author must be not only dedicated but also talented, if s/he is to realize the full range of *tour* in her/his writing and speaking. We are justified in associating with this quality a stylistic and intellectual brilliance rarely achieved, for the adept shading of light and dark in the expression of an idea is no easy accomplishment. *Tour* moves us beyond rote rhetoric into the realm of literariness.

Equally significant for the transition from pure mechanical technique to poetic inspiration in the search for a fabled *poésie du style* are the last two classifications under *elocutio*: tropes and sonorous harmony. The tropes (*Figuren*) include two different kinds of phrases: they can be mere puns and verbal play or they can be "the language of emotion" (*die Sprache der Affekte*). Wieland opines that the orator should not spend too much time on the former, intimating that punning is a poor application of this potent linguistic tool. Emotive eloquence, on the other hand, represents a powerful means of total communication with the audience. In order to preserve their forcefulness, these emotional appeals should be used sparingly and wisely.

The *numerus oratorius*, finally, is a pleasing, almost musical harmony of cadences, crescendos, retardation, and expansion created by the skillful arrangement of sentences and paragraphs. (We might borrow the musical term "period" to describe the point Wieland is driving at, for like the composer the writer groups phrases and measures together to complete a statement.) He portrays the *numerus oratorius* as "a hybrid of the slovenly sound of common prose and of poetic meter or versification." This indeterminate quality of language is similar to verve in that it contributes a special tone to prose writing and is very difficult to master. Here too the author must practice long hours and school himself/herself on the best authors.[37]

From the foregoing it is apparent that *elocutio* is the most emotive, subjective, and associative of the four main rhetorical categories. Its allusions, metaphors, tropes, cadences, and rhythms play upon the responsive chords of the heart rather than aim at perspicuity. Whereas the intellect has the upper hand in the accumulation and arrangement of evidence, intuition is allowed freer rein in the poetic expression of the ideas. In the consummate oration, then, a state of tension would seem to exist between reflection and imagination. The true orator endeavors to soften the manipulative purpose of the oration by expressing his ideas in an artistic manner. The proximity of the rhetorical ideal to essayistic writing is hard to miss. E.-O. Gerke remarks, for instance, in his study of Hugo von Hofmannsthal's prose writings, *The Essay as Artistic Form* (1970) that "the essay acquires its form in this field of tension between the intent of rational communication and the purpose of artistic configuration."[38]

Wieland's *Theorie und Geschichte der Red-Kunst und Dicht-Kunst* itself intimates the bond between the orator and the poet. Both kinds of artist draw upon distinct rules of composition, both should have an extensive knowledge of history and philosophy, and both must have a predisposition for elevating a work from the level of mere science (knowledge and rules) to that of artistic expression. Brute facts and technical mastery alone are insufficient.[39] Moreover, Wieland's view that a close correspondence must exist between poetic expression and the idea to be expressed, that a poet must have a lively imagination, fine wit, keen discernment, and an exquisite sensitivity to the nuances of language (AA, 4:349) is an echo of the prerequisites for the accomplished orator encountered elsewhere. He was, of course, following the lead of his mentors Bodmer and Breitinger, Cicero and Quintilian. Finally, the general interpretation of the nature of literature in the eighteenth century is not that dissimilar to the nature of rhetoric. Wieland's variation of the Horatian dictum regarding the general purpose of literature is: "instruct human understanding in a delightful manner while exciting the emotions" (AA, 4:397).

The historical survey of the era provided in the *Grundriß der Rhetorik* shows how representative Wieland's views are of the purpose of literature (and rhetoric) in the eighteenth century (see 126). Ueding and Steinbrink devote a lot of space to this aspect in their chapters on the period 1680–1815. In fact they attribute the high incidence of essay writing in the Age of Enlightenment to the preponderant influence of rhetoric, asserting that "rhetorical *Kunstprosa* or essayism is the product of the Enlightenment's efforts to popularize and aestheticize knowledge" (123). Concerning the intended impact of oratory, they conclude (259):

> *Delectare* and *movere* are certainly those affective modes which
> require an orator (or poet), while mere instruction is achievable
> without his special talents. Yet according to classical rhetorical
> theory these affective modes may not be used independently;
> their purpose is to shape persuasive arguments. . . . Thus it is
> not sufficient to impact upon only a part of human personality,
> judgment, or intellect. The emotions, the will, the sensations,
> and psychological forces must also be addressed in a manner
> suited to the particular line of argument pursued.

The significance of this total appeal to the recipient is evident in the writer's intent to incite action, not just emotion or thought (see Chapter V).

A brief look at those sections in Wieland's chronicle of the theory and history of literature which deal with prose composition (#11) and the authors of didactic poems (#19) will provide some specific examples of the interaction of rhetorical and literary qualities in prose writing.

As far as the *form* of a descriptive work is concerned, we are told that there are no prescriptive rules, that the composition of a poem is entirely at the hands of the individual poet. The critics have spent too much time devising rules to explain the composition of the *Odyssey* or the *Aeneid*, for example, and in doing so have overlooked the essential criterion: the author's native genius. "But the genius," Wieland explains, "cannot be bound by such rules; each and every poet is every bit as justified as Homer or Vergil in devising a plan as he sees fit. The only guideline is that of common sense" (4:348). The only binding organizing principle for longer or shorter works is the central idea (= *idea totali*) which should act like a huge magnet bonding the individual parts together. The individual parts must be arranged "so that one can comprehend the whole work at once without hesitation and commit it easily to memory" (AA, 4:348). However, the writer should not allow the dictum of clarity to lead to a mechanical organization of the material. The particular charm of the manifold must not be sacrificed to the call for clarity. From this nervous tension between unity and diversity the poetic work draws its energy. Suddenly, the distance between a "modern" theory of prose (cf. Mundt; also Iser, "The Reading Process," 65ff.) and the Enlightenment position seems much shorter.

The attentive author realizes that the reader's interest must be maintained in order to facilitate quick comprehension and appreciation of the work. Lucid argument and emotive language must be complementary. Consequently, the writer should strive to enlist the reader's active participation by establishing a sense of suspense as to the course of development in the composition and the unravelling of the main idea. The interaction of ideas and stylistic techniques, in other words, must be finely tuned. A literary piece, executed in this manner, will establish a certain rapport with the reader. Wieland's conclusion concerning poetic composition is worth citing in full, for it attests to his scrupulously reasoned theory of the poet's relationship to the text and via the text to the potential reader:

> Aside from these rules, from which no poet may dispense himself, there are several others which are rooted in *the rapport of the poem with the readers* [my italics] and are no less indispensable. Among these are (1) the requirement that the images [*Gemälde*] in a larger work be arranged so that they place the preceding and ensuing ones in relief, (2) that the poet not neglect the emotional needs of the reader or appeal to him in only a muted fashion, (3) that the impressions [*Scenen*] alternate artfully between expressive and serene, between awesome and charming, between tumultuous and tender so that the reader will not remain long in the same mood, but be subjected to a pleasant multiplicity of emotional responses. Observance of

these last rules imparts the greatest beauty to a poem. Yet [the rapport of the poem with the readers] is one of the most difficult principles to master because of the great potential for failure.[40]

While not suggesting here that the reader be engaged in a direct or personal manner, Wieland does stress the need for appealing to both reason and emotion. The rapport with the reader would seem to be more the result of the general ordering of the evidence, which is marked by a skillfull shading of ideas and feelings. Is this phenomenon not akin to George Poulet's concept of interiority which produces a "close *rapport* with my own consciousness" ("Interiority," 43)? Is there not a similarity between the animation of the reader in this fashion and the verve or sonorous harmony of the ideal oration?[41]

The concept of painted scenes in a poem places Wieland in the conservative tradition of the *ut-pictora-poesis* theory of literature (see Nivelle, 25–34), but his arguments elsewhere (AA, 4:336f.) align him more closely with the art of music than with the plastic arts. The musicality of his writing is a mark of his much lauded *poésie du style*. This quality was an ideal for many of the great writers in the later eighteenth century and not just for Mundt in the nineteenth.[42]

While Wieland directed the foregoing comments at epic writing, he soon turned his attention to shorter pieces such as the didactic poem, the epistle, and the satire, all of which are found under the rubric of didactic poem. The affinity of the didactic poem to shorter prose writing, especially of the *Abhandlung*, is brought out by Basedow in his *Lehrbuch prosaischer und poetischer Wohlredenheit* (*Textbook of Prosaic and Poetic Eloquence*, 1756) composed at the same time as Wieland's lectures (see Dell' Orto, "Audience," 118.). If we could put aside for the moment our modern prejudice of expecting essayistic compositions to be in prose, we would have little difficulty in perceiving parallels between Wieland's analysis of the art of the didactic poem and descriptions of essayism.

Any subject that arouses our curiosity, we are told, is appropriately treated in a didactic poem (or epistle or satire). In Antiquity the content was of an historical, philosophical, or practical nature. A fourth category of modern origin should now be included as well: topics dealing with nature and human psychology. As an example he cites Thompson's *The Seasons*. These topics comprise the content of essayistic writing.

Here as well as in rhetorical works, the writer's primary task is the arranging of the evidence which, as we have seen, is not limited to individual stages of the logical argument but also inclusive of "images, similes, anecdotes, and poetic descriptions" while tending to avoid "universal and abstract theorems" (see AA, 4:398). Moreover, the poet too must give the appearance of levity while pursuing a serious intent. In the epistle and satire, for example, he should write "as if he were only jesting or just jotting down a few ideas on paper" (AA, 4:398). The affinity between essayistic and this didactic category of writing is even more evident in the assertion that the poet must constantly engage the reader's attention through seeming digressions, poetic interludes, and appropriate anecdotes. Evidently, the accomplished didactic poet makes use of the same devices which stand the accomplished rhetorician in good stead. Both vary their presentations via fluctuating sentence rhythms, choice of salient metaphors and expressions, and brief, seemingly digressive passages in an attempt both to engage the audience and to drive the main point home. The vigilant orchestration of the diverse elements of a poetic work would necessarily result in a certain *poésie du style*.

The interweaving of literary and rhetorical techniques is attested to by the rhapsodic collection of epistles Wieland published at the time he was delivering his lectures on rhetoric and poetry, *Sympathien* (1756). There the young poet refers to the cooperative effort of oratory and perspicacity in the service of truth. In capable hands, he asserts, they are "ambrosial fruits and sweet, nourishing food for the soul."[43] In a later letter he repeats the assertion, adding that reason (*der richtigste Verstand*) and rhetoric (*die süßeste Beredsamkeit*) are capable in unison of making truth a three-dimensional reality with a soothing effect on even the wildest of dispositions (H, 3:160).

Continuity in Contrast: Emotionalism and/or Rationalism?

In surveying the nexus of rhetorical traditions and prose writing from Thomasius to Wieland, we have noted the insistent call for naturalness, for the correspondence of idea and expression. Beginning with the ideal of gallant style, natural spontaneity gained constantly in value over studied moves. The role of rhetoric has evolved as a kind of midwifery for literary expression. Yet we have not heard a clear demand for the unmitigated expression of emotion except in apparently isolated and atypical instances so that the need still exists to examine the emotive element a little more closely.

One of young Wieland's mentors in Zurich, Johann Jacob Breitinger (1701–1776), a professor of Hellenic and Hebraic cultures and an influential literary critic, accorded strong emotions a more central role in his poetics than Gottsched had done. In his *Critische Dichtkunst* (*Critical Poetics*, 1740), Breitinger devotes an entire chapter to affective stylistics. He begins by stating the intention of this *modus scribendi*: its purpose is to impart to the reader a sense of the passion expressed through language. It is a figurative language which conjures up images before the readers' eyes as if they were actually present before them.[44] Its chief characteristic is the rejection of grammatical and logical ordering principles in arranging the words, phrases, and sentences (= a periphrasis for anacoluthon). Instead the reader is confronted with a rapid sequence of expletives and impassioned feeling which lend the passage a definite verve (*Schwung*; see also *die raschen Vorstellungen, die Wuth der Leidenschaften*) (Breitinger, *CD*, 2:354f.). It is a natural language free from all artifice and studiousness. The heart speaks seemingly without the aid of reason. Or does it?

In the opening sentences of the first chapter of his *Critische Dichtkunst*, Breitinger explicitly informs his reader that his system of poetics is based on Christian Wolff's understanding of philosophy as the science of all possible things (1:4–5). It is not surprising, therefore, that Breitinger defines *Affektensprache,* or the language of emotion, in terms of the Wolffian concept of perception (derivative, in turn, of Leibniz's ideas on knowledge). The accepted view was that there are two basic kinds of knowledge: distinct and indistinct. While distinct knowledge is made possible by the higher human faculties of *Verstand* and *Vernunft*, indistinct knowledge results from the operation of the lower faculties (*Empfindungen* and *Einbildungskraft*). Sensations provide knowledge of the present material world, the imagination recalls the past, projects into the future, and conjectures about possible variants of observed phenomena. Indistinct knowledge is always only a prelude to distinct knowledge. The function of the understanding (*Verstand*) according to Wolff is to compare, to judge, and to draw conclusions while reason (*Vernunft*) — the highest form of cognition — is metaphysical in nature. It aims at comprehending universals.[45]

In line with that view Breitinger contends that the *Affekten* (strong emotions) are indistinct ideas of good and evil which are activated by the imagination rather than by rational argument. As a result, he argues with Quintilian that "oratorical and poetic images . . . are nothing more than the natural language of these emotions which have been awakened in our bossom." By themselves these rhetorical and poetic twists and turns are empty, mere artifice. Vigor and energy is imparted to them by the strength of emotion felt by the individual (Breitinger, *CD*, 2:362). This would seem to be a call for individualistic and forceful, even arational expression of emotion in Enlightenment writing which is supposed to be only lucid, plain, and subdued. Again we encounter an instance of boundary crossing; here between reason and emotion, expository and affective style, philosophy and rhetoric.

Johann Gottfried Herder (1744–1803) picked up on the notion of the emotions as having their own language and raised it a notch above the ideal of tempered expression. Even though young Herder reacts against the intellectualism of the Enlightenment, he continues many of its basic assumptions and convictions while adjusting them to his particular purpose of speaking to the common man. In order to do so, he logically argues in his early treatise *Wie die Philosophie zum Besten des Volkes Allgemeiner und Nützlicher Werden Kann* (*How Philosophy Can be Made More General and Useful for the Benefit of the People*, 1763), writers must speak the common man's language. That language is based on real things not empty words; their way of thinking is lively, not clear and definite and not demonstrative. Herder contends that language evolved as a means of expressing emotions first and ideas second. This holds true, he asserts, for all humanity, not just the common people.[46]

In an essay of 1767 titled "In der Dichtkunst ist Gedanke und Ausdruck wie Seele und Leib, und nie zu trennen" ("In Literature the Idea and its Expression are Like the Body and Soul and Never to be Separated") and published in *Über die neuere deutsche Literatur. Fragmente* (*On Modern German Literature, Fragments.* 1766–67), Herder directly addresses the problem of how to express emotions via dead words.[47] He attacks here the perceived widespread separation of idea and expression in the usual poetic handbooks, arguing that belles-lettres are supposed to express natural feelings, but books deal with words, and words are dead. Thus it proves very difficult to evoke a sense of vital emotions through writing. The means of expressing emotion are physical: the eyes, the face, the tone of voice, and gestures. Herder writes: "Im Auge, im Antlitz, durch den Ton, durch die Zeichensprache des Körpers—so spricht die Empfindung eigentlich und überläßt den toten Gedanken das Gebiet der toten Sprache" (In one's eye and countenance, through the tone of voice and the language of the body—that is how feeling seeks expression. The realm of dead language is left for dead thoughts, Suphan, 1:394–96).

He commiserates with the poor poet who must pour his heart out in a text of lifeless signs, asking how abstract words can possibly duplicate the living language of spontaneity and the body? Here would seem to be Herder's main contention with the Enlightenment. While the Enlightenment seemed to favor the appearance of spontaneity and intense feeling, Herder forcefully advocates unmitigated emotion and affective stylistics, urging his reader "to see and hear via the reading act itself" (1:395). An apparent contradiction exists between the language of words—the mainstay of the Enlightenment—and the language of emotion (*Affektensprache*) after all. Placed in this light, Breitinger's solution would amount to a glossing over of the problem. From Herder, an inaugurator of the tumultuous Storm and Stress movement and himself an *Originalgenie*, we might expect an ingenious solution to the apparent dilemma of how to convey emotions in the garb of words. Unfortunately, any joyful expectation that we might entertain at the prospect of a felicitous resolution to the problem is soon thwarted. Herder, in fact, offers no radical break with the traditional notions of rhetoric and literature unrolled in this chapter.

It is clear in any event that Herder's venom is directed at the ultraconservative and pedantic wing of the Enlightenment, which relied solely on the power of words. These were the same "false" enlighteners satirized by Gellert in his Magister of *Die zärtlichen Schwestern* (*The Tender Sisters*, 1747), by Lessing in *Der junge Gelehrte* (*The Young Scholar*, 1747), and by Wieland in *Sympathien* (1755). (It is a motif continued in the 1770s and 1780s by Nicolai in *Sebaldus Nothanker*, by Goethe in *Werther* and *Urfaust*, and by Schiller in the opening scene of *Die Räuber*). Herder is bothered by the false enlighteners' lack of sensitivity to the wholeness of experience and language. His attack amounts to a Rousseauean plea for the reunion of idea, feeling, and formulation in an age of growing specialization.

Herder's critique of language and style emphasizes the continuity of theorectical reflection even as Wieland's *Theorie und Geschichte der Red-Kunst und Dicht-Kunst* underscores how knowledgeable writers in the eighteenth century were of writing strategies, how attuned they were to the power of language, and of how consciously they plied their trade. Many of the boundaries between pure poetry and pure rhetoric were dismantled in the consummate expression of ideas and emotions so that the two merged together. These writers were, in short, truly literate, not just capable of writing and reading, but sensitive to and in total control of the manifold uses of language.

Obviously, Herder felt that some Enlightenment writers plied their trade a little too consciously. The great error of these fellow writers, he contends, is that they sought "to capture the thought process without feeling" (*das Denken ohne Ausdruck erhaschen*, Suphan, 1:396). That misperception caused them to focus on the individual elements of linguistic expression, blinding them to the unity of the parts. By concentrating on the rational component, that is, on the idea that stands behind every formulation, they neglected the emotional one. And according to Herder the emotional element cannot be identified with this or that strategy, with words and phrases; instead, it evolves from and is integral to the perception of the whole. It is not the mouth that speaks nor the hand that writes; no, the soul is at the center of literature.

Thus, he urges authors to imbue their writing with heart-felt feeling, enumerating the most effective vehicles for this purpose: sentence structure, organization and linkage of words, images. Moreover, the writer must be in total control of his language, attuned to its simplicity as well as to its opulence with all its vigor and hues in order to approximate the effect of speech and gesture. Herder sums up this notion in the exclamation: "Wie sehr klebt hier alles am Ausdrucke, nicht in einzelnen Worten, sondern in jedem Teile, im Fortgange derselben und im Ganzen" (How everything adheres to expression! Not as rendered by individual words, but by each part and their development to a [harmonious] whole! Suphan, 1:395). Such writing is an act of self expression of one's whole being; and the reading it occasions is a self-conscious, dynamic process.[48]

What is really new in all this? Not all that much. Since Thomasius theorists had pointed to the importance of *tour, numerus Schwung, Zierlichkeit,* and *poésie du style.* Each has to do with the artistic unity of opposites which contribute to a harmony of the whole. Of course, the Enlighteners emphasized the integrity of idea and expression, but had not forgotten to enhance that nexus with a dose of strong emotion as Breitinger and Wieland had done. Theoretically, then, the basis for Herder's emotive theory of prose already existed. He did not alter the parts, he stressed their cumulative unity. The degree of emphasis is perhaps novel and welcome for our purposes in delineating a rhetorically based theory of prose writing disposed to the genesis of the German essay in a period of supposed bloodless cogitation. But we must not overlook the fact that even Herder's Storm-and-Stress response is essentially a continuation of Enlightenment rhetoric in the sense of a *rhetorica contra rhetoricam* (cf. Ueding and Steinbrink, *Grundriß,* 113).

These views on the nature of rhetoric and literature were very persistent. In addition to the usual handbooks on eloquence, poetics, and rhetoric the essential principles of oratory are echoed in numerous articles and journalistic pieces in the latter half of the eighteenth century. I focus here on two writers who form a link with such prominent authors as Gellert and Wieland and who were neglected by Ueding in his *Grundriß der Rhetorik.*

Johann Carl Wezel (1747–1819), a young novelist and critic between Enlightenment and Storm and Stress, began as a disciple of Wieland. In the treatise, *Über Sprache, Wissenschaften und Geschmack der Teutschen* (*On the Language, Sciences, and Taste of the German*, 1781), Wezel draws upon the principles of oratory to defend German writers against Friedrich II's judgment that Germany had not produced respectable literature. Yet he readily grants that the literary scene in Germany is dominated by second-rate authors (*Schönschreiber, Periodendrechsler, Wortwähler*) and that there are only a few first-rate prose writers.[49] The second-rate authors fail to realize that the essence of good style is an inner music resultant from the harmonious interaction of the constitutive parts of the composition. Thus they do not heed the fine points of the art of writing: *numerus oratorius, oratorischer Wohlklang, Anordnung der Sätze und Perioden* (Wezel, 3:83f.). "We must pay more attention," he exhorts, "to the *rhetorical* and not *grammatical* euphony" (Wezel, 3:82). Critical for Wezel is the resultant melody and harmony just like in music. While melody is achieved through the proper alignment of sounds, syllables, and words, harmony results from the sentence structure, the arrangement of the periods, the cadences within each period as well as within the entire work, and from the unity of expression and idea or emotion (Wezel, 3:84). Although there is nothing new in these formulations, Wezel does provide a more detailed description of melodic and harmonic writing than hitherto encountered. He explains:

> Whoever avoids the harsh clash of consonants and the crowding together of monosyllabic words, whoever chooses and arranges his words so that his sentences—if one were to scan them—are marked by a richness and multiplicity of metrical feet, neither all lively dactyls nor monotonous iambs and trochees nor listless spondees, whoever observes these and similar rules, writes *melodically*. Whoever selects and arranges his words and arrays the sentences within his periods so that they alternately capture the vigor, dalliance, sublimity, and playfulness of his thoughts, or the rawness, tenderness, melancholy, and joy of his moods and expresses them in lines that either dance and skip with joy or move with heavy and tired step or that dawdle or soar as the case may be, that person writes *harmonically*.[50]

Wezel succeeds here in expressing succinctly the effect that all those rhetorical rules are supposed to achieve. Nor does he neglect the problematic question of strong emotions.

The young critic warns his reader not to conclude falsely that a writer need only count words and syllables. Like Neukirch, Breitinger, Wieland, and Herder before him, Wezel soundly rejects the notion. Fastidious observance of the individual rules will only lead to artificiality and stilt-edness. If an author wishes to express an idea robustly he must experience it intensely. In order to suit the language to the emotion, the formulations must flow easily from his pen without false starts and without hesitation. He must be able to make quick judgments about the suitability of words and phrases, and that means he must not only possess discernment but also be extremely familiar with the nuances of language (Wezel, 3:86).

Wezel's estimation of poetic prose stands squarely in the theoretical tradition of rhetorical prose. Although he does not exceed the established parameters of that line of thinking, he does provide a succinct summary of the essential elements of the new kind of writing advocated by edu-cators, philosophers, and writers since Thomasius and Leibniz. In its ideal form it is not plain, it is not merely distinct, it is not monotonous. It is alive and full of energy. One could even say that it is "popular."

Popular appeal was cited already by Leibniz and again later by Herder as a chief criterion of the new writing mode. In the late eighteenth century Christian Garve (1742–1798), professor in Leipzig and independent scholar in Breslau, can be seen as a kind of successor to Gellert with his popular appeal. He reflected on the popularity of prose writing in a number of articles. Pertinent here are above all his "Über die Popularität des Vortrages" ("On the Popularity of Discourse," 1793) and "Über die prosaische Schreibart" ("On Prose Style," 1798). Popularity of style, he remarks at the outset of the first, can refer either to the readability of a composition or to its mass appeal. In the first instance, the work is written for a generally educated audience (the approximately 250,000 persons referred to in Chapter V) and is not aimed exclusively at scholarly read-ers. In the second case the work is composed for the common man (*der gemeine Mann, das Volk*).[51] It quickly becomes clear that Garve empha-sizes the first connotation of popular, for he ultimately rejects the notion that a writer must "speak the common man's language" in order to make himself understood. In almost the same breath he praises France for having developed a prose style common to both the academic community and the broader, educated public.[52]

The primary consideration for any writer should be audience reaction to the work. There can be no reaction on the part of the reader if the work in incomprehensible or unreadable. Although he does not specifically state the notion, Garve was surely convinced that no reader could be as interested in *reading* the composition as the author is in *having it read*. What Garve does state is that the piece must be clearly argued. The prerequisites for clarity are drawn from rhetorical tradition: mastery of the language with all its connotations, control of the rules of grammar, a unity of language and idea, select use of images and concrete examples, avoidance of abstract theorems, and so on.

The single, distinguishing trait of a cultivated prose style, however, is a certain agility of expression which is a meta-quality of the individual components capable of immediately communicating ideas and emotions. This quality is achieved only with effort but vanishes as soon as the effort becomes obvious. It cannot be achieved by virtue of reason alone; only in combination with the imagination can a writer hope to compose prose with broad appeal and style. Without the aid of the imagination, the thought process is slow and tedious; stirred by imagination (and feeling) rational thought soars; the sentences and "periods" become vibrant and intense, the composition throbs with life ("Popularität," cf. 2:1046ff.). This first part of Garve's argument, which defines popularity as an appeal to the larger cultured reading public rather than to the masses, culminates in a summarizing paragraph notable for its compactness. Garve specifically refers to the treatment of philosophical ideas in popular garb.

> Hence: that philosophical treatise is capable of affecting the broader cultured audience which combines a naturally easy flow of ideas with the consummate didactic discourse and which weaves into its argument as much historical fact or poetic inspiration [*Geschichte oder Poesie*] as is necessary to explain the abstract concepts or to confirm universal theorems ("Popularität," 2:1049).

What we have here is nothing less than a definition of essayistic writing. The foregoing arguments regarding the tradition of prose theory in the eighteenth century place us in a position to espy the lineaments of rhetorical as well as poetical notions that combine to create Garve's ideal of popular prose. His formulation is a compact rendition of the essential elements of a consummate "rhetorical prose" envisioned by thinkers preceding Garve by as much as one hundred years. (Incidentally, it embodies the essential qualities of later essays penned by such masters as Emerson.)

We encounter it again in the assessment by Friedrich Schlegel (1772–1829) — the classic German theoretician of essayism. Schlegel describes the hermaphroditic and dialogic quality of essayistic writing in terms reminiscent not only of Garve but also of Lessing, Gellert, and Thomasius. Essayistic compositions are to be written, he states, as if we were "writing a letter or speaking freely on a moral topic in neither a philosophical nor a poetic style" (Schlegel, *Kritische Werkausgabe,* 18/2: 206). In this context we can also recall Schlegel's praise of Georg Forster's style which throbs with life because of the simultaneous appeal to the mind, the imagination, and the emotions. The effect of this broad appeal to the lower as well as higher human faculties is labelled "genuine popularity." Because the passage is frequently cited as an early description of essayistic writing, we would do well to look at it here again. Schlegel writes:

> [Forster] begins with the individual phenomenon, understands however how to give it a turn to the universal and everywhere draws connections to the eternal. He never occupies the imagination, the feelings or reason alone, but instead animates the entire person at once ("Karakteristik," *DE,* 6:223).

Historians of the German essayistic tradition generally quote only this far and then stop. But for our purposes of drawing an intimate connection between the cultivation of an original prose in general in the eighteenth century and the rise of essayistic writing in particular, the subsequent sentence is most revealing. The next sentence, namely, reveals the continuity of Schlegel's ideal essayistic style with notions promulgated by Thomasius and Leibniz:

> To cultivate all the powers of the soul in oneself and in others in an equally intense and harmonious fashion—that is the foundation of genuine popularity, which does not simply consist in uniform mediocrity (*DE,* 6:223).

The consistency of prose ideals from Baroque to Romanticism would therefore seem to be self-evident. At least it was my intent in reviewing the philosophy of prose to show how similar the late seventeenth and the early nineteenth centuries really were in their aspirations for a new manner of writing. The writer's desire for genuine popularity around 1700 is no less acute around 1800. It was no fluke that Schiller turned in 1794 to Garve for a contribution on the topic of a genuinely popular style for *Die Horen.* Schiller scholars know just how important the question was for him, especially in his early stage of authorship.[53]

Finally, the overall impact of this affective, essayistic writing tends to anticipate essential elements of modern reader-response criticism, especially as a means of experiencing life through a process of continual modification. In Iser's words: "In whatever way, and under whatever circumstances the reader may link the different phases of the text together, it will always be the process of anticipation and retrospection that leads to the formation of the virtual dimension, which in turn transforms the text into an experience for the reader."[54]

Garve's piece, "On Prose Style," echoes the same ideas presented in "On the Popularity of Discourse." But that is not the reason why we now turn to it. "On Prose Style" is noteworthy in our context because it is actually a response to the announcement by the Deutsche Gesellschaft in Mannheim of an open writing competition on the question: "Why, according to their own best authors, do the Germans lag behind the Greeks and Romans and perhaps the French and English as well in regard to good prose style, and what is the most characteristic merit of the best German prose writers?" ("Warum stehen die Deutschen, nach dem Geständniß ihrer besten Schriftsteller, in Ansehung einer guten prosaischen Schreibart, gegen Griechen und Römer, vielleicht auch gegen Franzosen und Engländer zurück? Und welches ist der besten deutschen Prosaisten charakteristisches Verdienst?" 1798). Unfortunately, Garve's reply remained fragmentary. Fortunately, he chose to answer the second part of the question first. This is a fortunate turn since we are most interested in qualities of *German* prose.

Garve answers the question in terms reminiscent of Herder's cultural relativism. He states that to compare Germans with Greeks or Romans with the French and so on would not be all that fruitful since a common point of comparison between these idosyncratic languages is lacking and a judgment would be essentially a subjective matter wholly dependent on the viewer (63). He then goes on to assert that the Germans do possess excellent prose writers, naming as examples Moses Mendelssohn (1729–1786), Gotthold Ephraim Lessing (1729–1781), and Johann Jakob Engel (1741–1802). Each is exemplary in a different way. Because these authors will be discussed in the hermeneutical section of this study, we need not pursue the matter here. Yet Garve's characterization of Engel's prose style is so striking because of its affinity to the classical essayistic style that it warrants citation as an expression of the ideal of prose writing authors had striven for since the beginning of the Enlightenment:

> [Engel's] specific talent—rarely encountered among us Germans—is a mixture of philosophical penetration and poetic imagination . . . . While delving deep into the nature of his subject matter, he does not neglect to depict its outer shell graphically. Moreover, he knows how to illuminate the immaterial qualities

of his topic through well-chosen images. His definitions are precise, his line of reasoning clear and cogent, his conclusions are novel and persuasive. But the twists and turns [*Wendung*] which he gives to his analyses are the work of the imagination; his elucidations are poetic, his style is appropriate to the subject matter [*die Sachen*]. This style is at the same time precise and florid, its diction is perfect not only for expressing the thing itself but also for its pleasing sound. Finally, its "periods" are scrupulously rounded off, but it would appear, only as a result of the complete development of the ideas themselves.[55]

The most valued feature of this kind of writing is the cooperation of mechanical technique and inspiration in achieving a balance of philosophy and poetry. Again the overall quality is described in the familiar terms of rhetoric which—because of the emphasis on the *total* impression of the composition—moves resolutely into the realm of belles-lettres. This kind of prose, Garve concludes, has universal appeal; its attraction is not limited just to experts and philosophers as would seem to be the case with Mendelssohn's and Lessing's style.[56]

In arguing that excellent prose writers in German did exist, Garve is supported by the judgment of several contemporaries. Goethe in "Literarischer Sansculottismus" (1795), Friedrich Schlegel in "Georg Forster: Fragment einer Karakteristik der deutschen Klassiker" (1797), and Karl Morgenstern in "Plan im Lesen" (1805) all advance the same opinion even though each represents a different literary school of thought. Other writers cited for their excellent prose style include Gellert, Lichtenberg, Goethe, Schiller, Wieland, Forster, Johannes Müller, Herder, Johann Heinrich Voss, Garve, and even Leibniz. Their work is distinguished by its harmonious appeal to the human being in his or her wholeness, that is, by a simultaneous appeal to the head and heart, to reason and sensibility. This writing is "classical," as Morgenstern states, because it pursues a purely human purpose by cultivating humanity's innate sense of the true, the good, and the beautiful. And it does not matter whether the writing occurs in the realm of poetry, rhetoric, history, or philosophy.[57]

Both Morgenstern and Schlegel agree that classical writing promotes active reader involvement, for its true value lies in the process of being read, not in the static state of having been read. The pleasure granted by the writing is the stimulation to think and feel along with the writer, to discover new thoughts and to savor dormant emotions anew, to enter into the soul of the writer and experience the common bond of humanity uniting writer and reader. Each rereading enhances the sense of joy and pleasure as it contributes to the perfection of human potential. The reader who is capable of reading in this manner is a "classical" reader, that is an *alter auctor* (see Morgenstern, 79f.; Schlegel, "Forster," *DE*, 6:220).

The description of the "classic" interaction with the text was previously described by Wieland as a rapport of the poem with the reader. In the twentieth century Wolfgang Iser concludes that the production of the meaning of a literary text results from the reader's projection of consistency onto the text (*Konsistenzbildung*) and "entails the possibility that we may formulate ourselves and so discover what had previously seemed to elude our consciousness."[58] The possibility of this kind of literary production is, for the eighteenth-century critic, predicated on the equality of author and audience who are esssentially attuned to one another by the bond of "sympathy." This bond assumes that the reader's projection of consistency is consistent with the text's inherent logicalness or *analogon rationis*. It is a fundamentally rhetorical quality of the text that has been referred to in various ways. Kant spoke of a "discursive way of looking at things" (*diskursive Vorstellungsart*; Kant, *Anthropologie*, Weischedel, 12:571), while Mundt remarked on the "dialectic of movement and thought" ("die Dialektik der Bewegung . . . muß sich . . . der Dialektik des Gedankens anschließen," Mundt, *Kunst*, 123). Finally, Hinderer labelled it a "popular and productive way of speaking and writing" ("diese populäre und produktive Vortragsweise;" Hinderer, "Kurze Geschichte," 234).[59] The perspective of discourse had been undergoing dialectical development since Thomasius and totally informs both the philosophy and the rhetoric of written communication in the Enlightenment. It derives, no doubt, from Leibniz's and Wolff's conviction that "the fundamental phenomenon of the mind . . . consists in activity not in mere passivity" (Cassirer, *Philosophy*, 121).

Generations of writers learned from one another, each perfecting the style just a little more. In his response to the criticism that the Germans lacked classical prose authors Goethe could point to this "invisible school" of writers, claiming that the literary achievements of the late eighteenth century would not have been possible without the pioneering work of authors in early century (Goethe, "Literarischer Sansculottismus," 12:243). Far from being a vacuous age, the eighteenth century was vibrant with seemingly boundless philosophical, rhetorical, and artistic energy. That energy, Goethe suggests, is reflected in the best examples of prose from the era. He writes: "A significant piece of writing is like a significant oration; it is merely the result of life." Goethe urges us to be mindful, therefore, of the changing conditions of life. Because of the rich, indigenous tradition to draw upon, the final decades of the eighteenth century were most favorable for the practice of classic prose. Because there was less of a tradition to draw upon in the early decades of the era, conditions for the practice of classical prose writing were less favorable. Goethe admonishes his reader: "Compare the conditions which favor a classical writer, especially a prose writer, to those under which the best Germans of this century labored and—if you are capable of seeing clearly and judging fairly—you will wonder at their accomplishments and commiserate respectfully with their failures."[60]

We turn now to an analysis of those prose efforts as they found expression in essayistic attempts from Thomasius's "An die Studierende Jugend" (1687) to Adam Müller's "Vom Gespräch" (1816). In doing so we will endeavor to judge their merits not by the standards of so-called classical prose, but according the goals set by their own times and conditions as revealed in the history of boundary crossings between rhetorical technique and aesthetic conception in the communicative art of essayism.

Notes

1. Eric A. Blackall, *The Emergence of German as a Literary Language, 1700–1775* (Cambridge: Cambridge University Press, 1959), 147f.
2. Johann Jakob Bodmer, *Anklagung Des verderbten Geschmackes, Oder Critische Anmerkungen Über den Hamburgischen PATRIOTEN, Und Die Hallischen TADLERINNEN* (Frankfurt and Leipzig, 1728), in Johann Jakob Bodmer and Johann Jakob Breitinger, *Schriften zur Literatur*, ed. Volker Meid (Stuttgart: Reclam, 1980), 38.
3. See Gerd Ueding, *Grundriß der Rhetorik: Geschichte, Technik, Methode.* 2nd ed. (Stuttgart: Metzler, 1986), 105: "Vereinfacht ausgedrückt verläuft die Aneignung der Rhetorik im 18. Jahrhundert bis in die vierziger Jahre hinein nach diesem Muster, die emotionale Überzeugungsherstellung durch Erregung der sanften Gefühle oder der heftigen Leidenschaften wird *nur* als Zugeständnis an die menschliche Unvollkommenheit gewertet und *die eigentliche Aufgabe der Rhetorik in der Aufklärung des Verstandes,* also in der rationalen Wirkungskomponente *(docere) gesehen"* (my emphasis).
4. See Herman Meyer, "Schillers philosophische Rhetorik" (1959), in *Begriffsbestimmung der Klassik und des Klassischen,* ed. Heinz Otto Burger (Darmstadt: Wissenschaftliche Buchgesellschaft, 1972), 411–467; here 429n.
5. Theodor Mundt, *Die Kunst der deutschen Prosa: Ästhetisch, Literaturgeschichtlich, Gesellschaftlich,* ed. Hans Düvel (1837; rprt. Göttingen: Vandenhoeck and Ruprecht, 1969), 39: "Ideal aller Sprache und Darstellung ist bloß *der Gedanke.* Von dem richtigen Verhältniß des Gedankens zu seiner Darstellung, wovon zugleich das Maaß aller zu gebrauchenden Kunstvortheile und der Schönheit selbst abhängt, ließe sich am allerersten ein akademischer Canon aufstellen. Wenigstens ist eine *Philosophie des Stils*

denkbar und zu versuchen [my emphasis], welche, der genialen Willkür der Production allen Spielraum übrig lassend, das allgemein Nothwendige, auf dem jede treffende und das Leben erschöpfende Darstellung beruhen muß, zum Bewußtsein brächte."

6. This argument has been repeated most recently by Robert S. Leventhal, "Semiotic Interpretation and Rhetoric in the German Enlightenment 1740–1760," *Deutsche Vierteljahresschrift für Literaturwissenschaft und Geistesgeschichte.* 60/2 (1986), 223–248.

6a. Heinrich Küntzel, *Essay und Aufklärung. Ursprung einer originellen deutschen Prosa im 78. Jahrhundert* (Munich: Fink, 1969).

7. A notable exception is Eberhard Wilhelm Schulz's "Winckelmanns Schreibart," in *Studien zur Goethezeit. Eric Trunz zum 75. Geburtstag,* ed. Hans-Joachim Mähl and Eberhard Mannack (Heidelberg: Winter, 1981), 233–55, which makes specific reference to Küntzel's concept of an original prose. While Schulz does not examine Winckelmann's prose style as essayistic writing, he does determine its qualities as *Ausdrucksprosa,* rooted in the principles of precise and graphic representation. He concludes: "Seine Sprache ist vielmehr sinnlich, voller Leben, sie gleicht dem Marmor seiner Skupturen, in den das Licht eindringt . . . . es kündigten sich in ihr zukünftige Stilentwicklungen in der deutschen Prosa an" (255). Historians of aesthetic theory have generally been more judicious than historians of essay writing. Like Küntzel, Armand Nivelle, *Literaturästhetik der europäischen Aufklärung* (Wiesbaden: Athenaion, 1977), also stresses the continuity or at least the non-disruptive evolution of aesthetic thought in the eighteenth century. He points out that Leibnizian concepts of the *analogon rationis* and of the dream inform literary theory throughout the age. Nivelle speaks of the "continuity between the rational and the irrational" regarding the initial, spontaneous impressions objects make on us, which are then approved by the intellect. Leibniz explains this harmony as resultant from a divinely ordained correspondence between clear and opaque perceptions (Nivelle, 34f.; see also 15, 30, 40f., 62ff. on the continuous development of emotionalism and relativity). The non-disruptive evolution of aesthetic theory in our time frame functions as a leitmotif in Silvio Vietta's, *Literarische Phantasie: Theorie and Geschichte. Barock und Aufklärung* (Stuttgart: Metzler, 1986) (see, e.g., 71ff.). Leventhal's analysis of the semiotic and rhetorical aspects of aesthetic thinking in the eighteenth century falls short of Nivelle's and Vietta's niveau. His view of the Enlightenment is undifferentiated, his understanding of rhetoric somewhat naive, and he places too much emphasis on the principle of "hermeneutic economy" as a constitutive factor in Enlightenment aesthetics. According to Leventhal that principle "teaches that the interpreter should only attribute that sense to the signs, expression and text which is in accordance with the principles of reason and which correspond to the perfections of the human soul: clarity, completeness, comprehensibility, authenticity, truth and virtue" (238). Although this rational principle was operative, it was not without balance by the irrational.

8. Dell Orto, "Audience," misrepresents the thrust of Küntzel's argument
    when he contends that the German equates the origination of the essay with
    the "creation of a prose free from the strictures of rhetorical formulae"
    (111).
9. Gerd Ueding and Bernd Steinbrink, *Grundriß der Rhetorik: Geschichte,
    Technik, Methode,* 2nd ed. (Stuttgart: Metzler, 1986), 111ff., 122f.
10. Long after Wayne Booth had drawn attention to the nexus of literature and
    rhetoric in English literature, critics of the German setting have begun to
    accord the topic its deserved due. The *Grundriß der Rhetorik* (2nd ed.,
    1986) can be recommended as one of the most competent assessments of
    rhetoric available today. A product of the only institute in the Federal
    Republic of Germany for the study of rhetoric, the *Grundriß* is both a
    critical assessment of the history of rhetoric from classical antiquity to the
    present as well as a *Lesebuch* on the subject. Hard-to-find sources from the
    Middle Ages to the late eighteenth century are cited extensively in an effort
    to communicate a sense of the historical debate on the theory and practice
    of rhetoric. The book is divided into two major parts. The first deals with
    the history of rhetoric, while the second offers a detailed treatment of its
    concepts, techniques, and typical genres. An exhaustive bibliography com-
    pletes the study. In brief, the *Grundriß* is a most useful work. Shorter
    renditions of the topic include those by Klaus Kockhorn, *Macht und
    Wirkung der Rhetorik. Vier Aufsätze zur Ideengeschichte der Vormoderne*
    (Berlin, 1968); W. Hinderer, "Kurze Geschichte der deutschen Rede," *Über
    deutsche Literatur und Rede. Historische Interpretationen* (Munich: Fink,
    1981); Hans-Wolff Jäger, *Politische Kategorien in Poetik und Rhetorik der
    zweiten Hälfte des 18. Jahrhunderts* (Stuttgart: Metzler, 1970), and Ued-
    ing's own *Rhetorik des Schreibens. Eine Einführung* (Kronberg/Ts: Athe-
    näum, 1985). One of the most concise and readable studies of the concept
    and practice of classical rhetoric is provided by Werner Eisenhut, *Ein-
    führung in die Antike Rhetorik und ihre Geschichte* (Darmstadt: Wissen-
    schaftliche Buchgesellschaft, 1974).
11. Hans-Otto Rößer, *Bürgerliche Vergesellschaftung und kulturelle Reform.
    Studien zur Theorie der Prosa bei Johann Gottfried Herder und Christian
    Garve,* Gießener Arbeiten zur neueren deutschen Literatur und Literatur-
    wissenschaft, 9 (Frankfurt a.M.: P. Lang, 1986), 3f. See my critical review
    of this book in *Internationales Archiv für die Sozialgeschichte der deutschen
    Literatur* 13 (1988).
12. Eschenburg's, *Entwurf einer Theorie und Literatur der schönen Wissen-
    schaften,* 2nd ed. (Berlin and Stettin: Nicolai, 1789), is subdivided into two
    main sections: poetry and rhetoric. The second part is labelled "Allgemeine
    Theorie der prosaischen Schreibart" and includes chapters on epistolary,
    dialogic, dogmatic, and historical writing as well as on rhetorical compo-
    sitions. Herman Meyer, "Schillers Philosophische Rhetorik" (1959), in *Be-
    griffsbestimmung der Klassik und des Klassischen,* ed. Heinz Otto Burger
    (Darmstadt: Wissenschaftliche Buchgesellschaft, 1972), 426–436, discusses
    the role of Eschenburg (and Johann Georg Sulzer) in the development of a
    theory of rhetoric and of prose in the second half of the eighteenth century.

13. See Hans-Wolf Jäger, "Lehrdichtung," *Hansers Sozialgeschichte der deutschen Literatur*, ed. Rolf Grimminger (Munich: dtv, 1980), 3/2:500–544.

14. Wilhelm von Humboldt, *Über die Verschiedenheit des menschlichen Sprachbaus*, ed. Nette (1949), 207. Cited by Detlef Rasmussen, "Georg Forsters Stil als gegenständliches Denken und Beschreibung der Dinge," in *Goethe und Forster. Studien zum gegenständlichen Dichten*, ed. D. Rasmussen (Bonn: Bouvier, 1985), 42.

15. Leventhal points out that the two kingpins of his analysis, J. M. Chladenus (1710–1759) and G. Fr. Meier (1718–1777) never "worked out a theory for the interpretation of specifically literary texts" (235ff.). One cannot help but wonder why, then, he chose to focus on them. On the theory of poetic prose see, in addition to Nivelle and Vietta, David Wellbery, *Laokoon: Aesthetics and Semiotics in the Age of Reason* (Cambridge: Cambridge University Press, 1984).

16. Johann Christoph Gottsched, *Der Biedermann*, facsimile ed. Wolfgang Martens (Leipzig, 1727–29; rprt. Stuttgart: Metzler, 1975), 2:22; see also 1:1.

17. See Hinderer, "Kurze Geschichte der deutschen Rede" (1981), 244, and Ueding, *Grundriß*, 122. In general Hinderer understands the tradition and practice of rhetoric one-dimensionaly and even though he acknowledges its underlying philosophy (i.e., its contribution to the cultural education of humanity), he is guided in his interpretation by its manipulative function which dominates political orations (241, 248). A major difference between the *Rede* and the essay is the latter's penchant for stimulating independent thought, while the political *Rede* tends to be prescriptive.

18. Gottsched, *Ausführliche Redekunst. Nach Anleitung der alten Griechen und Römer, wie auch der neuern Ausländer; Geistlichen und weltlichen Rednern zu gut, in zweenen Theilen verfasset und mit Exempeln erläutert* (Leipzig, 1736; rprt. Hildesheim and New York: Gerstenberg, 1973), 33f.: "Die Wohlredenheit drückt nach dem Klange des Wortes nichts weiter aus, als eine Fertigkeit wohl, das ist zierlich, und anmuthig zu reden, oder zu schreiben. Sie besteht also fast gänzlich in einer guten Schreibart, oder in vernünftigen und wohl ausgedrückten Gedanken." Cited by Ueding, *Grundriß*, 122.

19. See McCarthy, "Gallant Novel and the German Enlightenment (1670–1750)," *Deutsche Vierteljahresschrift für Literaturwissenschaft und Geistesgeschichte* 59/1 (1985), 76f.

20. On the distinction between *galant homme* and *homme galant* see Dieter Kimpel, *Der Roman der Aufklärung (1670–1774)*, 2nd ed. (Stuttgart: Metzler, 1977), 53, 57.

21. Heinz Otto Burger, "Europäisches Adelsideal und deutsche Klassik" (1963), demonstrates the continuity of this anthropological ideal from antiquity to Weimar Classicism, noting the central role that rhetorical concepts played in its evolution. However, Burger does not cite Thomasius's input and refers to the ideal of the *honnête homme* instead of the *gallant homme* (although the notions are related). See H. O. Burger, "Europäisches Ideal," *Begriffsbestimmung der Klassik und des Klassischen* (Darmstadt: Wissenschaftliche Buchgesellschaft, 1972), 177–202.

22. Christian Thomasius, "Christian Thomasius eröffnet der Studierenden Jugend zu Leipzig in einem Discours Welcher Gestalt man denen Frantzosen in gemeinem Leben und Wandel nachahmen soll? Ein Collegium über des Gratians Grund-Reguln/ Vernünfftig/klug und artig zu leben," *Deutsche Litteraturdenkmäler des 18. und 19. Jahrhunderts*, No. 52/2, new series No.2/3 (Stuttgart, 1895; rpt. Nendeln/Liechtenstein: Krauss, 1968), 11, 33.

23. NS 2/3:23–25; similarly in "Von der Klugheit, sich selbst zu raten" (1705): NS 2/3:80–97.

24. Benjamin Neukirch, *Anweisung zu Teutschen Briefen* (1721), 11. Buch, 10. Kap., 103ff.; reprinted in *Der galante Stil, 1680–1730,* ed. Conrad Wiedmann (Tübingen: Niemeyer, 1969), 32.

25. See McCarthy, "The Gallant Novel," 60–68.

26. Friedrich A. Hallbauer, *Anweisung zur Verbesserten Teutschen Oratorie* (Jena, 1725; rprt. Kronberg/Ts., 1974), 496: "Zu einem guten stilo wird erfordert, daß er richtig 1), rein 2), deutlich 3), üblich 4), zusammenhängend 5), ungezwungen 6), gleich 7), zierlich 8), und nach der Materie, den Lesern oder Zuhörern, auch nach der Absicht gerichtet sey 9)." Cited by Ueding, *Grundriß,* 111.

27. Hallbauer, *Anweisung,* 500ff.; Cited by Ueding, *Grundriß,* 111f.

28. Johann Jakob Bodmer, "Anklagung Des verderbten Geschmackes, Oder Critische Bemerkungen Über Den Hamburgischen PATRIOTEN, Und die Hallischen TADLERINNEN," in Johann Jakob Bodmer and Johann Jakob Breitinger, *Schriften zur Literatur* (Stuttgart: Reclam, 1980), 36–40.

29. See my "The Gallant Novel," 47–78, and "Lektüre und Lesertypologie im 18. Jahrhundert (1730–1770). Ein Beitrag zur Lesergeschichte am Beispiel Wolfenbüttels," *Internationales Archiv für Sozialgeschichte der deutschen Literatur* 8 (1983), 66–77 et passim; also Wolfgang Martens, *Die Botschaft der Tugend* (Stuttgart: Metzler, 1968), 441–469 et passim.

30. Gottfried Honnefelder, "Christian Fürchtegott Gellert," in *Deutsche Dichter des 18. Jahrhunderts. Ihr Leben und Werk,* ed. Benno von Wiese (Berlin: Erich Schmidt, 1977), 127.

31. C. F. Gellert, *Die epistolographischen Schriften,* facsimile of the 1742 and 1751 Eds. (Stuttgart: Metzler, 1971), 47f.: "Man bediene sich also keiner künstlichen Ordnung, keiner mühsamen Einrichtungen, sondern man überlasse sich der freywilligen Folge seiner Gedanken und setze sie nach einander hin, wie sie uns entstehen: so wird der Bau, die Einrichtung, oder die Form eines Briefes natürlich seyn."

32. C. M. Wieland, *Theorie und Geschichte der Red-Kunst und Dicht-Kunst,* in *Wielands Werke,* ed. the Akademie der Wissenschaften (Berlin: Akademie der Wissenschaften, 1909ff.), 4:303: "Wir verstehen unter der Red-Kunst eine auf die Kenntniß der Reglen gegründete Fertigkeit, wohl zu reden, d.i. durch seine Reden die Zuhörer zu überzeugen, sich ihrer Affekten zu bemeistern und sie zu dem Zweck zu lenken, den man sich vorgesetzt hat; denn das Vermögen, zu reden, ist uns von der Natur zu keinem andern Zweck gegeben, als damit wir dadurch einander unsre Gedanken beybringen und einander determiniren könnten, uns in unsern Absichten beförderlich zu seyn; oder, mit andern Worten, vermittelst der Rede würken

wir auf den Verstand und auf den Willen der andern Menschen. Es folgt also von selbst, daß nur derjenige wohl reden kann, der andern durch seine Vorstellungen würklich bewegen kann, etwas zu glauben oder zu thun." Hereafter this edition is cited as AA.

33. AA, 4:306f. Cf. also Eisenhut, 82. Ueding speaks of the *genus iudicale*, and *genus demonstrativum* with regard to the eighteenth century and mentions the *genus deliberativum* only in connection with later eras (*Grundriß*, 123–126, 172f.).

34. Nivelle warns us not to attach too much weight to the shift from didacticism and entertainment (*docere et delectare*) to *Rührung* (*movere*; English, *passion*; French, *émotion*) in the aesthetic experience which came to the fore in the last third of the eighteenth century. The stress on emotion is not a simple lapse into a rhetorical tradition. Despite the parallels between them, *ästhetische Rührung* is more encompassing than *movere* (40f.).

35. AA, 4:311. Bernhard Sowinski, *Deutsche Stilistik. Betrachtungen zur Sprachverwendung und Sprachgestaltung im Deutschen* (Frankfurt a.M.: Fischer, 1973), 128–178, demonstrates by his detailed discussion how stylistically important sentence structure is. James Wardell (Dissertation, University of Michigan, 1986) seems unaware of the attention classical rhetoric pays even to the minutest details of writing/speaking. Otherwise he would not have found it necessary to introduce such concepts as macrostructure and microstructure in his discussion of style.

36. "Es bestehet eigentlich in derjenigen Art des Ausdrucks, wodurch ein Gedanke lebhaft oder unerwartet oder erhaben oder fein oder neu wird. Diese Kunst, die Gedanken zu wenden, kann nicht anders, als durch aufmerksames Lesen der schönsten Schriftsteller und eine lange Übung erlangt werden" (Wieland, AA, 4:312).

37. "Unter dem *numerus oratorius* versteht man eine gewisse wohlklingende Harmonie, wodurch dem Ohr geschmeichelt wird, und die aus dem geschickten Arrangement der Sätze und Perioden entspringt. Es ist ein Mittelding zwischen dem nachlässigen Klang der gemeinen Prosa und zwischen dem poetischen *Metro* oder der Versification . . . . Sie gehört aber auch unter diejenigen, die nur durch die Übung und Lectur erlangt werden" (Wieland, AA, 4:312). On the relationship of rhetorical cadence to musical periods, see Christian Winkler, *Elemente der Rede. Die Geschichte ihrer Theorie in Deutschland von 1750–1850.* Dissertation Erlangen 1931 (Bausteine zur Geschichte der deutschen Literatur, XXXII) (Walluf and Nendeln: Sändig-Reprint, 1975), 83–105.

38. E.-O. Gerke, *Der Essay als Kunstform bei Hugo von Hofmannsthal* (Lübeck und Hamburg, 1970), 22: "In diesem Spannungsfeld zwischen rationalem Mitteilungszweck und künstlerischer Gestaltungsabsicht gewinnt der Essay seine Form."

39. AA, 4:313f. See also the section in the *Grundriß* on the nexus of rhetoric and poetics (113–14). Eisenhut concludes his study of classical rhetoric and its significance for Hellenic and Roman literature with the telling statement: "The master—whether poet or orator—uses the techniques in a sovereign fashion; only the dilettante (*Nichtkönner*) thinks that following the rules is the main thing" (94).

40. "Außer diesen Reglen [sic], von welchen sich kein Dichter dispensieren darf, gibt es noch einige andre, die ihren Grund in dem Rapport des Gedichts mit den Lesern haben und ebenso nothwendig beobachtet werden müssen. Dergleichen sind, daß die besonderen Gemähsde in einem großen Gedicht so placiert seyn müssen, daß jedes denen, die vor oder nach ihm stehen, einen Relief gebe, daß der Poet das Herz des Lesers niemals lange ungerührt oder in gar zu ruhiger Bewegung lassen muß, — daß die pathetischen Scenen mit ruhigern, die schrecklichen mit anmuthigen, die ungestümen mit sanften auf eine geschickte Art abgesetzt seyn müssen, so daß der Leser nicht allzulange in dem gleichen Affect bleibe, sondern durch eine angenehme Mannigfaltigkeit von Gemüths-Bewegungen geführt werde. Die Beobachtung dieser letzten Regeln gibt einem Gedicht die größten Schönheiten; sie ist aber wegen der vielen Abwege, in die man dabey gerathen kann, in der *pratique* eine der schwersten" (Wieland, AA, 4:349).

41. Leventhal misrepresents the true nature of classical rhetoric when he describes this call for a multiple appeal to the soul's representational powers as "a divergence from traditional rhetoric." What Leventhal says about the aesthetic text is also true of classical rhetoric at its finest: "Rather, the aesthetic text must represent beautiful thoughts in such a way as to maximize and enhance all the cognitive faculties in a harmoization of the soul's conflicting powers. Aesthetic persuasion functions not simply to affect the lower sensible forms of cognition, but the playful interaction of all of the soul's representatinal powers" (240). Theorists since Neukrich recognized the need for a toal engagement of the recipient to achieve genuine enjoyment of the text. See, e.g., Herder *Über die neuere deutsche Literatur, 1. Sammlung* (1767).

42. See *Grundriß*, 136, 299, et passim; also Lessing *Laokoon*, LM, 14:431–34, and Rasmussen, "Georg Forsters Stil als gegenständliches Denken und Beschreibung der Dinge" (1985), 20–26 and 42–48. Moreover, Rasmussen's analysis of Georg Forster's essayistic style mirrors the prose ideal as envisioned by Wieland at mid-century.

43. Christoph Martin Wieland, *Werke* (Munich: Hanser, 1966ff.), 3:126. This edition (cited as H) is used because of its ready availability.

44. Johann Jakob Breitinger, Chapter 8: "Von der herzrührenden Schreibart," *Critische Dichtkunst*, 2 Vols., Reprint of the 1740 Edition, ed. Wolfgang Bender (Stuttgart: Metzler, 1966), 2:352–98. The demand for graphic representation that would cause the audience to visualize the argument is typical of rhetoric. See Hinderer, "Kurze Geschichte," 234; cf. Ueding, *Grundriß*, 245–255.

45. See Cassierer's Chapter 3: "Psychology and Epistemology" (93–133); Ueding and Steinbrink, *Grundriß*, 106; Vietta, Chapter 1: "Erkenntnistheorie der Frühaufklärung," 23–42; and Nivelle, 34ff. With his holistic notion of *Vernunft*, Herder later departs from the Thomasian scheme. On Herder's divergent views, see Wulf Koepke, "Herder's Craft of Communication," in *The Philosopher as Writer: The Eighteenth Century*, ed. Robert Ginsberg (Cranbury, NJ: Associated University Presses, 1987), 114ff.

46. J. G. Herder, "Wie die Philosophie zum besten des Volkes allgemeiner und nützlicher werden kann," *Sämmtliche Werke*, 33 vols., ed. B. Suphan (Berlin: Weidmannsche Buchhandlung, 1877–1913), 32:31–61, here 49ff.

47. Herder, "In der Dichtkunst ist Gedanke und Ausdruck wie Seele und Leib und nie zu Trennen," in *Über die neuere deutsche Literatur, Fragmente* (Suphan, 1:394–400).

48. Suphan, 1:395; see Koepke on the notion of wholeness in Herder's concept of literature: "Herder's Craft of Communication," 94–21.

49. Johann Carl Wezel, *Ueber Sprache, Wissenschaften und Geschmack der Teutschen* (Leipzig, 1781), in *Kritische Schriften*, 3 vols., facsimile ed. Albert R. Schmitt (Stuttgart: Metzler, 1971–75), 3:19.

50. Wezel, *Kr. Schr.*, 3:16f: "Wer den rauhen Zusammenstoß der Konsonanten und die Zusammendrängung der kleinen Wörterchen vermeidet; wer seine Worte so wählt und ordnet, daß in jedem Satze, wenn man ihn skandirte, eine Mannichfaltigkeit und Abwechslung von Silbenfüßen, weder lauter hüpfende Daktylen, noch lauter einförmige Iamben, Trochäen oder träge Spondäen enthalten wären; wer diese und ähnliche Regeln beobachtet, der schreibt *melodisch*, wer seine Wörter so wählt und stellt, die Sätze seines Perioden so anordnet, daß bey starken, spielenden, erhabnen, scherzhaften Gedanken, bey rauhen, sanften, düstern, fröhlichen Empfindungen auch die Rede munter und fröhlich dahinhüpft, oder schwer und träge fortschleicht, tändelnd oder feyerlich wird, der schreibt *harmonisch*."

51. Cf. Klopstock, *Gelehrtenrepublik*, 186, where we find a more restrictive definition of *Volk*. Herder had defined the *gemeiner Mann* as *kein Büchergelehrter* (Suphan, 2:29).

52. Christian Garve, "Von der Popularität des Vortrags," *Popularphilosophische Schriften über literarische, ästhetische und gesellschaftliche Gegenstände*, facsimile ed. Kurt Wölfel (Stuttgart: Metzler, 1974), cf. 2:1045, 1049, 1058). Hans-Otto Rößer, *Bürgerliche Vergesellschaftung* (1986), examines Garve's concept of popular style in great detail (184–224), placing it in the context of the Enlightenment's optimistic expectation of universal progress (210). Rößer's analysis contains a running criticism of Garve because he aimed his popular writings at the educated classes who were in fact capable of reading in the fashion Garve envisioned for them. Rößer seems to feel that the broader masses should not have been neglected. My approach takes a decidedly different tact than Rößer's marxist-informed perspective.

53. For a discussion of Schiller's views on the ideal style, see my "Die republikanische Freiheit des Lesers. Zum Lesepublikum von Schillers *Der Verbrecher aus verlorener Ehre*," *Wirkendes Wort* 1 (1979), 28–43, esp. 28–31.

54. W. Iser, "The Reading Process," 56; cf. also *Der Akt des Lesens*, 182f., 20f.

55. Christian Garve, "Über die prosaische Schreibart," *Popularphilosophische Schriften* (Stuttgart: Metzler, 1974), 2:1191f.: "Sein [Engels] eigenthümliches und ein unter uns Deutschen seltnes Talent ist eine Mischung von philosophischem Scharfsinn mit dichterischer Einbildungskraft . . . . Er geht tief in die Natur der Sachen hinein, welche er untersucht; er weiß zugleich

ihre Außenseite sehr anschaulich darzustellen, er weiß ihre unsichtbaren
Eigenschaften durch sehr glücklich gewählte Bilder aufzuhellen. Seine Begriffe sind bestimmt, seine Ideenfolge ordentlich und bündig, die Resultate
seiner Schlüsse neu und überzeugend. Aber die Wendung, welche er seinen
Untersuchungen giebt, ist das Werk der Imagination, seine Erläuterungen
sind dichterisch, sein Styl ist den Sachen ähnlich. Er ist zugleich präcis und
blumenreich, seine Worte sind sehr gut gewählt, sowohl für den Ausdruck
der Sache als für den Wohlklang: seine Perioden sind sehr genau abgerun-
det, aber, wie es scheint, nur durch die vollständigste Entwickelung der
Ideen selbst."

56. Garve, "Über die prosaische Schreibart," 2:1193, 1185. Theodor Mundt
feels that Engel's prose was overrated and rejects him as a shallow thinker
(*Kunst*, 117).

57. Karl Morgenstern, "Plan im Lesen. Rede bey Bekanntmachung der Preisaufgaben für die Studirenden der kaiserlichen Universität zu Dorpat. Gehalten den 12. Dec. 1805," in K. S. Morgenstern, *Johann Müller oder Plan
im Lesen* (n.p., 1808), 69. The copy in the Herzog August Bibliothek in
Wolfenbüttel was used: Signatur:Ac 256.

58. Iser, "The Reading Process," 68; also *Akt des Lesens*, 204f., 210.

59. Given the discursive/dialectical nature of texts for the true Enlighteners
from the beginning to the end of the century, we must reject Leventhal's
basic premise "of the collapse of the Enlightenment view of the written text
as a sign of the spoken discourse" as not wholly justified. Nor, as we have
seen, was the Enlightenment model of interpretation simply "semiotic-
rhetorical and ideational" (246f.).

60. "Eine bedeutende Schrift ist, wie eine bedeutende Rede, nur Folge des Lebens. . . . Man halte diese Bedingungen, unter denen allein ein klassischer
Schriftsteller, besonders ein prosaischer, möglich wird, gegen die Umstände,
unter denen die besten Deutschen dieses Jahrhunderts gearbeitet haben, so
wird, wer klar sieht und billig denkt, dasjenige, was ihnen gelungen ist, mit
Ehrfurcht bewundern und das, was ihnen mißlang, anständig bedauern"
(Goethe, "Literarischer Sansculottismus" (HA, 12:241).

CHAPTER 7

The Dialectic Muse Awakes: Essayistic Writing 1680–1750

Toward a History of Early German Essayism

The history of essayistic writing in the Age of Enlightenment has yet to be written. In the 1950s Klaus Günther Just had planned to write the chronicle of the German essay from its beginnings in Germany. It was to have been descriptive and inclusive of minor as well as major authors. Unfortunately, he was never able to follow through with the project.[1] Ludwig Rohner himself does not present us with a *history* of the writing mode in his expansive study but rather with the indispensible documents—as the subtitle states: *Materials for the History and Aesthetics of a Literary Genre*. While he includes a number of textual analyses by way of illustration of the kinds of essayistic writing, he does not aim at a history of the attitude. It seems almost as if the chameleon-like nature of essayistic writing not only eludes definition, but also thwarts attempts to write its history.

Attempts, however, have been made. There is Bruno Berger's *Der Essay. Form und Geschichte* (1964) which includes forty pages of scant remarks on the development of the mode from Lessing to Ludwig Curtius. He does not offer any real textual analyses. There is also the study by Helmut Rehder with the very promising title "Anfänge des deutschen Essays" ("Beginnings of the German Essay," 1966). Yet like Berger Rehder begins at mid-century, specifically with Friedrich Carl von Moser's *Politische Wahrheiten* (composed 1759–61, published 1796). While he does go beyond Berger by actually analyzing a text in some detail (Moser's *Political Truths*), Rehder by and large also presents us with only a catalogue of names: Thomas Abbt, Johann Georg Zimmermann, Christian Wilhelm Dohm, Albrecht von Haller, Johann Georg Hamann, and others. Like Berger and Rohner, Rehder concludes by stating that much work remains to be done. While Heinrich Küntzel (1969) provides exemplary stylistic analyses, he again addresses the situation in the latter half of the century.

In recent years additional strides have been taken to provide the individual case studies long cited as prerequisite for writing the history of the mode (Rohner, *Essay*, 782). These more recent publications include several dissertations as well as a number of contributions to the *Jahrbuch für internationale Germanistik*.[2] Not all of these studies are devoted to our time frame, and those that are tend to gravitate to a handful of canonical writers: Lessing, Lichtenberg, Goethe, Georg Forster, Friedrich Schlegel, and Wieland. Nevertheless, they advance us toward the ultimate objective of a more encompassing history of essayism. Although Jürgen Jacobs specifically draws attention to the novelty of essayistic writing in his *Prosa des 18. Jahrhunderts* (1976), he does not include it in his analysis of prose from that era. Other new literary histories of the eighteenth century are equally silent on the central question of essayistic writing 1680–1815.[3] Nor does anyone make reference to the role played by women writers in this regard.

Only Vincent J. Dell'Orto clearly recognizes the native roots of the German essay in the period *before* 1750. He examines its origins in the Moral Weeklies, epistolary handbooks, and rhetorical doctrines of the early eighteenth century. The strength of Dell' Orto's "Audience and the Tradition of the German Essay in the 18th Century" (1975) lies in his discussion of three phases of the early essay.[4] The first is associated with Gottsched, the second with Theodor Lebrecht Pitschel, the third with Klopstock. Most convincing are the arguments regarding phases one and two. In addition to Dell' Orto's emphasis on the critical role of audience awareness in the emergence of the essay, a second noteworthy conclusion is that already by 1750 *two* kinds of essayistic writing had evolved: one objective and *sachbezogen*, the other popular and entertaining.[5] In the following we will have occasion to return to these insights.

My purpose in this and the ensuing chapters is to make amends for past omissions. By providing a number of textual readings spanning the years 1680–1815, I hope to accomplish two objectives. First, I wish to illustrate the practice of essayism as determined by a communicative theory of literature in the Age of Critical Thinking. Second, by systematically sampling essayistic prose (essayistic verse must unfortunately be excluded for reasons of space), I hope to contribute to the chronicling of the mode in a more significant manner than has been hitherto achieved. I undertake my task in recognition of the need for "exact linguistic and stylistic analyses" (Haas, *Essay*, 83) as well as in the hope of reconstructing essayistic practice in a specific literary epoch (Berger, 193). Although I profit from previous attempts, I intend to go beyond the mere cataloguing of documents and names, which seems so commonplace in essay research, by exposing the nexus of attitude and form in representative works from Thomasius to Müller. I am guided generally by the view that only the analysis of the mode's constituent epistemological and structural features within a stated historical framework will enable us to assess accurately its uniqueness as a morphologically separate manner of aesthetic expression.[6]

While I do not wish to discount the significance of leading intellectual lights of the age (e.g., Shaftesbury, Bayle, Gottsched) nor to make light of Warren and Wellek's recognition that "books are influenced by books," I prefer to highlight the questioning attitude of the age inherent in those thinkers and books.[7] Consequently, I will continue the emphasis of the foregoing sections of this inquiry by concentrating on the nature of essayistic writing as a bridge uniting science and poetry, function and form.

Because of the overwhelming richness of material, my purpose cannot be to present a full-fledged history of the practice of essayistic writing in eighteenth-century Germany and Austria. An attempt to describe the history of essayistic writing for even a limited time frame would produce a thick tome. Thus I will have to be more modest in my aspirations here. I must be selective, and my selections will not meet with everyone's approval. My diachronic approach must be augmented by a synchronic one which would illuminate essayistic activity decade by decade. Also many more case studies of individual authors are necessary before the complete history of essayism in the eighteenth century can be written. Definite desiderata here include: J. J. Bodmer, G. W. Rabener, J. H. Merck, Fr. J. Riedel, J. G. Herder, J. von Sonnenfels, K. Ph. Moritz, Sophie La Roche, Jean Paul, Elisa von der Recke, J. C. Wezel, Chn. Garve, and J. G. Fichte as essayists.

Whose Influence? The French and English Connections

It has become traditional in studies of the essay to recount in some detail its development in France and England as a preparation to a focussed discussion of the German situation since the German mode is part and parcel of the European tradition. Moreover, it is assumed that the German tradition owes its existence to the French and English ones (cf. most recently Wardell, 132–201).

It is customary to date the beginnings of the German essay from around 1750. Although note is taken of Montaigne's indirect influence via England on Germany, no one seems really interested in tracing the mode's roots back further than mid-century. The reason seems to be the researcher's preoccupation with the key-figure theory in essay research. The premise of that school is that we must identify direct lines of influence from one writer to another. The important question for that school is whether Bacon or Montaigne is the key figure. And since they are so different in style how can they both be considered fathers of the essay? Is one to be judged more genuine than the other?

Exemplary of this stance is Rohner who places the beginning of conscious essayistic writing in the second half of the eighteenth century. He states that "it was the eighteenth century which discovered Montaigne again, and paradoxically in English guise" (*Essay*, 69). Oddly enough Montaigne's direct stylistic influence was not felt until the late nineteenth century, although the first German translation of the *Essais* was published by Johann Daniel Titius (Tietz) in 1753 as *Michaels Herrn von Montaigne Versuche* and a second translation by Johann Joachim Christoph Bode appeared 1793–1797 as *Michel de Montaignes Gedanken und Meinungen über allerley Gegenstände* (*Essay*, 70, 77). Apparently, even Montaigne's *indirect* influence was not critical for the rise of essayism in the eighteenth century, for Rohner speaks of "essays avant la lettre" in his anthology (*DE*, 1:84). The combination of English and French in the title is designed to underscore the double origins of the genre. The implication is that the practice of the essay occurred in Germany and was valued aesthetically by the reading public before writers theorized about the concept —or before Montaigne (and Bacon?) could influence them directly. The practice of essayistic writing thus preceded its theory and the clear impact of its presumed kingpin models by approximately fifty years. There seems to be little reason to recount the history of key-figure influence here, if the mode could evolve without their direct influence. Furthermore, we shall see that Montaigne and Bacon were only two of a number of ancient and modern models for the new attitude.

Of interest in our connection is also the implied opposition between the subjective and sober styles of the two modern originators of essayistic writing, Montaigne and Bacon. That divergence can be explained away without much difficulty. The two essayists actually complement one another. The holistic approach of the European Enlightenment to the human condition easily accounts for their commonality. A hallmark of Enlightenment anthropology is the newly (re-)emerged consciousness of the individual either as man reflecting or man acting. "Reflective man" began to examine his/her relationship to society and the universe in a new light. When the emphasis is cosmological, the tone of essayism is more detached or philosophical. When, on the other hand, the social or personal context is foregrounded, the tone becomes more immediate and vibrant. Emerson's "Man Thinking" characterizes the first situation, finding expression in German works such as Schiller's "Die philosophischen Briefe" ("Philosophical Letters," 1786). The second instance could be described as "Man Acting" or "Social Man." That stance characterizes Emilia von Berlepsch's "Über einige dem Glück der Ehe nothwendige Eigenschaften und Grundsätze" ("On Some Character Traits and Principles Indispensible to Marital Contentment," 1791). Both the philosophically detached and the personally involved attitude could be considered phenomena of the Copernican era.[8]

Furthermore, the stylistic tendency toward the objective or subjective pole can be explained in terms of the relative absence or superabundance of rhetorical technique. Of course both Bacon and Montaigne were heavily indebted to classical rhetoric (witness their stylistic models: Socrates, Cicero, Quintilian). With the desire of enlightened writers to convey their ideal of the polished, self-assured cosmopolite (= *galant homme*) to an ever widening public, their use of rhetorical techniques increased. The strategies and the substance for these writers were practically one and the same. Neither Bacon nor Montaigne served the advocates of the gallant attitude or of the rhetorical middle style as a dominant model.

Within the context of the theoretical thrust of *Crossing Boundaries*, it makes more sense to acknowledge the *general* influence of basic tenets of pan-European Enlightenment thinking than to fix on *direct* lines of supposed generic influence from Montaigne and Bacon or any other single model (e.g., Shaftesbury, Swift, Bayle, or Montesquieu). The indirect intellectual paths are of greater interest to me because of their pan-European nature. We can accept the clear crisscrossing of ideas between England and the continent as fact and leave it at that.

Breaking with Tradition

Christian Thomasius

As a popularizer of Enlightenment views in the late seventeenth century, Christian Thomasius (1655–1728) certainly broke with tradition. Although the myth about his being the first professor to lecture in his native German at the University of Leipzig is untenable, we cannot deny that he was most instrumental in ushering in a new style of lecturing in the sacrosanct Latin halls of higher learning. While his philosophical tracts, *Ausübung der Vernunft-Lehre (Practice of a Theory of Reason,* 1691) and *Ausübung der Sittenlehre (Practice of Theory of Ethics,* 1696), attest to his interest in practical philosophy, his lectures such as *Kurtzer Entwurff der Politischen Klugheit sich selbst und andern . . . wohl zu rathen . . . (A Brief Sketch of Political Sophistication,* 1710) and journalistic pieces in the *Monats-Gespräche (Monthly Conversations,* 1687–88) give evidence of his desire to reach out to a large anonymous public, one not limited to the university-trained. Thomasius is, in fact, credited with having taken large strides in the creation of a new, enlightened reading public in the first half of the eighteenth century.

All of these efforts are of interest to us in tracing the origins of essayistic writing in Germany. Thomasius's celebrated lecture of 1687 on the imitation of the French, "Discourse on the Manner in which One Should Imitate the French in Every-Day Life: A Course on Gracian's Doctrine of How to Live Sensibly, Wisely, and Gracefully" (*Christian Thomasius eröffnet der Studirenden Jugend zu Leipzig in einem Discours Welcher Gestalt man denen Frantzosen in gemeinem Leben und Wandel nachahmen solle? Ein Collegium über des Gratians Grund-Reguln/Vernünfftig/ klug und artig zu leben*) can serve us well as an example not only of the professor's manner of thinking but also of his innovative style of writing.

The long, descriptive title—so typical of the Baroque era—does not at first appear to offer hope of originality. Nor are we predisposed to perceive in his lecture essayistic traits reminiscent of Montaigne or Bacon when we discover that neither is mentioned in the 36-page article while scores of other French, English, Greek, and Roman writers are introduced. Finally, his concluding remark that "a modest man . . . should not speak of himself at all, especially in published papers" seems unfavorable to a confessional style in Montaigne's manner.[9] At the same time the length of Thomasius's lecture clearly separates it from Bacon's pithy, aphoristic writings.

Yet the topic—the art of living—is dear to the heart of all essayists in the wake of Montaigne and Bacon. More importantly the style is marked by a surprisingly light touch, lively movement, and ironic twists little evident in the prose production of the seventeenth century, except perhaps in the narrative fiction of Johann Jacob Christoph von Grimmelshausen (1621–1676) and Johann Beer (1655–1700). The alteration in tone evident in "On the Imitation of the French" is all the more amazing since it echoed in the halls of hallowed academe, an institution that took itself even more seriously then than now.

Thomasius's broad, far-ranging topic is in essence a critique of the deplorable state of education in Germany. His point of departure is maxim # 67 from the Spanish moral philosopher Baltasar Gracian's (1601–1658) *Arte de prudencia* (1647) in the French translation of Nico-las Amelot de la Houssaie (1634–1706). The maxim succinctly states the need for the harmonious interaction of rhetorical, historical, and philo-sophical techniques in formulating the most felicitous expression of ideas best designed to engage the listener. Close examination of his tract reveals that Thomasius adeptly followed the maxim. Throughout his treatment Thomasius tests his ideas against Dominique Bouhours's (1628–1702) ideal of the *honnête homme*, widely subscribed to at the time. The lecture, which Thomasius grants has grown longer than he anticipated (36), is neatly divided into five subdivisions: a lively introduction (5–7), a defi-nition of terms (7-12), a protracted discussion of the central concept of *honnête homme* (12–31), an examination of *le bon goût* (31–33), and the conclusion (33–36). Throughout he gravitates to the reasons for educa-tional reform and how that reform can best be achieved.

Thomasius begins by painting a disparaging picture of the pedantic state of learning and of the foppish, indiscriminate imitation of things foreign. He follows up that dreary portrait with innovative suggestions for change. These recommendations include a proper understanding of what the French ideal of the *honnête homme* really is, what a true scholar should be, what role the vernacular must play in the cultural elevation of the Germans, why women have a right to study at the universities, why they are actually more educable than men, and how prejudice can be overcome through the cultivation of critical thinking. In sum he defines genuine imitation of the French as emulation of *honnêteté, Gelehr-samkeit, beauté d'esprit, un bon goût* and *galanterie*. When all of these qualities come together in one person "un parfait homme Sage oder ein vollkommener weiser Mann" is made possible (33). Thomasius obviously addresses himself to very important cultural questions of the day (they continue to persist in the twentieth century), so that we can easily classify Thomasius's essay under Just's second category, the culturally investiga-tive essay. According to Just, that type focuses on humankind as creative subject in a broadly cultural context, and historical facts figure domi-nantly in the argument. But as noted earlier, the content is not decisive in the essayistic mode, while the art of presentation is. We will concentrate on the stylistic qualities here as a reflection of Thomasius's attitude to-ward his audience and subject matter.

"On the Imitation of the French" was presented as a lecture. As was the custom, the lecture was also published. This practice is reflected in the text itself when Thomasius casually explains that it is appropriate for his quill to pause in its writing (33). Since the text is a university lecture, we would expect it to abound in scholarly allusions. And we are not disappointed. Scholarly erudition is everywhere evident in the allusions to writers of Greek and Roman antiquity, European Renaissance personalities, and contemporary seventeenth-century continental and English scholars. We would require a small catalogue to list all the persons cited. On the other hand, Thomasius was instrumental in reintroducing rhetoric to the University of Leipzig. Thus we would expect the treatise to bear the marks of rhetorical technique and oral presentation as well. Again we are not disappointed.

The opening sentence evokes an image of ancestral Germans returning to "modern" seventeenth-century Germany being shocked at the changes in German society wrought by blind imitation of all things French from the noble to the mundane. Although the opening sentence runs for twelve and one half lines, it is clear and forceful. Subdivided by semicolons into two major, distinctly delineated segments, the sentence is immediately comprehensible. The first part of the sentence is straightforward, almost professorial, while the second part introduces an appealing touch of ironic humor. The first portion of the sentence reads: "Es ist kein Zweifel, und schon von vielen angemercket worden, daß wenn unsere Vorfahren die alten Teutschen anitzo auferstehen und in Teutschland kommen solten, ihnen im geringsten nicht düncken würde, daß sie in ihren Vaterlande und bey ihren Landsleuten wären, sondern sie würden sich vielmehr einbilden, daß sie in einem frembden Lande bey unbekanten und gantz andern Menschen sich aufhielten."[10] The use of the subjunctive form forces the listener/reader to imagine the contrary-to-fact situation along with the speaker/author. Some if not many persons in the academic audience surely recalled the topos of returning ancestors as being a favorite among sixteenth-century humanists, such as Johannes Fischart. In any event the device has the effect of drawing the listener immediately into the text who is now attentive to the criticism levelled at the pervasive French influence.

In the next, pithier sentence Thomasius details the areas of life affected by the French mania: clothing fashion, cuisine, household goods, language, and customs. The list takes an unexpectedly humorous twist at the end with the addition of two additional phenomena resultant of the rage for things French: "French sins" (sodomy) and "French disease" (syphilis). The shift in focus from the normal cultural areas to those of morality and health is a well prepared surprise for the listener/reader. By implying the spiritual and corporeal ill side-effects of the wanton imitation of the neighbors to the west, Thomasius realizes the greatest effect of his sharp criticism which he later clearly formulates as: "Eine Nachahmung ist allezeit lobenswürdig, wenn die Sache selbst nichts scheltwürdiges an sich hat" (Imitation is always laudable when the thing imitated is not reproachable, 5).

The note of irony soon turns to sarcasm as Thomasius imagines the further reaction of the German forefathers who would reject present-day Germans as "unechte Kinder, Bastardte" (illegitimate children, bastards) and "weibische Memmen" (effeminate cowards) worthy perhaps of a severe scolding or scornful laughter but certainly not of praise (3f.). The entire first page of the lecture is a wonderful example of the classic *exordium*. The ensuing pages offer a learned critique of the oft-repeated criticism of the phenomenon, and the implications of the opening sentence are repeated in their explicit historical context. In doing so he draws upon the arsenal of rhetorical technique of which he proves himself a master: allusions to historical events, evocation of authority figures, rhetorical questions, personal appeals, graphic language, examples drawn from daily life, metaphors, similes, tropes, prolepses, and litotes. A fine example of Thomasius's light touch is the following series of rhetorical questions (a favored, recurring technique) which is enlivened by his ironic use of French words in playful mockery of the dominant fashion in the Academy, at court, and in the burgher salon:

> Denn wie kommts doch, daß wan von uns Teutschen iemand in Franckreich reiset, ohnerachtet er *propre* gekleidet ist, und sehr geschickt von einen Franztzösischen Braten oder *fricassée raisoniren* kan, auch *perfect parliret* und seinen Reverentz so gut als ein liebhafftiger Frantzoß zumachen weiß, er dennoch gemeiniglich als ein einfältiges Schaff ausgelachet wird, da hingegen die Frantzosen, so zu uns herausser kommen durchgehends Liebe und Verwunderung an sich ziehen?[11]

Thomasius's use of French here is clearly parodic; it is not primarily attributable to the fashionable, affected mixing of languages typical of the period. (The text abounds with other examples of this strategy.)

Also typical of the style is the frequent occurrence of metaphor which is used with great effect. For example, in arguing for equal opportunities for women in higher education, he uses the metaphor of the writing tablet to illustrate the resiliency of the human mind. The more a writing tablet has been used, the less distinct are the new letters because the old ones leave residual shapes in the background. New tablets absorb the chalk more readily because their pores are not cluttered with the dust of past scribblings. Imagine, he urges his listeners, how difficult it is to erase writing of long-standing and how nigh impossible it is to eradicate inscriptions on skins of asses, i.e., on dim-witted individuals. In the original the passage has a quiet brilliance: "Eine neue Schreibetaffel nimmet das jenige so man drauff schreibet gar leicht an: wenn aber eine Schrifft eine geraume Zeit darauff stehen blieben, wie schwer gehet es doch zu, wenn man hernach das erste auswischen will? ist dann das erste gar auff eine Eselshaut geschrieben worden, so wische man wie man wil es werden die alten Buchstaben oder Zahlen noch allezeit herfür gucken."[12] In other words, Thomasius argues that women can learn more easily because they have not been corrupted by the old academic ways he wishes to replace. His new method of learning would stress critical reflection as a means to understanding, not rote memorization and mechanical repetition. Whether in writing or in conversation, the truly educated individual will have mastered the rules of sound reasoning, clarity of organization, good judgment, and lively presentation (22f.).

Because of the rhetorical variations used to perk up his argument, the lecture does not seem long. Again and again the audience is drawn into the deliberations in a communicative manner and is invited to consider the appropriateness of the criticisms levelled as well as the recommendations proffered. One example will have to stand for many.

Drawing near his conclusion, Thomasius illustrates the foibles of false gallantry in graphic fashion. He puts together a string of rhetorical questions, using commonplace examples and lightly humorous diction. Having delineated the benefits of educational reform and use of the vernacular for raising the cultural level of the nation, he returns to the reality of student social life. The contrast of the mundane reality with the noble aspirations for a new Germany is striking. Thomasius asks:

> Was gehen nun da für *galanterien* vor? Wie zutrampelt man sich vor dem Fenster, ob man die Ehre haben könne, die Jungfer, oder doch an deren statt die Magd oder die Katze zu grüssen? Wie viel verliebte Briefe, die man aus zehen *Romans* zusammen gesuchet hat, und die mit vielen flammenden und mit Pfeilen durchschossenen Hertzen bemahlet sind, werden da abgeschicket, gleich als ob man des guten Kindes *affection* damit *bombardiren* wolte? Wie lässet man sichs sauer werden, eine *galante* Nacht-Music zu bringen? Wie spielet man mit denen verliebten Minen überall, auch wohl in dem GOTTES-Hause?[13]

The image of an unruly band of lovelorn youths storming the citadel of love with bad music and paper missiles inscribed with borrowed phrases and clichéd icons captures the reader's imagination. The regression from refined *Jungfer* to uncouth *Magd,* and finally to the ridiculous *Katze* exemplifies in salient fashion the inanity and foolishness of the galant fad which shows no respect even before the sacred altar of the Divine. The words with the most effect are: *zutrampeln, Katze, bombardiren, sauer werden,* and *Minen.* Each in its own way captures the vacuousness of the German manner of emulation so that we are reminded of earlier French characterizations of the German people as inept with their "coarse temperaments and massive bodies" (28). Coming at the close of his conjectures, the negative image seems designed to incite continuing audience response long after the text has ended.

Thomasius's inaugural lecture of 1687, therefore, would seem to be an auspicious beginning to a German tradition of essayistic writing. However, it would not be accurate to claim solely endemic roots for the mode, for Thomasius is clearly inspired by the Spanish skeptic Gracian, the French moralists (Bouhours, Malebranche, Scudéry, Bayle), and ancient thinkers (Lucian and Epictetus). He not only lists them in the body of his text, he exhorts his students to cultivate their understanding and sentiment by reading the works of the *autorum classicorum.* Clearly, books influence books.

Gottfried Wilhelm Leibniz

The importance of Gottfried Wilhelm Leibniz (1646–1716) for the German Enlightenment is well known. His main contribution to the *Aufklärung* lies in his advancement beyond Cartesian logic. Substituting a pluralistic universe for Descartes's dualism, he stressed the concept of becoming. Ernst Cassirer calls this change an extension of Cartesian thinking: "the logic of 'origin' and . . . the logic of individuality" which "leads from mere geometry to a dynamic philosophy of nature, from mechanism to organism" (Cassirer, *Philosophy,* 35f.). He was also a catalyst for a rethinking of aesthetic theory by such disciples as Christian Wolff, Johann Christian Gottsched, and Alexander Baumgarten. The dynamism of Leibniz's intellectual views no doubt favored an essayistic mode of writing.

Of the philosopher's numerous shorter writings, I have selected his epistle of 1683 entitled "Ermahnung an die Teutschen, ihren Verstand und Sprache besser zu üben, samt beigefügten Vorschlag einer teutschgesinnten Gesellschaft" ("A Call to the Germans to Make Better Use of their Reason and Language, Together with a Proposal for a Pro-German Society").[14] The "Ermahnung" and its companion piece "Unvorgreifliche Gedanken" (c. 1709) have been identified as representing a clear break with the stylistic concepts of the Baroque era. Although it was not published until 1846, the "Ermahnung" is to be analyzed here rather than the more widely known "Provisional Conjectures" (published by Gottsched in 1717) because it is the earlier form of the piece and is more detailed.[15] Like Thomasius's "Discours Welcher Gestalt man denen Frantzosen in gemeinem Leben und Wandel nachahmen solle," Leibniz's epistle raises cultural and literary questions.

In twenty-one pages Leibniz presents an appeal to his countrymen to upgrade their langauge which was considered far inferior to that of the English, French, and Italian (69). This argument is presented in two principal parts with a clear demarcation between the two stages of reasoning and the clearly formulated, concluding summation of the proposal's intent. Generally speaking, the first part of the argument (60–68) presents a positive view of the German situation, while the second (68–79) takes a more critically negative look at the same conditions. The first part culminates in a utopian vision of a highly civilized Germany (67f.), the second with the proposal to found a "Teutschgesinnte Genossenschaft" whose purpose would be to further the ideal of an enlightened Germany (80). Despite this clear organization the argument is not presented in a straightforward, strictly syllogistic manner. The markers for the division are all internal with no external signs to guide the reader through the train of thought. The length, topic, and style mark "Ermahnung an die Teutsche" as a representative example of a progressive form of writing around 1700. While Thomasius's lecture might be aligned with informal essayistic writing, Leibniz's epistle tends more to the formal. Like Thomasius's work, nonetheless, this one can be classified as a culturally critical essay.

Leibniz begins by conjuring up a thoroughly positive image of the Holy Roman Empire of the German Nation with depictions of its wealth and superfluity throughout all the social classes. Nowhere are natural resources more abundant, the aristocracy more competent, the numerous free city-states more prosperous, or freedom more prevalent than in the empire. Even the peasantry is better off with excellent prospects for future improvement (61–64). These images of prosperity and growth potential are designed to arouse the reader's sense of patriotism to which Leibniz had appealed in his opening paragraph (*exordium*). The Germans' national and cultural identity is derived above all from their common customs and language (60). Leibniz concludes from his detailing of Germany's blessings that the Germans' happiness and contentment as outlined in his utopian vision is dependent solely on the individual's will to be happy and content. All the prerequisites are present. The time for reform is now.

Obviously, the reader expects to learn what Leibniz's suggestions are, but is held off in two ways. First the author raises the reader's sense of expectation through a series of prolepses which rule out all forms of official state action—improved communications network, establishing a fixed constitution, common coinage, promotion of commercial centers, introduction of a unified legal code—as means of translating the imagined utopian state into reality. Then he asks rhetorically, what's left? What other action could be taken? And he immediately responds: nothing, that is, if all of the above political problems had truly been resolved. Instead of introducing his proposal at this point, Leibniz begs the question.

Drawing back from the main point, he employs the essayistic strategy of weighing the different possibilities and rejecting each one by turn (the rhetorical technique of anticipating counterarguments or prolepsis): "One might think that a reform of the schools and the universities was being considered but no, that is not the purpose" (66). Next Leibniz introduces a diversion by way of heightening the suspense; he speaks of the audience he wishes to cultivate, an audience which is new and not comprised of scholars or politicians. His intended reader is the generally educated citizen regardless of social rank. In this Leibniz parallels Thomasius. The difference between the educated class and the common man is drawn in vivid terms.

Leibniz uses easily intelligible diction and similes with a delightful touch of irony (= litotes) to explain the difference between these two groups. For instance the common people are characterized as "dummes Volk ohne Erregung und Feuer" (a dumb people without spirit or fire). They delight in slandering their neighbors and amuse themselves with "bestial drunkenness or mischievous card playing." They think only of eating, live only for each day, and are as nimble as cattle. Historical accounts are the same to them as fairy tales; descriptions of other countries and customs mean nothing to them. Furthermore, they are so ignorant of religious matters that they are as capable of appreciating a magnificent concert as is a person born deaf.

By contrast the educated classes are freer in their movements and outlook, an attitude reflected by their choice of reading matter. They are inquisitive of mind, sociable in manner, and noble in spirit. Because they are far-sighted they have a greater understanding of the difficulties encountered by the government and are therefore more useful to the state.

In everything s/he does, the generally educated person reveals more sensibility and good sense than the average individual. Leibniz concludes the first part of his argument with the assertion: "The more citizens of this type in a country, the more that nation is polished and civilized; consequently all citizens will be happier and more resolute" (67f.). But even this statement is not the proposal the reader has been led to expect. In ironic fashion Leibniz instead assesses the consequences of the as yet unstated proposal. By means of this strategy the reader's level of curiosity is raised yet another notch. All of these elements are essayistic traits but nurtured by rhetoric.

The axis of the two-part treatise finally formulates Leibniz's reform suggestion: the establishment of a Pro-German Society (*Teutschgesinnte Gesellschaft*). It is only by means of such a society that the goals outlined in the first part of the essay can be achieved (68). The first step is to create and enlarge the new cultural group referred to as the *Gebildeten*.

The focus of part two shifts to the function of language in this reform effort, for it is through language than we learn refined thinking (68). Language is ultimately viewed as an "interpreter of the human spirit and as a guardian of science" (80). As such it mirrors a person's level of understanding and eloquence. Before formulating that concluding statement, however, Leibniz first addresses himself to questions also raised by Thomasius: his countrymen's cultural backwardness, the stilted and obtuse quality of German writing, the lack of felicitous translations, blind imitation of foreign models, and lack of true understanding (71ff.)

In the second part of his presentation, Leibniz has greater recourse to rhetorical strategies than in the first. We find the full range of such tactics from the use of simple examples and proverbs to paradox, prolepsis, and hendiadys. Their effect is to produce a more forceful and graphic presentation. Thus the philosopher speaks of German books as uninspired and lifeless (*ohne Kraft noch Leben, ohne Schmack oder Saft,* 68). Or he refers to them metaphorically as worthless chaff (*Eicheln, Spreu und Kleye*) which has been substituted for finely winnowed wheat (*wohl gesichtete Weizen,* 68). Even the most common reader could understand the agrarian images.

Leibniz expands the metaphor to include plant and garden motifs. The world of German writing is depicted as a garden bed in which all kinds of plants (flowers, fruit, and herbs) must grow side by side so that overall prosperity will be assured: "Our German garden dare not contain only exquisite lilies and roses; it must also include sweet apples and healthful herbs. The former quickly lose their beauty and pleasant scent, the latter prove much more useful" (72). An allusion to the *Fruchtbringende Ge-*

sellschaft (1617–1680), a society founded for the promotion of the German language and its literature, serves to equate poetry to flowers and scholarly writing to fruit-bearing plants. The name of the society, Leibniz contends, was a misnomer for it did not produce fruit. Rather it brought forth only tender blossoms that die quickly if not nourished with the powerful nutrients of immortal art and science.

The advantages of a refined mother tongue—insightful thinking, mature judgment, and fine sensitivity (as was the case in France or England) did not filter down to the generally educated in Germany because German scholars were slavishly attached to Latin and a non-German way of thinking (71). The German spirit needed to be liberated, and use of the vernacular was the way to do it. At the turn from the seventeenth to the eighteenth century, the German vernacular was limited to belles-lettres. Consequently, authors had experience in writing poetic German, but none in a more popular vein designed to instruct as well as to entertain. The tide of incompetent writing had risen so high that the beneficial influence of belles-lettres was no longer sufficient to stem it. Much more vigorous writing was called for (*ander Zeug von mehr Gewicht und Nachdruck*). To stress his point Leibniz uses striking, salient similes.

Just as a strong arm cannot toss a feather as far as a stone, neither can the sharpest intellect achieve as much with literature which is designed only to amuse (71). A new kind of writing is required which combines intellectual profit with aesthetic pleasure. The nucleus of such writing is composed of weightier matter, something for the intellect as well as for the senses. This hybrid style is more effective than either erudite or literary prose alone. Profound substance must be paired with poetic lightness. Leibniz writes: "Muß also der Nutzen mit der Annehmlichkeit vereiniget werden gleichwie ein Bolzen, so von einem stählinen Armbrust in die Ferne getrieben werden soll, sowohl mit Federn versehen, als mit Metall gekrönet zu sein pfleget" ("Utility must be paired, therefore, with pleasantness just as an arrow must be equipped with feathers and crowned with a metal tip if it is to be shot from a crossbow over a great distance through the air") (71). The feathers at the end of the arrow stand metaphorically for the light touch of poetry, while the heavy metal tip represents the weightier substance of scientific studies. The allusion to weapons suggests the need for forceful liberation from the bonds of linguistic and cultural slavery perpetuated by stuffy academicians. Only by cultivating German as the language of science and learning can the German people hope to close the cultural gap between themselves and their neighbors.

Leibniz is quick to grant that his proposed language reform might appear a futile effort to some people. Would it not be better to let oneself go, to swim with the current (72)? This occurrence of prolepsis is followed rapidly by a second one protracted over the next few pages which anticipates yet another possible objection, namely, that French evolved from a mixture of Old French and Latin. Why could German not evolve in similar fashion? There is evidence of German writers who quite effectively employ foreign expressions in their works. Is it necessary to ban all foreign phrases? Leibniz responds to the first objection by drawing an analogy to a dam constructed to stem the tide of a ponderous writing style. The problem lies not in the reform effort itself but in the quality of the materials used to build the "dam": the sand, the stone, the earth (72). His proposed reform project would be constructed of firmer stuff. Leibniz's response to the second objection is that negligence and laziness are no excuse for not practicing a polished German style purified of extraneous elements. Appropriate German terms could be found for the foreign ones, while preserving the sense of refinement.

Interspersed in these two prolepses are personal appeals to the reader to reject obtusely macaronic style and barbaric customs (73). Moreover, Leibniz's case is strengthened by personal anecdotes (73, 75) as well as by contrasting the apparent decline of German culture into chaos with the dawning of a new age of enlightened harmony everywhere else (73). Examples of excellent writing composed by non-scholars in a universally intelligible and appealing style are cited from history (76f.) to show that the reform effort would not be in vain. History moves in cycles; the signs of enlightenment elsewhere indicate that the twisted state of German customs can also be reversed. The style of those historical documents are held up as models for imitation, for they reveal (1) an elegance of diction, (2) clear reasoning, (3) inventive conceits, (4) precise formulations, (5) natural integration of the parts, and (6) a sense of harmonious unity.

The traits cited here by Leibniz as worthy of imitation evolved in a most natural manner as a kind of dialogue between author and reader. They are free of all patent artifice and are fully commensurate with the classical method of the literary essayism which Ludwig Rohner characterizes as "tranquil, graceful, conciliatory, and familiar" in tone (*Essay*, 307). In a sense Leibniz enumerated those qualities which set his own dialogic discourse apart from the usual sedate fare. A careful reading of Leibniz's essay reveals that the philosopher is not interested in presenting us with the results of his cogitation. He is more concerned with leading us through the thought processes themselves so that we might become fully convinced of his conclusions, yes, so that his conclusions might become our conclusions. If we were seeking a description of the early German essayistic style, we could stop right here. We can consider Leibniz's "Ermahnung an die Teutsche" both as an early example of essayistic writing and as an early theory of essayistic style in general. Leibniz comes pretty close to Friedrich Schlegel's famous ruling at the end of the eighteenth century: "We should write an essay as if we were just thinking a thought through for the first time, writing just for ourselves, speaking freely on a topic, or composing a letter—in each case focusing on a moral topic out of pure interest without philosophic or poetic intent."[16] While Leibniz does not think of essayism in terms of a genre, he does specify key traits of essayistic writing, he does envisage the critical role of audience awareness for the reading act, and he does recognize the need for an author to wax enthusiastic about the topic (for example, Leibniz writes that he has argued his point "not without emotion"; 79).

At a decisive point in his argument, Leibniz contends that German scholars were largely unsuccessful in their writing because they wrote only for one another. If they were to take aim at the generally educated reader, at the courtier, and at women, as authors in France and Italy do, they would also learn to write in a lighter vein (70). The repeated designation of language as "a true mirror of the mind" (*ein rechter Spiegel des Verstandes*) is an implicit reference to the interrelationship of audience and style (cf. 73, 76). Both the new audience and innovative language are marked by reasonableness and elegance.

The proximity of Leibniz's "Ermahnung an die Teutsche" to essayistic writing is evident. It partakes of the provocative, avant-garde tendencies of the essay and is, like that mode, a dialectic hybrid of scientific tract and artistic *tour de force*. Cognizant of his audience, Leibniz the essayist approached his task in a non-philosophical, that is, non-syllogistic manner. His writing is gauged to lead the reader on a dynamic journey of encirclements which, while revealing the ambiguity of the situation at hand, suggests possible solutions. Neither aphoristic nor effusive, neither pedantic nor flowery, Leibniz's engaging prose composition foreshadows Friedrich Schlegel's ideal essay: "The essay is a mutual galvanism of author and reader; it is, moreover, an inner charging of each one alone, that is, a systematic alternation between paralysis and palpitation. The essay should bring about movement, it should combat intellectual arthritis and promote nimbleness."[17]

Reaching Out

Johann Christoph Gottsched

The efforts of Thomasius and Leibniz to promote a new, clear and engaging manner of writing while advancing the goals of the Enlightenment found staunch support among the mostly anonymous composers and publishers of Moral Weeklies in Germany beginning with Bodmer's and Breitinger's *Diskurse der Malern* (1721–23) and continuing well into the second half of the century. The broad impact of the Weeklies was a critical factor in the emergence of German as a literary language, directly through practice in writing mellifluous prose and indirectly by preparing the reading public for the more literary fare of other journalistic endeavors such as *Belustigungen des Verstandes und Witzes* (1741–45), *Bremer Beiträge* (1744–57), *Briefe, die neueste Literatur betreffend* (1759–65), and *Der teutsche Merkur* (1773–1810). The pages of these journals contained the work of the promising literary talent of the era. Some of these writers passed on to posterity, most are now scarcely known. Among those writers are numbered K. Chrn. Gärtner, Gellert, Hagedorn, Klopstock, Lessing, Mendelssohn, Pitschel, Rabener, J. E. Schlegel, Wieland and Zachariae. We can deal with only a few here.

This situation is described by no less a personage than Goethe himself who commented in his autobiographical *Dichtung und Wahrheit* on the great strides made in journalistic style by mid-century. He speaks of the overcoming of Germany's literary vacuous age (*wäßrige, weitschweifige, nulle Epoche*) through the emergence of a new kind of non-fictional writing which wrought a revolutionary change in the quality of literature.[18] Critical elements of that new prose style are the salutary qualities of "firmness, precision, and pithiness" noted elsewhere. Important in our context is the fact that Goethe is less interested in belletristic writers than he is in non-fictional ones, such as philosophers, theologians, preachers, government officials, and lawyers. Noting that a pleasing style of writing was fast becoming a necessity by the 1760s, Goethe claims that writers appeared from all quarters, "who endeavored to write about their studies and professions for the expert as well as the layman in a clear, intelligible, and penetrating fashion" (Goethe, HA, 9:276). That revolution was the result of the earlier efforts of the Moral Weeklies.

Gottsched (1700–1766) is one of the most celebrated Enlighteners from the first half of the century and one of its most effective journalists. Much maligned as a pontifical pedant by Lessing and the Storm and Stress generation, Gottsched's importance for literary life in the eighteenth century went long unacknowledged. He deserves wide recognition for his translations, his contributions to the theory of literature, his reform of the theater, and his radical revamping of the traditional stage repertoire. Increasing attention is now being paid to the positive effect of his many-sided reform efforts, not the least of which were his translations and journalistic activities in the 1720s. Of greatest significance for our present purposes are his prose contributions to his two journals *Die vernünftigen Tadlerinnen* (1725–27) and *Der Biedermann* (1727–29), which he published in imitation of Addison's and Steele's *The Tatler* (1709–11), *The Spectator* (1711–12), and *The Guardian* (1713).

Moreover, as a disciple of Thomasius and Christian Wolff (1679–1754), he applied their principles of clear and critical thinking to the making of literature, finding in those principles the ultimate justification for belles-lettres. Such was the motivation behind his translations of Bernhard le Bovier de Fontenelle's (1657–1757) *Dialogues des Morts* (1683; German transl. 1727) and Pierre Bayle's (1647–1706) *Dictionnaire historique et critique* (1695–97; German transl. 1741). In threefold manner, therefore, Gottsched served as a harbinger of the new ideas and styles to the Holy Roman Empire of the German Nation lauded by Goethe. He is truly a pivotal figure in the rise of the German's cultural identity. The search for a national identity was still being advocated by the likes of Adam Müller in the early nineteenth century.

Vincent J. Dell' Orto cites Gottsched as an example of the early essayists who were constrained to reach out to an anonymous reading public, referring to his articles in *Der Biedermann* as essays *in nuce*. Whoever is schooled in classical rhetoric will immediately note its centrality to Gottsched's mode of popular writing in his journals, be it in his claim that one best conquers an adversary with *Gelindigkeit* and deference than through a brutal frontal attack or in his judgment "that an orator and poet, in order to be able to write well, must first strengthen his understanding and his will through an acquaintance with psychology and morality."[19] In the first instance Gottsched's reference point is Thomasius, in the second it is Wolff. As examples of the new kind of writing seasoned with reason and ethics, Gottsched also refers his reader to Cicero, Quintilian, Horace, Persius, St. Evremond, and Montaigne. The literary potentate himself gives samples of this kind of prose writing, even as he delivered models for tragedy and comedy. In *Der Biedermann*, of course, his purpose was to transmit enlightened, yet devout thoughts on the individual's relationship to God, society, and nature. These musings were presented, as Wolfgang Martens has noted, "unsystematically, under different guises, and on various occasions."[20] Let us analyze the untitled piece published as # 74 and # 75 of volume 2 (October 4 and 11, 1728) in this respect.

The first striking feature about the composition is that it is only five pages long. The second salient feature is that it was not published in one piece. Page five appeared one week later. The explanation for the extension over two numbers of the journal is simple enough: each number encompassed one sheet in quarto. Gottsched was unable to fit the composition onto four pages. The composition is nevertheless—to mix metaphors—cut from the same cloth. As is frequently the case in Moral Weeklies, the prose piece is in the form of a fictive letter to the editor. Gottsched calls the contribution "ein schönes Philosophisches Schreiben" (a pleasant, philosophical piece, 2:93) which contains "moralische Betrachtungen" and "lehreiche Gedancken" (moral meditations, instructive reflections, 2:98). The fictive author himself refers to his letter as "diese zufällige [sic] Gedancken so, wie sie mir in die Feder geflossen" (these incidental thoughts as they flowed through my pen, 2:98). On the basis of such references to the casualness and subjectivity of the writing, we would be justified in expecting an article similar in style to an informal essay by Montaigne. In actuality, however, the letter is closer in tone and structure to Bacon's manner of the formal essay and is reminiscent of the character sketches so popular in the sixteenth and seventeenth centuries (e.g., Brantôme, La Bruyère).

The "philosophical prose piece" is clearly structured into a narrative part and a subsequent interpretation of it. The writing is lucid and straightforward without the rhetorical finesse of either Thomasius or Leibniz, although rhetorical strategies are obviously at work here. It seems closer to the sermon than the far-ranging essay. The first portion contains a parable about two persons, Sperantius and Timorine, who are opposite in character. As their names indicate, Sperantius's main trait is his uninhibited sense of hope and trust that all will work out to his benefit, while Timorine suffers from extreme temerity in all respects. While Sperantius gives no thought to possible calamity, Timorine is paralyzed by the constant fear of losing what she has or failing to achieve what she desires. Sperantius counts his chickens before they hatch; Timorine is afraid to count her hatched chickens. In each case Gottsched vivifies their respective hopes and fears by means of numerous commonplace examples drawn from family and private life, professional careers, politics, economics, nature, and so on. The first two pages are devoted to a characterization of these two figures; page three turns to an initial interpretation of the allegory.

The message is formulated in quintessential form: "*Furcht* und *Hoff-nung* sind die beyden Axen, um welche sich das menschliche Gemüth in diesem Leben herum drehet. Stehen diese nicht in ihrer gehörigen Ord-nung, so verfället der Mensch aus dem Kreise der richtigen Bewegung in einen gefährlichen Abhang."[21] God in his wisdom granted these emotions to humans for their benefit, and their use is totally dependent upon the individuals themselves. The beneficial qualities of hope are rendered in metaphorical terms: it is the sweetener (*Zucker*) of human existence, the stabilizing anchor in this tempestuous existence, a consolation for the suffering, and a picker-upper for the depressed. The crescendo of meta-phors culminates in the triumphant claim that hope "causes the miner to rejoice in the deepest pit, the slave to exult in the heaviest chains" (2:95).

Because hope can obtain so much it must be used wisely. Wisely means sensibly. "Whoever wishes to hope sensibly," we are informed, "dare not love himself insensibly" (2:96). Insensible self-love is explained immedi-ately as being too attached to the things of this world, for all earthly goods are transient. Excessive attachment to them can never assure inner peace (*Ruhe*) which is the ultimate goal and function of hope. The shift in focus to eternal values allows Gottsched to elaborate upon this ulti-mate objective in loving detail. His conclusion draws the sum of the foregoing: "Sie [Hoffnung] befestiget unsere Zufriedenheit. Sie vereiniget unsern Willen mit der göttlichen Ordnung, und unser Wohlseyn mit seiner weisen Fügung. Sie bringet unsere Eigenliebe in gehörige Ordnung, und ermuntert uns den Zweck zu suchen, wozu wir erschaffen sind."[22]

In similar fashion Gottsched praises the potentially beneficial effects of anxiety, which he calls "the mother of wisdom" (2:96) and which should serve humankind as a "guiding light" (*Leitfaden*, 2:97). God, he argues, is not a tyrant but rather a loving father. Anxiety has not been imparted to humans to torment and paralyze but to promote peace and tranquility. As he did in arguing the virtues of hope, Gottsched launches into a series of reasons why anxiety too is a mainspring of human life. Even as hope placed in eternal reward guarantees peace of mind in the vagaries of earthly fate, fear only of eternal torment grants the strength of will to bear the temporary misfortunes of existence on earth with patience and calm.

Perhaps because of its devout theme, this essay seems less progressive than those by Thomasius and Leibniz. We sense less of the writer's personality in "Über Hoffnung und Furcht" than in "Ermahnung" or "Nachahmung." Nevertheless, we would appear to be dealing here with what was later to become known as the formal essay with its sober, no nonsense stance. Examination of other contributions to *Der Biedermann* testifies to Gottsched's penchant for the clear and simple style, embellished only slightly by rhetorical strategies. Gottsched's report of November 10, 1727, on the lark hunt near Leipzig gives ample evidence of this tendency.

In four pages of concentrated, yet readable prose, Gottsched narrates in systematic order: (1) the conduct of the hunt, (2) a calculation of the number of birds caught in a season (2,160,000 pairs), (3) the marketing of the birds in Leipzig, (4) their role in foreign trade, (5) an assessment of the economic advantages for Leipzig, (6) reasons for the greater economic value of the larks caught at night, (7) reflections upon their feeding habits, and (8) the size of the geographical area necessary to support these numbers of birds. Gottsched is not insensitive to the needs of the reader. Even as my reader might find the detailed enumeration of these points a bit tedious, Gottsched anticipated that his reader might be put off as well. In a fine use of prolepsis, the journalist begins his penultimate paragraph with the remark: "Wenn meine fremde[n] Leser, die nicht gebohrne Meißner sind, mit dieser Menge von Lerchen, die ich ausgerechnet habe, ihren Spott treiben, oder mir es verdencken wollten, daß ich sie so mühsam beschrieben, so habe ich ihnen zweyerley zu antworten."[23] The hint of self-irony (i.e., litotes) is appreciated. While expecting the inhabitants of the Meißen area to have a natural interest in the report, Gottsched is fully aware that others might find it slightly ridiculous. The promised response is two-pronged: the first is practical, the second allegorical. Or we might say secular and sacred.

Leipzig is part of Germany and is therefore a concern of all Germans. More importantly, however, is the following consideration. If the birds were not hunted in such extravagant numbers, their population could not be kept at manageable levels. If, for example, the more than four million birds caught had been allowed to breed another season, as many as 60,480,000 pairs of larks would descend upon the fields a year later. Unchecked, these birds would plague all of Germany within ten years time.

Gottsched's clinching argument, however, is the concluding exhortation to be astonished at the wonders of God's creation. A blessing can easily turn to a plague. Thus it behooves mankind to be watchful: "Wer weise ist, der mercket auf!" (Whoever would be wise, let him be on guard! 1:112).

Although Gottsched's style seems uninspired and indebted to traditional thinking, it is marked by a dialectic of sorts. The reader is encouraged to calculate with the author how many birds there are, what benefits they produce, how many attributes of hope and fear can be identified, and so on so that s/he can conclude independently whether to accept or reject the argument. At this early stage of essayistic writing, it is not unduly surprising when the writer is more directive than in a later era which had been cut loose from the firmly established world-view and divine order. Within that philosophical/moral framework, Gottsched moves as nimbly as possible. More important than the external characteristics of the piece as a "formal essay" in the determination of whether we are dealing with essayistic writing or not is, however, the internal epistemologic and poetic structuring principle. Typical of that method is, to speak with Haas, "the intellectually playful moment" (*das gedankenspielerische Moment*) and the author's reflection upon the act of writing itself ("Zur Geschichte und Kunstform," 16). And here we sense both criteria although Gottsched is not as associatively innovative as Leibniz or Thomasius. "Die Lerchen-jagd" tends more to Bacon's moralistic, closed style than to Montaigne's meandering, searching manner. In any event, we cannot simply dismiss the prose pieces of the Moral Weeklies with a nonchalant wave of the hand as unimportant for the emergence of an original prose in the eighteenth century. If not all of them are full-blown essays, they at least attest to the mode's generic development.[24]

Johann Michael von Loen

Loen (1694–1776) is perhaps best known to literary historians for having married Sibylla Lindheimer, the sister of Goethe's grandmother Textor. In *Dichtung und Wahrheit* and in *Wilhelm Meister* (the figure of the uncle), Goethe immortalized his great uncle by mentioning him. Yet aside from that illustrious connection, Loen can lay claim to fame for his numerous writings on sociological, economical, political, religious, historical, military, and moral questions. Between 1724 and 1768 (when he went totally blind), Loen composed some 137 works, ranging from poems to satires, miscellaneous observations, translations, and novels. Most famous of these writings is the early Enlightenment novel, *Der redliche Mann am Hofe* (*The Upright Man at Court*, 1740). Less known are the shorter prose pieces written in German, French, and Latin and originally published anonymously in Moral Weeklies and other journals before being collected in four volumes in 1751.

The editor, Philipp Heinrich Hutter, calls the anthology "ein morali-sches Malereycabinet" and Loen himself refers to the journalistic works as "moralische Schildereyen," as "zufällige Gedanken," and "Briefe und Betrachtungen über allerhand Materien" in which spiritual and secular topics are depicted as being intrinsically intertwined. His expressed models are Theophrast, La Bruyère, St.-Evremond, and Fénelon. Like them in their character studies, Loen endeavors to describe only what he has seen and observed: "I speak of them as one who thinks freely and who loves the truth . . . . I speak of the general welfare as a person who is affected by it and who would wish to advance it if possible."[25] The proclivity of Loen's attitude to that of Montaigne is manifest. As a sampling of this popular writing, let us consider his characterization of Switzerland and its people based on observations made on two trips to that country in the years 1719 and 1724. I cite the text according to the readily available edition in Rohner's anthology, *Deutsche Essays. Prosa aus zwei Jahrhunderten.*

Like Gottsched's "Hoffnung und Furcht", Loen's "Die Schweitz im Jahr 1719 und 1724" (1749) is a character sketch; only Loen sketches the character of an entire nation, while Gottsched gives us an allegorical portrait of man. Both are nevertheless concerned with *homo moraliter.* The opening sentence of Loen's composition immediately draws the reader into his subject through its use of the "if then" construction and of the motif of *e pluribus unum*: "Wenn man ein freyes und glückseliges Volk sehen will, so muß man in die Schweitz reisen. Es ist zu verwundern, wie so verschiedene Menschen in der Religion, in den Sitten und in der Sprache ungleich, sich mit einander in eine so genaue und unverbrüchliche Vereinigung haben einlassen können, daß daraus eine so mächtige Republik, wie die Schweitz, entstanden ist; deren Bande nun desto dauerhafter sind, je mehr sie aus Einfalt und Neigung zur Freyheit sind zusammen geflochten worden."[26] The topic of freedom was widely discussed throughout the eighteenth century, so an author could count on a ready audience for a treatment of the theme. By citing freedom as the salient trait of the Swiss—a general association in eighteenth-century Europe—Loen ensures himself wide appeal because his reader was either for or against freedom. The citation of unity despite ethnic, religious, and linguistic diversity arouses the reader's intellectual curiosity.

Thus it readily becomes apparent that the motif of freedom is, in a sense, a mere ploy. The observer next grants that Switzerland is predisposed toward a life of freedom because of natural barriers to intrusion from the outside. The geographical barriers help protect against the importation of discord, and the Swiss people stand ready to repel an attempt by neighboring states to annex any portion of the Alpine country. Besides, the mountain republic is not rich in natural resources; its real wealth, Loen explains, is the citizenry. And with that, he has arrived at his real purpose: to talk about the character of the Swiss. The introductory remarks culminate in the rhetorical question: "Was kann man nicht mit ihnen ausrichten, zumahl mit solchen, die mäßig, frisch, gesund, arbeitsam, redlich und behertzt, wie die Schweizer sind?" ("What limits can be set to the employment of such people, especially with those who are as moderate, spirited, healthy, industrious, honest, and plucky as the Swiss?" 1:86f.). The initial three paragraphs, in other words, form the *exordium*. The reader has been won over, the parameters of the discourse established, and expectations aroused.

Immediately following the effective use of the rhetorical question to focus our attention, Loen launches into the second of the five phases of his characterization. Phase 2 (87–89) deals with reasons for the Swiss's famed industry and honesty, while phases 3, 4, and 5 (89–91) treat their customs, language, and manner of thinking respectively. In keeping with his remark that his shorter prose pieces reflect his incidental thoughts without any specific organization, the conclusion (phase 6) is not really a conclusion but rather "a footnote" (*eine Anmerkung*, 91) to the foregoing depiction. Interjected in the middle of phase two is an explanation that we must distinguish between the French and German sections of Switzerland.

In the French section prosperity abounds because of the richness of the soil. In the larger German area the citizenry must work very hard to eke out a living, be it in the mountain meadows, manufactories, or marketplace. As a consequence of the differing environments, character differences between the two parts of the republic have evolved. The French speakers are "much more spirited and much more given to sensual pleasure than [are the inhabitants] of the harsher mountainous region." Superfluity seduces the senses to dangerous intemperance. Thus, we are informed, "there are two versions of Switzerland and of the Swiss" (88). But because the harsher German section is dominant, the virtues and character traits of its people are generally taken to be representative of the whole. This assessment of the Swiss nation echoes that of Albrecht von Haller in his didactic poem praising the natural beauty and customs of his homeland, *Die Alpen* (1729).

The reader is prepared for this important differentiation between the French and German life-styles by a striking metaphor at the beginning of phase 2: "Ein Schweizer ist ein Holz aus dem sich alles schnitzen läßt. Doch mit Unterschied: es giebt auch viele unnütze Pengel in einem Wald" (A Swiss is like wood from which anything can be cut. Yet with one difference: there are many useless trees in a forest; 87). Although Loen does not return to the comparison, the image is so strong that it recurs whenever the theme of diversity and disparity arise.

The Swiss people are praised for making a virtue of necessity, for turning frugality into contentment, for living simple and honest lives as dictated by their environment. Their ability to live according to their real needs rather than according to perceived needs sets them apart as models for imitation by the rest of Europe. Loen pithily remarks: "It seems to me that Switzerland is the true home of reason" (89), adding later "their manner of thinking is uncommon; they examine things deeply and judge them keenly without appearing to be profound or astute" (91). It is in Switzerland where free thinking is as highly developed as the art of living freely. Despite those intellectual advances, however, religious strife between the Catholics and Protestants cause the Swiss to act occasionally like an ill-tempered married couple who love to fight at home but protect one another from outside intervention (91f.).

Loen's final comments then seem to meander away from his focus; he speaks of the occurrence of superstition in the Catholic areas, of the military preparedness of the people, citing the ability of the Bernese canton to arm 20,000 men in twenty-four hours, or to alert the entire country to the danger of enemy attack within fifteen minutes. It would seem, indeed, that the reader is presented with merely incidental, disconnected thoughts of a passing observer. Thus a certain tension arises between the internal structuring of the entire composition and the openness of the conclusion. It is like the alternation between the peaks and valleys of the countryside itself, even as the moral strength of the inhabitants derives from their dependence on the geographical peculiarity of their situation. What Haller specifically states in *Die Alpen*, Loen merely implies in *Die Schweitz im Jahre 1719 und 1724*: the Swiss have been able to preserve themselves from the decadence and immodesty of the rest of Europe because of their physical isolation and hard lives. Life close to nature promotes moral vigor. Whatever conclusion of this type the reader draws from Loen's composition, s/he must draw it alone, for Loen does not prescribe all the steps. With this prose piece we have drawn closer to the informal type of essayistic writing which gives individual impressions and stimulates further reflection. At the same time it includes foreign quotations, verse citations, and historical references which are marks of the classical essay of later generations.

Christian Fürchtegott Gellert

Gellert (1715–1769) was possibly the most beloved of the German writers at mid-century, reaping nigh universal praise for the fluidity of his writing and his commonsense views. Simple, cordial, and naive, yet elegant and noble: such were the accolades of his brother poets in the eighteenth century. Renown for his fables and narratives (1746, 1748), lectures (1770) and model epistles (1751)—all of which contributed significantly to the general refinement of German writing style—Gellert was a worthy successor to Thomasius and a colleague of Gottsched at the University of Leipzig, where he lectured for many years on rhetoric, literature, and morality. Among his students were Johann Andreas Cramer (1723–88) and Goethe, both of whom reported on Gellert's extraordinary effectiveness as a lecturer. It is perhaps appropriate to analyze an appeal of 1768 to the students in Leipzig to restore law and order to the streets of Leipzig after several days of rioting. Because of his good standing with the student body, Gellert was asked by the authorities to urge them to refrain from further disorder. The result was his "Ermahnung an die Studenten der Universität Leipzig."[27]

The brief address is a model of rhetorical technique and is fully representative of his highly lauded lecturing style. It is included for discussion here, firstly, because it continues a tradition initiated by Thomasius with his appeal of 1687 and, secondly, because Gellert's "Ermahnung" is highly personal in tone which is designed to bond speaker/writer and listener/reader in intimate discourse. The bonding process is promoted by direct addresses (*meine Herren, ich bitte Sie*), by signs of his respect for them (*Edelmüthige, Lernbegierige Jünglinge*) by insinuating his friendship for them as almost his equals (*theureste Commilitonen, academische Mitbürger, Freunde*), and finally by appealing to their sense of filial devotion (*Söhne dieser Akademie, meine väterliche Bitte*). The levels of appeal rise steadily to culminate in the ultimate suggestion that they look upon him as their spiritual father who desires only what is best for them.

The effectiveness of these personal appeals is heightened by his successful differentiation between the vast majority of the students in his audience who are peace loving and law abiding and those handful of thoughtless agitators who are behind the disturbances in the city. These unthinking troublemakers do not deserve student support, because they show no respect for the student body or for anyone else. In a few years they will be gone from Leipzig and will lose contact with their academic fellows. Is it right to condone civil disorder by those who do not care about you? Moreover, Gellert makes it clear that he has come to them at the behest of the authorities and not on his own. He does concur, nevertheless, with the view that the lawless acts must stop and encourages his listeners to help restrain the frivolous few. Through a repetition of the striking phrase, "to [these thoughtless few] I am to state what they surely did not consider" ("Denen soll ich sagen, was sie wohl nie mögen erwogen haben"). After each occurrence the professor graphically describes violations of the rights of the general citizenry ranging from disturbance of their much needed sleep to the threat of physical harm. Civil order is a sacred right because it is divinely ordained. Gellert asks rhetorically: "And who are you, young man, to disrupt with cool contempt God's order?" (1:259) and: "Would you not be embarrassed to demand openly by day what you seek to wrest by force cloaked by the darkness of night?" (1:260). Are there not enough pleasant distractions available in the city as it is? Are there not enough support mechanisms for the students such as stipends and free meal tickets? Are the state, city, and university not run by understanding and well disposed magistrates? Gellert concludes his string of rhetorical questions with the conciliatory yet threatening remark that he will be forced to renounce his position at the university if his "fatherly request" is not granted. In sum, peace or else. Cramer's eyewitness account attests to the effectiveness of Gellert's rhetorical skills. The students were so moved that the rampaging ceased (1:258).

A skeptical reader might protest that the lecture format of Gellert's address disqualifies it as a sample of essayistic writing for it is much too ephemeral and situation specific. Despite its specificity, however, the "Ermahnung" is imbued with qualities that preserve its freshness and appeal. Thus like Thomasius's famous exhortation or Schiller's lecture on the nature of universal history, Gellert's oration can be read again and again with profit and pleasure.

The Literary Journals of the 1740s

The intimate style of the "Ermahnung an die Studenten der Universität Leipzig" is symptomatic of the newly emerged personal style in the first half of the eighteenth century. That manner is directly traceable to the ideal of the gallant epistle as championed by Thomasius and Benjamin Neukirch and applied to the Moral Weeklies by Hallbauer and Gottsched.[28] Evidence of this continued development is provided by such Moral Weeklies as *Der Gesellige* (Halle, 1748–50), *Der Redliche* (Nürnberg, 1751), and *Der Mensch* (Halle, 1751–56) as well as by the early journalistic writings of Lessing and Wieland around 1750. But in keeping with the implicit focus on the pivotal role of Leipzig and its academics in the emergence of an original way of thinking and writing, let us consider instead the literary journal, *Belustigungen des Verstandes und des Witzes* (1742–45), edited by Johann Joachim Schwabe (1711–1784), one of Gottsched's prize students.

Aside from the historical significance of its early numbers for illustrating the theoretical quarrel between the two main schools of thought at the time—Leipzig (Gottsched) and Zurich (Bodmer/Breitinger)—the *Belusti-*

gungen is important as the first noteworthy forum for belletristic and innovative writing.[29] In keeping with its stated goals, the journal favored the shorter literary forms such as odes, bucolic poetry, cantatas, elegies, didactic poems, fables, and satires. However, fictive letters and prose pieces dealing with moral-didactic topics in the manner of the Moral Weeklies also found their way into the journal. Everything was acceptable as long as the dictum to entertain while educating was observed. By 1740 that meant a cordial, engaging dialogic style. In his *Formgeschichte der deutschen Dichtung* (1949), Paul Böckmann cites the practice of presenting didactic maxims in pleasing garb as the most characteristic feature of the *Belustigungen*. He sees the tactic as being related to the light, conversational manner of the Rococo era: "Die ganze Zeitschrift erscheint in einer Form des witzigen Sprechens, die nahe bei der Ironie steht und jedenfalls aus dem Ernst des direkten Sagens herausgetreten ist."[30] Repeatedly we read that the style of this journal is anchored in an ironic stance, for the contributors endeavored to avoid dogmatic stances. In his foreword to the inaugural volume, Schwabe explains what the reader can expect to encounter: "Es sollen darinnen Abhandlungen aus allen Teilen der Weltweisheit und von allen Arten der freien Künste vorkommen. Man wird historischen, kritischen, philologischen u.a.d.g. Aufsätzen einen Platz in diesen Blättern einräumen . . . Alle Gattungen von Schriften, die ins Reich der Dichtkunst und Beredsamkeit können gezogen werden . . . , wird man in dieser Sammlung aufnehmen. . . . und *alle kleine* [sic] *Werke, welche der Verstand nur hervorbringen mag, ohne sich pedantisch dabei zu erweisen,* sollen allhier einer gütigen Aufnahme und Fürsorge genießen."[31] Striking is the reference to poetry and rhetoric in the same breath. More striking is Schwabe's ultimate purpose; he wishes to demonstrate how accomplished Germans have become in expressing themselves with *esprit* and *élan*. The concluding remark concerning the acceptability of "all short forms" free of pedantry and dryness deserves our special attention, for it signals an appreciation of what was to become known as essays, or better, essayistic writing. The *Belustingungen des Verstandes und Witzes* are, in short, a very important document for the history of non-fictional writing.

Furthermore, the list of contributors to the periodical reads like a Who's Who of the literary world in Northern Germany in the 1740s. Local luminaries such as L. Chn. Gärtner, Gellert, Gleim, Gottsched, Hagedorn, E. von Kleist, Rabener, J. E. Schlegel, and Zachariae published in its pages. The presence of these authors encouraged aspiring writers to submit their prose and verse pieces as well. Thus the journal, which proved to be a great success, offers extraordinary insights into the literary and stylistic tendencies of the day. Many of the articles, satires, and poems published here were never reprinted or reissued in revised form. A look at the "poetisch-produktive" (poetically creative)[32] compositions of long forgotten aspirants to the Parnassus will serve to balance and round out the portrait of original prose[33] in the early eighteenth century in the wake of reform efforts from Thomasius to Gottsched.

On the basis of an analysis of prose compositions such as the anonymous "Briefwechsel zwischen einer Mannsperson und einem Frauenzimmer" ("Correspondence Between a Man and a Woman," Vol. 1), Johann Elias Schlegel's "Der junge Herr" ("The Young Gentleman," Vol. 1), and Kästner's "Betrachtungen über den Beruf" ("Meditations on a Profession," vol. 2), Böckmann concludes that the writing in the *Belustigungen* exhibits a refined understanding of penetrating wit and ironic playfulness (520ff.). For his part, Vincent J. Dell' Orto values the essays of Theodor Lebrecht Pitschel (1716–1743)—for example, "Von dem unphilosophischen Leben der Weltweisen" ("On the Unphilosophical Life of the Philosophers," 2:42–65)—as successful parodies of ponderous academic prose (*Abhandlung*). What makes them so successful is their playfully ironic and unexpectedly familiar tone. The high point in "On the Unphilosophical Life of Philosophers" is reached, for example, when Pitschel reports that his pen rebels at the thought of making numerous scholarly notations. The footnote apparatus, he laments, serves only to display the writer's erudition and is inherently detrimental to the communicative process. No one, he continues, is really interested in the information contained in them, so the author succeeds only in removing himself yet further from his audience. Through a similar use of litotes and exhortations to reflect upon what is actually being written, Pitschel aims to involve his reader in a dialogue with himself via the text. The ultimate purpose of "Von dem unphilosophischen Leben der Weltweisen" is to reject the traditionally aloof and sober relationship between author and reader in favor of a new intimate nexus (Dell' Orto, "Audience," 116f.). The writing thus reflects the journal's openness to innovative aesthetic forms.

In his "Schreiben an einen Freund, bey Uebersendung eines Briefes von einem Freygeiste" ("Note to a Friend on the Occasion of a Letter from a Free Thinker," 1742, 2:393–398) Pitschel intones his missive in similar fashion to the *Weltweisen*; that is, he provides it with a long introduction which doesn't say all that much and is clearly ironic. He recognizes his reader's antipathy towards "Ciceronian letters . . . from which we learn only that the writer is writing" and assures the reader his own letter will not be any different from what he has been accustomed to (394f.). It is only on the third page of the article that Pitschel finally gets around to his topic: freethinking. And even then his purpose is merely to initiate a dialogue, and for that reason he has recourse to the various rhetorical devices suited to that purpose. He concludes by remarking that his letter is too long for an introduction to the article on freethinking which he has enclosed. Any further discussion will evolve from his interlocutor's response (= synecdoche).

The strange mixture of whimsical and serious tone is even more evident in a subsequent "Schreiben von der Stärke der einmal angenommenen Meynungen" ("Letter on the Intractability of Opinions Once Formed," 1743, 85–93). Almost in counterpoint to the foregoing letter, Pitschel begins by remarking that his correspondent is correct to chide him for composing mini-treatises (*kleine Abhandlungen*) instead of letters (85). Far from being devoid of import, his letters fairly overflow with observations and philosophical reflections (*Betrachtungen und philosophische Gedanken*). However, he is so acutely conscious of the ineptitude of his insights (*Durftigkeit meiner Einsichten*) to expect someone to collect them as "choice new insights."

Following these remarks Pitschel draws an important distinction between and epistle and a philosophical treatise. Far from wishing to expand philosophical theory into unaccustomed realms, he desires only to engage "in a brief conversation with a friend" (86). Since he is uninterested in discovering new truths but rather in reflecting on known ones, he can let several, even contradictory, observations stand side by side without having to make a value judgment. And because these views occur in an exchange of letters with a comrade, he is under no pressure to develop a single thought fully. Instead he can begin to unfold an idea in one letter and continue refining it in another. In short, Pitschel argues that the informality of letter writing does not bind the writer to an unyielding system: "Ich bin indeß nicht gebunden, und habe ein weiteres Feld vor mir" (I am not bound in any way, having in front of me an open field. 88). These reflections on the posture of letter writing take up half of the essay.

With a playful twist Pitschel creates the transition to his ultimate reason for writing. As he is not of a mind to begin using a new sheet of paper and most of the present one is almost filled, his reader can rightly surmise that he will soon get around to his topic (88f.)! The analogy of a diplomatic visit underscores the drawn-out ritual of introduction. The remainder of the letter recounts the story of a harmless village teacher who was drummed out of the district because he attempted to improve the diction of his little charges. The report of the harsh treatment the teacher suffered at the hands of the bigoted farmers illustrates effectively the power of prejudice. The contrast between the witty, engaging meandering style of the first half of the essay and the simple narrative of the second half heightens the reader's ability to react in a productive manner to the poetic piece. Pitschel trusts that his attentive reader will recognize the connection between the two disparate parts of his seemingly digressive composition.

Similarly engaging for their masterful rhetorical and organizational skills are Steudnitzer's satiric treatment of physiognomical analysis, "Yahoonoologie, das ist, Philosophische Abhandlung von dem Verstande der Menschengesichter" (1744, 307–317) and J. D. Overbeck's "Was ein großer Kopf sey?" (1744, 421–427). In comparison with Pitschel, however, neither Steudnitzer nor Overbeck display the same exuberance or light touch as he. Clean-cut like crystal, "Yahoonoology" and "What is a Great Thinker?" are more formal in tone without seeming too detached from the perceived audience. In any event these few examples confirm that the stylistic traits discovered by Böckmann and Dell' Orto are indeed typical of the *Belustigungen*. Together with its sister journal, *Neue Beyträge zum Vergnügen des Verstandes und Witzes* (1748–57), it represents an important milestone in the rise of essayistic writing in the Age of Reason.

Notes

1. L. Rohner, *Der deutsche Essay* (Berlin and Neuwied: Luchterhand, 1966), 784, reports that Just had informed him privately of such a plan to expand the succinct and informed overview published in *Deutsche Philologie in Aufriß*.

2. Among the more significant dissertations on the topic are: James Raymond Wardell, "The Essays of Christoph Martin Wieland: A Contribution to the Definition and History of the Genre in Its European Context." Dissertation University of Michigan, 1986; James M. van der Laan, "The German *essay* of the Eighteenth Century: An Ecology." Dissertation University of Illinois at Urbana/Champaign, 1984; Robert Victor Smythe, "Christoph Martin Wieland as Essayist." Dissertation University of Texas at Austin, 1980. Contributions to the *Rahmenthema*, "The Poet as Essayist and Journalist," include studies by Gerhard Haas, Vincent J. Dell' Orto, John McCarthy, Ruth Dawson, Joachim Wohlleben, and Raymond Immerwahr. See the bibliography for complete details.

3. Jürgen Jacobs, *Prosa der Aufklärung. Kommentar zu einer Epoche* (Munich: Winkler, 1976), 45; Hans-Friedrich Wessels, *Aufklärung. Ein literaturwissenschaftliches Studienbuch* (Königstein/Ts: Athenäum, 1984). Despite his stated purpose of offering a reappraisal of Enlightenment literature by opening it up to non-canonical literary forms, Wessels totally overlooks essayistic writing in the age. The most logical place to have

included such writing would have been in Berghahn's chapter on the dominant role of periodical literature in the spread of Enlightenment thought. Neither R. Grimminger, *Sozialgeschichte der deutschen Literatur,* Vol. 3: *Deutsche Aufklärung* . . . (Munich: Hanser, 1980) nor V. Zmegac, *Geschichte der deutschen Literatur vom 18. Jahrhundert bis zur Gegenwart* (Königstein/Ts: Athenäum, 1978) treats essayistic writing in systematic fashion.

4. Vincent J. Dell' Orto, "Audience and the Tradition of the German Essay in the 18th Century," *Germanic Review,* 50 (1975), 111–25. James Van Der Laan's more recent treatment in the *Lessing Yearbook* (1986) of the eighteenth-century essay fails to take note of the specific work on the era, whether by Küntzel, Rohner, Rehder, or Dell' Orto and does not follow any strict chronological sequence. In all fairness, however, we must state that Van Der Laan is not interested in analyzing individual essays, but rather in arguing that essayistic writing is on the whole a symptom of the entire stochastic age. Consequently, he organizes his study along thematic lines: the essay as a sign of emancipation, of cultural disintegration, experimentation, and of a new epistemology (189). Therein lies the real value of his undertaking, not in the cataloguing of long-forgotten essayists (e.g. note 2, 192f.), although the thorough documentation is appreciated.

5. Vincent J. Dell' Orto, "Audience and the Tradition of the German Essay in the 18th Century," *Germanic Review* 50 (1975), 111–125.

6. See Haas, "Zur Geschichte und Kunstform des Essays" (1975), 11, and more recently Klaus Weissenberger, "Der Essay," in *Prosakunst ohne Erzählen. Die Gattungen der nicht fiktionalen Kunstprosa,* ed. Klaus Weissenberger (Tübingen: M. Niemeyer, 1985), argues: "Nur eine so weiter betriebene Strukturanalyse der Gattungskonstituenten erlaubt es, zu einer umfassenderen morphologischen Gattungsbestimmung und Typologie vorzustoßen, die die Ganzheit und Geschlossenheit des Essays aus dem synergetischen Zusammenspiel seiner historischen Voraussetzungen mit seinen ästhetischen, strukturellen und erkenntnistheoretischen Konsituenten erkennen läßt (105).

7. Van Der Laan took this route in his, "The German Essay of the 18th Century: Mirror of its Age" (1986), concluding that we could appropriately refer to the century as "the age of the essay" (179). Klaus Weissenberger concurs in this assessment ("Essay," 110f.).

8. Cf. Hans Blumenberg, *Die kopernikanische Wende* (Frankfurt a.M.: Suhrkamp, 1965). Wardell, on the other hand, rejects the notion that a definition of the essay incorporating both basic types can be refined enough to distinguish the essay from related small-format compositions. He writes: "To include both bodies of essays [i.e., those of Bacon and Montaigne] one would have to formulate a concept of the essay that would not be able to show how the essay differs from such related genres as article, epistle, tract, dialogue, or discourse" ("Essays of Wieland," 128). Obviously, I cannot share this view. Moreover, Wardell does not seem to be aware of the inherent contradiction in his statement: if he accepts Bacon and Montaigne as the fathers of the modern essay, then it *must* be possible to incorporate both

kinds of writing in a definition of that writing. Wardell encounters difficulties, I believe, because of his insistence upon speaking in terms of a *genre*. I endeavor to skirt the inadequacy of such an approach by speaking in terms of a *mode* or of authorial and reader *attitudes*.

9. Christian Thomasius, "Christian Thomasius eröffnet der Studirenden Jugend zu Leipzig in einem Discours Welcher Gestalt man denen Frantzosen in gemeinem Leben und Wandel nachahmen solle? Ein Collegium über des Gratians *Grund-Reguln Vernünfftig klug und artig zu leben,*" in *Deutsche Literaturdenkmale der 18. und 19. Jahrhunderts,* ed. August Sauer, New Series 2/3 (Nendeln/Liechtenstein: Krauss Rpt., 1968), 52/2:5–36, here 36.

10. "Many have already commented that there could be no doubt about the sense of surprise our forefathers, the old Teutons, would experience upon being resurrected in present-day Germany. They would not suspect in the least that they were in their homeland among their countrymen, but rather would assume that they were in a foreign country among a strange and unknown people" (Thomasius, "Nachahmung," 3).

11. "Why is it that we Germans are ridiculed as nitwits when we travel to France even though we are dressed in the latest fashion, can hold forth about a French roast or reflect upon a *fricassée* so artfully, even speak French perfectly, paying our respects as good as any Frenchman, while the French who come to Germany are treated universally with love and admiration?" (Thomasius, "Nachahmung," 6f.).

12. "A brand new writing tablet absorbs markings quite easily. However, when writing has been left to stand a long time, how difficult it is to eradicate it. If, furthermore, the first markings have been inscribed on the skin of a jackass, you can scrub what you will: you will not be able to get rid of the original letters or numbers" (Thomasius, "Nachahmung," 25).

13. "And what about all those gallantries? How the young men push and shove in front of the window in hopes of having the honor to greet the fair damsel—or if not she herself, then her maid-in-waiting or maybe just her cat? How many lovelorn letters (copied out of ten novels), how many arrow-pierced hearts painted in flaming colors are sent off as if to storm the young lady's affection with them? To what ends will they go to present a gallant serenade? They play the amorous fool everywhere, even in the House of God. (Thomasius, "Nachahmung," 32).

14. G. W. Leibniz, *Politische Schriften,* ed. H.H. Holz (Frankfurt a.M.: Europäische Verlagsanstalt, 1967), 2:60–80. The ensuing discussion has been adopted from my chapter, "The Philosopher as Essayist: Leibniz and Kant," in *The Philosopher as Writer: The Eighteenth Century,* ed. Robert Ginsberg (Cranbury, NJ: Associated University Presses, 1987), 48–74; especially 51–63.

15. Blackall, 3-9; Paul Böckmann, *Formgeschichte der deutschen Dichtung* (Hamburg: Hoffmann and Campe, 1967), 482f.

16. Friedrich Schlegel, *Sämmtliche Werke,* Kritische Ausgabe, ed. Ernst Behler (Paderborn: F. Schöningh, 1963), 18/2:206.

17. Schlegel, 18/2:221. For a more detailed analysis of Leibniz's prose piece see my "The Philosopher as Essayist: Leibniz and Kant" in *The Philosopher as Writer: The Eighteenth Century*, ed. Robert Ginsberg (Cranbury, NJ: Associated University Presses, 1987), 48–74.

18. Johann Wolfgang von Goethe, *Werke*, Hamburger Ausgabe, Vol. 9, *Autobiographische Schriften I* (Munich: Beck, 1981), 269. See also Walter Jens, *Von deutscher Rede* (Munich: Piper, 1969), 14 who refers to the demise of scholastic rhetoric around 1750 prompted by new pressures in the evolving literary life.

19. J. Ch. Gottsched, *Der Biedermann, Eine Moralische Wochenschrift*, facsimile ed. Wolfgang Martens (Leipzig, 1727–29; rprt. Stuttgart: Metzler, 1975), 2:108, 22.

20. Wolfgang Martens, "Nachwort" to *Der Biedermann* (Stuttgart: Metzler, 1975), 32.

21. "Fear and hope form the axis in this life around which human emotions revolve. If these sensations do not stand in appropriate relationship to one another, the individual is thrown from his proper orbit into a dangerous spiral" (Gottsched, *Biedermann*, 2:95).

22. "Hope is the staff of contentment; it unites our individual will with the divine plan, our welfare with His wise judgment. It places the proper restraints on our self love and encourages us to realize our purpose for existing" (Gottsched, *Biedermann*, 2:96).

23. "If my foreign readers, that is, those who are not natives of Meißen, are tempted to poke fun at the large number of larks which I have calculated or fault me for having described their habits so painstakingly—to them I have two things to say" (Gottsched, *Biedermann*, 1:112).

24. Berger rejects the articles in the Moral Weeklies as lacking artistic roundness, a cosmic view, and a sovereign attitude, concluding that it would be a disservice to label them essays" (*Essay*, 200). Similarly Helmut Rehder believes that the Moral Weeklies retarded the development of the true essay ("Beginnings," 29). On the other hand, Klaus Günther Just ("Essay," col.1914) and V. J. Dell' Orto ("Audience," 112) both see the connection as fruitful. Weissenberger ("Essay," 110) duly notes that Bacon's broad stylistic influence was primarily due to the intermediary role of the weeklies while Wardell ("Essays of Wieland," 202ff.) recognizes the importance of the Moral Weeklies in the genesis of essayism without going into detail.

25. *Des Herrn von Loen gesammelte Schrifften*, 3rd Ed., ed. J. C. Schneider (Frankfurt and Leipzig: Philipp Heinrich Huttern, 1751). Cited according to L. Rohner, *Deutsche Essays*, 1:93f.

26. "If you would see a free and happy people, you must go to Switzerland. It is amazing how so many dissimilar people—different in religious belief, in customs, and in language—could have entered into such a perfect and indestructible union from which such a powerful republic like Switzerland could evolve. Their unifying bonds are the more enduring, the more they are woven of straightforwardness and love of freedom" (Loen, *DE*, 1:86).

27. See Johann Andreas Cramer, *Christian Fürchtegott Gellerts Leben* (Leipzig: Weidmanns Erben und Reich, 1774), 164–167. Gellert's text is cited according to *Deutsche Reden, Part I*, ed. W. Hinderer (Stuttgart: Reclam, 1973).

28. See chapter VI of this study and Dell' Orto, "Audience," 113f. It is interesting to note that Gottsched was granted membership in the "Deutschübende Poetische Gesellschaft" shortly after to moving to Leipzig in 1724. He quickly became president of the society, renaming it the "Deutsche Gesellschaft" and transforming it into a national organization for the promotion of the German language and literature. Thus he stands in direct line with Thomasius and Leibniz.

29. Jürgen Wilke, *Literarische Zeitschriften des 18. Jahrhunderts (1688–1789)*, Part 2 (Stuttgart: Metzler, 1978), 19.

30. Paul Böckmann, *Formgeschichte der deutschen Dichtung*, Vol. 1: *Von der Sinnbildsprache zur Ausdruckssprache. Der Wandel der literarischen Formensprache vom Mittelalter zur Neuzeit* (Hamburg: Hoffmann and Campe, 1967³), 521: "The entire periodical is in the form of a witty conversation, almost ironic—at the very least far removed from the usual earnestness of direct statements."

31. "Articles from all disciplines of world philosophy and from all branches of the arts will be published in these pages. The editors will accept historical, critical, philological, and all similar kinds of treatises for publication. . . . All kinds of literary or rhetorical writing are . . . appropriate. . . . Furthermore, *all kinds of short pieces which the mind can possibly produce without becoming pedantic in tone*, will be welcome and well received here" (*Belustigungen*, 1:12–15; my emphasis).

32. Robert Prutz uses this term in his *Geschichte des deutschen Journalismus*, Part 1 (Hannover, 1845). See Wilke, 2:19.

33. Heinrich Küntzel, *Essay und Aufklärung. Zum Ursprung einer originellen deutschen Prosa im 18. Jahrhundert* (Munich: Fink, 1969) uses the term original prose as the touchstone of his inquiry.

CHAPTER 8

The Dialectic Muse Soars I:
Essayistic Prose 1750–1790

Fermenta Cognitionis

Momentous changes in the tenor of literary life began to occur around 1750, all of which had nothing to do with the birth of Goethe on August 28, 1749. For example, Friedrich Gottlieb Klopstock (1724–1803) left Zurich in 1750 for Copenhagen to complete his monumental epic, *Der Messias*, under the patronage of the Danish king, Frederick V. About the same time Gotthold Ephraim Lessing (1729–1781) abandoned his studies in Leipzig in order to pursue a writing career in Berlin, and Christoph Martin Wieland (1733–1813) abandoned *his* studies in Tübingen to enter a writer's apprenticeship with Johann Jacob Bodmer in Zurich. For years these ambitious men struggled to establish themselves as professional writers, eventually succeeding in emerging as dominant literary figures. They represented a new breed of writer between the North Sea and the Alps. Yet none of them quite realized his goal of becoming an independent professional writer.

Important within our context, however, is the fact that they subscribed to the ideal of an apolitical, asocial *transzendentale Publizistik* which offered a new channel of communication between writer and audience. Derivative of the stance of the Moral Weeklies, the new brand of journalism is called "transcendental" because it transcended all religious, ethnic, political, or social classifications of the individual.[1]

It was, nevertheless, directed at a specific group of readers who felt and thought in similar fashion as the writer-journalists addressing them. Whether these persons were called "cosmopolites," "Freemasons," or merely "friends," they all had one characteristic in common: sensitivity to the common bond of "sympathetic feeling,"[2] which seemed to be an extension of the intimate bond between writer and reader cultivated by

the essayist-publishers of the Moral Weeklies. Those journals, we will
recall, continued to flourish into the second half of the century. Klopstock's own essayistic contributions to *Der Nordische Aufseher* (*The
Nordic Guardian*, 1757) entitled "Vom Publico" ("On the Reading
Public") like the anonymous article, "Von Lesen und Lesern" ("On Reading and Readers") in *Der Mensch* (*The Human Being*, 1751), draw attention to the new writer's enhanced awareness of the need to identify
"his" segment of the new anonymous and diversified audience. As an
example of the kind of writing that sought to create an intellectual community beyond the usual political and social boundaries, we can turn to
Klopstock, Wieland, Lessing, and their circles.

Friedrich Gottlieb Klopstock

During the late 1750s Klopstock frequently contributed articles on
literary practice and theory as well as on general cultural themes to
Johann Andreas Cramer's *Der nordische Aufseher*. A number of these
publications such as "Von der Sprache der Poesie" ("On the Language of
Poetry") in which he addresses the degree of refinement between
"prosaic" and "poetic" language in the Europe of his day, his article
entitled "Von dem Fehler, andere nach sich zu beurteilen" ("On the
Fallacy of Judging Others According to Oneself") which treats the much
discussed notion of virtue in the sober style of Francis Bacon, or his
"Gedanken über die Natur der Poesie" ("Thoughts on the Nature of
Poetry") which he openly labels "dispersed thoughts" (*zerstreute Gedanken*) on the nature of poetic writing are representative of a pronounced
shift to a consciously literary style and to literary topics.

Klopstock's definition in the latter composition of the true difference
between prosaic and poetic writing is an anticipation of the concept
underlying the formulation borrowed from Lessing: *fermenta cognitionis*. Klopstock writes in "Gedanken über die Natur der Poesie"
("Thoughts on the Nature of Poetry"): "Das Wesen der Poesie besteht
darin, daß sie, durch die Hülfe der Sprache, eine *gewisse Anzahl* von
Gegenständen, die wir *kennen* oder deren Dasein wir *vermuten*, von einer
Seite zeigt, welche die *vornehmsten* Kräfte unserer Seele in einem so
hohen Grade *beschäftigt*, daß eine auf die andere wirkt und dadurch die
ganze Seele in Bewegung setzt."[3] Each of the italicized traits is readily
identifiable as a quality of the evolving essayistic style which draws
equally upon rhetorical and analytical techniques. Like Kant was later to
do in his famous "Beantwortung der Frage: was ist Aufklärung?" ("What
is Enlightenment?"), the poet uses the opening passages of his text to

clarify in detail each of the stressed characteristics. To achieve his purpose Klopstock uses other rhetorical strategies like prolepsis, antithesis, tropes, and exclamation.

His "dispersed thoughts" on the subject all gravitate to the central notion that genuine literary expression is capable of causing motion, of evoking an inner emotional and spiritual response which contributes significantly to our sense of pleasure. For this reason Klopstock argues that his definition of poetry is equally applicable to "high" and "low" literature (*höhere* and *angenehme Poesie*). In all fairness we must note that he also disdains what he calls "versified prose" (*versifizierte Prosa*) which would include essayistic writing, for as an elitist writer Klopstock considered only verse to be the appropriate vehicle of poetic expression (Aufbau, 259).

Nevertheless, his thoughts on the quintessence of literariness are applicable to prose writing as well since it too uses language, polyperspectivity, reality, and probability to animate the entire person of his reader in the evocation of life on the printed page. Klopstock himself draws attention to this expanded view of literature in later writings on the art of depiction included in his *Die Gelehrtenrepublik* (*The Republic of Letters*, 1774). We need recall only his important distinction between "depiction" (*Darstellung*) and "analysis" (*Abhandlung*). While the latter offers a static final judgment, the former creates the impression of an ever-energetic present (Aufbau, 267). The distinction is significant for assessing the qualitative difference between the formal and the informal essay vis-à-vis other short prose forms.

Christoph Martin Wieland

Recent research on the eighteenth-century essay has tended to use Wieland as a touchstone of the art.[4] Those recent contributions to our understanding of Wieland's position within the context of the eighteenth-century essay should be consulted for a more thorough analysis of individual texts than can be provided here. The sheer volume of Wieland's essayistic writing and the sixty-year duration of his active writing career make it unfeasible to attempt anything more than a *Kostprobe* of his essayistic style. The Swabian began contributing articles to journals and periodicals in the early 1750s and continued into the next century.

Wieland's earliest essayistic prose (1752–56) can stand as an example of the state of writing at mid-century. Fortunately, we possess a detailed study of this early phase by Fritz Budde who examined these anonymously published works with an eye toward verifying Wieland's authorship. By comparing and contrasting known contributions by Wieland's mentor, J. J. Bodmer, to the same journals with the anonymous pieces whose authorship by Wieland was in question, Budde identified some key traits of Wieland's early prose style. The writings scrutinized by Budde were "Zufällige Gedanken bey Durchlesung von Joseph und Zulika" ("Occasional Thoughts Upon Reading *Joseph und Zulika*," 1753), "Anzeige von Q. Horatii Flacci opera" ("Announcement of the Collected Works of Horace," 1754), and the "Vorbericht an die Deutschen zur Sammlung der Zürcherischen Streitschriften" ("Preface for the German People to the Anthology of Polemical Writings from Zurich," 1753).[5]

One of the extraordinary features of Wieland's early prose is the carefully orchestrated pattern of argumentation which is obviously indebted to rhetorical technique. In addition to the tendency to express several related ideas in one sentence, there is the more stylistically important inclination to clearly delineate the logical sequence of thoughts to cover several sentences, in fact to encompass an entire piece. This integration of the *ideas partium* with the *idea totali* was accomplished by repeating key words, combining conjunctions (*und da endlich*), inserting pleonasms (*dies tat er damals, als; daher daß*), and the preferred grouping of several clauses together by means of the conditional. Not only is the logical connection between the parts made lucid in this manner, but Wieland also achieved varying degrees of retardation in the rhythm of his cadences. A major characteristic of his prose, this aspect serves to emphasize the main points of his argument.

Quite striking in the arrangement of sentences is the contrast between the unaccentuated cadence of one sentence followed by the upbeat of the next one with dramatic results for the rhythmic flow of the words and thoughts. Furthermore, the young author achieved variation and liveliness by beginning sentences with proper names, personal addresses to the reader, or expressions of opposing points of view. Unusual in this regard is Wieland's habit of beginning a prose piece with a dependent clause. The dramatic effect of the technique is transparent. The care which the poet gave to structuring the elements of each sentence is also characteristic of his paragraphing technique. With surprising adroitness the novice writer alternated longer retarding cadences with abrupt, almost staccato-like phrasing, regulating the rhythm by means of rhetorical questions, curt factual statements, and effective repetition of words or formulations.

In concert these various strategies (e.g., anadiplosis, anaphora, anastrophe, antithesis, enumeratio, hendiadys, hyperbole, synecdoche, and variatio) lend a melodious quality to the prose. Appropriately, to take the musical analogy a step further—the conclusion, whether a single phrase or an entire movement, struck a commanding note. Thus the conclusion avoided close stylistic integration into the preceding passages, while succinctly summarizing the composition's main theme. The final chord was consequently quite emphatic. As a fledgling creative writer Wieland surely composed such supple prose intuitively. Yet our earlier analysis of his *Theorie und Geschichte der Red-Kunst und Dicht-Kunst* has demonstrated his familiarity with rhetorical structuring devices.[6] Let us turn to a major, yet much neglected, work of the 1750s to exemplify the author's essayistic talent as portended in his earliest journalistic pieces. I have selected the "Sympathien" published in 1756 for closer scrutiny.

Addressed to a coterie of women friends in Zurich and Bern as well as to more distant like-minded thinkers, the "Sympathien" is conceived as a series of "remembrances and exhortations" (*Erinnerungen und Ermunterungen*).[7] It is a transitional work in the author's development toward a more aesthetic and philosophic stance. Extending over more than fifty pages, the collection of seventeen loosely joined, frequently rhapsodic letters is on the long side for the typical essay. Yet it displays qualities which identify it as essayistic. First, its range of topics is typical for essayism, whether it is the indispensability of communicative discourse in the fulfillment of human destiny (3:117), the need to develop critical thinking (3:125), the criticism of shallow social customs (3:133), the conviction that the soul senses itself only in the process of conscious reflection (3:137), the notion that humans are accorded only fragmentary glimpses of universal truths (3:139), the dialectical nature of the thought and life processes (3:145), the question of self-knowledge or an understanding of philosophy as the art of living (3:146–149), or the benefit of pairing rhetoric with poetry (3:160).

It speaks, moreover, directly to the role of language and literature in refining human sensibilities and improving the general quality of life. Finally, it is also addressed to an intimate circle of friends who share the bond of *Sympathie* and think in similar fashion. They were further united in their vision of the perfectibility of humankind through the process of self-knowledge. While not all of these "friends" were personally known to Wieland, they were all related to him through an almost mystical bond (3:110). This overriding concept determines both the title and the motto ("as Soul approaches Soul") of this essay. The sense of brotherhood (or sisterhood) with the clearly defined target audience marks "Sympathien" as a product of "transcendental journalism." In fact Wieland occasionally addresses his preferred reader as a *Weltbürger* (citizen of the world, 3:118, 149).

Martini considers the "Sympathien" to be a prime example of truly artistic prose which anticipated in strong fashion the bathos and linguistic sophistication of Classic-Romantic expression.[8] We can agree with this conclusion despite the occasional tendency in the work to preach or to wax too obtuse. Whenever that happens, Wieland catches himself, apologizes for the preachy tone or the anagogic obtuseness and returns to a lucid style of short sentences, graphic tropes, and proverbs to enliven the expression of his ideas. The third letter (3:115–119) abounds in direct appeals, short sentences, rhetorical questions interspersed with exhortations, and tropic language. As a sampling of his talent for tropic and metaphoric language, I offer the following:

> "stehet unerschüttert im Sturm, wie eine Ceder Gottes" (121)
> "denkendes Antlitz," "Purpurwolken," "Frühlingslüfte" (123)
> "eine glänzende Seifenblase, ein buntes Nichts!" (123)
> "diese Würmerseelen, die, von niedrigen Begierden gedrückt, auf deinen Wangen kriechen" (123)
> "die erste Morgenröte einer schönen Seele" (131)
> "die Milch der Weisheit" (132)
> "ein elendes Handwerk, eine Arbeit der Finger, wozu ungefähr so viel Geist erfordert wird als zum Wollespinnen" (150)
> "du läßest die schreibenden Dunsen durchwischen" (163)
> "die pedantischen Klein-meisterischen Magister" (164)
> "die Herrschaft der Vernunft, ohne welche unser Planet nur ein großes Tollhaus ist" (166)
> "der gemeine Haufen der After-Gelehrten, und der Blinden, die sich von diesen Blinden leiten lassen" (166).[9]

Important in our context is not only the asseveration of bathos, lively imagery, and rhapsodic tone but also the nature of these seventeen letters as fragmentary expressions of an all-encompassing idea. They are like planets circling a common sun, alternating between light and dark, drawing nearer to and further away from the center of attraction at varying rates of speed. Many of the concepts and formulations here echo or anticipate qualities in Klopstock's, Herder's, and Schiller's work.

Although the text of the "Sympathien" is marked by rhapsody, it also reveals a dialogic quality and a personal warmth toward the reader. The affable quality of the author-reader relationship becomes clear in the very first letter. Wieland does not talk down to his interlocutor. Instead he treats her/him as an equal partner in a dialogue and in the ensuing letters exhorts, encourages, consoles, and cajoles each individual interlocutor (each "half of his soul," 3:110) to strive for the common goal. The introductory letter begins with a rhapsodic intonation designed to induce a similar response by the initiated reader. The perspective gradually expands in scope to include the skeptical reader, and concludes with an exhortation to the *Sympathetischen* not to mock those who have not yet learned to see and think in their heightened manner. The bifurcation of the focus compels the writer to resort to the rhetorical devices of persuasion.

In the ensuing twelve letters, Wieland addresses himself specifically to his intended reader, taking up in each letter a different topic many of which recall the concerns of Montaigne's *Essais*. A gradual shift from the private to the public sphere becomes manifest until it reaches its high point in letter # 14 (3:141–151) where the central idea of the "Sympathien" is expressed with all its consequences. That core idea is expressed as a categorical imperative pointing forward to Kant's thinking and anticipating the Classical language of Schiller. Wieland states:

> Bemühe dich nur so viel du kannst deine Erkenntnis zu lauter Licht und Wahrheit, und deine Liebe immer reiner und ausgebreiteter zu machen. Hiedurch wirst du zugleich in der Demut und in der Vollkommenheit zunehmen. Denn unsre Vollkommenheit besteht darin, daß wir uns immer mehr von unsern natürlichen und erworbnen Fehlern, von Unwissenheit, Irrtum, Eitelkeit, und allen unrichtigen oder übermäßigen Affekten reinigen, eine Arbeit mit der auch die Heiligsten in diesem Leibe des Todes nie zu Ende kommen.[10]

The passage marks the work as a product of enlightened religous thought. It also represents a climax in the line of subtle reasoning in the letter. Following it Wieland shifts his interest more and more toward the role of writer and writing in the betterment of society. Because of its pivotal role in the overall composition, we will analyze the epistle more closely here.

Through a series of essayistic encirclements (*Einkreisungen*) Wieland comes in letter # 14 to a discussion of humility. Genuine humility is a central concept of self-awareness which is anchored in Christian humanism with its ideal of the wise person promulgated around 1700 by such writers as Christian Thomasius.[11] The fourteenth letter begins on an upbeat, which is simultaneously a simple statement of fact and a provocation: "Die meisten Menschen, o Arete, sind von Empfindung ihres eigenen Werts aufgeblasen, weil sie nicht wissen, was der wahre Wert eines Menschen ist."[12] This simple statement contains the two poles between which the energized charges of the author's ensuing analysis oscillate: a false and a true sense of worth. The very next sentence sounds the crux of his argument: "Sie kennen sich selbst nicht, weder was sie sind, noch was sie sein sollen" (They do not know themselves, neither who they are nor what they should become, 3:141f.). When the wise man considers that his/her true worth is judged by God and not by one's fellow humans, all the external signs of his worth—physical beauty, wit, wealth, social position—are exposed as worthless, since God considers none of these accidentals in judging mankind. When humans view themselves stripped naked of earthly paraphernalia, how can they help but become humble? What really counts? What does one really possess? With this insight the wise person strives to please God, not man, and imperceptibly moves toward perfection. However, in keeping with the doctrine of synergism, the wise person realizes that s/he has many faults and cannot reach perfection, nor earn eternal happiness on one's own. Both are possible only through the grace of God.

At this juncture a false sense of humility might arise, Wieland observes, one that exaggerates human inadequacies and the role of divine largess. Since humans cannot achieve perfection independently, they might be tempted to belittle the meager powers imparted to them. Humankind must guard against this pernicious temptation, the author advises, for it saps the will to act. The reader comes full circle from the writer's opening statement when s/he next reads: "denke nicht zu gering von dir selbst" ("Do not hold yourself in too low regard." 3:145). Humankind should consider itself neither too high nor too low in the scale of creation. Wieland's often cited penchant for the golden mean is readily evident here.

The poet then formulates the already quoted crux of this letter and the essential import of the entire "Sympathien": humans must strive for self-knowledge, must endeavor to purify and increase their capacity for love. Both knowledge and love lead to perfection and hence to God. Perfection is then defined as the vanquishing of ignorance, error, vanity, and false or excessive emotion (*unrichtige oder übermäßige Affekte*, 145). After reaching this climax, Wieland interjects a paragraph that tends to retard the rush of logical consequences. He pauses to shift his focus from the allegorical wise individual (referred to as Arete, Greek for virtue) to a real person: Amyntor (i.e., Ludwig Gleim). However, Gleim's name is not mentioned until two paragraphs later. In the intervening passage, Wieland repeats his central idea in succinct and direct fashion: "kenne dich Selbst" (know yourself, 146). The repetition accentuates the importance of self-knowledge, a concept clearly adopted from the Platonic tradition. In addition the significance of that admonition is underscored by the introduction of the logical extension of self-knowledge: action. In order to be all that one is capable of becoming, one must act. This exhortation occurs at the mid-point of this essayistic fragment.

The first half of the letter is theoretical and abstract. With the formulation of the phrase "know thyself," the tone and style of the text become more graphic and agitated. The bifocal quality of the opening letter (the *exordium* of the "Sympathien" seen as a whole) emerges here in full flower. The admonition to fulfill the ultimate purpose of life entails personal involvement for the improvement of society. The insights gained from self-knowledge "should guide all [of Amyntor's] actions" (147). Shifting the focus away from the enlightened individual to society, Wieland dwells upon what is wrong with the world. His descriptions of misplaced values and false concepts rise in a carefully orchestrated crescendo of Baroque imagery and impressions, interspersed with pointed exhortations and rhetorical questions. Although the sentences are protracted—implying the extent of the abuses—they are organized with clear markings:

> Andre, deren Verstand umnebelt ist, die zu schwach sind den Eindrücken der sinnlichen Dinge, und den Reizen phantasierter Glückseligkeiten zu widerstehen, mögen Wollust oder eitle Ehre zu dem Endzweck ihrer Bestrebungen machen; sie mögen alle Schärfe ihres Geistes dazu anwenden, wie sie sich in diesem Schattenleben, in dieser vergänglichen Welt, als wie für die Ewigkeit etablieren wollen, welches eben soviel ist, als ein Gebäude auf Wasser gründen: andre mögen vor den Fürsten und ihren Günstlingen kriechen; sie mögen immerhin Titel, Ordensbänder, Bedienungen, für beneidenswürdige Güter halten, und vor Begierde sie zu besitzen verdorren, wie der Geizige über seine Schätze zum Gerippe wird.[13]

The physical separation of *andre* from its verb emphasizes the difference between the virtuous, those few who see clearly, and "the others," whose reason is clouded and whose sensuality is unchecked. A sense of their hollow lives is evoked by such terms as *phantasiert, eitel, Schattenleben,* and *vergängliche Welt*—Baroque impressions which culminate in the first of two striking metaphors: *ein Gebäude auf Wasser.*

With that simile of a house built on the uncertain element of water a plateau is reached from which a new onrush is launched. *Andre* is repeated to tighten the focus, *mögen* recurs two more times to express the author's own indifference to the values of this world and establishes a closer tie between writer and addressee. *Kriechen* and *verdorren* are introduced to imply the vainness of such attitudes. Then, finally, the impact of the second simile: the miser's bleached skeleton still grasping his amassed fortune. The style, the sentence rhythm, are thus constructed to impress upon the reader the necessary consequences of "befogged reason" (*umnebelter Verstand*).

Next the author remarks that Amyntor and the "secret society" of like-minded thinkers must attempt to spread enlightenment to the uninformed. No help can be expected from the ranks of the intellectuals, the traditional preceptors of the people. The poets have abandoned their lofty calling in search of popularity. Instead of poets in the old mold, the new age has spawned "eine Menge leichtsinniger und nichtswürdiger Witzlinge" (a bunch of frivolous and unworthy wags). These poetasters cater to the whims and prejudices of the masses (*Pöbel*) with their impudent triflings (*Tändeleien*, 148).

Similarly, the wise philosophers of old (*philosophischer Kopf*) who tackled practical problems with "herculean courage" have been supplanted by haughty school men (*aufgedunsene Schulgelehrte*). Wieland's description of their metaphysical rambling and arrogance continues a lively humanistic tradition since the fifteenth century. His acerbic formulation distinctly foreshadows Goethe's and Schiller's indictments during the 1770s and 1780s:

> Ja diese glücklichen Tage sind nicht nur verschwunden, sondern
> unsre Sophisten und Dunse sind so sehr verblendet und von
> ihrer gelehrten Unwissenheit berauscht, daß sie von erleuchteten
> Zeiten schwatzen, und vom Gipfel ihrer aufeinander getürmten
> Bücher, deren Wert sie beim Pfund abwägen, auf die großen
> Genien des Altertums mit dummer Verachtung hinabsehen,
> ohne zu wissen daß Leute von ihren Fähigkeiten zu Platons Zeit
> kaum zu Abschreibern gut genug gewesen wären.[14]

These words could have been spoken by Faust or Karl Moor—except of course that they antedate those two characters by a good twenty years. Whereas philosophy formerly dealt with the art of living, it had now degenerated into sophistry. The striking picture of the arrogant little man among his piles of books seems most effective.

As a *Weltbürger* Amyntor has the task of working for the general welfare. Every divinely inspired individual who has cultivated a sense of order and beauty is eager (*voller Aktivität*) to promote these qualities in others (149). Yet the world of politics, the court, is anathema to persons like him. Princes and rulers cannot tolerate honest and just advisers, and will not allow them to act in accordance with their ideals. Wieland therefore advises his friend to look for a different means of "spreading truth . . . through the various estates and classes of men" (150). The means is the medium of literature. Once again an expression of enlightenment through print.

A combination of Homer's epic grandeur, Plato's graceful dialogues, and Lucian's friendly satire are best suited to lead men to beneficial insights, not just to amuse them. Amyntor (i.e., Gleim) was suited to this lofty office and Wieland concludes this letter which began with an examination of humility with a fervent appeal for public activity on the part of gifted writers. The high office of yore has been "usurped" by insipid poetasters who compose just to see their names in print or because they do not know what else to do. Wieland sums up: "Die Kunst zu schreiben ist, wie die edelsten Künste alle, in unsern Tagen, ein elendes Handwerk geworden, eine Arbeit der Finger, wozu ungefähr so viel Geist erfordert wird als zum Wollespinnen" (The art of writing—like all the noble arts in our day—has been reduced to the most deplorable trade, a mere product of the fingers for which about as much imagination is necessary as for spinning wool, 150). The salient image of busy work dominates the final section of the piece. Wieland then concludes his culturally critical epistle with a question expressing the hope that Amyntor would help restore the profession of the writer to its former luster. By ending the piece with a query, the essay is not really over. A resolution has not been found, and perhaps it cannot be: "Willst du nicht helfen, Amyntor, diesem erhabenen Beruf seinen alten Glanz wieder zu verschaffen? Willst du nicht einer von den wenigen sein, für welche Schäftesbury seine Erinnerungen nicht umsonst gegeben hat?" ("Will you not help, Amyntor, to restore this sublime profession to its old glory? Will you not be one of the select few for whom Shaftesbury has not composed his meditations in vain?" 151). The concluding exhortation to translate thought into action coupled with the synecdochic reference to Shaftesbury's *Characteristics* reaffirm the place of Wieland's "Sympathien" in the tradition of the European essay.

The reader is struck by the contrast between the beginning and the conclusion of this brief letter. What starts off seraphically ends as a call for a socially engaged writing posture. The "digression" from the religious to the social is only superficial. In the context of the Enlightenment and pietism, recognition of the truth implied active engagement to reshape human life in accordance with that recognition. From the cocoon of self-introspection, the visionary must rise to an ideal state. Obviously, given the conditions of absolutism in eighteenth-century Germany which allowed the likes of Wieland and Gleim to engage only "in thinking and

wishing" (*nur zu denken und zu wünschen,* 150), the pen was the only
way they could effect their dream of universal equality. The importance
of the writer in the moral and aesthetic improvement of society is reem-
phasized when Wieland returns to the topic in the concluding letter (#17)
of the "Sympathien." There we find a satiric characterization of the state
of arts and letters coupled with an appeal to write in the manner of
Christian Liscow to rid the world of "the pedantic, small-minded academics" (*die pedantischen Klein-meisterischen Magister,* 164) and the
"general horde of half-learned scholars" (*der gemeine Haufen der After-
Gelehrten,* 166). Once they are quieted, real education through print can
take hold.

Wieland's rhetorical and artistic talent is evident in this early product
of his journalistic pen. His tone alternates rhythmically between philosophical earnestness and personal warmth, the perspective frequently
changes from the private to the public revealing how interwoven the two
spheres are. He utilizes the full register of rhetorical and poetic strategies
to engage a willing and informed reader in a critical review of contemporary issues of timeless value. And his understanding of writing and
reading as ethical acts preliminary to overt activity is everywhere manifest.

Our analysis of letter fourteen in the collection "Sympathien" is representative of Wieland's essayism in the 1750s. As the writer gained
expertise he produced many more essayistic pieces which more fully
mirror the "classical" manner of the nineteenth-century mode. Examples
of that latter work range from interludes in his novel, *Die Geschichte des
Agathon* (1766/67) (e.g., Book 3, chapter 5: "Der Anti-Platonismus in
Nuce"), contributions to the *Teutscher Merkur* such as "Was ist Wahrheit" (1776), "Fragment über Erasmus" (1776), the satirical "Sendschreiben eines Nachdruckers an den Herausgeber des T.M." (1781),
"Über die ältesten Zeitkürzungsspiele" (1781), or the dialectical "Für
und Wider. Ein Göttergespräch" (1793). Because these and other essayistic samples have been analyzed elsewhere, we can make do here with a
general characterization of their dominant traits.[15]

What is striking about these later works is not so much the "con-
creteness and clarity" of their language as Martini suggests ("Nachwort,"
3:995), since those qualities are evident already in the "Sympathien," but
rather their greater stylistic agility and the intellectual equality of the
interlocutors. The participants in the dialogues of the 1780s and 1790s
treat one another with respect. Each realizes the other is capable of
grasping a line of argument or a subtle allusion and of expanding upon

it. This is not to say that some speakers are not bigoted and blind; their function is to catapult the discourse forward toward a higher level of understanding.

Wieland himself adopted an objective stance, mediating between opposing views, and illuminating a question from many different vantage points.[16] Only from that superior standpoint of inner detachment, from the symbolic pinnacle of Mount Olympus can one enjoy an unrestricted syncretic panorama of the totality. Far from being dogmatic, Wieland is conciliatory in his writing. Sometimes he even appears digressive or merely associative without a clear purpose. In the post-1770 era his essayistic compositions continued the discursive quality of his earlier work but took on the even more refined quality of Horace's epistles which he so admired. Wieland had translated those letters in 1781 providing critical introductions and commentaries. In his analysis of the epistle to L. Calpurnius Piso and his sons, Wieland characterizes Horace's manner of proceeding in a highly significant manner for our purposes. He describes it namely as a leisurely walk:

> Der Gang unsers Autors in diesem Discurse hat . . . das Ansehn eines Spaziergangs, wobei man nichts anders beabsichtigt, als zu gehen; wo ein kleiner Abweg nichts zu bedeuten hat, und man bald bei einer schönen Aussicht stille steht, bald seitwärts ablenkt, um eine Blume zu pflücken oder der Kühlung eines schattenreichen Baumes zu genießen; wo immer der nächste Gegenstand, der in die Augen fällt, das Gespräch fortführt, und man doch am Ende, ohne zu wissen wie, sich auf einmal da befindet, wohin man wollte. Er verweilt bei keiner Materie lange genug, um die Wißbegierde zu befriedigen; bestimmt selten eine Regel genau genug, um ihre Anwendung für einen Schüler der Kunst leicht und sicher zu machen; kommt alle Augenblicke vom Besondern wieder aufs Allgemeine.[17]

What Wieland states here about Horace's epistolary style and method is equally true of his own writing. The passage is strongly reminiscent of Montaigne's self-evaluation of his musings as a leisurely stroll which gave rise to one of the chief topoi of essayistic writing.

From beginning to end Wieland's essayistic stance can be viewed as attempts to achieve that special, all-encompassing point of view aimed at encouraging the same syncratic perspective and graceful expression in his readers. Thus his essayistic articles can be interpreted as being fragments of a public dialogue which we have designated *transzendentale Publizistik* and which was designed to improve general aesthetic sensitivity while promoting critical thought.

Gotthold Ephraim Lessing

The available evidence would seem to belie the traditional wisdom that the genre of the literary essay began at mid century with Gotthold Ephraim Lessing (1729–1781), the so-called father of the German essay. That contention was fueled by Friedrich Schlegel's high praise of Lessing's role in the development of an innovative prose. In his assessment of the author, "Lessing. Wege der Kritik" (1801), Schlegel cites above all else Lessing's combinatory method (*das Kombinatorische*) as an original feature, concluding: "Diesen originellen Stempel wird nicht leicht jemand in den Lessingschen Fragmenten verkennen können; und ich denke, daß auch in Rücksicht der kühnen und überraschenden Kombinationen das Ganze derselben dem Begriff der aufgestellten [vierten] Gattung so sehr entspricht, als nur immer möglich, daß ähnliche Schriften anderer noch größer Massen von Ideen aus der inneren Fülle der verschiedenartigsten Wissenschaften und Künste in noch gedrängterer Kürze enthalten; in Rücksicht jener kühnen Kombinationen aber und des seine Sprünge und überraschenden Wendungen so glücklich nachbildenden und ausdrückenden genialischen Stils wird Lessing nicht so leicht übertroffen werden."[18] The key phrase for our present purposes would seem to be Schlegel's remark that Lessing's supple and engaging style cannot easily be outdone by other writers.

Even earlier Herder had praised Lessing's style as a clear reflection of the writing process itself, with all its uncertainties and false starts.[19] Perhaps more vividly than with any previous writer, Lessing's writing style mirrors his innermost manner of thinking. Today it is common practice to speak of his "intellectual gymnastics," a phrase adopted from Lessing's friend and contemporary, Moses Mendelssohn.[20] The term refers to the dialectical agility and epistemological polyperspectivity of his never-ending quest for truth. Convinced that the totality of representation could be approximated only by an ever-changing point of view, Lessing considered his articles and fragments to be "nothing more than the fermentations of his thinking," i.e, *fermenta cognitionis*.[21] The manner of conception and expression which desires to stimulate further contemplation and to counteract the hardening of thought and belief into rigid systems lies at the heart of essayism. For that reason Lessing's formulation of *fermenta cognitionis* can serve as an expression of essayistic writing in general. It is, in any event, an appropriate title for this chapter subsection.

Lessing's own explanation of his epistemologic method in the *Duplik* (1778) has frequently been cited as an early definition of essayism. Our purposes are well served by recalling that famous formulation here: "Nicht die Wahrheit, in deren Besitz irgendein Mensch ist oder zu sein vermeint, sondern die aufrichtige Mühe, die er angewandt hat, hinter die Wahrheit zu kommen, macht den Wert des Menschen. Denn nicht durch den Besitz, sondern durch die Nachforschung der Wahrheit erweitern sich seine Kräfte, worin allein seine immer wachsende Vollkommenheit bestehet."[22] The similarity between the tentativeness of the essayistic approach and the methodological probing of Lessing's philosophical inquiry is self-evident. If we add to this intellectual stance Lessing's insistence upon the reader as a necessary factor in the dialectical process of thinking and writing, yet another similarity to essayism is discernible.

Nevertheless, the legitimacy of the claim that the first signs of a nascent essayistic style are to be found in the works of Lessing (Berger, *Essay*, 197) requires revision. We have come to recognize that literary forms do not evolve spontaneously, that they experience a growth cycle like all living things, and that it is not possible to state simply that "the essay is the external form of essayism."[23] Moreover, it is clear that Lessing was imbedded in the philosophical and rhetorical traditions of his age dating back at least to Thomasius. Nor are we better served by suggesting that another writer, for instance Johann Peter Sturz (1736–1779) with his skillful short forms of the 1770s (epistles, dialogues, fragments, anecdotes), was the originator of the essay in Germany.[24] Thus it would behoove us to guard against precipitous judgments. Even Lessing's much lauded consciousness of an adjudicating public was anticipated by a Thomasius, Gellert, or Pitschel. The awareness of ultimate audience participation in the writing act must be seen as a general mark of the new prose style. We can, in any event, treasure Lessing as a consummate essayist, although he hardly ever published separate, rounded essays.

During the 1750s and 1760s Lessing was busy writing reviews and articles for journals like *Die Berlinische privilegierte Zeitung* (1749–55) or collections such as the *Literaturbriefe* (1758–61) and the *Hamburgische Dramaturgie* (1767–69). There is good reason to select an early example of Lessing's essayistic writing from these works. Yet because a definite continuity in Lessing's style is detectable from start to finish, we will consider *Ernst und Falk*, a collection of five dialogues written and circulated among his friends during the mid 1770s but not published until 1778 (#1 to #3) and 1780 (#4 to #5). Additionally, they have been frequently examined as statements of his political or anthropological views, while seldom treated as belletristic creations. Moreover, they are similar to Pitschel's letters in *Die Belustigungen des Verstandes und Witzes* in that the argument continues from one installment to the next, with the first three dialogues forming a distinct unit culminating with Ernst's decision to become a Freemason. The fourth and fifth dialogues take place several weeks after the first three. Each discourse can, nonetheless, stand alone.

Ernst und Falk is truly a literary jewel because of its pristine clarity and deft engagement of the reader. The topic discussed by the two friends, Ernst and Falk, is the true nature of Freemasonry which Lessing, via his spokesman Falk, equates with the advancement of humanity and the treatment of individuals as autonomous agents rather than passive pawns. The forms which Freemasonry has assumed in the eighteenth century are far removed from the original intent. Accidentals have replaced the essence, so that we are left mostly with externals (*Schema, Hülle, Einkleidung,* LM, 13:399). While emphasizing what is essential, each of the five dialogues strives to expose the falseness of a movement which has become commercialized and politicized. Thus "good deeds" like the organizing of orphanages in Stockholm and Dresden or schools like Basedow's Philanthropic Institute in Dessau must be viewed in the proper light (first dialogue; LM, 13:349). The real actions of the Freemasons do not readily meet the eye, Lessing claims. The truly important activities of the genuine Freemasons do not require publicity, for their aim is the refinement of humanity in the long run. This argument is subtle and sometimes enigmatic, an effect which Falk readily admits. In order to ensure that Ernst properly understands his meaning, Falk engages him in a Socratic discourse. Like Ernst the internal interlocutor, the skeptical reader is also engaged in dialectical interplay, is encouraged to think critically, and is cajoled by rhetorical or poetic technique to comprehend Falk's meaning.

If it were merely a matter of the reader being manipulated into seeing things more distinctly like Falk with his falconine vision, we could hardly consider *Ernst und Falk* to be essayistic. Thus we must stress that Lessing's use of rhetoric is not intended to deprive the reader of her/his intellectual independence but rather to nurture a critical stance toward generally accepted notions. In so doing Lessing fulfills the purpose of the dialogue form as formulated in Johann Georg Sulzer's *Allgemeine Theorie der schönen Künste* (*General Theory of the Fine Arts,* 1771): "The dialogue is thus an imitation of a conversation among people who expose their manner of thinking and feeling to one another in such a manner that their unobserved audience is granted a view into their innermost souls."[25] Such was Lessing's intent in all of his essayistic pieces. For the sake of economy, the following analysis is restricted to the first three dialogues published together in 1778.

The first three discourses are introduced by the "Vorrede eines Dritten" ("Preface by a Third Party") which acts as an *exordium*, alerting the reader to the importance of what follows. The directness and terseness of the opening lines of the dialogue immediately arrest the reader's attention:

> Ernst: Woran denkst du, Freund?
> Falk: An nichts.
> Ernst: Aber du bist so still.
> Falk: Eben darum. Wer denkt, wenn er genießt? Und ich genieße des erquickenden Morgens.[26]

Every reader has had the experience of just sitting and enjoying the morning calm without thinking of anything in particular, especially if one is on holiday (Falk is relaxing at a spa = *Brunnenkur.*). Lessing uses that commonplace experience (that is, commonplace within his target audience) in order to underscore the connection between thinking and acting at the outset. Immediately thereupon Falk remarks that there is nothing better in the whole world than candid discourse with a friend: "Nichts geht über das *Lautdenken* mit einem Freunde" (Nothing is finer than *thinking aloud* with a friend, LM, 13:342). His remark reminds us of a cardinal prerequisite of essayism: writing is tantamount to thinking aloud either to stimulate action or as a reaction to an external stimulus. This perception is analogous to Habermas's understanding of communicative action discussed in Chapter III.

Moreover, there is also the hint of the topos of the leisurely walk which has been identified as a major mark of the essayism. Although Ernst and Falk do not meander about, they are located near a spa in the peaceful countryside far from the hubbub of the city and are thus at leisure to think about anything if they are so inclined. Ernst is inclined. He turns to Falk and asks point blank: Are you a Freemason? Translated into today's parlance, the query had an impact similar to: are you a communist? Falk's response is seemingly evasive: he remarks that it is not the proper question. To Ernst's insistence upon an answer, Falk replies: "Yes, I think I am." Even Falk's choice of words (*glaube es zu sein*) is symptomatic of the skeptical, essayistic stance. Nothing is known or can be known with absolute certainty. Falk subsequently explains that he phrases his response so tentatively out of deference for others. He has no desire to impose his convictions on anyone (LM, 13:342). And his conviction is that Freemasonry is a necessary part of human existence, that it is part and parcel of human nature and human society.[27]

However, it is not easy to express the quintessence of Freemasonry because every attempt to put the concept into words is subject to inaccuracy and misinterpretation. Falk touches here upon the underlying difficulty in any discursive act: how can one communicate one's innermost thoughts and feelings reliably if the speaker does not possess the facility to formulate exact meanings? Citing the misuse of language by poets and orators (*Hyperbel, Probewerk, Jüngerarbeit*), Falk concludes that the most reliable channels of communication are the individual's actions themselves; Ernst calls them "sprechende Taten" (self-revealing deeds, LM, 13:349). (This line of reasoning is a continuation of Klopstock's remarks on the nature of language as semiotic signs.)[28] For this reason Falk is hesitant to equate philanthropic projects with the essence of Freemasonry. For him their true deeds are "so big, so forward-looking that several centuries will have to pass before one can say: this is what the Freemasons did." Their essential actions, therefore, are not readily discernible, although they are all directed at making the world a better place. Their ultimate goal is to make all so-called good deeds expendable (LM, 13:352). Ernst is understandably confused by these equivocating responses to his direct inquiries.

Lessing guides the reader through the maze of his essayistic meandering by posting metaphors as sign posts. At the critical point of Falk's argument regarding the genuine deeds of the Freemasons, Lessing has him interrupt himself to chase after a butterfly. This gives Ernst time to ponder the paradox of good deeds whose goal is to make good deeds unnecessary. He goes off to a nearby tree to watch a hord of ants busily pursuing their chores. On those two notes the first discourse comes to an end. The attentive reader suspects that the butterfly is a symbol of truth which flutters about, now distant, now near, but always out of reach. The anthill, on the other hand, probably symbolizes organized activity in pursuit of the common good. The practiced reader suspects that the diametrically opposed images are somehow interrelated.

The second discourse begins with an explanation of each metaphor. Falk returns from his hunt without the butterfly which has eluded him. Thereupon Ernst answers that he has had no better luck with his reflections on the paradox of the need to make good deeds superfluous. He tells us: "I won't catch it either, that beautiful butterfly!" (LM, 13:352). He then points to the anthill he has been observing. The well organized activity of the ants allows the colony to operate smoothly. Falk remarks that the ant community is like the beehive. The metaphorical significance becomes clear with the next exchange between Falk and Ernst: an orderly society must be possible without the interference of a governmental apparatus. Yes, Ernst opines, when each member of the society is capable of self-regulation, then government will disappear. Falk asks wistfully: will human society ever develop to that point? With that Lessing has arrived at the central idea of his second colloquy: is humankind a means or an end? (LM, 13:360). Both interlocutors agree that the state exists for humankind and not vice versa. Any official regulation that occasions the repression of even a minority is labelled the "cloaking of tyranny" (*Bemäntelung der Tyrannei*, LM, 3:361) and is not to be tolerated.

This idea is further elucidated in the remaining eight pages of the twelve-page conversation through the use of direct appeals, concessions, analogy, syncrisis, allusions, repetition, and periphrasis. The effect of the conclusion is maximized by the introduction of an adage followed immediately by a simile. "Whoever wishes to enjoy the fire," Ernst remarks, "has to put up with the smoke." True, Falk enjoins, but just because smoke is inseparable from fire, that does not mean that we should refrain from actions which would make the experience more enjoyable. Far from being antipathetic towards fire, the inventor of the chimney flue (*Rauchfang*) has enhanced its usefulness and pleasure. Falk then applies the simile to his interpretation of the state which joins individuals together while creating systems for smooth and enjoyable operation. These systems or separations (*Trennungen*) are a necessary part of society. Yet every thinking person should strive to reduce them to the barest minimum in order to ensure the greatest happiness of each member. Ernst's reply to each supposition made by Falk is a reverberating: "Recht sehr zu wünschen!" (That would be great!) which ultimately culminates in the exclamation: "Ein schöner Traum!" (What a beautiful dream!) at the thought of a utopian society (LM, 13:373f.).

At the conclusion of this series of suppositions and responses, Falk surprises Ernst by returning to the topic of the Freemasons. Ernst is nonplussed, for he has not suspected the connection. The unexpected twist is an instance of *sustentio*, a rhetorical strategy used here with great effectiveness, for Falk then abruptly breaks off the conversation. The breakfast bell has sounded and he wishes to go off to eat! He urges Ernst, whose curiosity is at a high, to forget the remark. Breakfast is more important and they will surely "find a more worthy topic of conversation in the larger group" than that of Freemasonry (LM, 13:374). The belittling of his topic is typical of essayistic writing in general, following in the manner of Montaigne. This strategy is used expertly, for example, at the conclusion of Justus Möser's "Harlequin, oder Vertheidigung des Groteske-Komischen" ("Harlequin, or In Defense of the Grotesquely Comic," 1761). Even though his composition treats essential human qualities, Möser apologizes for having detained his reader from pursuing more important activities during the hour it took to read through the article!

The third exchange takes place at the end of the same day. No opportunity had presented itself for Ernst and Falk to continue their conversation. The limiting of the action to one day reminds us of the dramatic unity of time. The oneness with the preceding two discourses is further emphasized by the recurrence of Falk's coyness in responding to his interlocutor's pressing queries as well as the repetition of the eye motif sounded in the "Vorrede eines Dritten." Fearing that most readers would fail to understand the import of *Ernst und Falk*, Lessing had drawn the distinction in the preface between "impaired sight" (*blöde Augen*) and intellectual openness (*gesunde Augen*) (LM, 13:341). In the third dialogue he allows Falk to return to that divergence.

First Falk mentions that the evidence he cites should be obvious to even the "most shortsighted person" (*das kurzsichtigste Auge*, LM, 13:371). Then he reinvokes the eye motif just prior to making the critical point in his summation. In contrast to the general notion of secret societies, the Freemasons have consistently acted in full public view (*vor den Augen der ganzen Welt*) with regards to a basic tenet of their philosophy. That principle is to accept any worthy individual (*Mann*) regardless of ethnic, religious, or social differences into their order (LM, 13:372). In other words, the Freemasons practice a democracy of the spirit.

Ernst's eagerness to satisfy his curiosity about the Freemasons' real goal of reducing the ethnic, religious, and social distances between human beings as members of society mirrors the astute reader's own animated inquisitiveness. Falk's initial coyness in responding to that interest serves to enhance the atmosphere of expectancy. As he did when originally asked whether he was a Freemason, Falk pauses when Ernst requests proof that the Freemasons are really sincere about a democratic revolution of the spirit: "You are silent? — You're thinking about it?" (LM, 13:372). Falk hesitates, not because he is lacking an answer, but because he is startled that Ernst would ask such a question. The interlude serves to clear the air between the two discussants. Neither wishes to be misunderstood as being willfully deceitful, sophistic, or starry-eyed.

The move is critical to the general intent of the three discourses. If genuine communication, that is, a common ground of understanding and action is to evolve, it can only happen on the basis of mutual trust. Moreover, it can only eventuate if both parties are attentive. Ernst has grown tired and is no longer able to follow Falk's argument. In reply to Falk's piqued question whether Ernst is dreaming, the latter explains: "No, my friend, but I've had enough. Enough for tonight. Tomorrow at the crack of dawn I am returning to the city." The two take cordial leave of one another and exit. A postscript explains that a spark had nonetheless been struck. Ernst returned to the city and became a Freemason. His experiences as a lodge member is the topic of discourses four and five.

Lessing's *Ernst und Falk* is exemplary of literature's use as an intellectual stimulus. The dialectical interplay of the textual interlocutors prefigures the dialogue which should take place between author and reader with the text as the medium. In the manner of classic essayistic style, the argument remains open and in need, therefore, of continuance. The label *cognitionis fermenta* is apt to compositions of this quality.

The Philosopher as Essayist

Lessing provides an appropriate transition from the realm of belletristic writing to that of philosophic analysis and speculation because his writing is intensely informed by philosophic and specifically epistemologic concerns. *Ernst und Falk* like Wieland's *Was ist Wahrheit?* (1776) or *Sechs Antworten auf sechs Fragen* (1789) points to the predilection of the essayistic mode for philosophic questions. It is as if philosophy blends into literature or literature into philosophy.[29] Concurrent with Lessing's emergence as an innovative writer, Immanuel Kant's (1724–1804) fame as an innovative philosopher began to spread.

Prized as a rigorous thinker, Kant is not valued for graceful formulations. Quite the contrary. He himself recognized the contorted style of such works as the *Critique of Pure Reason* (1781).[30] Yet it would be surprising indeed if he did not profit in his shorter, journalistic pieces from the stylistic strides made since the turn of the century by such writers as Gottsched, Gellert, Pitschel, Wieland, and others. Because of the affinity between essayism and philosophical concerns we might further expect a philosopher's writing to reveal essayistic traits.[31] In the early years in Königsberg, Kant penned a series of articles in the service of the Enlightenment for a broader reading public. The following journal pieces with their typically essayistic formulations come to mind:

1. "Betrachtungen über das Erdbeben von Lisabon" (1756);
2. "Versuch über den Optimismus" (1759);
3. "Versuch über die Krankheiten des Kopfes" (1764);
4. "Träume eines Geistersehers erläutert durch Träume der Metaphysik" (1766).[32]

Wilhelm Windelband discerns in these early writings a "lively, fresh, and for the most part very witty" use of language.[33] The impetus for the "untypical" style for Kant might very well lie in the English model, for Kant was an avid reader of English literature during the 1750s and 1760s. In his study of the German essay Bruno Berger argues that even some of the specifically philosophical studies from these years, such as the "Beobachtungen über das Gefühl des Schönen und Erhabenen" ("Observations on the Sensation of the Beautiful and Sublime," 1764) approach the character of the essay (Berger, 212).

However, because of its seminal role in discussions of eighteenth-century Enlightenment, Kant's "Beantwortung der Frage: Was ist Aufklärung?" ("An Answer to the Question: What is Enlightenment?"), first published in the December 1784 issue of the *Berlinische Monatsschrift*, has been selected for scrutiny here. With its mere ten paragraphs covering but seven pages, the article closely approaches the "ideal" length of the essay form. The compactness of structure lends the piece an air of focused forcefulness. As a careful logician, Kant placed importance on systematic analysis so that we find here a sparkling, transparent house of crystal.

The publication of "Was ist Aufklärung?" in the popular *Berlinische Monatsschrift* bears witness to Kant's intention to reach out to a broader audience. He had not fixed his gaze on his fellow philosophers, but had his eye more on the amateur thinker. Nevertheless, he did expect the anonymous reader to bring a modicum of interest to the task. Even though he could presume interest on the reader's part because the topic was a hot issue in the 1780s, Kant made extensive use of the rhetorical devices of repetition, personal appeal, figurative language, striking metaphors, and rhetorical questions to involve his reader more deeply in his thought process.

The tone is set in the opening paragraph (the *exordium*) with its direct and precise definition of terms:

> *Aufklärung ist der Ausgang des Menschen aus seiner selbst verschuldeten Unmündigkeit. Unmündigkeit* ist das Unvermögen, sich seines Verstandes ohne Leitung eines anderen zu bedienen. *Selbstverschuldet* ist diese Unmündigkeit, wenn die Ursache derselben nicht am Mangel des Verstandes, sondern der Ent-

schließung und des Mutes liegt, sich seiner ohne Leitung eines andern zu bedienen. Sapere aude! Habe Mut dich deines *eigenen* Verstandes zu bedienen!, ist also der Wahlspruch der Aufklärung.[34]

These lines are a typical instance of the literal or determinate concept.[35] As the essay unfolds, however, the dichotomy of art and science becomes evident with the introduction of the metaphorical and indeterminate. The reader's attention is immediately caught by the opening sentence. Because it is italicized the sense of electricity underlying it is enhanced. The statement is electrifying precisely because of its clarity and directness. The reader is induced to read on in order to learn how human beings are themselves responsible for their intellectual dependency. The immediate repetition of the italicized word *Unmündigkeit* (tutelage) at the beginning of the second sentence draws one on. The third sentence uses the same technique with *selbstverschuldet* (self-incurred). In each instance the key term is concisely defined. The concluding sentence makes unmistakably clear the intent of the preceding definitions: humanity must dare to use reason freely. The repetition of the Latin *sapere aude* (dare to know) in German paraphrase lends greater weight to the exhortation. Finally, that exhortation is identified as the motto of the *Aufklärung*. Instead of curbing the reader's curiosity, the matter-of-factness of these opening lines unexpectedly kindles intense interest. The economy of words is classic in its impact.

Kant does not let up. In the second paragraph he immediately moves to the causes of the intellectual dwarfishness: laziness and cowardice (*Faulheit und Feigheit*, 55), for which he provides a series of examples: "Habe ich ein Buch, das für mich Verstand hat, einen Seelsorger, der für mich Gewissen hat, einen Arzt, der für mich die Diät beurteilt u.s.w., so brauche ich mich ja nicht selbst zu bemühen." And he concludes using again the inclusive first person pronoun *ich* to invite reader identification: "Ich habe nicht nötig zu denken, wenn ich nur bezahlen kann; andere werden das verdrießliche Geschäft schon für mich übernehmen."[36] The pointed reference to money characterizes the reluctance to think for oneself as a luxury which, in the long run, one can ill afford. Kant follows up the money motif and its implications of privilege with the metaphor of the unthinking majority of citizens as domestic cattle (*Hausvieh*) tethered by their guardians (*Vormünder*) to a cart with harness (*Gängelwagen*) who have become too timid to attempt independent action. In his first two paragraphs Kant succeeds in totally captivating his reader. The writer is firmly in control; the reader plunges on.

The third paragraph is closely integrated into the line of movement established by the preceding two. This continuity is achieved on two levels: by means of the literal argument and by means of tropes. The argument is clear: because individuals are unpracticed in the free use of reason, they find it difficult to think for themselves. Besides, the force of habit has something comforting about it. Only in isolated instances has an occasional person succeeded in breaking free of the set patterns, thereby liberating the powers of reason. The immense difficulty of achieving this freedom is underscored by images of shackles (*Fußschellen*) and an uncertain gait (*unsicherer Gang*). Kant argues that most of those few individuals who succeed in ridding themselves of the "shackles of continuing dependence" are scarcely able to leap over the smallest ditch (56). Only the rare individual is able to walk with sure step. The allusions to walking and jumping echo similar motifs of the second paragraph where Kant speaks of "den Schritt zur Mündigkeit" (the move toward intellectual maturity) and of an individual's inability to venture a "Schritt außer dem Gängelwagen" (step from the harness cart) in which one is held captive (55). In view of the frequent use of metaphors (*Gängelwagen, Hausvieh*) and images (*Fußschellen, unsicherer Gang*), we recall that aesthetic ideas included for Kant such rhetorical devices as similes, tropes, metaphors, and poetic analogies. The metaphor for Kant was not just ornamental but also of cognitive value. Indeed, "the metaphor raises important questions concerning the origins and limits of knowledge," while also serving as "the hallmark of artistic genius."[37]

The same rhetorical techniques are repeated in paragraph four, which begins to focus more clearly on the essential element of freedom in this process of liberation. Given the opportunity to develop their critical faculties, the people would naturally strive for self-realization. The sine qua non, however, is that the "yoke of tutelage" (*das Joch der Unmündigkeit*) must first be thrown off. Kant introduces at this important juncture the idea that enlightenment evolves gradually, whether for the fortunate individual or for the commonweal. Revolution might free the individual from political or economic oppression, but it would never lead to a genuine reform of one's mode of thinking (56). True and permanent change only comes with the eradication of prejudice.

In four brief paragraphs Kant leads his reader deep into the labyrinth of his thinking without the reader having suspected how demanding the philosopher's line of reasoning really is. The impression of ease in moving from one idea to the next is conveyed largely by Kant's judicious and appropriate use of images, all related to the need to walk and move about freely. But we are not dealing here with the topos of the leisurely walk which may occasion all sorts of thoughts and has become the hallmark of the literary essay.[38] The reader is completely persuaded to follow Kant's lead on a journey of exploration. Thus, the reader hardly realizes that the next two paragraphs (5 and 6) run on for four pages (each paragraph covers two pages of print) and form the crux of the philosopher's argument. The main idea of paragraph five is the concept of *Freiheit* in Kant's specific context, while paragraph six explores the idea of moral responsibility for bringing about enlightenment. The ideas of freedom and obligation were first sounded in paragrpah four. The middle part of the essay is thus devoted to an elaboration of views introduced in the first page and a half.

The protracted discussion of freedom avoids tediousness by employing devices such as definition, prolepsis, repetition, variation, rhetorical questions, direct quotation, and examples drawn from everyday experience. As he had done before, Kant begins the fifth paragraph with a definition, this time of freedom: "to make public use of one's reason without restraint" (*von seiner Vernunft in allen Stücken öffentlichen Gebrauch zu machen,* 56). This definition is immediately followed up by a series of terse sentences which anticipate objections and thus form a prolepsis. they also have a dialogic quality designed to engage the reader more intensely. The prefatory comment, "Nun höre ich aber von allen Seiten rufen: *räsonniert nicht!*" (But I hear on all sides: *Do not think!*), introduces variations of the main dictum. Exhortations not to think are heard from such pillars of society as a military officer, a finance minister, and a cleric. Each has his own reason to urge the citizenry not to think (for example, "obey, pay, believe"). The sole exception to this litany of "do-nots" is Friedrich II's exclamation: "*räsonniert, so viel ihr wollt, und worüber ihr wollt; aber gehorcht!* (*think* as much as you will and about whatever you will, *but obey!* 56), which is cited parenthetically here. Kant's use of the statement lent it great notoriety. Its function is to underscore how diametrically opposed to freedom are all the usual *räsonniert nicht!* commands.

To his rhetorical question about what is beneficial or detrimental to enlightenment, Kant replies that we must distinguish between public and private use of critical thinking. Public use of one's reasoning powers is equated to views published in print for a general audience, whereas private use designates the application of reason by persons in public service who are required by their positions to execute the will of others. While the *öffentlicher Gebrauch* of reason can tolerate no restrictions, the *privater Gebrauch* is frequently subject to curtailment. Restrictions in the latter area are not detrimental to the ultimate evolution of critical, enlightened thinking.

In speaking of the need for compliance to a general will in the government sector, Kant refers to the administrative apparatus of society as a machine which necessarily must operate in a mechanical way (*ein gewisser Mechanismus notwendig, Maschine, 57*). The use of the machine image to designate the nature of government is noteworthy apart from all the associations it can evoke because Kant reintroduces the concept at the conclusion of his essay to imply the opposite of its designation in its current context.

In an effort to explain fully the differentiation between public and private use of reason, Kant cites several examples of public persons—an officer, a taxpayer, a cleric, a teacher—acting in both a public and a private capacity. In the moment of battle, for instance, the officer may not question decisions. However, after the battle he may—and should—analyze in public view mistakes in deployment, timing, tactics, and so forth. Only by means of such public analysis can military strategy be improved. Analogous cases are made for the benefit to other areas of government and church administration. Whenever an expert addresses himself "through print to the actual public, namely the world" on matters within his jurisdiction, s/he enjoys unrestricted freedom in the use of reason and in the expression of personal views (58). It would be nonsensical, the philosopher concludes, to claim that the cleric (or officer or teacher) has knowledge of his profession only when speaking as a functionary of church or state but not as an individual human being. In Kant's words: "Denn daß die Vormünder des Volks . . . selbst wieder unmündig sein sollen, ist eine Ungereimtheit, die auf Verewigung der Ungereimtheiten hinausläuft" (That the guardians of the people . . . should themselves be incompetent is an absurdity which amounts to the eternalization of absurdities. 58).

Paragraph six begins with a classic example of a prolepsis. Kant anticipates the counterargument that the clergy could agree to advance officially and individually always and everywhere the same views, that is, to create an "unceasing guardianship" over the people. The prolepsis is effective because the reader is now taking every step with the writer. Kant's ploy is to narrow the focus to freedom of thought in religious matters. His response to the anticipated objection is clear and curt: "Ich sage: das ist ganz unmöglich" (I say it is altogether impossible. 58). The ensuing rationale is apodictic, much more syllogistic than metaphorical. The only rhetorical attempt to persuade the reader to accept his view is the allusion to the *Obervormundschaft* (guardianship) as "ein Verbrechen wider die menschliche Natur, deren ursprüngliche Bestimmung gerade in diesem Fortschreiten besteht," adding "und die Nachkommen sind also vollkommen dazu berechtigt, jene Beschlüsse, als unbefugter und frevelhafter Weise genommen, zu verwerfen."[39] Enlightenment is a moral obligation that no individual may deny others or even oneself. Enlightenment and human nature are identified so intimately that they prove inseparable. You cannot have the one without the other.

Kant reverses the argument in the best rhetorical tradition. Not only do those in authority *not* have the right to prescribe beliefs for others, they carry the primary responsibility for ensuring the progress of enlightenment from generation to generation. Thus the monarch must safeguard the right to freedom of speech. Unnecessary and excessive censorship is tantamount to supporting the spiritual tyranny of the few over the many. To underscore his point, Kant has recourse to the tried rhetorical technique of citing authority. he interjects the apparent quotation in Latin: "Caesar non est supra grammaticos" (Caesar is not above the rules of language [that is, above the law], 60). After the long, intellectual argument of paragraph six, these words impart the final impression. They also succinctly summarize Kant's overall argument. No monarch, no bishop, no officer can deprive the individual of the innate right to freedom of thought.

As if sensing that the unusual length and cerebral quality of the last two paragraphs might have overtaxed the reader's willingness to think his thoughts, Kant resumes the technique of segmenting his ideas into more manageable size. The final four paragraphs frame the central argument regarding freedom and moral obligation by mirroring the structure of the opening four paragraphs. The first and final sections of the essay, therefore, provide an attractive symmetry. Moreover, the tripartite structure is a feature of many essayistic compositions.[40]

Paragraph seven shifts the reader's attention to the question of whether the current age is an enlightened one. The response takes the form of a word play: no, author and reader were not then living "in an *enlightened age* . . . but rather in an *age of Enlightenment*" (60). The substitution of *Aufklärung* for *aufgeklärt*—a rhetorical device known as *polyptoton*—stresses the process rather than the completion of the development. The paragraph concludes with the suggestion that the age could also be labeled *das Jahrhundert Friedrichs,* an allusion to the dominant role played by Friedrich II in the political world. With that the topic of the ensuing paragraph is sounded.

Friedrich is honored in this manner because he granted his subjects freedom of thought in matters of conscience. The free use of reason in religious questions was an important first step. The reader's half-conscious inquiry as to whether this freedom is restricted to the realm of religion is answered almost in the same breath: we read that the spirit of open inquiry had already begun to spread to political concerns (60).

In the penultimate paragraph Kant explains why he has addressed himself first and foremost to enlightenment in religious matters. The answer, Kant implies, is self-evident "because our rulers have no interest in playing the guardian to the arts and sciences" (61). Besides, tutelage in questions of dogma is the most serious kind of prescriptive guidance. To indicate that the free use of reason is equally applicable to the political situation, Kant employs an oblique reference as a means of inviting the reader to complete his line of thought: "Aber die Denkungsart eines Staatsoberhaupts, der die erstere begünstigt, geht noch weiter, und sieht ein: daß selbst in Ansehung seiner *Gesetzgebung* es ohne Gefahr sei, seinen Untertanen zu erlauben, von ihrer eigenen Vernunft *öffentlichen* Gebrauch zu machen, und ihre Gedanken über eine bessere Abfassung derselben, sogar mit einer freimütigen Kritik der schon gegebenen, der Welt öffentlich vorzulegen."[41] Without naming him, the reference to the chief of state is sufficient to prompt the reader to conclude that Kant means Friedrich II.

Even as the repetition of the term *öffentlicher Gebrauch* (*public* use) recalls its previous occurrence, so does the concluding paragraph act as a summation of the entire article. It achieves its impact by implementing the device of anaphora, which involves the repetition of key terms and ideas at the beginning of successive clauses/sentences. Friedrich's remark (*räsonniert, so viel ihr wollt*) is repeated in its entirety. The benefit of greater political autonomy for an enhanced atmosphere of intellectual independence of inquiry is acknowledged, but the preeminence of "Freiheit des *Geistes*" (intellectual freedom) is emphasized as the critical factor. Thereupon Kant reminds his reader that humanity is destined to think freely and critically (*Hang und Beruf zum freien Denken*) and that it is only a matter of time before human potential (and rights) evolve fully. Freedom of thought will naturally and logically lead to liberty of action, action based on reasoned choice. For Kant a natural affinity exists between rationality and moral sovereignty. *Mündigkeit* proves, therefore, to be a rational category.

The final sentence of the essay offers another striking synecdoche, achieved by an allusion to Julien Offray de Lamettrie's celebrated work, *L'homme-machine* (1748). The reintroduction of the motif of mechanicalness in this new context highlights an important parallel between the bureaucratic machinery mentioned earlier and the genesis of the human spirit as envisaged in the final paragraphs. Both administrative bodies and the human personality operate according to a set of internal laws. However, the *punctum saliens* in their dissimilarity lies in the preeminence of the individual human being whose destiny is to evolve in a morally and intellectually unrestricted manner. This predisposition of humanity for emancipation is seen as the nucleus (*Keim*) of civil life. By contrast, governmental bureaucracy is bound by non-vital laws which allow no deviation from a self-prescribed path. These external structures of society are referred to as this hard shell (*diese harte Hülle*).

Placed in this light, the concluding allusion to the mechanism of the human individual is reversed, for the government must eventually recognize the disjuncture, acknowledging that the human being is "nun mehr *als Maschine*" (61). Forced to cede the point, the guardians of state would then be moved to treat the individual as the free agent that every person is and not like an automaton programmed to execute the official will. Consequently, the philosopher infers, the bodies of state and church would be restructured according to the human propensity and vocation to free thinking (*Hang und Beruf zum freien Denken*).

Kant expresses these complicated ideas in the final sentence with an admixture of philosophical rigor and poetic imagination: "Wenn denn die Natur unter dieser harten Hülle den Keim, für den sie am zärtlichsten sorgt, nämlich den Hang und Beruf zum *freien Denken*, ausgewickelt hat: so wirkt dieser allmählich zurück auf die Sinnesart des Volks (wodurch dieses der *Freiheit zu handeln* nach und nach fähiger wird), und endlich auch sogar auf die Grundsätze der *Regierung*, die es ihr selbst zuträglich findet, den Menschen, der nun mehr *als Maschine* ist, seiner Würde gemäß zu behandeln."[42] The concluding words poignantly express the underlying conviction of this brief discourse: humankind must be treated with dignity according to its basic nature. The external shell of restrictive convention must be pierced and peeled away so that the inner being might evolve freely, thereby providing the basis for social and political reform.

The reference to the intimate relationship between the expression of ideas (through print) and resultant action is strikingly parallel to arguments previously encountered in Klopstock's thinking. Kant's affective use of language in this regard gives evidence of the philosopher's ability to enlist the power of poetic image and turn of phrase to formulate philosophic ideas more expressively. The technique is a clear indication that even for such a rigorous thinker such as himself (aesthetic) theory without communication is an empty exercise.

The predominance of rhetorical strategies in a work not normally considered for its aesthetic qualities might raise the question of whether Kant was not functioning merely as a rhetorician. Yet Kant did distinguish between mere rhetoric and genuine poetry. The latter he valued as an ally in scientific argumentation. His comment in the *Kritik der Urteilskraft* on these functions can be applied with as much validity to his own "Was ist Aufklärung?" There Kant argued that rhetoric promises something serious while giving only an "entertaining play of the imagination." Poetry, on the other hand, promises only amusement while accomplishing "something worthy of being made a serious business, namely, the use of play to provide food for the understanding, and the infusion of life in its concepts."[43] Like Leibniz almost a century earlier, Kant's journalistic prose mixed science, rhetoric, and poetry in the essayistic mode. "Was ist Aufklärung?" is a fine example of Just's category, the "conceptual essay."

A similarly extensive textual analysis of Moses Mendelssohn's *Briefe über die Empfindungen* (1755) or his *Phädon oder über die Unsterblichkeit der Seele* (1767) or of his response in the *Berlinische Monatsschrift* (September 1784), "Über die Frage: was heißt aufkl ären?", would demonstrate their stylistic proximity to the "conceptual essay."

A good friend of Lessing and a fellow philosopher with Kant, Mendelssohn breathed the same air, admired the same writers, and strove for the same felicity of expression in his writing. As a disciple of Leibniz and Wolff he did not follow their doctrines slavishly, but in the tradition of true Enlightenment advocated the ever renewed quest and testing which lie at its heart. It is, of course, the stance of the essayist. Although it is true that he rejected the shallow thinking and pre-packaged ideas of the French *philosophes* and their German imitators, the *Popularphilosophen*, it would be precipitous for that reason to deny their less rigorously philosophical writing any claim to essayism as Bruno Berger does so offhandedly.[44]

Despite its length of more than eighty printed pages, *Phädon* is actually a series of three dialogues of approximately twenty-five pages per piece. Seen separately, each constituent dialogue locates closer to the external size of an essay. More significantly, it utilizes the Socratic method and personal tone (with the prerequisite stroll through nature) prefiguring Lessing's *Ernst und Falk* a decade later. The movement in these dialogues is one of encircling a major, indisputable, enigmatic truth. And it is done in a soothing, engaging manner which often belies the philosophical earnestness. Thus we can readily understand why *Phädon* was so highly lauded by contemporaries for its stylistic sophistication.

The second dialogue, for instance, deals with the essential characteristics of truthseeking. The two fundamental concepts of thinking as an act
are dynamic in nature: expansion and motion (*Ausdehnung und Bewegung*). However, Socrates endeavors to convince his interlocutor, Sim-
mias, that these qualities are not characteristic of a composite thing
(*Zusammengesetztes*), but paradoxically of the unified whole (*das Ein-
fache*). This instance of syncrasy is conceived in the manner of Leibniz's
Monadologie. The diversity of the multiple converges here "as if in a
single point" where that diversity, multiplicity, spatial separation, and
movement cease to exist—at least as separate categories. The dialogue
culminates the idea in a salient extended metaphor:

[Die Menschen] irren, die Wahrheit suchend, auf den Meeren
der Meynungen auf und nieder, bis ihnen Vernunft und Nachdenken, die Kinder Jupiters, in die Segel leuchten, und eine
glückliche Anlandung verkündigen. Vernunft und Nachdenken
führen unsern Geist von den sinnlichen Eindrücken der Körperwelt zurück in seine Heimat, in das Reich der denkenden
Wesen, vorerst zu seines Gleichen, zu erschaffenen Wesen, die,
ihrer Endlichkeit halber, auch von andern gedacht und deutlich
begriffen werden können. Von diesen erheben sie ihn zu jener
Urquelle des Denkenden und Gedenkbaren, zu jenem alles be-
greifenden, aber allen unbegreiflichen Wesen, von dem wir, zu
unserm Troste, so viel wissen, daß alles, was in der Körperwelt
und in der Geisterwelt gut, schön und vollkommen ist, von ihm
seine Wirklichkeit hat, und durch seine Allmacht erhalten
wird.[45]

The passage is filled with energy and movement that imitates the continually altered perspective of the one and the many. Like a Jacob's ladder
the ideas and sentiments rise out of the individual souls into the universal
one and return from that original source to its mirror image *en miniature*.
The tone and topic recall Wieland's "Sympathien" and like that piece is
anchored in a Platonic-Leibnizian world. Even if the reader does not
understand the individual parts and phrases, the dominant image of
returning home and seeking like-minded souls imprint themselves on the
reader's mind.

It is not possible to pursue the likelihood of Mendelssohn's essayism
any further here. The danger of a study that strives to cross the traditional
(and artificial) boundaries of literary history is that it will lack all shape
and conciseness. Thus even this inquiry must succumb to the demands of
limitation, to the need to curtail and classify. Without that restraint

clarity of argument would suffer. Let it suffice to remark how necessary
it is to engage in many more individual studies of eighteenth-century
writers before we will possess a satisfactory picture of the genesis and
forms of essayism in the period 1680–1815.

The Popularizers
Johann Gottfried Herder

Johann Gottfried Herder (1744–1803) was a central figure in the literary life of the second half of the eighteenth century in Germany. A
prolific author, he has just recently begun to attract increased critical
attention from many sides. This scholarly interest is well deserved and
long overdue. Herder wore many hats and wore them well. He was, for
example, an innovative cultural historian, an early semiotician, a sensitive
literary critic, a pioneering language theorist, and a popular preacher.
Some would argue that his significance for the world of eighteenth-
century thought rivals that of Kant himself. At the very least it could be
argued that "Herder was as valid a stylistic model as Goethe, Wieland, or
Lessing."[46]

Although not normally numbered among the *Popularphilosophen,*
Herder (like Thomasius, Gottsched, Wieland, Garve, and Johann Bernhard Basedow) was intent upon reaching out to an anonymous,
educated—but not pedantically scholarly—audience. In part his stature
as a central figure is attributable to his success in disseminating his views
on historical and cultural relativism in a lucid, intriguing style. Both his
manner of expression and his way of thinking were echoed by Storm-
and-Stress and Romantic circles. His writings through the 1770s bear the
marks of the middle, natural style advocated by the popular philosophers; that is, his writing is broadly accessible, his ideas clearly conceived,
his topics of practical consequence.[47] Consequently, his opus is particularly rich in informal, essayistic compositions. This is true whether we
consider his earlier or later compositions. I am thinking, for instance, of
his fragments in the wake of Lessing's, Nicolai's, Abbt's, and Mendelssohn's *Briefe, die neueste Literatur betreffend: Über die neuere deutsche Literatur. Fragmente (Letters on Contemporary Literature,
Fragments,* 1767) and his *Kritische Wälder (Critical Forests,* 1769). The
articles in these periodicals often assume the posture of the informal
essay, while his mature works such as *Ideen zur Philosophie der Ge-*

schichte der Menschheit (*Ideas on the Philosophy of the History of Mankind*, 1784–91), *Gott* (*God: Some Conversations*, 1787), and *Briefe zu Beförderung der Humanität* (*Letters for the Advancement of Humanity*, 1793–97) tend more to the tradition of the formal essay.

The introduction to the first collection of fragments on German literature is entirely symptomatic of Herder's free, exploratory style. There he informs his reader what to expect. While the *Fragmente* are designed as a continuation of Lessing's *Literaturbriefe*, they are not intended as the last word on literary criticism. He tells us: "Ich sammle die Anmerkungen der Briefe, und erweitere bald ihre Aussichten, bald ziehe ich sie zurück, oder lenke sie seitwärts. Ich zerstücke und nähe zusammen, um vielleicht das bewegliche Ganze eines Pantins zu verfertigen. Dazu habe ich Freiheit, wie ich glaube: denn wenn die Briefe sich durch das Fruchtland anderer Wege bahnten, so kann ich ja zum Vortheil des Besitzers diesen Weg wieder überpflügen."[48] Herder's open attitude toward his subject matter is the same as that of the essayist. His style makes copious use of metaphors and similes to bring his thoughts to life. Mind and method are similar in both cases. The search for answers, the expansion and restriction of the perspective, the development of an idea are of paramount importance. He assures us that he is offering us only his private opinions and reflections on cultural matters of public concern. The attraction that his vivid style and meandering thought held for his own contemporaries have retained their appeal for the modern reader. They continue to stimulate and challenge.

Herder's reflections (*Einfälle*) on the genesis of language and literature are of particular significance for the incidence of essayistic prose in our time frame because he sees human perfection achievable through the medium of language, especially poetic language. In the first installment of his *Über die neuere deutsche Literatur*, for example, he speaks of the organic development of all branches of arts and science within their cultural setting. He identifies four ages of development analogous to the human aging process: (1) childhood, (2) youth, (3) maturity, (4) advanced age. Additionally, Herder refers to three levels of language use associated with the stages of human development: (1) poetic, (2) prosaic, and (3) philosophic. These categories correspond to increasing levels of ratiocination and abstractness.

Herder contends that poetic language is most obvious in the first two stages of human and cultural development where the idea and its expression are spontaneous and inseparable. As a culture refines its thinking via the use of language to express exactly the idea involved, it begins to exert

closer control over the manner of expression. When the richness of youthful exuberance is moderated but without destroying its idiotisms and free
associations, the age of maturity is achieved. In terms of linguistic expression it is the period of "beautiful prose" (*Periode der schönen Prose*).
In the advanced stage of development the tendency is to value only the
accuracy and correctness of thought but not its aesthetic expression. That
period Herder labels "the philosophic age of language" (*das Philosophische Zeitalter der Sprache*).[49] We are most concerned here with "the
manly age of language" since it is marked by aesthetically pleasing formulations. It partakes equally of poetic verve and philosophic specificity,
holding the balance between the language of sensation and the language
of reason.

Moreover, Herder felt that his own era was nearing the end of that
third phase and rapidly entering the fourth and least poetic stage: the
philosophic. *Das männliche Alter,* it would seem therefore, is equivalent
to the age of essayism, since it saw the rise of poetry in prose. Let us
review the central passage from Herder's *Über die neuere deutsche Literatur*:

> Je mehr [die Sprache] Kunst wird, je mehr entfernet sie sich von
> der Natur. Je eingezogener und Politischer die Sitten werden, je
> weniger die Leidenschaften in der Welt wirken, desto mehr ver-
> lieret sie an Gegenständen. Je mehr man an Perioden künstelt,
> je mehr die Inversionen abgeschaffet, je mehr bürgerliche und
> abstrakte Wörter eingeführet werden, je mehr Regeln eine
> Sprache erhält desto vollkommener wird sie zwar, aber desto
> mehr verliert die wahre Poesie.
> Jezt ward der [sic] Periode der Prose geboren, und in die Runde
> gedrehet: durch Uebung und Bemerkung ward diese Zeit, da sie
> am besten war, das Alter der schönen Prose . . . die den Eigen-
> sinn der Idiotismen einschränkte, ohne ihn ganz abzuschaffen,
> die die Freiheit der Inversionen mäßigte, ohne doch noch die
> Fesseln einer Philosophischen Construction über sich zu neh-
> men, die den Poetischen Rhythmus zum Wohlklang der Prose
> herunter stimmte, und die vorher freie Anordnung der Worte
> mehr in die Runde eines Perioden einschloß:—dies ist das
> männliche Alter der Sprache.[50]

The qualities of artistic prose detailed here recall the traits of original
prose identified in chapter VI of this study. A distinguishing characteristic
of all poetic discourse—whether in verse or prose—was the intimate

nexus of idea and formulation. In other words, the text attempts to engage the reader on two levels: through rational argument and through the implementation of images.

For Herder perception and cognition were interdependent. He believed in the wholeness of existence, trusted in the reliability of the senses, and believed in the inseparability of reality and sensation. Because of this vitalistic conception of psychology, the role of metaphor as a structuring system dominated in his thoughts on language. Herder expressed the unity of sensation and cognition preeminently in metaphorical terms.[51] Like the harmonious workings of body and soul in the individual, language and idea interact in natural unison. The more expressive words are of body language (*die Zeichensprache des Körpers,* Suphan, 1:394; *DjH,* 24), the more poetic their effect. That is, the closer the language of words approximates the original natural language of the body, the higher the incidence of metaphors, similes, analogies, and images will be. The result is "beautiful prose." Thus "artistic" language is best understood in Herder's system as a "Sinnbild der Seele" (symbol of the soul) or "einen Boten des Gedanken" (a messenger of thoughts) (Suphan, 1:399; *DjH,* 27).

Herder's piece on Shakespeare, composed in 1771 but not published until 1773, has been selected for examination for two reasons. First of all, it demonstrates his anti-intellectualism and desire to accord the experience of art a special status.[52] The composition counteracts, therefore, the tendency in the prose of his day to be too abstract, too syllogistic, and too preoccupied with technical correctness at the expense of "verve" or *tour.* Secondly, the essay first appeared in the manifesto of the *Sturm und Drang* and was widely received. Published by Herder under the title *Von deutscher Art und Kunst. Einige fliegende Blätter (On German Art,* 1773), the manifesto contains five essays; two by Herder (in addition to "Shakespeare," the fragmentary "Auszug aus einem Briefwechsel über Oßian und die Lieder alter Völker"), one by Goethe ("Von deutscher Baukunst"), another by Justus Möser ("Deutsche Geschichte"), and finally a piece by Paolo Frisi ("Versuch über die Gothische Baukunst"). The collection's subtitle ("Some Loose Pages") as well as the individual titles themselves underscore the tentative, exploratory nature of this work.

"Shakespeare" is a cardinal example of young Herder's rhapsodic, energetic style. At twenty pages it has almost the preferred length of the essay form. Its topic and style would identify it as an informal, *literaturkritischer* or—because of its broad sweep—*kulturkritischer Essay.* The essentially rhapsodic tenor of the article is generated by his expert use

of anacoluthon to draw the reader along at breakneck speed (*DjH*, 87f).
The sense of urgency is enhanced by the plethora of exclamation marks
and frequent use of *variatio* and *repetitio* on practically every page. The
predominance of italics (*Sperrdruck*) makes individual ideas literally
jump out of the page at the reader. Inversions, omissions of expected
parts of speech (verbs and subjects), and anaphora add to the sense of
vitality. Examples would be such formulations as:

> Hier ist kein Dichter! ist Schöpfer! ist Geschichte der Welt!
> (*DjH*, 87);

or:

> Als Puppe ihm noch so gleich; der Puppe fehlt Geist, Leben,
> Natur, Wahrheit—mithin alle Elemente der Rührung—mithin
> Zweck und Erreichung des Zwecks—ist's also dasselbe Ding
> mehr? (*DjH*, 81);

and finally:

> Alles Kostume der Geister erschöpft! Hahnkräh und Pauken-
> schall, stummer Wink und der nahe Hügel, Wort und Unwort—
> welches Lokal! welches tiefe Eingraben der Wahrheit! Und wie
> der erschreckte König kniet, und Hamlet vorbeiirrt in seiner
> Mutter Kammer vor dem Bilde seines Vaters! und nun die an-
> dre Erscheinung! Er kam am Grabe seiner Ophelia! Der
> rührende good Fellow in allen den Verbindungen mit *Horaz,
> Ophelia, Laertes, Fortinbras*! (*DjH*, 88).[53]

Everything seems to be occurring in the present; nothing is past, nothing
future. The several direct appeals to the reader (who is addressed as
"friend") ensures that the latter is not left behind in this whirlwind review
of Shakespeare's dramatic art.

Perceiving himself as "an interpreter and rhapsodist" (*Ausleger und
Rhapsodist, DjH*, 84), Herder is little interested in demonstrating to his
reader in a clearly structured and rational manner the greatness of
Shakespeare. In the *exordium* the writer explicitly takes a position against
the *Letternkultur* (alphabet culture) of his day: enough has been written
"about, for and against Shakespeare" to fill whole libraries. He himself
has no desire to add to the paper waste. Moreover, he hopes that no
member of his select audience will feel obligated to take pen in hand to
defend, excuse, or denounce the dramatist. Herder prefers to convey a

feeling for Shakespeare: "aber zu erklären, zu fühlen wie er ist" (but to explain, to feel what he is like; *DjH*, 74), for the dramatist appears to him to speak "die Sprache aller Alter, Menschen und Menschenarten" (the language of all ages, all people, all races) and to be a "Dolmetscher der Natur in all' ihren Zungen" (interpreter of nature in all her tongues) (*DjH*, 84). Consequently, he makes minimal appeal to the reader's sense of logic or desire for rational clarity.

The *exordium* can be seen as a reaction to Lessing's interpretation of Shakespeare's dramatic art as a silhouette of the immortal creator's universe.[54] Even though Lessing valued Shakespeare's creative genius, considering his creations to be more natural than the products of French classicism, Herder explains, Lessing still tended to see the plays in terms of literary theory. As such they continued to abide by rational principles. Herder goes a step further. He sees Shakespeare's dramas as history itself and history, on the other hand, as dramatic event. Consequently, Shakespeare's artistic work presents an arational, emotional unity rather than a rationally ordered world.[55]

Instead the entire composition consists of a rapid flow of words, images, and sounds designed to incite an intuitive approach to Shakespeare. His dramatic art essentially encompasses the entire spectrum of human emotion. At the conclusion of his tribute, Herder comments to his reader that his purpose has been to excite him/her with a sense of Shakespeare's greatness even as he himself has been awed (*DjH*, 94). The remark makes clear that the purpose of Shakespeare's art is to arouse a whole range of emotions. And in his rhapsodic oration Herder attempts to imitate the effect of his model. For this reason he waits until the *conclusio* to press to "the heart of his analysis" (*DjH*, 92). It is understandable then that the rhetorical technique of *synecdoche* is so predominant since it effects greater communication between reader, text and author by inducing the recipient to complete the writer's fragmented thoughts and to understand the allusions.

Yet the article is far from illogical. It is, in fact, a fine example of the "unmethodological method" often associated with essayistic style. The inner logic of the piece consists in a series of encirclements which serves as a major ordering principle here. Herder's central idea is that Shakespeare is life itself in all its diversity, fullness, and chaotic frenzy. His plays represent a *Wunderganzes* (a wonderful whole), are filled with *Menschengeist* (human spirit), recall Spinoza's *Pan! Universum!* and offer *Geschichte und Weltseele* (history and world spirit) (*DjH*, 83, 85, 89, 94). The individual parts of this world (*ideas partium*) exist only in relation to the whole (*idea totali*). The constant encircling of his subject matter, his almost mystical sense of awe at the hugeness yet wonderful simplicity of life, and his rapid association of ideas all serve to underscore *das Wunderganze* which is Shakespeare, the "interpreter of nature in all her tongues" and the "new Sophocles" (*DjH*, 83f.). By contrast French tragedians appear to be soulless puppets going through empty motions.

The rhetorical structure of this rhapsody on art readily meets the eye. A schematic rendition would look like this:

> *exordium*: page 74
> *expositio*: pages 74–75
> *divisio*: pages 75–78 (origins of tragedy and comedy, principle of
>   unity)
> *confutatio*: pages 78–80 (state of French theater)
> *divisio*: page 81 (real purpose of drama)
> *confutatio*: page 82
> *confirmatio*: pages 83–92
>   concepts of genius and the organic growth of cultures
>   with their natural diversity and arguments directed *a*
>   *honesto, a necessario, a testimonio, a exemplo,* and *a*
>   *contrario*
> *conclusio*: pages 92–94.

In nuce Herder's argument runs as follows: beginning with a rejection of all previous Shakespeare scholarship (*DjH*, 74f.), he points out that critics have overlooked the one important question, namely, what is the *purpose* of dramatic art in terms of the origins of Greek drama? (*DjH*, 75–82). He then argues that the preconditions for Shakespeare's theater were basically different than those of Sophocles (*DjH*, 83f). Thereafter he launches into a rhapsodic discussion of several Shakespearean plays (*DjH*, 84–90), before zeroing in on his main thesis regarding the concept of totality (*DjH*, 90–94) by reintroducing into the discussion the role of the three unities (time, place, and action).

Because of the nexus of literature and culture in the wider sense which lies at the heart of this composition, it is not clear that the label *literaturkritisch* is quite appropriate. "*Culturally* critical" (*kulturkritisch*) would appear to be more exact. In any event, the unity of form and idea is eminently clear, and the reader is engaged on an emotional as well as intellectual level.

Johann Jacob Engel

Like Lessing and Wieland, Johann Jacob Engel (1741–1802) pursued a career as a free-lance writer, theater critic, and essayist especially during 1765–76 in Leipzig, before he was called to a professorship at the Joachimsthalschen Gymnasium in Berlin (1776ff.) where he became a central figure in the Berlin Enlightenment. A friend of Chr. F. Weiße, Christian Garve, and K. W. Ramler and educator of Alexander and Wilhelm von Humboldt as well as of Friedrich Wilhelm III of Prussia, Engel was successful as a playwright of popular comedies. In addition to his plays (and novels), he also penned numerous prose compositions, publishing them in the leading journals of his day.

Of particular interest to us in our present connection is his own journal, *Der Philosoph für die Welt* (1775f.) and the collection of shorter prose works, *Kleinere Schriften von J. J. Engel* (Berlin, 1795). Each is rich in essayistic compositions. While the majority of prose pieces in *Der Philosoph für die Welt* are from his own pen, the journal also published the work of Kant, Mendelssohn, Garve, David Friedländer, and Eberhard.[56]

Most notable among these contributions are Garve's "Brief über den Werther" (1775) and "Das Weihnachtsgeschenk" (1777) as well as Engel's own "Briefe über Emilia Galotti" (1775). Equally noteworthy is Engel's theoretical piece, *Fragmente über Gegenstände der schönen Wissenschaften* (*Fragments on Topics of Belles-Lettres*) contained in the *Kleinere Schriften* of 1795, but published earlier. In fact, the *Fragmente* appeared in 1774, one year earlier than the critique of *Emilia Galotti*. The study bore the original title "Über Handlung, Gespräch und Erzählung" and was first published in Weiße's *Neue Bibliothek der schönen Wissenschaften und der freyen Künste*, vol. 16 (Leipzig, 1774), 177–256. Its casual tone and fragmentary nature mark it—despite its considerable length and scholarly notes—as an essayistic attempt.

More importantly, however, it and the "Letters on *Emilia Galotti*" reflect Engel's endeavor to translate his theory of popular style into practice. His own prose writings approximate the ideal of the dramatic which he presented as a contrastive style to the narrative in "Über Handlung, Gespräch und Erzählung." The latter treatise was composed in reaction to J. G. Sulzer's *Allgemeine Theorie der schönen Wissenschaften* (*General Theory of the Fine Arts*, 1771). Essential to both dialogue and narrative is action or event (*Handlung*). However, Engel sees the former as being more dynamic. He posits the difference between the two as being one of development versus completion. While the dialogue creates a sense of immediacy by presenting an event or idea *as it arises*, the narrative mode presents it as a *fait accompli*. For the dialogue writer everything occurs in the present.[57] Ernst Theodor Voss argues that Engel based his journal, *Der Philosoph für die Welt*, on this principle, seeing it as a means of involving the reader in the active thought processes themselves, not as passive observers but as active participants.[58]

In his *Anfangsgründe einer Theorie der Dichtungsarten* (*Fundamentals of Genre Theory*, 1783) Engel returns to the distinction drawn earlier between the "dramatic" and the "narrative" mode which he had posited as a refinement of Sulzer's differentiation between "didactic" (*lehrend*) and "descriptive" (*schildernd*) dialogues.[59] He first suggests replacing the earlier terminology with the designations *dialogische* and *undialogische Form* (dialogic and non-dialogic form). A few pages later he suggests *darstellend* (representational) and *berichtend* (expository). While the former emphasizes present time and immediacy, the latter operates in the past and deals with that which is not immediately present before the onlooker. By way of clarification Engel writes: "Es ergiebt sich, daß dort *die Sache*, an welcher sich die Veränderungen ereignen, *selbst vorgeführt*, und wir zu unmittelbaren Zeugen dieser sich eben itzt entwickelnden Veränderungen gemacht werden; dahingegen hier die Sache uns nicht selbst vorgeführt wird, ihre Veränderungen sich nicht in unsrer Gegenwart entwickeln, sondern ein fremder Zeuge . . . uns von ihnen schon geschehenen Dingen Bericht erstattet. Das einemal *wird, geschieht*; das andermal *ist geworden, ist geschehen*."[60] The distinction drawn here is reminiscent of the division of essayistic writing into formal and informal, a tendency noted by Dell' Orto and others. With his general emphasis on *Ausdruckspsychologie* (affective psychology) Engel can be seen in a line of tradition with Wieland, Herder, and Garve with whose prose style and theories he would seem to have many similarities.[61]

Above all we must stress that the difference between the two modes is qualitative, but not valuational. Whether a writer chooses the "representational" or the "expository" mode, each kind of writing is a valid vehicle of essayistic expression. In the first instance the weight is shifted toward the poetic (Herder's "Shakespeare"), in the second toward the philosophic (Kant's "Beantwortung der Frage: was ist Aufklärung").

Christian Garve

Like Engel Christian Garve had dreams of living the life of a free-lance writer. Like other writers in Leipzig before him, he was not entirely successful. Yet there is no doubt about his prolixity as a writer, especially as an essayist in the last third of the century.[62] His compositions appear as *Briefe, Versuche, Abhandlungen, Betrachtungen, Anmerkungen,* and *Gedanken* as in such noted works as "Betrachtung einiger Verschiedenheiten in den Werken der ältesten und neuern Schriftsteller" ("Observation on some Differences in the Works of Ancient and Modern Writers," 1770), "Vermischte Anmerkungen über Gellerts Moral, dessen Schriften überhaupt und Character" ("Miscellaneous Notes on Gellerts Moral Sense, His Works in General, and Character," 1771), and "Einige Gedanken über das Interessierende" ("Some Thoughts on That Which We Find Interesting," 1772) all of which first appeared in *Neue Bibliothek der schönen Wissenschaften und der freyen Künste.*

By contrast essayistic works dating from the 1790s were simply titled "*On* such and such." Examples of this practice are "Über die Moden" (1792), "Über die Rolle des Wahnwitzigen in Shakespeares Schauspielen" (1796), "Über die Muße" (1796), "Von der Popularität des Vortrages" (1793), and "Über einige Schönheiten der Gebirgsgegenden" (1798). These essays were published in collections revealingly labelled *Versuche über verschiedene Gegenstände aus der Moral, der Litteratur und dem gesellschaftlichen Leben* (*Essays on Various Topics of a Moral, Literary, or Social Nature*; 1792, 1796) or *Vermischte Aufsätze welche einzeln oder in Zeitschriften erschienen sind* (*Miscellaneous Essays Previously Published Separately or in Journals,* 1796). The formulations recall the method of Shaftesbury's miscellaneous reflections contained in *Characteristics of Men, Manners, Opinions, Times* (1711). Although we nowhere encounter the term essay, there is little doubt that we are dealing here with the essayistic mode. The topics Garve feels drawn to are clearly the preferred topics of the classical essayists of any period.

In this regard Garve's preface to Part One of his *Versuche* (Breslau, 1792) is enlightening.[63] Like later essayists he speaks of his writings as *eine kleine Gabe* (a trifling) which he does not consider to be all that momentous (2:3). The topics he treats are so commonplace (*populär*) that they will not astound by their novelty. Moreover, he writes for a small group of readers within the broader anonymous public who think and feel as he does. These "sympathetic" readers (to borrow Lessing's and Wieland's term) will know how to appreciate his individual observations. Also in the manner of the essayist, Garve confesses to having reservations about the observations he presents. Thus he invites the reader to examine his remarks and correct them where necessary. Actually, his hope is that his observations will stimulate further reflection (2:5f.).

Finally, Garve makes explicit reference to the patrons of his style of writing: Montaigne, Pascal, and La Rochefoucauld (2:7, 16). He mentions these authors because of the value they placed on the social graces (*Umgang mit Menschen*). Like Montaigne before him, Garve proceeds from personal to generalized observations about human nature and society. He hopes, even as Montaigne did, that the reader will come to know and value *him* and not merely value the book. The book is his person (2:7). And like Pascal Garve believes that every person should be valued as a human being, not because of any social status s/he might enjoy. Garve speaks of the desire of being seen as an *"honnête et galant homme,"* a designation we know well from our examination of Christian Thomasius's social ideal! Like La Rochefoucauld he prefers to write about his own past experiences, since he knows them best. Although that approach leaves him open to the criticism that time has passed him by, that his views are no longer applicable, or that his observations are so minutely restricted as to be untransferable to others, Garve believes that his empirical method will ultimately stimulate "more new ideas and reveal the more latent attributes of an object of study" than the speculative or generalizing kind of inquiry (2:17).

Thus his compositions are offered in the spirit of experimentation and in the hope of stimulating further thought. The ultimate purpose of these reflections, present and future, is to advance human perfection (cf. 2:9). Garve's conception of his prose writing style resembles the essayistic posture to a very high degree. There is, in fact, sufficient evidence to number him among the "classical" essayists.

Rohner includes "Über einige Schönheiten der Gebirgsgegenden" in his collection of essays from our time period, considering it exemplary of the "graphic essay" (*gegenständlicher Essay*). Because of the attention already accorded the piece, we can turn to other samples from Garve's pen. An analysis of any one of the above mentioned compositions would reveal their qualities as formal essays of either the graphic, conceptual, or culturally investigative type. Their tone is a far cry from the hymnic raving of Herder's "Shakespeare." Most are written in a popular yet clear and objective style like his "Von der Popularität des Vortrages" and "Über die prosaische Schreibart" (1799) considered in Chapter VI of this study in connection with a theory of prose in the eighteenth century. Though factual and sober, they reveal the impact of both rhetoric and inspiration in the manner of Francis Bacon.

Intriguing for our purposes is Garve's early piece from the year 1777, "Das Weihnachtsgeschenk" ("The Christmas Present"). I say intriguing for two reasons; first it contains *in nuce* a life-long conviction of its author encountered repeatedly in his later writing such as "Von der Popularität des Vortrages" ("On Popular Discourse," 1796), "Einige Beobachtungen über die Kunst zu denken" ("Some Observations on the Art of Thinking," 1796), and "Über die öffentliche Meinung" ("On Public Opinion," 1802). Secondly, the article addresses itself to a major concern of *Crossing Boundaries*. The title leads the reader to expect an anecdote or short narrative. Yet upon closer scrutiny, the composition turns out to be an extraordinary discourse on the nexus of reading, writing, and thinking. The title refers to a book given by a father to his daughter on Christmas day. However, the exact significance of the book as a *Christmas* gift is not explained; that determination is left to the reader.

The *exordium* is truly effective because it has an anecdotal quality. It consists of a brief nine-line narrative in which we learn that the narrator casually picked up a book from the dressing table of a young female acquaintance. She quickly grabbed the book away from him before he could open it. His immediate suspicion is that the book contained embarrassing material, for the complaints about inappropriate reading selections for young women had already grown into a topos by the mid 1770s. The fact that she turned beet red reinforced his suspicion. Realizing the wrong impression she had given, the young women read the first few pages aloud to her friend. The pages were penned by her father and contained an exhortation to use the book well. The friend was so impressed by what he heard that he subsequently asked her for a copy of them. The following five and one half pages of "Das Geschenk" contain the father's dedication to his daughter. With an impressive economy of words Garve has drawn his anonymous reader fully into his text. But even though the narrator disappears after the brief *exordium*, the reader is not left to wallow in the text; ultimately s/he is led out again, not by any guiding narrator, but by the thought processes themselves. The text, in other words, encourages the peruser of the pages to apply the individual experience to her/himself.

The book is striking because—except for the father's introductory comments—it consists of blank pages. Those pages are reserved for the daughter's own miscellaneous thoughts and reflections upon experiences and books read. That is the only means of ensuring that the reading act fulfills its ultimate purpose of refining the individual's critical thinking ability. The father recalls the historical evolution of modern society from the Enlightenment point of view: "As long as humankind could not communicate by speech, it merely saw, heard, felt, and tasted without thinking. As long as humankind could not write, it reflected little and expressed itself badly. It is due to the tongue and the quill that mankind has evolved to its present state."[64] In keeping with the idea of "enlightenment through print" since Thomasius and Leibniz, Garve clearly suggests that the ultimate purpose of writing and reading is to improve the lot of humankind. That is why the father gives the daughter an empty book. Like the religious celebration of Christmas, the blank book represents a new beginning. What happens after that spiritual rebirth is dependent upon the individual her/himself. The real fruit of reading, of listening to others, as the father remarks, is to develop the ability to think independently. Thus he exhorts her: "From a [mere] reader turn yourself into a writer!" (1:20). Previously he had stated that women as readers had become so commonplace that it could no longer be considered a sign of distinction. The real mark of distinction is for a young women to read to enhance her knowledge, refine her judgment, and improve her morals (1:18).

All of this could sound sexist to the modern ear if taken out of context. In context it can be seen as the continuing thrust of progressive intellectuals since the early eighteenth century to include women in the emancipatory process. Now that they had mastered the mechanics of reading, it was time for them to master the *art* of reading and writing so as to enter onto equal footing with other intellectuals in society.[65] The emancipation of humankind via the process of critical reflection is learned by imitating others first. As Garve expresses the idea: "Ehe wir selbst denken, müssen wir erst einem andern nachdenken lernen" (Before we can think for ourselves, we must first learn to think like another. 1:19). That transitional process is best achieved by synthesizing the thoughts of others expressed in written form.

At first it is merely a matter of noting the ideas of others. But as time passes we begin to add our own ideas to the "imported" ones. In fact the mere act of writing forces us to formulate someone else's ideas in a manner characteristic of our own personalities. The act of writing is not to be misconstrued with mechanical copying. In writing we hit upon new thoughts, and those thoughts lead to yet others. "The ideas generate one another," we are informed, "like electrical sparks" (1:20). By nature a dynamic process, thinking via the writing and reading acts will carry itself to final fulfillment once initiated. On this note, Garve concludes his little essay. The final words of the father's reflections read: "Cogitation accords us with such pure and lively enjoyment that s/he who has tasted the pleasure but once in her/his life will never be able to do without it again" (1:21).[66]

The effectiveness of the piece is traceable to the conceit of a father's advice to his daughter, the dismissal of a textual narrator after a mere nine lines, and the economy of diction to drive the main point home. Free of grammatical and syntactical flourishes, unencumbered by learned citations and notes, Garve's "Das Weihnachtsgeschenk" is couched in crystal clear, widely accessible language. It is an essayistic gem, different in quality from the work of other writers sampled, but not less engaging. Having completed the piece, the tendency is either to go back and read it again or merely to sit and muse upon its content and style. Such is the effect of truly creative writing that it forces us to transcend the boundaries between the self and the other in the communicative act of creative reading.

The quality of writing represented by Wieland, Lessing, Engel, Herder, Kant, and Garve analyzed thus far is broad, but is unified by the commonality of approach toward subject matter and audience awareness. We can perceive a continuance of the essayistic traits noted in compositions of the 1750s to 1770s in later works of the same authors. Examples would include Wieland's "Sendschreiben an einen Nachdrucker" ("Open Letter to a Pirate Publisher," 1784) and his *Neue Göttergespräche* (*New Dialogues of the Gods*, 1791) as well as Lichtenberg's "Über einige wichtige Pflichten gegen die Augen" ("On Some Important Duties For One's Eyes," 1791), and Herder's "Von den Gefahren der Vielwißerei und Vielthuerei" ("On the Dangers of Sciolism and Officiousness," 1801). Similar qualities are discernible in other contemporary writers who do not belong to the canon of eighteenth century literature. Helferich Peter Sturz's "Erinnerungen aus dem Leben des Grafen Johann Ernst von Bernstorf" ("Memoirs of the Life of Duke Johann Ernst von Bernstorf," 1777), Adolph von Knigge's "Meine eigene Apologie" ("My Own Apology," 1784), and Theodor Gottlieb von Hippel's novel, *Kreuz- und Querzüge des Ritters A bis Z* (*Chivalric Sorties in All Directions From A to Z*, 1793–94), which contains essayistic passages (very typical of the age), belong here.[67] We might also mention Georg Forster's "Über Leckereien" ("On Tidbits," 1789) and "Die Kunst und das Zeitalter" ("Art and the Age," 1789), although he does not enter the scene until the 1780s.[68] (Forster could just as easily be discussed in connection with the Classic-Romantic era as with the Enlightenment.)

Moreover, there is a pressing need in eighteenth-century research to examine the non-fictional prose contributions to journals edited by women for women. Sophie von La Roche's *Pomona, für Teutschlands Töchter* (1783–84) comes readily to mind, but there were others such as Charlotte Henriette Hezel's earlier *Wochenblatt für das schöne Ge-*

schlecht (1779), and Marianne Ehrmann's *Amaliens Erholungsstunden* (1790–92) or her *Die Einsiedlerinn aus den Alpen* (1793–94) which followed La Roche's editorial lead. We are only at the threshold of inquiry into the active role women played not only as readers but also as writers in the literary life of the *Aufklärung*.

Yet the spectrum of essayistic styles (if not of the authors) is well expressed in the few examples discussed here. Within the space limitations of my current inquiry, I can only hope to transmit a sense of the richness and breadth of the new writing mode. Perhaps because it was tied so closely to journalistic endeavors in search of a large audience, the essayistic mode cannot be made to respect epochal boundaries as rigidly as literary historians would like. In any event, the usual boundaries are crisscrossed.

It is now our purpose to place the canonical writers of German Classicism and Romanticism in the context of our discussions of the theory and history of essayistic prose 1680–1815. It will become manifest from our limited focus on essayism that the ongoing endeavor to tear down the walls separating Classicism and Romanticism from other literary/cultural developments is justified on many grounds.

Notes

1. See Ernst Manheim, *Aufklärung und öffentliche Meinung. Studien zur Soziologie der Öffentlichkeit im 18. Jahrhundert* (1933; rprt. Stuttgart and Bad Cannstatt: frommann-holzboog, 1978), 50ff.
2. On the question of *Sympathie* as the distinguishing character trait of truly enlightened individuals see my articles: "Das sicherste Kennzeichen einer gesunden, nervösen Staatsverfassung," *Lessing und die Toleranz*. Special Supplement to the *Lessing Yearbook*, ed. Peter Freimark et al (Munich: edition + kritik, 1986), 238f. and "Die gefesselte Muse?" in *MLN* 99 (1984), 454f.
3. Fr. G. Klopstock, *Klopstocks Werke in einem Bande*, ed. Karl-Heinz Hahn (Berlin and Weimar: Aufbau, 1979), 258: "The essential characteristic of poetry consists in its ability to depict with the help of language a *certain number* of objects—whose existence we either know or suspect—in a *light* which *affects* the *highest* powers of the soul to such a degree that one faculty activates the next until the *entire* soul is animated" (Klopstock's emphasis).
4. In addition to my 1980/81 study, "The Poet as Essayist and Journalist: C.M. Wieland," *Jahrbuch für internationale Germanistik* 12/1 (1980), 104–138 and 13/1 (1981), 74–137, see also Robert Victor Smythe, "Christoph Martin Wieland as Essayist," Dissertation University of Texas (1980); James van der Laan, "The German Essay of the Eighteenth: An Ecology," Disser-

tation University of Illinois at Urbana/Champaign (1984); and James Raymond Wardell, "The Essay of Christoph Martin Wieland: A Contribution to the Definition and History of the Genre in its European Context," Dissertation, University of Michigan (1986).

5. Fritz Budde, *Wieland und Bodmer* (Berlin: Meyer and Müller, 1910), 68ff. The ensuing discussion of Wieland's essayistic style has been adapted from my analysis in *Jahrbuch für Internationale Germanistik* 13/1 (1981), 108–114.

6. Given this fact there is no need to introduce even more terminology to the confused scene of poetics. Thus it makes little sense to adopt Wardell's building blocks of style: form, macrostructure, microstructure, and genre structure. Particularly pleonastic in his framework are the last three terms. While "microstructure" refers to the structuring of sentences, "macrostructure" covers all larger segments of the text. Rhetoric already accounts for the organization of the parts as well as of the whole. Why not stick to rhetoric? "Genre structure" seems to beg the question. Wardell's purpose is to define the essay genre in very delimited terms. To use a principle such as "genre structure" to define essay in an area of investigation fraught with confusion doesn't seem to offer much relief. The designation "genre structure" implies that Wardell already knows where he wants to end up before he begins his inquiry. If a form does not fit the preconceived notion, does one deny it essayistic qualities? Is there a real difference between essay and essayism? See Wardell, "The Essays of Chr. M. Wieland," Dissertation, University of Michigan (1986), xxv et passim.

7. The text is cited according to: Chr. M. Wieland, *Werke*, ed. Fritz Martini and Hans Werner Seiffert (Munich: Hanser, 1967), 3:109–166; here 112 and again 139. This work is cited as Hanser.

8. Fritz Martini, "Nachwort," to Wieland, Hanser 3:960.

9. "stands unbending in the storm like the cedar of God" (122); "thoughtful countenance," "purple cloud," "spring breezes"(122); "a gleaming soap bubble, a colorful nothing" (123); "these worm-like souls, oppressed by their lowly desires, crawl around on your cheeks" (123); "the first morning rays of the beautiful soul" (131); "the milk of wisdom" (132); "a deplorable trade, the mere product of the fingers which requires about as much imagination as the spinning of wool" (150); "you . . . let the scribbling blockheads get away" (163); "the pedantic, small-minded academics" (164); "the rule of reason, without which our planet would be one big insane asylum" (166); "the common bunch of pseudo-scholars and of the blind who allow themselves to be led by the blind" (166). All citations from Wieland, "Sympathien," Hanser, 3.

10. "Do whatever you can to distill your knowledge to pristine truth and to make your love ever purer and more encompassing. In doing so you will increase in both humility and perfection because perfection consists in the elimination of our innate and acquired faults: of ignorance, error, vanity, and all inappropriate or immoderate emotional states. This is a task which will never cease even for the most godly among us in this vale of tears" (Wieland, "Sympathien," Hanser, 3:145).

11. See, e.g., Christian Thomasius, *Politische Klugheit*, Chapter 4: "Von der Klugheit, sich selbst zu raten" (1705), rprt. in *Deutsche Literaturdenkmale des 18. und 19. Jahrhundert*, ed. August Sauer (Nendeln/Liechtenstein: Krauss Reprint, 1968), 52/2:80–97.

12. "Most humans, Arete, are inflated with an exaggerated sense of self-worth because they do not know what the real value of a person is" (Wieland, "Sympathien," Hanser, 3:141).

13. "Let others, whose understanding is clouded, who are too weak to withstand the assaults of sensual reality or the charms of imagined bliss, choose sensual pleasure or vain honor as the ultimate goal of their striving; let them use the sharp edge of understanding to establish themselves in this shadowlike life, this transitory world, as if they were working for eternity; that is tantamount to building a house on water. Let others kowtow to princes and their lackeys; well may they consider titles, ribbons of distinction, servants as enviable goods, wasting their lives in search of them even as the miser turns into a skeleton still grasping his gold" (Wieland, "Sympathien," Hanser, 3:147).

14. "Yes, these happy days are not only gone, but our sophists and blockheads are so deluded and taken with their own ignorance that they carry on about enlightened times. From the top of the books piled up around them—which by the way they value by the pound not the page!—they look with stupid disdain upon the great geniuses of antiquity, not realizing that people of their caliber would hardly have been worthy of being a mere copyist in Plato's age" (Wieland, "Sympathien," Hanser, 3:149).

15. See my analyses of these compositions in *Jahrbuch für Internationale Germanistik* 13/1 (1981), 114–133. See also Lieselotte E. Kurth, "Wieland and the French Revolution," *Studies in Eighteenth-Century Culture* 7 (1978), 79–103. Wardell (1986) analyzes numerous essays from the post 1770 era (see 318–396).

16. In his "Meine Erklärung über einen im St. James Chronicle Jan. 25, 1800, abgedruckten Artikel" (*NTM*, 65 [1800]) Wieland succinctly formulates his life-long conviction of the proper manner of judging mankind and its world: "Meine natürliche Geneigtheit, Alles (Personen und Sachen) von allen Seiten und aus allen möglichen Gesichtspunkten anzusehen, und ein herzlicher Widerwille gegen das nur allzu gewöhnliche *einseitige Urtheilen* und *Parteynehmen*, ist ein wesentliches Stück meiner Individualität." Reprinted in *Wielands Werke*, ed. Heinrich Düntzer (Berlin: Hempel, 1879ff.), 34:373.

17. Chr. M. Wieland, "Horaz: Über die Dichtkunst. An L. Calpurnius Piso und seine Söhne": "The manner of our author in this discourse . . . gives the impression of a leisurely stroll, whereby one has no other purpose than to walk. A small digression means nothing; one pauses to enjoy a beautiful panorama or turns aside to pick a flower or to enjoy the cool shade of a tree. It is a manner of proceeding in which the nearest object, which catches one's eye, determines the course of the conversation. Yet in the end the walkers arrive at their destination without really knowing how they got there. [Horace] does not dwell on one topic long enough to satisfy our curiosity, seldom defines a rule clearly enough so that it can be used as an easy and

sure guide for the student of art, and at every turn moves from the specific to the general" (Hanser, 5:598f.). Although Wieland's translation of Horace's epistles occurred in 1781 and were published in 1782, his interest in the Roman dates from his years in Klosterbergen and Zurich.

18. Friedrich Schlegel, "Lessing. Vom Wesen der Kritik," *Schriften und Fragmente* (Stuttgart: Kröner, 1956), 57: "No one will easily overlook this original caste of Lessing's fragments. Moreover, I think also in regard to the bold and surprising combinations evident in them that the whole corresponds so perfectly to the concept of the proposed [fourth] genre. Additionally, I believe that similar works by other authors contain in even greater succinctness an even fuller wealth of ideas drawn from the richness of the most diverse branches of the sciences and the arts. However, with regard to his bold combinations and his mimetic, expressively genial style which reflect so successfully the sudden jumps and surprising twists of his mind, Lessing will not be easily excelled." See also Haas (1975), 23.

19. See Wolf Koepke, "Herders Totengespräch mit Lessing," in *Aufnahme— Weitergabe. Literarische Impulse um Lessing und Goethe*, ed. John A. McCarthy and Albert A. Kipa (Hamburg: Helmut Buske, 1982), 125–142. Koepke stresses the common philosophico-anthropologic basis of the two writers while indicating how Herder continued Lessing's style.

20. Moses Mendelssohn, *Gesammelte Schriften*, 7 Vols., ed. G. B. Mendelssohn (Leipzig, 1843–45), 7:702. On the modern view of the thinking/writing nexus in Lessing's work see *Humanität und Dialog. Lessing und Mendelssohn in neuer Sicht*, ed. E. Bahr, E. P. Harris, and L. G. Lyon (Detroit: Wayne State University Press; Munich: edition + kritik, 1982), Part 2: Podiumsgespräch: "Denkstrukturen bei Lessing," 123–73.

21. "Meine Gedanken mögen immer sich weniger zu verbinden, ja wohl gar sich zu widersprechen scheinen; wenn es denn nur Gedanken sind, bei welchen sie Stoff finden, selbst zu denken. Hier will ich nichts als 'Fermenta cognitionis' ausstreuen" (Lessing, 95th number of the *Hamburgischen Dramaturgie*, LM, 10:188. I have discussed this aspect of Lessing's thinking elsewhere: "'Das sicherste Kennzeichen einer gesunden, nervösen Staatsverfassung:' Lessing und die Pressefreiheit," in *Lessing und die Toleranz*, ed. P. Freimark, F. Kopitzsch, and H. Slessarev (Detroit: Wayne State University Press; Munich: edition + kritik, 1986), 225–244, esp. 229–232.

22. "The value of a human being is not determined by the truth which s/he has or thinks s/he has, but rather by the sincere effort expended to arrive at truth. This is so because human powers are expanded not by the possession, but by the search for verity. Increased perfection results only from the latter" (Lessing, LM, 13:23f.).

23. Berger writes: "Die äußere Form der Essayistik, der Essay" (*Essay*, 189). The equation of *Essayistik* (not: *Essayismus*?) with *Essay* does not work in a great number of instances, for example when the essay is embedded in a novel or appears in the form of a letter. How problematic Berger's insistence is to delimit the nature of essayism to one isolated short (prose) form becomes transparent when he states a few pages later that "Lessing spürte also schon die Möglichkeit der *notwendig gewordenen literarischen Kunstform* voraus und *verwendete nur aus Tradition* die eingespielte Briefform

. . . " (199, my italics). If Lessing recognized the essential nature of essayism
(= Berger's *Essayistik*) and the need for a specific literary art form and
chose nevertheless not to write essays, he obviously felt it possible to have
the one without the other. Thus Berger's adamancy regarding the equation
of "die äußere Form der Essayistik" and "der Essay" is unreasonable as well
as untenable. And his discussion of Lessing's significance for the genesis of
the essay is troubling.

24.   See, e.g., *Deutsche Dichtung im 18. Jahrhundert,* ed. Adalbert Elschen-
       broich (Munich: Hanser, 1960), 683n.

25.   Johann Georg Sulzer, *Allgemeine Theorie der schönen Künste,* Part 1
       (1771), Artikel: "Gespräch," 473–76; rprt. in Johann Jakob Engel, *Über
       Handlung, Gespräch und Erzählung,* facsimile, ed. Ernst Theodor Voss
       (Stuttgart: Metzler, 1964), 109–114, here 110.

26.   "Ernst: What are you thinking of, my friend?
       Falk: Nothing.
       Ernst: But you are so quiet.
       Falk: Yes, precisely for that reason. Who thinks when he is enjoying him-
             self? And I am enjoying this lovely morning (LM, 13:342).

27.   This view is echoed by other Enlighteners. See, e.g., Theodor Gottlieb von
       Hippel, *Kreuz- und Querzüge des Ritters A bis Z* (Berlin, 1794), 2:52–63,
       rprt. in *Deutsche Dichtung des 18. Jahrhunderts,* ed. Eschenbroich (1960),
       444–450; and Wieland, *Geschichte der Abderiten,* book 2, chapter 6
       (Leipzig: Weidmann, 1781).

28.   Klopstock speaks of "Zeichen des Gedanken." See "Gedanken über die
       Natur der Poesie" (Aufbau, 261) and "Für junge Dichter" (Aufbau, 268).

29.   See Robert Ginsberg's introduction to *The Philosopher as Writer: The Eigh-
       teenth Century,* ed. Robert Ginsberg (Cranbury, NJ: Associated University
       Presses, 1987), 7–11.

30.   See the preface to the second edition of the *Kritik der reinen Vernunft*
       (1787), B xliii. For an analysis of Kant's writing style in the *Critique* see
       Stephen F. Barker, "The Style of Kant's *Critique of Reason,*" in *The Phi-
       losopher as Writer* (1987), 75–93.

31.   The entire volume of *The Philosopher as Writer* bears witness to the cor-
       ollary between essayistic and philosophic interests. See specifically Gins-
       berg's introductory remarks (7-10). My current comments on Kant's
       contribution have been adapted from my chapter on Leibniz and Kant in
       The Philosopher as Writer, 48–74.

32.   Immanuel Kant: "Observations on the Earthquake in Lisbon" (1756)
       "Essay on Optimism" (1759), "Essay on Mental Illness" (1764), "Visions
       of a Seer Annotated by the Visions of a Metaphysician" (1766).

33.   Wilhelm Windelband, *Geschichte der neueren Philosophie* (1911), 2:11.

34.   The following edition is used: Immanuel Kant, *Was ist Aufklärung? Auf-
       sätze zur Geschichte und Philosophie,* ed. Jürgen Zehbe (Göttingen: Van-
       denhoeck and Ruprecht, 1975), 55–61 (= Akademie Ausgabe, 8:35–42):
       "*Enlightenment is humankind's release from self-incurred tutelage. Tute-
       lage is the inability to make use of one's understanding without direction
       from another. Self-incurred is this tutelage when its cause lies not in the lack*

of reason but in the lack of resolution and courage to use it without guidance from another. Dare to know! Have the courage to *think independently!* That is the motto of the Enlightenment" (Zehbe, 55; Kant's emphasis).

35. Francis X. J. Coleman, *The Harmony of Reason: A Study of Kant's Aesthetics* (London: University of Pittsburgh Press, 1974), 167, 181.

36. "If I have a book that understands for me, a pastor who has a conscience for me, a physician who decides my diet, and so on, I need not trouble myself. I need not think for myself, if I can only pay; others will readily undertake the irksome work for me" (Kant, Zehbe, 55).

37. Coleman, *Harmony of Reason*, 159–61.

38. Haas, *Essay* (1969), 47f.

39. "That would be a criminal act against human nature itself, the foremost destiny of which lies precisely in the advancement of enlightenment; and future generations would be fully justified in rejecting those decrees as having been made in an unwarranted and malicious manner" (Kant, Zehbe, 59).

40. Rohner, *Essay* (1966), 309.

41. "But the way a monarch thinks, who favors the former [religious enlightenment], goes even further, recognizing that there is no danger even to his lawgiving in allowing his subjects to make public use of their reason and to publish their thoughts as a better formulation of that legislation" Kant, Zehbe, 61).

42. "When nature, therefore, has uncovered from under this hard shell the seed which she most carefully nurtures—namely, the propensity and vocation to *free thinking*—then this kernel gradually affects the people's way of thinking (by means of which they gradually become ever more capable of *free action*). Ultimately, the premises of governance are affected as well so that the *governing body* will find it advantageous to treat all persons—who are now recognized as more than mere *machines*—according to their inherent dignity" (Kant, Zehbe, 61; Kant's emphasis).

43. Kant, Akademie Ausgabe, 5:321.

44. Berger, *Der Essay* (1964), 200. See Alexander Altmann's monumental study of Mendelssohn as writer and thinker for a thoroughgoing assessment: *Moses Mendelssohn: A Biographical Study* (University, AL: Alabama University Press, 1973).

45. Moses Mendelssohn, *Phädon oder über die Unsterblichkeit der Seele*, ed. Dominique Bourel, introduction by Nathan Rotenstreich (Hamburg, 1979), 101: "In the search for truth humankind is thrashed about by the waves of opinion until reason and reflection—these offspring of Jupiter—fill its sails, promising a safe landing. Reason and reflection lead the human mind away from the sensual perceptions of the corporeal world back to its true home, that is, into the realm of sentient beings. Above all it is a movement toward beings of the same type, to created beings who, because of their finiteness, can be clearly conceived and comprehended. They raise [the seeker] up to the source of all that is capable of thinking and conceiving, to that source

which comprehends everything although it itself is incomprehensible. Of this source we gratefully know enough to realize that everything good, beautiful, and perfect in the physical and spiritual realms originates in and is maintained by that supreme source."

46. Koepke, "Herder's Craft of Communication," *The Philosopher as Writer*, ed. R. Ginsberg (1987) 94–121; here 95. He describes Herder's writing style in detail, reaching similar conclusions about Herder's craft of prose as I do about the nature of creative writing and reading. The renewed interest in Herder's many accomplishments is attested to by recent publications such as the essay collections *Johann Gottfried Herder: Innovator Through the Ages*, ed. Wulf Koepke, Modern German Studies 10 (Bonn: Bouvier, 1982) and the *Herder-Kolloquium 1978*, ed. Walter Dietze (Weimar: Hermann Böhlau, 1980). They offer an overview of research trends as well as concise analyses of Herder's specific contributions to cultural reform in the eighteenth century.

47. On the middle style and popular philosophy in general see Gert Ueding, "Popularphilosophie," *Hansers Geschichte der deutschen Literatur*, ed. Rolf Grimminger (Munich: dtv, 1980), 3/2:615–621.

48. "I gather the commentaries of these letters, now expanding their points of view, now restricting them or giving them a new twist. I tear [them] to pieces and sew [them] back together in hopes of creating the pattern of a dynamic whole. I believe I have the freedom to do that. If the letters [Lessing's *Literaturbriefe*] opened other paths through the fertile countryside, I can plough over this path to the advantage of its owner (Herder, Suphan, 1:135).

49. *Der junge Herder*, ed. Wolfdietrich Rasch (Tübingen: Niemeyer, 1969), 19–23 (= *Sämmtliche Werke*, 33 Vol., ed. B. Suphan (Berlin: Weidmannsche Buchhandlung, 1877–1913), 1:147–158.

50. "The more polished language becomes, the more removed it becomes from nature. The more rigid and socially determined (*politisch*) customs become, the less room there is for passion in the world, so much more does the world lose its graphic quality. The more refined the clauses become, the less pronounced the inversions, the more dominant political (*bürgerlich*) and abstract vocabulary becomes, the more rule-conscious language becomes, that much more perfect does language become while losing to the same degree the potential for genuine poetic expression.

    The age of prose was born and made its rounds. Through practice and theory this most favorable phase became the age of beautiful prose, restricting the caprice of idioms without eliminating them entirely. That new style restrained the free use of inversions without adopting the rigor of philosophical constructions which reduced poetic rhythm to the harmony of prose and which enclosed the previously free word order into more balanced clauses. This was the mature age of language" (Suphan, 1:154f.; *DjH*, 23).

51. On Herder's epistemology and concept of "*Ganzheit*" see Koepke, "Herder's Craft of Communication," *The Philosopher as Writer* (1987), 97ff.

52. The text of Herder's "Shakespeare" is cited according to *Der junge Herder*, ed. Wolfdietrich Rasch (Tübingen: Niemeyer, 1969), 74–94 (= Suphan, 5:208–231).

53. "This is no poet! This is a god! This is world history!" (*DjH*, 87). "It resembles him like a puppet; the puppet lacks spirit, life, nature, truth—it lacks in sum all abilities to animate—it lacks purpose and the realization of that purpose. Can it, therefore, still be the same thing?" (*DjH*, 81). "Everthing created a cloak of the spiritual reality! The crowing of the rooster, the resounding of trumpets, the silent wink, the hill close-by, words and nonsensical sounds—what an atmosphere! What depth of truth! And how the horrified king kneels, how Hamlet staggers past his father's image in his mother's room! And now the other scene! At the grave side of his Orphelia! The moving good fellow in all his ties to Horatio, Ophelia, Laertes, Fortinbras!" (*DjH*, 88).

54. cf. Lessing, *Hamburgische Dramaturgie*, 73. Stück.

55. See Herbert von Einem, "Anmerkungen" in Johann Wolfgang von Goethe, *Werke*. Hamburger Ausgabe (Munich: Beck, 1981), 12:692.

56. See Ernst Theodor Voss, "Nachwort," *J. J. Engel. Über Handlung, Gespräch und Erzählung*, facsimile, ed. E. Th. Voss (Stuttgart: Metzler, 1964), 21–25.

57. J. J. Engel, *Über Handlung, Gespräch und Erzählung* (1964), 250ff. et passim.

58. Voss, "Nachwort," *Über Handlung, Gespräch und Erzählung*, 27.

59. J. G. Sulzer, "Gespräch," *Allgemeine Theorie*, Part I, 474: "Wir haben also zwey Arten des Gesprächs zu betrachten; die eine Art schildert die Sinnesart der Menschen, die andre setzet gewisse Wahrheiten in das helleste Licht. Wir wollen Kürze halber diese lehrende, jene schildernde Gespräche nennen" (Reprint edition, 111). Sulzer considers the former to be "eine höchst schätzbare Gattung der Beredsamkeit, bequämer als irgend eine andre Gattung, die wichtigsten Beobachtungen der Vernunft in der höchsten Einfalt und Deutlichkeit vorzutragen. Dieses ist gerade das, was der Philosophie noch am meisten fehlet" (*Allg. Theorie*, I, 475; rprt. 111f.). Of the "descriptive" dialogue Sulzer states: "Es hat eine genaue und lebhafte Kenntnis des Menschen zur Absicht. . . . Das ganze Gespräch ist so eingerichtet, daß der Leser sich einbildet, er höre einem Gespräche, da die unterredenden Personen ihn in das Innerste ihrer Seelen hinein schauen lassen, ihnen unbemerkt zu. . . . Solche Gespräche sind in dem eigentlichsten Sinn Schilderungen der Seelen, und solche Schilderungen, die nicht, wie Gemählde, vor uns stehen, sondern lebendige Abbildungen, da wir selbst auf der Scene stehen, wo alles vorgehet. Alles was im menschlichen Gemüthe schätzbar und liebenswürdig, was verächtlich und abscheulich ist, wird dadurch fühlbar gemacht" (*Allg. Theorie*, I, 475f.; rprt. 112f.). Not only is the relevance of these determinations to essayistic writing manifest, but they also show that Sulzer anticipated key elements of Engel's theory of the dialogue.

60. J. J. Engel, *Anfangsgründe einer Theorie der Dichtungsarten. Aus deutschen Mustern entwickelt*, Part I (1783), in *J. J. Engels Schriften*, Vol. 11 (Berlin:

Mylius, 1806), 541f. Chapter 9 of this work is reprinted in *Über Handlung, Gespräch und Erzählung*, ed. E. Th. Voss (1964), 144–153. The cited passages are found on 146f.: "The result is that in the former the *thing itself becomes visible* as it undergoes change, and we are transformed into eyewitnesses of this process. In the latter case, on the other hand, the thing itself is not represented nor are we given its development; rather . . . we learn of completed affairs thirdhand. In the one case, things *happen*, they *develop*; in the other, things *have been done*, they *have developed* (Engel's emphasis).

61. Cf. *Deutsche Dichtung im 18. Jahrhundert*, ed Eschenbroich (1960), 679n.

62. Berger expresses grave doubts about including any of the *Popularphilosophen* in a study of essayism, but then he has grave doubts about many things. The only work by Garve he accords any value as an essay is Garve's "Über die Rolle des Wahnwitzigen in Shakespears Schauspielen." Otherwise he abides largely by his judgment that: "Mit wenig Ausnahmen fehlt jedoch fast allen diesen *Zerstreuten prosaischen Aufsätzen* (Campe) [but he means the writings of the *Popularphilosophen*] künstlerische Rundung, Weite des Blicks und Überlegenheit der Haltung; der mitteilende Charakter (der als essayistisch verstanden werden könnte) ist meistens nur lehrhaft, oft pedantisch; die wissenschaftliche Haltung ist platt und popularisierend oder nur dahingeplaudert. Es handelt sich fast nur um bessere oder schlechtere feuilletonistische Arbeiten, und es wäre eine Abwertung der Gattung, sie als Essays zu bezeichnen" (*Der Essay*, 200). It is surprising that Berger feels justified in making such a sweeping statement without the benefit of individual textual analyses.

63. Reprinted in Christian Garve, *Popularphilosophische Schriften*, facsimile, ed. Kurt Wölfel. Deutsche Neudrucke, Reihe Texte des 18. Jahrhunderts (Stuttgart: Metzler, 1974), Anhang, 2:3*–20*.

64. Christian Garve, "Das Weihnachtsgeschenk," *Popularphilosophische Schriften*, 1:16–21, here 19. Originally published in *Philosoph für die Welt* (Leipzig, 1777), 15. Stück, 2:18–23. Hereafter the reprint edition is cited in the text.

65. See Chapters III and IV of this study and the pertinent bibliographical citations for a more information on the roles of reading, writing, and women in the Enlightenment. Barbara Becker-Cantarino has recently published a thorough study of the role of women in the intellectual and literary life of the Renaissance to Enlightenment period. See her *Der lange Weg zur Mündigkeit. Frau und Literatur (1500–1800)* (Stuttgart: Metzler, 1987). On women as writers during the Enlightenment, see also Ruth P. Dawson, "Women Communicating: Eighteenth- Century German Journals Edited by Women," *Archives et Bibliotheques de Belgique* 54 (1983), 95–111, and "'Der Weihrauch, den uns die Männer streuen': Wieland and Women Writers in *Der Teutsche Merkur*," in *Christoph M. Wieland 1733–1813. North American Contributions to the 250th Anniversary of his Birth*, ed. Hansjörg Schelle (Tübingen: Niemeyer, 1985), 225–249.

66. Garve concludes his article, "Über die öffentliche Meinung," with the remark that the desire for knowledge and independent thinking, once it has been awakened, must be disseminated throughout all classes of society to preserve orderly government while ensuring individual happiness. See Garve, *Popularphilosophische Schriften*, 2:333f.

67. On Sturz see Jaikyung Hahn, *Helferich Peter Sturz (1736–1779). Der Essayist, der Künstler, der Weltmann* (Stuttgart: Heinz, 1976). Knigge und Hippel are yet to be analyzed as essayists.

68. On Forster as essayist see Ruth P. Dawson, "Georg Forster, Essayist," in *Jahrbuch für internationale Germanistik* 9/2 (1977), 112–25. She considers Forster to be "a perfect writer of essays" who was inspired by the attitudes and beliefs of the Enlightenment to adopt the essayistic mode from his earliest attempt, "Ein Blick in das Ganze der Natur," c. 1783), to his *Ansichten vom Niederrhein*, 1790). Ludwig Rohner, *Der deutsche Essay* (1966), 139–151, gives a detailed interpretation of "Über Leckereien," 1788) as an example of the conceptual essay (*begrifflicher Essay*). Thomas P. Saine provides an engrossing account of Forster in his *Georg Forster*, TWAS 215 (New York: Twayne, 1972), but places the writer's beginnings as an essayist during the years 1788–92 (see Chapter III).

CHAPTER 9

The Dialectic Muse Soars II: Essayistic Practice 1770–1815

The Dioscuri

No discussion of historical developments can follow strict chronological lines. Time is a relative concept. So too is the chronicle of history. Especially with regard to literary history, I wished to avoid visually separating an examination of the Classic-Romantic writers from the treatment of the Enlighteners in order to underscore emphatically what Rehder has called the "consistency in structure and purpose" of the essay "that can only testify to a strong linkage between romanticism and rationalism."[1] However, the wealth of material forced a division somewhere in order to make it manageable.

The previous chapter discussed the work of many authors who can be considered classical essayists. Their careers began in the 1740s, 1750s or 1760s and continued in some instances far beyond the traditional beginnings of German Classicism around 1787 and German Romanticism about a decade after that. Thus although this chapter optically isolates Goethe, Schiller, Schlegel, Kleist, and Müller from Wieland, Lessing, Herder, Garve, and Kant (as they in turn were isolated from their predecessors), the reader should conceive of the boundaries as fluid. The works of these writers from different schools overlap and are frequently even simultaneous. Moreover, I include in this chapter a sampling of those writers born in the 1750s and 1760s who have not been asigned to any literary school simply because they have been grossly neglected by literary historians. I am referring to the women writers who rose to the fore in the waning years of the century: e.g., Emilia von Berlepsch, Elisa von der Recke, Friederike Brun, and Caroline Pichler. A synchronic view of literature would be a necessary complement to our present diachronic perspective. In fact, it is a pressing desideratum.

I begin with my typical disclaimer. Because Goethe's (1749–1832) and Schiller's (1759–1805) writing careers spanned more than forty years beginning around 1770, it is not possible to convey an encompassing picture of their essayistic endeavors. We must be highly selective. On the other hand, I do not wish to accord the Classic Duo larger prominence in the history and theory of essayism than is seeming. Since a selection must be made, I endeavor to identify a common denominator aside from the essayistic traits themselves. This procedure allows us to highlight thematic continuities in the eighteenth century apart from our primary concern with the authorial stance which marks essayism as defined in *Crossing Boundaries*.

Johann Wolfgang von Goethe

Fortunately, we possess a focused study by Joachim Wohlleben of Goethe as essayist which details the evolution of his essayistic method and prose from beginning to end.[2] However, Wohlleben opts to discuss Goethe's essayism outside the context of previous essay research. Consequently, he fails to differentiate between the essay and related forms (e.g., aphorism, letter, treatise, and character study). He also complicates the usual terminology further by speaking of *der gnomische Essay* (45), *der virtuelle Essay* (46), *der Briefessay* (47) *die Essay-Skizze* (47), *der eingreifende Essay* (48), *der romanhafte Essay* (54), *der serielle Aufsatz* (54), or *Essay-Entwurf* (105). All these designations are redundant in one way or another and are of little use for determining the quintessence of essayistic style. Finally, Wohlleben's attempt to organize Goethe's essayistic compositions according to content criteria seems problematic in light of our theoretical considerations on the nature of the essay (see Chapter III). Despite these failings, the book is a useful introduction to Goethe as an essayist, and we are grateful for Wohlleben's demonstration of the consistently gnomic tendency in Goethe's writing (44 et passim).

The following compositions immediately come to mind when we think of Goethe as essayist: "Zum Shakespeares-Tag" ("On Shakespeare's Name-Day," written in 1771, but not published until 1854)), "Von deutscher Baukunst" ("On German Architecture," 1773), "Granit" (1781), "Literarischer Sansculottismus" ("The Literary Left," 1795), "Winckelmann" (1805), "Sanct Rochus-Fest zu Bingen" ("The Saint Rochus Festival in Bingen," 1814), or "Shakespeare und kein Ende" ("Shakespeare Without End," 1813–16). They represent the essay as literary critique, cultural criticism, graphic description, and biographical treatise. They also span the final 45 years of our period of inquiry, crossing the boundaries from Storm and Stress to late Enlightenment, Classicism, and Romanticism. Elements of each literary phase have found their way into these representative works. In the following we will concentrate on the two Shakespeare critiques since they represent the beginning and end of the current phase under scrutiny.[3]

Actually, "Zum Shakespeares-Tag" is not literary criticism, for Goethe is engaged here in self-exploration. In typical Goethean fashion he intones the sketch with the words: "*Mir* kommt vor" (It seems to *me*; my emphasis). And the second paragraph begins: "Ich! Der ich mir alles bin, da ich alles nur durch mich kenne!" (Me! I am everything unto myself because I know all things only through myself!). His concern is with his own poetic genius which grants immortality, so that we might see the oration as a fulfillment of Lessing's judgment that "a genius can be inspired only by another genius" ("17. Literaturbrief"). Thus, we cannot readily say whether this composition should be labelled a literary critique, a culturally investigative essay, or biographical sketch.

The influence of Herder's rhapsodic tone during the Strasbourg phase is readily apparent in Goethe's piece with its many exclamation marks and rapid-fire sequence of images and allusions. Originally, Herder's composition was supposed to have been delivered on October 14, 1771, as part of a celebration honoring the great Englishman in the home of Goethe's parents in Frankfurt. Herder's oration was not held, but Goethe's was. While Herder celebrated Shakespeare as a phenomenon of history, Goethe shifted the emphasis under the added influence of Shaftesbury solely to the dramatist as a "second creator" and thus as a phenomenon of nature and genius.[4]

The loose structure of the mere four pages which constitute "Zum Shakespeares-Tag" is emphasized by the dominant impression of human existence as an indefinite pilgrimage. Moreover, the poet warns his audience at the beginning not to expect him "to write much or in an organized manner" because the occasion calls for a festive and not a somber tone (HA, 12:224). Finally, he admits at the end that he is concluding his remarks "even though [he] has scarcely begun" (HA, 12:227). His manner of proceeding is therefore in the best manner of the essay—associative, additive. Also in the best manner of the classical essayist, Goethe speaks only about that which he knows best: himself. His own artistic personality forms the nucleus toward which his ideas and feelings gravitate.

Readily granting that he has *thought* little about Shakespeare, Goethe stresses that he has *intuited, felt* much (HA, 12:224). For that reason he has little to say about Shakespeare's place in the history of the drama and is incapable of explaining exactly what he experienced upon reading Shakespeare. All that he can state is that he has felt his own experience expanded immeasurably by the encounter with the English dramatist (HA, 12:225). Shakespeare is thus his friend, his companion, his mentor. His concluding appeal to awaken the "sympathetic souls" (*alle edle* [sic] *Seelen*) from their aesthetic half life (*Schattenleben*) in the Rococo landscapes of myrtle and laurel sounds the call to a fuller experience of life as art in the Storm-and-Stress custom. It simultaneously recalls the *exordium* in which Goethe remarked upon the human tendency to fall short of its goals because we wax too lax to live life to its fullest, thereby slipping back into the "general non-existence" from which we all issue. Using Shakespeare as the inspiration, Goethe is really urging all like-minded souls to realize their full individualistic potential (*der Keim in uns, das Eigentümliche unsres Ichs,* HA, 12:224, 226).

Although this sketch barely provides the contours of the author's topic, it is so abundant in inspired thoughts and tropes that the reader responds by reflecting further upon what s/he has read. Goethe's frequent appellations to the audience to react to Shakespeare like himself contributes to a breakdown of the walls separating individuals from one another. The affected reader/listener is supposed to call out with Goethe: "Laßt mir Luft, daß ich reden kann!" (Let me catch my breath that I might speak! HA, 12:227).

"Shakespeare und kein Ende," composed in March of 1813 (Parts I and II) and early 1816 (Part III), is decidedly different in tone despite the commonality of concepts and subject matter. While young Goethe could only wax enthusiastic about the great master, the mature Goethe feels the need to specify the dramatist's unique position in literary history. By employing the methodology of analysis and synthesis, he hopes to arrive at an objective assessment of Shakespeare's significance based on theory and not mere feeling. That theory is the content of section two: "Shakespeare, verglichen mit den Alten und Neuesten" ("Shakespeare Compared With the Ancients and Most Modern Writers," HA, 12:290–95). Using the notion of the "Querelle des anciens et des modernes" and the differences between them as a point of departure, Goethe stylizes Shakespeare as neither an ancient nor a modern although he shares qualities with both parties. By way of clarification the poet sets up a set of seven antitheses between the two schools:

ancient—modern
naive—sentimental
heathen—Christian

heroic—Romantic
real—ideal
necessity—freedom
duty (*Sollen*)—volition (*Wollen*) (HA, 12:291).

The first six pairs were common in the eighteenth-century debate on the preeminence of the one or the other aesthetic school. The final pair, however, echoes a new note introduced first by Kant and Schiller into the discussion.[5] The remainder of the composition centers on the notions of Sollen and Wollen.

As in 1771 Shakespeare still appears as the advocate of a *Weltgeist*-concept of reality (HA, 12:289) and as a *wahrer Naturfromme* (a veritable devotee of nature, 12:294). Moreover, Goethe more explicitly labels him "a decidedly modern poet" (12:291) whose greatest talent is that of an *Epitomator* (i.e., one who summarizes or joins together, 12:297). But he is no longer simply a colossal phenomenon of nature which is beyond analysis and can only be appreciated as a gigantic moment of existence as in 1771.

Like the classical essayist Goethe encircles his subject, drawing close to this central idea and then pulling back again. That is the movement from part I to II and III. The reader is engaged in a process of gradual discovery; s/he is not merely overwhelmed with verbiage and enchanted with metaphor, but is also encouraged to consider the playright from various vantage points. Thus, for instance, Goethe begins his inquiry in a sober tone which contains no direct appeals to the reader, but which nevertheless garners her/his attention because he details his manner of proceeding. Each part is then tagged separately: I—"Shakespeare als Dichter überhaupt" ("Shakespeare as Poet in General"); II—"Shakespeare, verglichen mit den Alten und Neuesten" ("Shakespeare Compared with the Ancients and Most Modern Writers"); III—"Shakespeare als Theaterdichter" ("Shakespeare as Dramatist"). Interpolated between parts II and III is a transitionary paragraph in which Goethe attempts to bridge the chronological gap between the publication of parts I and II in 1815 and part III in 1826 (although composed in 1813 and 1816 respectively).

The approach used here is the practical application of Goethe's quasi-theory of essayistic writing formulated in the preface to his *Zur Farbenlehre* (*On Chromatic Theory*, 1808). A book which treats natural phenomena (and we can consider Shakespeare to be a natural phenomenon), the poet/scientist writes, will be enjoyable and useful only if it presents its material in vivid fashion. Just as the drama only comes to life when it is performed on stage, the scientific text lives only through the active participation of the reader's powers of imagination. Goethe explains: "Wenn [das Buch] genossen, wenn es genützt werden soll, so muß dem Leser die Natur entweder wirklich oder in lebhafter Phantasie gegenwärtig sein. Denn eigentlich sollte der Schreibende sprechen und seinen Zuhörern die Phänomene, teils wie sie uns ungesucht entgegenkommen, teils wie sie durch absichtliche Vorrichtungen nach Zweck und Willen dargestellt werden können, als Text erst anschaulich machen; alsdann würde jedes Erläutern, Erklären, Auslegen einer lebendigen Wirkung nicht ermangeln."[6] This notion echoes Goethe's concept of style which is based on "the most fundamental principles of cognition and is informed by the essence of things." By stripping the accidentals away from the object being described, the artist exposes its essence. In the process the unity of the whole is also revealed.[7] Moreover, it sounds suspiciously like the roles envisioned for poets and rhetoricians since the days of Leibniz and Gottsched!

Earlier in the same preface Goethe had outlined his conception of how conscious reflection operates. We will never be satisfied, he argues, with merely looking at an object; we must also theorize about what we experience. We must consciously reflect upon the interrelationships of phenomena and upon their significance for our own self-definition. If experience is to be truly useful it must be analyzed in animated fashion. The approach presupposes an uncommon freedom and flexibility of thought. Goethe labels that method "irony," a concept of great importance to the Romantics. Because the passage is so central to our considerations of essayism and critical thought since Thomasius, I cite it in full:

> Denn das bloße Anblicken einer Sache kann uns nicht fördern. Jedes Ansehen geht über in ein Betrachten, jedes Betrachten in ein Sinnen, jedes Sinnen in ein Verknüpfen, und so kann man sagen, daß wir schon bei jedem aufmerksamen Blick in die Welt theoretisieren. Dieses aber mit Bewußtsein, mit Selbstkenntnis, mit Freiheit und, um uns eines gewagten Wortes zu bedienen, mit Ironie zu tun und vorzunehmen, eine solche Gewandtheit ist nötig, wenn die Abstraktion, vor der wir uns fürchten, unschädlich und das Erfahrungsresultat, das wir hoffen, recht lebendig und nützlich werden soll.[8]

In other words, irony connotes a distancing of the thinker from her/himself during the very act of thinking. Only by remaining objective toward our own conceptualization process in this self-distancing manner can we hope to achieve a semblance of truth in our observations of the world and of the self. Goethe calls this stance "bold" (*gewagt*) probably because the term irony was already ambiguous. He did not mean to imply humor, satire, parody, understatement, litotes, or any other aspect of a traditional understanding of irony. Rather his meaning in the cited passage points to an interpretation of irony in the manner of Jean Paul or of the Romantics; that is, irony designates a bifocal view of the world resultant from the simultaneous awareness of subject and object. It is furthermore informed by the view that the context of the observing subject is in a state of flux. Because of the lack of stasis in the universe, the observer—whether poet or scientist—is highly conscious of the tentativeness of his/her insights. All dogmatic statements about that larger context and humankind's position within it become suspicious. By analogy this bifocality extends to a consciousness of the simultaneity of the individual and the universal, the real and the ideal. Goethe applies this bifocal (or ironic) approach to his observations on Shakespeare's position within cultural history, to which we now return.

Reminiscent of Herder's essay on Shakespeare is Goethe's remark that so much has been written about the dramatist that we could hardly expect to discover anything new. Yet it remains true that one mind is always capable of stimulating another (*die Eigenschaft des Geistes, das er den Geist ewig anregt,* HA, 12:287). Moreover, Goethe sees his work "only" as an attempt (*Versuch,* 12:295).

The central concept which Goethe is at pain to illucidate seems to be that "the highest goal to which the human being can aspire is the awareness of her/his own sentiments and thoughts" (HA, 12:287). The medium of this consciousness raising is Shakespeare's art. It forces a confrontation of the individual with the world thereby advancing an awareness of the world (12:288). By focusing on the Shakespearean dramatic method, Goethe contributes to the reader's own growing self awareness via his text. It is thus fitting that the third section of this essayistic attempt concludes with a reference to the audience's participatory role in realizing Shakespeare's theatrical objective. Without the active participation of the onlooker's imagination, all the words would be empty. Goethe had said as much early on in the oration when he averred: "Shakespeare nun spricht durchaus an unsern innern Sinn; durch diesen belebt sich zugleich die Bilderwelt der Einbildungskraft und so entspringt eine vollständige Wirkung, von der wir uns keine Rechenschaft zu geben wissen."[9] Shakespeare's appeal is directed at our inner being, that which makes us free-acting agents rather than merely reactive objects jostled about by natural forces. How that creative event within one's inner self occurs remains a mystery.

Upon further reflection Goethe's reader begins to realize that the "economy of the whole" (*Ökonomie des Ganzen*) characteristic of Shakespeare's plays also marks Goethe's "Shakespeare und kein Ende." Even as Shakespeare constructed each play around a central concept (*Begriff*, HA, 12:297), this little composition is centered on a unifying notion which one will never completely fathom so that Goethe could, years later, add a third segment to his argument without altering the overall quality of the work. The unifying idea is that Shakespeare occupies an historical and intellectual space *beyond* the ancients and the moderns. In fact, Shakespeare is aligned with the *most* modern (*die Neuesten*).

The purpose of Part II is to establish the theoretical basis for Goethe's claim. Essentially, he argues that the mentality of the ancients or if you will, their self-awareness, was marked by a moral imperative (*Sollen*) in the relationship between the individual and the world plan. This duty is despotic like a rational category and ineluctable like the natural laws of evolution. Destined by an external fate to strive for the unreachable, mankind is condemned to frustration and tragedy. The modern mentality, by contrast, has substituted volition (*Wollen*) as the motivator in the concept of destiny. The self-imposed directive in the modern ("romantic") world appears as free, individual, liberating, and ultimately uplifting (HA, 12:292). The influence of Schiller's moral aestheticism is so readily discernible in this line of reasoning that I fail to understand why Wohlleben considers it deprecating. Nor is it clear why he refers to Goethe's argument as digressive and inexact.[10]

Goethe avoids ponderosity in the abstract middle section of his article by employing several rhetorical techniques ranging from antithesis to periphrasis, tropes, and synecdoche. These strategies are designed to enhance the aesthetic and communicative pleasure of the essayistic piece. For example, Goethe draws a parallel between poetry and card games. The rules of the game and the central role of chance are analogous to the ancients' sense of fate. The player's decisions reflect the element of *Wollen*. In this manner Goethe sees whist as a metaphor of antiquity, since the role of chance is starkly reduced as is individual volition. *L'hombre* [a popular eighteenth-century card game], on the other hand, reflects the modern way of thinking and writing (HA, 12:292). Similarly, the poet explicitly addresses his public with the hope that it will apply the foregoing "preliminary observations" (*Vorbemerkungen*, HA, 12:293) to an interpretation of Shakespeare. He nevertheless offers his own analysis.

It is here that Goethe suggests that Shakespeare's unique historical position is marked by a unity of opposites. He encompasses both the

Sollen of the ancients and the *Wollen* of the moderns. In his capacity as a member of society (*Charakter*) the individual person (*Person*) is called to limitation (i.e., *Sollen*); but as a human being (*Mensch*) the individual enjoys an avocation to the all encompassing. (Goethe's separation of the *Person* into the constituent functions of object and subject is parallel to Kant's distinction between the human being as *Bürger* and as *Mensch*.) Goethe argues that Shakespeare complicates the matter further by introducing an external *Wollen* which subjugates the internal will to its greater force (HA, 12:294). The vertices of internal and external forces converging in the duty-oriented volition of the tragic figure represents for Goethe Shakespeare's unique contribution to the history of a mentality.

Despite the intervening forty odd years and its altered tone, "Shakespeare und kein Ende" does not offer a radically different assessment than the "Rede zum Shakespeare-Tag." In 1771 Goethe opined that while the Englishman's plays lack plot in the usual sense, they all revolve around a hidden, mysterious axis. As yet undetected by any philosopher, this center point is the locus of the clash between the freedom of the individual and the necessity of the whole. Goethe writes: "Seine [Shakespeares] Plane sind, nach dem gemeinen Stil zu reden, keine Plane, aber seine Stücke drehen sich alle um den geheimen Punkt (den noch kein Philosoph gesehen und bestimmt hat), in dem das Eigentümliche unsres Ichs, die prätendierte Freiheit unsres Wollens, mit dem notwendigen Gang des Ganzen zusammenstößt" (HA, 12:226).[11] The essay of 1813–16 leans more toward the conceptual and thus must treat the artistic whole of the work in segmented fashion; that is, as theoretician Goethe must analyze by separating that which naturally, sometimes even paradoxically, belongs together.

Part III returns the reader to the point of departure in Part I. The *Scheinparadox* (apparent paradox) as presented at the beginning of Part III proves to be the fitting preparation for the concluding suggestion of the entire composition; namely, that Shakespeare's role as a writer for the theater can only be successful if the spectator is willing to add what is missing from the presentation on the stage. To do so the onlooker must engage her/his inner eye and not just see with the physical one (cf. HA, 12:288). This inner eye is capable of apprehending the mysteries of the world spirit (*Weltgeist*, HA, 12:289); the corporeal eye perceives only the external form.

The active participation of the audience in the theatrical experience can be seen as a variation of the synecdochic method. Without it the stage event could not became what Shakespeare envisioned it to be. In the meanwhile we have come to recognize in this rhetorical strategy of forcing the audience to complete thoughts a classical technique of the creative writing and reading processes. Goethe's renewed discourse with Shakespeare's work "frozen" in this essayistic endeavor could not *be* what its author intended without *our* active involvment in *his* presentation. Placed in this light the title, "Shakespeare und kein Ende," alludes to the never-ending process of consciousness raising via the encounter with the word—oral and written. As with all true literature it is not a question of meaning but of meanings. Specifically with regard to the quality of this work as essayistic, we would do well to recall Saul Morson's explanation that the reader becomes a codeterminer of the text together with the author. The decoding process must be related to the encoding one without having to renounce the element of free choice. True communication occurs between the lines.

Friedrich Schiller

Friedrich Schiller (1759–1805) contributed numerous compositions to the tradition of essayistic writing beginning with his school oration in 1779, "Rede über die Frage: Gehört allzuviel Güte, Leutseeligkeit und große Freygebigkeit im engsten Verstande zur Tugend?" ("Oration on the Question: Is Virtue in the Strictest Sense Dependent on a Great Deal of Kindness, Geniality, and Generosity?") to "Über den Gebrauch des Chors in der Tragödie" ("On the Use of the Chorus in Tragedy"), the preface to his *Die Braut von Messina* (1803). In between we find such well-known pieces as the dialogues, "Der Spaziergang unter den Linden" ("Stroll Under the Linden Trees," 1782) and "Der Jüngling und der Greis" ("The Youth and the Old Man," 1782); his Mannheim lecture, "Was kann eine gute stehende Bühne eigentlich wirken?" ("What Can a Good Standing Theater Actually Accomplish?", 1785); "Die philosophischen Briefe" ("The Philosophical Letters," 1786); his inaugural lecture in Jena, "Was heißt und zu welchem Ende studiert man Universalgeschichte?" ("What is Universal History and Why Study It?", 1789); his review "Bürgers Gedichte" ("Bürger's Poems," 1791); "Über Anmut und Würde" ("On Grace and Dignity," 1793); and "Über naive und sentimentalische Dichtung" ("On Naive and Sentimental Poetry," 1795).

From these and the numerous other essayistic compositions either embedded in Schiller's historical or appended to his dramatic writings, we will draw upon only a very few, concentrating on examples written during the 1780s in order to complement the chronology of previous analyses: "Die philosophischen Briefe" and "Was heißt und zu welchem Ende studiert man Universalgeschichte." There are two additional reasons to focus on these two pieces. First, they reflect the essential quality of Schiller's moral and anthropological thinking throughout his career as well as his practice of essayism. Second, "Die philosophischen Briefe" and "Was heißt . . . Universalgeschichte" summarize cardinal ideas underlying the premise of *Crossing Boundaries*. In a very definite sense, Schiller (like Garve) represents the sum of the new way of thinking and writing in the eighteenth century.

This avant-garde facet of his work is immediately evident in the opening lines of the *Vorerinnerung* (preliminary remarks) to the "Philosophical Letters": "Die Vernunft hat ihre Epochen, ihre Schicksale wie das Herz, aber ihre Geschichte wird weit seltner behandelt. Man scheint sich damit zu begnügen, die Leidenschaften in ihren Extremen, Verirrungen und Folgen zu entwickeln, ohne Rücksicht zu nehmen, wie genau sie mit dem Gedankensysteme des Individuums zusammenhängen."[12] Schiller's intent, therefore, is to address the reciprocal influence of the individual's mentality on his/her actions and passions as well as to see those reactions as signs of one's mentality. In implicit contrast to his approach in "Der Verbrecher aus Infamie" ("Criminal Through Dishonor," 1786), he proposes here to delineate the formative impact of the head on the heart, for "the head must educate the heart." In non-tropic terms that statement reads: man's rational faculties must exert formative control over her/his emotional response.

In the second paragraph of his introductory remarks, Schiller draws explicit attention to the reading and writing revolution occasioned by the *Aufklärung*. The thinking portion of the reading public has grown so large that the structural alteration of mores and social class is becoming everywhere apparent. The progress of reason, however, is not without its pitfalls, so Schiller feels compelled to warn us that the path to truth is rarely straightforward. We must expect many wrong turns and false starts before arriving at our goal (Hanser, 1:701).

In the ensuing paragraph the poet/philosopher makes clear just how tentative the ideas contained in the "Philosophische Briefe" really are. Thus he calls them an *Entwurf* (sketch), *der Anfang eines Versuchs* (the beginning of an attempt), and a collection of relatively true, sometimes even contradictory *Meinungen* (opinions) which nevertheless form a whole as will become clear with the continuation of the letters (Hanser, 1:701). Since the letters were not resumed, they must be considered fragmentary. The qualities enumerated above are all symptomatic of essayistic writing.

Finally, in the fourth paragraph Schiller defines skepticism and free-thinking as the "fevered paroxysms of the human spirit" (*Fieberparoxysmen des menschlichen Geistes,* Hanser, 1:702). The cure for these extreme states lies in their being allowed to run their course through self expression. The doubts and errors inherent in the polar drives of human thought can be overcome only through open discourse (Hanser, 1:702). That discussion, as Schiller had previously mentioned, takes place between friends of differing opinions, but motivated by a common love of truth and moral integrity (Hanser, 1:701). When put into print, the dialogue forms a kind of "transcendental publication."

Having stressed the need to read the letters from the proper vantage point, Schiller presents a brief exchange of letters between Julius and Raphael which establishes the dialogic and dialectical quality of the entire composition (Hanser, 1:702–707). Through his realistic stance Raphael endeavors to restrain Julius's unfettered flights of idealism. The remaining eleven pages of the "Philosophical Letters" reproduces a "fragment" penned by Julius sometime earlier with the title "Die Theosophie des Julius" ("The Theosophy of Julius," 1:707–718). This "interpolated" section has a dual function. On the one hand, it is integrated thematically and stylistically into the fragmentary letters; on the other hand, it can also stand apart from the "Philosophical Letters." In the latter capacity it appears as an essay clearly divided into sections designated "Die Welt und das denkende Wesen," "Idee," "Liebe," "Aufopferung," and "Gott" ("The World and Man Thinking," "Thought," "Love," "Sacrifice," "God"). An example of essayistic writing in its own right, the "Theosophie des Julius" contains the nucleus of the planned series of letters and of Schiller's concept of reason.

In its conception the "Philosophical Letters" derive from Schiller's years in the Karlschule and can be seen in conjunction with his school oration, "Rede über die Frage: Gehört allzuviel Güte, Leutseligkeit und große Freigebigkeit im engsten Verstande zur Tugend?" (1779), as well as with the two dialogues, "Der Spaziergang unter den Linden" and "Der Jüngling und der Greis." Because the roots of their origin reach back to the late 1770s, the fruits of his reading and studies during those years have left their mark on the tenor of this fragmentary piece. The tone of Julius's letters to Raphael is indebted to Goethe's *Werther,* while the rhapsodic quality of the "Theosophie" recalls the tenor of Klopstock's *Messias.* Intellectually, the interjected "Theosophie" is indebted to central concepts of Leibniz (theodicy, monads), Ferguson (moral philosophy), Lessing (tolerance, friendship, perfectibility), and Carl von

Linnaeus's botanical theories.[13] While Julius's letters to Raphael deal
with his sense of disillusionment wrought by Raphael's "bold assault of
materialism" upon his idealism (Hanser, 1:707), the "Theosophie" is
unmitigated in its Platonic, even anagogic rapture.

Because Julius conceives of the universe as Divine Thought, there exists
for him only the "Man Thinking" (*das denkende Wesen*) whose function
is to perceive the whole of creation by interpreting the "signs" of complex
phenomena (*Chiffre*, 1:708). Everything surrounding the human being is
a "hieroglyph of an energy" coursing through humankind itself. Schiller
writes: "Alles in mir und außer mir ist nur Hieroglyphe einer Kraft, die
mir ähnlich ist" (Everything in and around me is only a hieroglyph of an
energy that is like myself, Hanser, 1:707). Active thought process is
therefore a divine-like act of interpretation, using material reality as a
springboard to higher planes.

In the subsection "Idee" Schiller explains that the energy of the universe gives direction to human perfectibility. The individual appears as
simultaneously manipulated object and autonomous subject: "Wir selbst
werden das empfundene Objekt" (We ourselves become the perceived
object, Hanser, 1:709). As intellect the human being is self-directive; as
material object s/he is determined by external forces. The drive for perfection affects only the spirit not the physical substance of the individual
person. The second subsection, "Liebe," begins with a symbolic allusion
to having reached the mountain pinnacle. The reference is to the tediousness of segmented reasoning which must go from the particular to the
universal. Having ascended the mountain, the "Man Thinking" enjoys a
panoramic view of the whole. That panoramic vision is likened to the
holistic perception of man as "loving creature." Love is, moreover, a
lodestar which guides the wanderer upwards toward the ultimate goal of
mystical reunion with the Creator. Love is then "the all powerful magnet
in the spiritual world" and a reflection of the "primal energy" ("Urkraft,"
1:710f.). "Wenn jeder Mensch," Schiller writes, "alle Menschen liebte, so
besäße jeder einzelne die Welt" (If every human being were to love all
mankind, then every individual person would be in possession of the
world, Hanser, 1:712).

The contrast to that harmonic image is the portraiture of the modern,
self-absorbed egoist who is like a lost atom floating in a vast emptiness
(Hanser, 1:713). By loving only her/himself the egoist cuts off the flow of
life-giving energy surrounding her/him. Consequently, the ability to think
and to love an other are the distinquishing characteristics of Julius's
anthropology.[14]

In a brief penultimate subsection, "Aufopferung" ("Sacrifice"), Schiller further explores the dichotomy of *Liebe* and *Egoismus*—or *amour propre* and *amour de soi*, to adopt Rousseauean terms—before advancing to his final segment on the nature of God. This final portion contains his "confession of reason" (*das Glaubensbekenntnis meiner Vernunft*) although it is only a "fleeting sketch of [his] attempted creation" (*einen flüchtigen Umriß meiner unternommenen Schöpfung*, Hanser, 1:716). The cardinal idea is that the power of love unifies body and soul, the individual and the universal while drawing each person to the fountainhead of perfection: God. For this reason, love is referred to metaphorically as "the ladder on which we ascend toward divine likeness" (*die Leiter, worauf wir emporklimmen zu Gottähnlichkeit*) and as "the rapidly expanding mystery" (*das wuchernde Arkan*). God and nature, Schiller argues, are two great phenomena, separate but identical to one another. "Nature is an infinitely particularized God" (*die Natur ist ein unendlich geteilter Gott*, Hanser, 1:714). Just as the attraction of the physical elements wrought the creation of the appearance of nature as we know it, so too will the attraction of the spirits eventually produce God (*Gott hervorbringen*, Hanser, 1:714).

Via a series of poetic interludes, historical examples, prolepses, and the frequent use of rhetorical questions, Schiller underscores the tentative, searching quality of his thoughts. Granting that his ideas might not be based on strict logic (*strenge Vernunftschlüsse*) but rather on his vibrant imaginings and admitting his lack of familiarity with philosophical writings, Schiller nevertheless suggests that even our purest intellectual concepts are only interpretations. What we call truth is not a quality of the "idiom" to which it refers (the world) or which it employs (language), but only the result of syllogisms. Schiller states emphatically: "Unsre reinsten Begriffe sind keineswegs *Bilder* der Dinge, sondern bloß ihre notwendig bestimmte und koexistierende *Zeichen*" (Intellectual conceptualizations are in no way *reflections* of objects, but merely their necessarily definite and co-existent *signs,* Hanser, 1:716). Consequently, *any* conscious exercise of reflection, *any* product of wit or reason—whether true or false—contributes to our receptivity for truth (Hanser, 1:718).

The final paragraph sums up *en miniature* the attitude and thrust of the "Theosophie." After making a personal appeal to Raphael (*teurer Freund meiner Seele*) in the manner of Amyntor, Ernst, or Falk and overwhelming the reader with a rapid-fire sequence of physico-theological metaphors (*Spinngewebe, Sonnenbild, Tautropfen des Morgens, erdumgürtender Ozean, trüb wolkigte Sumpfe, Millionen Gewächse*), which recall the four elements, Schiller reminds us that nature is one despite its fantastic diversity. Just as there are four natural elements, there are also four essential components of the spirit: "the *ego, Nature, God,* and the *future.*" Moreover, just as there is an essential unity in nature, so too is there but *one* truth in the spiritual realm. All individual expressions of truth revolve around the same axis: "Vier Elemente sind es, woraus alle Geister schöpfen, ihr *Ich,* die *Natur, Gott* und die *Zukunft.* Alle mischen sie millionenfach anders, geben sie millionenfach wieder, aber *eine* Wahrheit ist es, die, gleich einer festen Achse, gemeinschaftlich durch alle Religionen und alle Systeme geht—'Nähert euch dem Gott, den ihr meinet.'"[15]

The concluding exhortation to draw closer to God in the best way one can is a salient reference to the essential need for action based on individual conditions. Both the style and topic of the "Theosophie des Julius" are indebted to an essentially essayistic attitude on the part of the writer. The reader is supposed to respond in kind. Furthermore, the inclusion of poems in his prose text helps Schiller to focus attention on key points; the ploy also anticipates the method of the "classic essay," Friedrich Schlegel's "Über die Unverständlichkeit."

"Was heißt und zu welchem Ende studiert man Universalgeschichte" is another prime example of essayism in the 1780s. Presented as a lecture in Jena, it obviously draws upon rhetorical technique. But it goes considerably beyond the confines of mere rhetoric. Topic and manner are typical of the essay as a mode of thinking. Schiller's theme is the usefulness of historical studies, especially of "universal history." The latter he characteristically defines as a dynamic method rather than as a static discipline. From the long chain of frequently disjointed, recorded past events, the "universal historian" endeavors to discover the unifying thread of human development. These efforts are necessarily teleological in nature for Schiller and his age. The new breed of historian is interested in the present and not really in the past. He writes: "Aus der ganzen Summe dieser Begebenheiten hebt der Universalhistoriker diejenigen heraus, welche auf die *heutige* Gestalt der Welt und den Zustand der jetzt lebenden Generationen einen wesentlichen, unwidersprechlichen und leicht zu verfolgenden Einfluß gehabt haben."[16] The traditional relationship of cause and effect is reinterpreted as "means and ends" (*Mittel und Absicht,* Hanser, 2:20) which proves applicable to all races and generations because "history alone . . . is a *Bürgerin* of all nations and times" (Hanser, 2:21). Finally, Schiller remarks that the value of a universal perception of history is to cure us of an exaggerated admiration of past ages. All previous ages, after all, were necessary to bring about the present refined state of culture in "our *humane* century" (2:22). Consequently, all historical phenomena are only fragments of a larger picture; each valuable in itself, but not complete without the (often unstated) broader context. The stance adopted by the historian of the whole is therefore the same attitude epitomizing the essayist.

This quintessential view of history is presented in a most engaging manner which does not merely dazzle the listener/reader, but animates his/her critical faculties as well. It is in this light that Schiller's classic portraitures of *der philosophische Kopf* and *der Brotgelehrte* must be seen (2:10–12). As as an advocate of syncrasy, "the philosophical thinker" is like the essayist (or Emerson's "Man Thinking") who looks upon the parts as fragments of the whole, whereas the *Brotgelehrte* (professionally oriented scholar) is small minded, conservative, and inflexible. In contrast to the "bread-and-butter scholar" who loves to divide and classify, the "philosophical thinker" is constantly crossing disciplinary boundaries in search of the total picture. The difference between them is, therefore, not *what* they study but *how* they see it Hanser, 2:12).

It is in this light that Schiller's relationship to his audience must be seen. He endeavors to depict his listeners as "thinking persons" (*denkende Köpfe,* Hanser, 2:12) not unlike the Freemasons or cosmopolites of the Age of Reason. His concluding exhortation is especially noteworthy. He calls upon his audience to become active participants in the future by acting consciously in the present. In this manner they (we) will be able to impart permanence to "our fleeting existence" by adding to the "eternal chain" of events (Hanser, 2:22). The argument in the "Theosophie des Julius" regarding the impact of every single venturesome thought is repeated here with regards to every individual event.

In between the reader encounters an impressive use of language marked by anacoluthon, effective repetition of words and phrases, inspired diction, fluctuating perspectives, varied sentence length, a pleasing alteration between excited exhortation and reflective rhetorical question, and illustrative examples drawn from the history of religion, philosophy, and culture. The multiplicity of appeals to intellect and sentiment combined with the repeated switching of focus from the separate event to the universal chain of development constantly reminds the reader/listener of the fragmented nature of all inquiry. While imparting a sense of verve to the overall composition, these strategies reveal an essentially non-dogmatic stance on the part of the writer-seeker. Although the author sees himself as praeceptor, he like the essayist operates on the belief that no one individual has sole claim to truth. Truth lies neither here nor there, but *both* here and there. The reader both *understands* the point and *feels* it too.

As in the case of the "Theosophie des Julius," even this academic lecture reveals Schiller's proximity to the style and content of essayism. Thus, like the difference between the "universal" and "conventional" scholar, the distinction between essayistic and expository writing lies not in *what* is depicted, but *how* it is presented. Is this view not a mirror image of Morson's notion of the proper reading act with regards to the hermeneutic *perplexity* of boundary or threshold literature? For Morson—and for the peruser of essays—it is not a question of *what* we read but *how* we read it.

The question of method is inextricably bound up with authorial intention. We might be going too far in claiming that Schiller intended his "Theosophie des Julius" or his piece on *Universalgeschichte* to be hermeneutically complex; that is, he purposely doubly encoded his text in order to obscure its meaning. That was most likely not the case given the circumstances of their origin. Nevertheless, we would do well to recall with Morson that the decisive factor in boundary works is not what the author intended the work to *mean*, but *how* s/he intended it to be read. It is left up to the reader to identify the structure of a work and to construct a hierarchy of relevance by foregrounding some details of the constituent whole. It is thus a question of a *method for discovering* meaning rather than of a particular reading.[17]

We can read Schiller's compositions as static reflections of his anthropological philosophy by emphasing the abstract concepts or—by stressing linguistic signs—as dynamic, incomplete visions of the shape of past, present, and future. In this latter capacity, Schiller sees things in a "new" light even as the German Romantics introduced innovative, broadening perspectives into the interpretation of the self and the world. The question of how Schiller wanted the reader to approach his own "documentary" writing is perhaps best resolved by the poet himself. He provides us, namely, with his own theoretical explanation of the writing and reading of prose compositions.

It is safe to say that Schiller's prose writing dating from the school oration of 1779 reveals his mastery of rhetorical skills while also betraying poetic nuance. In his early compositions as well as the late, the poet could not be totally subjugated by the rhetorician. (Nor for that matter could the philosophic thinker completely crowd out the poet.) In later works Schiller endeavored to analyze the elusive relationship between rhetoric and literature in systematic fashion. This he did above all in "Über die notwendigen Grenzen beim Gebrauch schöner Formen" ("On the Necessary Limits in the Use of Aesthetic Forms," 1795). Thus it is not surprising that the interplay of "science" (i.e., the principle of necessity or philosophic rigor in the development of ideas) and "poetry" (i.e., the principle of freedom or the free play of the imagination) is an integral part of almost all of Schiller's prose works. Despite their heavy leaning toward philosophical clarity, Schiller's essays are not merely "mechanical" efforts to induce a "reproduction" of his ideas and feelings in the reader. The richness of imagery, metaphor, and thumbnail sketches transform them into "organic" products of mind and heart.

Like the metaphorical belt of Venus which lends its wearer grace and wins her/him love, the aforementioned devices are clearly strategies to involve the passive reader in active recontextualization. Through the multidimensional interplay with the text and its underlying thought system, the reader is to be transformed her/himself into a coauthor of the text. Despite his own admission in a letter dated August 3, 1795, to Johann Gottlieb Fichte that the style of his philosophic writings in the preceding years was arduous, he did not mean to imply that they were intentionally obtuse. Instead he explains his style as being opposed to the generally lax tenor of the times which placed absolutely no demands on the reader. His purpose was not to win over an audience at all costs by adopting its attitude, "but to surprise it, to unnerve it, and to stretch [its vision] by the bold articulation of [his] way of thinking ."[18] The three styles open to a writer were the "aesthetic" (*schöne*), the "popular" (*populär*), and the "philosophical" (*wissenschaftlich*). These were defined in "Über die notwendigen Grenzen beim Gebrauch schöner Formen."[19]

In explaining his conception of the "proper" writing and reading attitudes, Schiller has recourse to anthropological and literary concepts encountered earlier in the writings of Thomasius, Leibniz, Herder, Klopstock, or Lessing (See chapters VII and VIII). "Our destiny," he writes, "is to acquire insights and to transform those insights into action" (Hanser, 2:521). Moreover, this destiny is seen as a moral obligation dependent upon freedom of choice (2:534). However, no idea can be catapulted into action unless it has first become part of the learner's own thinking (*der Besitz*); that action is itself proof of the free, active participation of the (initially) passive reader. Thus Schiller explains: "the mind possesses nothing except for that which it actually does" (*der Geist besitzt nichts, als was er tut,* Hanser, 2:528). While the effect of that which is aesthetically pleasing is immediate, truth is mediate; it must be studied and consciously analyzed in order to be grasped (Hanser, 2:533).

The contrast between the effect of the beautiful and that of the true seems unbreachable. Yet Schiller's category of the "aesthetic" style is posited as the bridge between reasoning and imagining. In this category the unregulated freedom of the imagination which flutters casually (*zu-*

fällig) from one mode of seeing (*Anschauung*) to another is harnessed by the mechanical structure of rational dialectics which interprets possible connections between the individual, seemingly unrelated *Anschauungen* of the imagination. In other words while the imagination conveys a sense of play (*frei, zufällig*) and draws upon the stuff of the real world of objects (*sinnlich*), reason evokes a sense of meaning (i.e., interconnection or the whole) underlying the phenomena and their interplay. Consequently, the needs of the imagination for unregulated activity (*Gesetzlosigkeit*) as well as those of reason for rules and regulations (*Gesetzmäßigkeit*) are satisfied (Hanser, 2:525). With its dual emphasis on nature and logic, the *schöne Schreibart* addresses itself to the totality of the human person. It speaks "als Natur zur Natur" (Hanser, 2:529). Schiller sought to achieve this quality in his own writing, especially in the pre-1790 phase when he was more optimistic about influencing a larger reading public.[20] He explicitly rejects the scholarly treatise as a means of communicating with a larger, anonymous audience. Its erudite, dry tone is ill-designed to stimulate interest. Since Schiller largely succeeded in combining scholarly precision with poetic license, his "philosophical" musings show little of the *blakende öllampe* (smoking oil lamp) Rohner attributes to the *Abhandlung* in Germany.

The "aesthetic" approach utilizes the manner of presentation to animate the spirit and to evoke the transition from emotional and intellectual passivity to action (Hanser, 2:528). Finally, it appeals to a select group of readers capable of simultaneously thinking critically and imagining vividly. Schiller labels this feat as "thinking representationally," describing the author who achieves this full effect as a "representational writer" (*darstellend denken, der darstellende Schriftsteller,* Hanser, 2:529). In connection with this particular distinction he explains the difference between the orator and the praeceptor (*Lehrer*). By the nature of his profession, the orator is interested in an immediate "sensual" (*sinnlich*) impact upon the audience. Since s/he has no guarantee that the audience will return a second time, the orator must present a self-sufficient argument. Moreover, because the orator's audience is not predisposed to rational exertion, s/he must avoid the rigors of strict reasoning.

The writer genuinely interested in the education of the reader, on the other hand, is marked by a different basic attitude toward subject matter and audience. The preceptor accepts an audience only on certain conditions. The audience must be willing to become active codeterminers of meaning and understanding. The *Lehrer* has more time to mull over ideas. The individual products of his/her pen must be seen as fragments of a whole (Hanser, 2:527). The differentiation between the attitude of the orator and of the preceptor exquisitly summarizes the essential difference between merely rhetorical and genuinely essayistic writing as defined in earlier sections of this study. The education of the audience via the printed word is, of course, in keeping with the goals of the Enlightenment, while the view of author and reader as codeterminers of heuristic significance anticipates the reader-response theories of the twentieth century.

The poet's observations on the respective roles of writer and reader as well as on the qualities of the aesthetic mode as compared to the philosophic or popular ones point toward an essayistic understanding of the writing and reading acts in the search for truth and aesthetic pleasure. Although Schiller does not consciously reflect upon the nature of essayism like his younger contemporary, Friedrich Schlegel, both share a common understanding of the relationship between producer and recipient as a "galvanization of author and reader." Thus we can see Schiller as a point in the continuum of the theory and practice of creative writing and reading from Thomasius to the Romantics. But before we move to representative Romantic writers themselves, we must treat two groups of writers who are situated in neither the Classical nor the Romantic school of literature.

Between Classic and Romantic

The title of this subsection does not have to be taken literally. It is an allusion to the unique status accorded such writers as Jean Paul (1763–1825), Friedrich Hölderlin (1770–1843), and Heinrich von Kleist (1777–1811) by literary historians who do not quite know where to locate them. I wish to extend the term to include largely ignored women prose writers such as Elisa von der Recke (1754–1833), Emilia von Berlepsch (1757–1830), Friederike Brun (1765–1835), and Caroline Pichler 1769–1843). (While not ignored as a writer, Sophie von La Roche still needs to be examined as an essayist.)[21] The attitudes expressed in the writing of the latter group of authors are indebted to the general mentality of the Enlightenment as a liberating force. Stylistically, they exhibit parallels to the Classical and Romantic movements as well as to the Enlightenment itself. Like their male counterparts, the women writers draw upon classical traditions of rhetoric to forge a new consciousness, in their case of women as intellectually equal partners in the cultural life of Germany.

Yet, I find myself in a bit of a conundrum. I cannot analyze all of the above-mentioned writers as essayists. I am forced to make a selection but according to what criteria? Jean Paul, Hölderlin, and Kleist are undeniably very major writers according to any standard. And while Jean Paul and Hölderlin have been widely studied as novelist and poet respectively, they have been little viewed as essayists. They should, therefore, figure largely in *Crossing Boundaries*. However, I have the old problem of spatial limitations; it is simply not possible to follow every lead uncovered in the course of my investigations into the nature and practice of essayistic writing 1680–1815. It would be valuable, for example, to analyze Jean Paul's prolific output for its reflections on and of essayism. A likely candidate would be his *Vorschule der Ästhetik* (1804) with its individual chapters ("Programme"), frequently ranging in length from ten to thirty pages and treating such essayistic topics as "Über das Genie" ("On Genius"), "Humoristische Totalität" ("On Humoristic Poetry"), or "Die Ironie, der Ernst ihres Scheins" (On the Impression of Earnestness in Irony).[22] He continues the method in *Levana* (1811) and *Politische Schriften* (1808–1817). Although less voluminous, Hölderlin's work contains short prose compositions worthy of examination as fertile ground for the theory and practice of essayism (e.g., "On the Manner of Proceeding of the Poetic Genius" and "Growth in Decay"). However, we will have to be satisfied with examining only one of these extraordinary writers and, then too, only one composition by him.

Heinrich von Kleist

Although Kleist (1771–1811) does not strictly belong to the Romantic school, he shares many stylistic and creative traits in common with them. More importantly he learned much from older generations of writers (Wieland, Jean Paul, Goethe, and Kant) and was a writer of major proportions contemporary with German Romanticism. An indefatigable dramatist and story teller, he was also a journalist and publicist, penning such rewarding essays as "Aufsatz, den sichern Weg des Glücks zu finden" ("Essay on the Surest Way to Find Happiness," 1799), "Über die Aufklärung der Weiber" ("On the Enlightenment of Women," 1800), and "Über das Marionettentheater" ("On the Puppet Theater," 1810). Here we will examine his "Über die allmähliche Verfertigung der Gedanken beim Reden" (1807/08).

"On the Gradual Development of Ideas in Discourse" addresses an essential quality of all essayistic writing and thinking; that is why it is included here for analysis. The poet sums up his message by citing the

French adage, *l'appétit vient en mangeant,* which is subsequently re-worded to read: "l'idée vient en parlant."[23] The outward form of Kleist's "essay" mirrors the conversational act itself in that it consists of one long, run-on paragraph couched in a relaxed, casual style. Even as he writes, his ideas take shape. Kleist describes the process as follows:

> Ich mische unartikulierte Töne ein, ziehe die Verbindungswörter in die Länge, gebrauche auch wohl eine Apposition, wo sie nicht nöthig wäre, und bediene mich anderer, die Rede ausdeh-nender, Kunstgriffe, zur Fabrikation meiner Idee auf der Werk-stätte der Vernunft, die gehörige Zeit zu gewinnen.[24]

Kleist states explicitly that clarity about our feelings and ideas evolves in and through the communicative act itself. The effect of that activity is similar to the impact of La Fontaine's fables which utilize discourse to represent graphically "the transition of the spirit from thought to expres-sion." Decisive is the association of ideas—underscored by allusions to historical and literary figures such as Mirabeau and La Fontaine (*DE,* 2:37–38).

Such writing is—as Lessing had already noted—tantamount "to think-ing aloud" (*DE,* 2:39). And that thinking is defined as the confluence of images, their linguistic signs, and the underlying sentiments of the speaker/thinker. Placed in this light, Kleist suggest, "Die Sprache ist als-dann keine Fessel, etwa wie ein Hemmschuh an dem Rade des Geistes, sondern wie ein zweites, mit ihm parallel fortlaufendes, Rad an seiner Achse" (Language is then not a tether like a brake shoe on the wheel of the mind, but rather is like a second wheel running parallel to the first and revolving around the same axis, *DE,* 2:39). The wheel metaphor has been encountered elsewhere as an interpretation of the common touchstone for thought, sentiment, and action. Playing upon the revolving motion of the wheel, Kleist elaborates upon the nature of thought development during the act of communication in conversation. Above all the thinking and conversational acts are by their very nature incomplete acts. When the wheel of the mind ceases to turn, the brain dies; when the discourse between persons loses its forward motion, it ceases to be true discourse. (Maybe that is why Kleist's essay is itself incomplete?)

The quality of discourse is further influenced by the emotional involve-ment of the interlocutors (*eine gewisse Erregung des Gemüts*) and their recourse to non-linguistic means of communication (*Gebärdenspiel*) to express intuitively arrived at insights for the expression of which they have not yet found the appropriate words (*DE,* 2:39). Thus even as

Schlegel praised *Unverständlichkeit* (unintelligibility) as a positive quality
of life and therefore of literary expression, so does Kleist cite the incomprehensible (*etwas Unverständliches*) as a trait of the easy conversational
discourse he considers exemplary.

Finally, the poet concludes that such interaction can be seen as "the art
of midwifery in intellectual affairs" (*die Hebammekunst der Gedanken,
DE*, 2:40). As such it stands in marked contrast to the academic exam-
inations so familiar to students of any era. In keeping with the image of
the harmonically attuned revolving wheels of mind and expression, this
one-paragraph essayistic interlude concludes with the remark: "continuation to follow" (*DE*, 2:40). Its central idea not yet fully developed, the
reader is expected to complete the author's line of reasoning. Is there any
wonder why Kleist's "Über die allmähliche Verfertigung der Gedanken
beim Reden" is seen as seminal to the theory and practice of essayistic
writing?

Women Writers

In keeping with my intent to draw attention to neglected connections
and authors, it is especially important to include an evaluation of a group
of writers who deserve a great deal more exposure than they have received. By including them in a treatment with canonical writers, the less
known authors might share in the limelight. The more obscure essayists
contemporaneous with Weimar Classicism and German Romanticism
tend to be women. While it is offensive to omit Georg Forster, Karl
Philipp Moritz, Jean Paul, and Hölderlin from this study or to treat Kleist
in cursory fashion, it would be an even greater offense to slight the role
of their contemporary women colleagues if for no other reason than they
have been slighted for so long. The grievousness of this latter omission in
treatments of the age (except for feminist studies) is manifestly apparent
when we consider that the first bibliographies of women writers appeared
concurrent with Weimar Classicism.[25] The attention accorded the
women in those first collections attests to the success they had experienced in their efforts to scale Parnassus.

The anonymous bibliographer's introduction to "Deutschland's Dichterinnen" published in June of 1803 in the pages of the *Teutscher Merkur*
draws specific attention to this success. He (she?) begins by citing a line
from John Owen (1560–1622) which is itself an indirect indictment of
the neglect women writers had traditionally experienced: "Musae sunt
generis mulieribus" (*NTM*, 1803. 3:258). For both the ancients and the
moderns, the mythological sources of poetic inspiration were definitely

female, although women were rarely admitted to the ranks of the poet laureate. More importantly, the bibliographer remarks upon the great strides women writers have made in German literature, especially since the 1770s, both in their numbers and in the quality of their writing, concluding that they can "hold their own" with their counterparts elsewhere.[26] The fact that the anonymous author chooses to compare women to women is perhaps a sign that he is male, a supposition supported by the ensuing comment that the history of women writers in the German language is best written by a "female historian" (*NTM*, 3:259), as if women writers were essentially different from male authors. One does not have to be a feminist to wonder at the curiousness of such a division.

As is my wont in *Crossing Boundaries*, I will also transgress this artificial barrier. The best way to do this is to judge the quality of writing as if it were a blind submission. In reality, this is not such a difficult task since journal editors frequently published the work anonymously and did not consistently indicate the writer's sex. We can not be sure in the case of essayistic writing whether the reader was aware of the fact that s/he was reading an article penned by a women when s/he took journal to hand. And that is as it should be. The following analyses will demonstrate that women writers in the late eighteenth century could "hold their own" not just with "their counterparts" in France or England but with any prose writer in the homeland. Furthermore, I must note that the women were not intent upon writing just for other women or just about women's concerns; they wrote for anyone who was willing to read them. Thus it is inappropriate to speak of a generically different *Frauendichtung*.[27]

Emilia von Berlepsch

Emilia von Berlepsch, married to Friedrich Ludwig von Berlepsch (1749–1818), privy judge, councilor, and publicist in Hannover, is considered here on the strength of her *Merkur*-article, "Ueber einige zum Glück der Ehe nothwendige Eigenschaften und Grundgesätze" ("On Some Character Traits and Principles Indispensable to a Happy Marriage," 1791).[28] Ostensibly advice in the form of a letter to her sister on the occasion of her impending marriage, the journal article is noteworthy for several reasons. To begin with, it is "the first prose essay by a woman in the pages of the *Teutscher Merkur*."[29] Secondly, it takes a bold stance on the question of equal rights for women. And thirdly, it happens to be a fine example of prose writing.

Published in two installments, the article runs to fifty-seven pages. However, there is a break between the first installment of thirty-six pages and the second of twenty-one pages. While part one treats Berlepsch's concept of *Sanfmut* (equinamity) — the virtue essential to marital contentment (she calls it a *Temperamentstugend, NTM*, 2:67) — the second part shifts the focus from the mental state of the marriage partners to the actual running of a houshold. This second function is discussed in terms of *Ordnung* (order). Berlepsch defines *Sanfmut* as "kindness, friendliness, equality of disposition, and tractability"; *Ordnung*, on the other hand, connotes "thrift and prudent industry" (*NTM*, 2:67). In the following, we will be concerned only with the first part of Berlepsch's essay, the one that deals with *Sanfmut*. Not only can it stand alone, it is also the more avant-garde composition since it deals with a radically new image of women as a free and equal partner (*das gleichgeschaffene freye Weib, NTM*, 2:91), which stands in marked contrast to the legal and anthropological views expressed in the same decade in the Prussian legal code, *Allgemeines Landrecht* (*Universal Civil Law*, 1794), and Johann Gottlieb Fichte's *Grundlage des Naturrechts* (*Foundations of Natural Law*, 1796).[30]

Originally composed around 1780, "Ueber einige zum Glück der Ehe nothwendige Eigenschaften" was expanded much later for publication in April of 1791.[31] To be sure, Berlepsch offers advice to women on how to regulate their relationships with men, yet she states at the outset in the manner of an essayist that her views are not "finished" or been resolved into a rigid moral system. Thus she presents her ideas as a stimulus to further reflection (*NTM*, 2:64).

Dawson considers Berlepsch's advice uneven in argument and style. At first glance that conclusion seems supported by the text. Beginning with an apparently conventional argument, Berlepsch slips into a more agressive tone after the *exordium*. Yet the consistency of agressive tone, Dawson feels, is not maintained. In fact, an implicit conflict between "conventional submissiveness and a new unconventional independence for women" is never resolved in the text ("'Weihrauch,'" 1984, 243). Despite this "failing" Dawson considers the document an important milestone in the history of the struggle for women's rights. She places it in the same category as Wollstonecraft's *Vindication of the Rights of Women* (1792) and Theodor Gottlieb von Hippel's *Ueber the bürgerliche Verbesserung der Weiber* (1792) which appeared two years later.[32]

While Dawson is certainly correct to point out the radical side of the argument, I do not agree that the piece is as uneven as she thinks. Placed properly in the tradition of self-determination and freedom from preju-

dice vigorously advocated by the Enlightenment, Berlepsch's essayistic
endeavor can be seen as a logical culmination of the general rethinking of
much older anthropological concepts. Yes, she does go beyond the male
orientation of the legal code and practices, but in doing so she uses the
arguments of the leading male figures of the European Enlightenment
regarding human rights and human nature. Let us first consider the argument.

Berlepsch is less intent upon a radical realignment of the legal rights of
the marriage partners than she is upon advocating the fulfillment of
enlightened moral objectives. Like others of her generation, she saw the
pursuit of happiness as the ultimate purpose of this earthly existence.
Maximum happiness translated for her age into a steady level of contentment in which the valleys and peaks of emotion are mitigated. For
example, she exhorts her sister/reader to bear patiently and magnani-
mously those irritations of married life *which do not affect her true
happiness* (NTM, 2:75). Her ensuing argument turns on an understanding of "true happiness."

The key to contentment is *Sanftmut,* which is a reformulation of the
classic Judeo-Christian virtue of *Gelassenheit* (inner composure, even
temper) advocated by Thomasius and argued so forcefully by Gellert in
Das Leben der schwedischen Gräfin von G* (1747) or by Sophie von La
Roche in *Die Geschichte des Fräuleins von Sternheim* (1771). In fact,
Berlepsch even uses the term *Gelassenheit,* stressing the need for "das
rechte Gleichgewicht in deiner Laune" (the proper balance in your mood,
2:72, 74–75). The tone of those passages echoes the traditional stance of
a Gellert or La Roche. Yet it must be emphasized that Berlepsch's concept
of equanimity is free of the pejorative connotations Dawson or Becker-
Cantarino attribute to "submissiveness," for the Enlightenment saw the
secularized version of *Gelassenheit* positively as the realization of the true
inner self, not as the denial of self in the face of an almighty force.[33]
Berlepsch herself informs us that she rejects all connotations of *Sanftmut*
which have to do with "sentimental affectedness, hypocrisy, and phleg-
matic stupor" (NTM, 2:67) while simultaneously rejecting the (male)
prejudice that would deny a woman her own will and courage to act. She
insists that "Sanftmut" be understood as nurturing cooperation, not as
enfeebling submissiveness. This is an important distinction (not acknowledged by Dawson) because it sets limits to the degree of "submissiveness"
in a woman.

Berlepsch states, for example, that "true well being" (*das wahre Glück*)
has to do with one's individual character. Yet not everyone can be pressed
into the same mold. Thus as a *Temperamentstugend,* equanimity cannot

be realized in every person to the same degree (*NTM*, 2:67f.). Not the dominance of one partner over the other, but a sense of support and respect is the true source of equinamity. As she states in summation: marital bliss cannot be ensured by civil law or tyrannical behavior (*bürgerliche Gesetze, gebieterische Haltung*, *NTM*, 2:99), but rather by nurturing friendship (*NTM*, 2:102). The notions of "ownership" and "egoism" are foreign to true love (*Liebe weiß von Eigenthum und Selbstheit nichts*, *NTM*, 2:92). Balance is the ideal from beginning to end for Berlepsch; balance first within the individual, then within the marriage, and ultimately within society at large.

The expansiveness of her interpretation is inherent in such assertions as: "Seelenherrschaft ist durchaus republikanischer Art, und muß in wilde Anarchie ausarten, sobald sie einen despotischen Anschein gewinnt, und bloß auf das Recht des Stärkeren sich gründen will" (Psychological dominance is positively republican in nature and it degenerates into wild anarchy as soon as it takes on a despotic tone, seeking to be based soley on the right of strength, *NTM*, 2:76; cf. also 2:67, 72–75, 93). Finally, she comments that *Sanftmut* is not genuine equanimity without *Selbständigkeit* (independence, *NTM*, 2:89).

Berlepsch drives her point home through the felicitous use of strong, metaphorical language, punctuated not only by stunning imagery but also by the effective use of various rhetorical strategies. The following passage can stand as a sample of the high quality of her rhythmic and well-rounded prose. The excerpt also succinctly summarizes her theoretical standpoint:

> Doch da sich die Gesetze der Natur nicht umstoßen lassen; da es ewig unmöglich bleibt, den hochstrebenden Adler zur girrenden Taube, das schnaubende Roß zum geduldigen Schaf, den Sturmwind zum Zephyr, und den lauten Donnerschlag zum sanften Flötenton umzuschaffen: so wird auch nicht leicht ein Weib von feurigem Geist, starker Empfindung und lebhafter Phantasie, der sanften Dulderin gleichen, die bey ungegründeten Widerspruch das Köpfchen hängt, und in einem stillen Thränchen nur das Gefühl des erlittenen Unrechts wegschwemmt.[34]

Berlepsch's easy use of a series of striking images drawn from unharnessed nature—the soaring eagle, the impatient steed, the raging wind, and the resounding thunder clap—as similes for the woman of spirit, feeling, and imagination is as good as any writing we have encountered in *Crossing Boundaries*. The effective contrast between the unbridled and the broken of spirit which culminates in the image of dispirited, hanging head with tear in eye can "hold its own" with anything Goethe, Schiller, or Kleist have to offer.

Long before Ibsen has Nora Helmsted come to realize the psychological connection between self-cultivation and service to others, Emilia von Berlepsch calls upon husbands and wives to lay the groundwork of a true marriage. Men are exhorted to support their wives in these efforts, not just for the wives' sakes but also for their own. Instead of dictating and belittling the woman's self-worth, they should help nurture it through "sanfte Pflege und Schonung" (gentle encouragement and forebearance) to a sound basis of genuine intimacy and interdependence (*Anhänglichkeit, NTM,* 2:76f.).

For this development to occur men must be reeducated to value the true qualities of women (*NTM,* 2:77–84). Berlepsch even draws upon the arch-chauvinist himself, Jean-Jacques Rousseau, to bolster her argument. She cites Rousseau's dictum that "no true love [can occur] without enthusiasm." Since according to Rousseau women are characterized by a penchant for enthusiastic love, men can best learn from them how to regulate interpersonal relationships (*NTM,* 2:84f.). Berlepsch asks rhetorically of the woman's response to the man: "Kann sie liebenswürdig seyn, wenn sie nicht liebt? Und kann sie lieben, wenn sie nicht geschäzt und verstanden wird?" (Can she be lovable if she does not love? And is she capable of love, if she is not respected and understood? *NTM,* 2:86). The ideal, as elsewhere in the text, is balance. The needs and expectations of the husband must be balanced against the needs and expectations of the wife. Berlepsch knew that she could not achieve her ultimate end by addressing women alone. If things were to change, women needed the support of the men. Individual effort does not translate into cooperative gain. She was surely aware that the law could not be affected by attack from an outsider; moral reform would provide the most solid basis for legal revision.

Throughout, the style is designed to encourage the reader to consider her point seriously. The balance between agressive and meek tone, conservative and progressive view, is a ploy to engage and retain a larger audience than possible with a purely renegade stance. While "Ueber das Glück der Ehe nothwendige Eigenschaften" addresses a specific female reader and can rightfully be viewed as an example of "women communicating with women" (Dawson's formulation), it would be a mistake to see the piece strictly as *Frauenliteratur.* True, Berlepsch does demand self-awareness and self-determination for women in unambiguous terms;[35] however, she could not afford to alienate her male readers if she wished to achieve her ultimate objective. Without the understanding and support of the husband, the wife could not learn to "stand alone" or become an equal partner in the marriage bond. Those passages which take cognizance of the male reader's presence as well as of women less progressive in their thinking than Emilia von Berlepsch are conciliatory and conservative in tone. Thus, the style and argument of "Ueber einige zum Glück der Ehe nothwendige Eigenschaften" incorporates radical elements into a conservative mold as a means of communicating essential truths in an approachable form. The purpose of her prose (to adapt Schiller's self assessment) was surely designed "to surprise [her audience], to unnerve it, and to stretch [its vision] by the bold articulation of her thinking."[36] But surely she could gain nothing by alienating the men.

Elisa von der Recke

A second representative woman writer of the Classic-Romantic period, Elisa von der Recke, appeared more frequently in the pages of the *Neuer Teutscher Merkur*, submitting both poetry and prose. After the publication in 1787 of her exposé of Cagliostro as a fraud, von der Recke was numbered among the most celebrated women authors of the era. In 1803 the *Neuer Teutscher Merkur* printed her biographical piece on the Dresden composer Johann Gottlieb Naumann (1741–1801).[37] It is a far-ranging composition which first offers the reader a general introduction before focusing specifically on Naumann's character as a human being and artist. Two years later she published a sketch of her Italian journey of 1805, calling it "Blick auf Italien" ("A View of Italy," *NTM*, 1805. 3:39–46). With its seven-and-one-half pages, the article more closely reflects the ideal length of the essay form. Von der Recke's last contribution to the periodical was also a journal sketch occasioned by a trip to the state of Salzburg in 1804: "Ueber die Salzburgischen Tölpel" ("On the Retarded in Salzburg"). Although penned earlier than the Italian sketch, the reflections upon the Schwarzbach region appeared in the March 1807 issue of the *Merkur* (*NTM*, 3:187–200).

The latter two compositions will be examined here since their length approximates the ideal of the essayistic mode more closely than the biographical sketch of Naumann. Moreover, their dates of publication place them at the zenith of the intellectual and literary currents associated with the Classic-Romantic period. They will help us augment the dominant perception of the canonical ideals in literature.

"Blick auf Italien" is a short, vivid commentary consisting of but two sections: an *exordium* of one brief paragraph and the body of the text consisting of one single paragraph as if to connote that everything else follows from the opening statement. Its title, "Blick auf Italien," places it in the tradition of the travel reportage and the German fascination with Italy. However, the introductory sentence opens up a perspective which leads beyond the usual report of travel experience. The reader is immediately alerted to the fact that von der Recke is concerned with deeper questions not with the overt experience itself. She begins with an exquisitely rounded statement that plays upon the reader's normal expectations to gain his/her undivided attention:

> Wer mit einem kränkelnden Körper und dem Wunsche, Italien mit Nutzen zu sehen, diese interessante Reise macht, kann nur selten den Vorsatz ausführen, seinen Freunden von Zeit zu Zeit eine Uebersicht dessen mitzutheilen, was die Aufmerksamkeit beschäftigte, den Geist anzog, das Gemüth aber oft schmerzhaft erschütterte. Denn in diesem Lande der Kontraste, wird die Seele mit Bildern überfüllt, der Körper ermüdet, wenn man nur einigermaaßen die Gegenstände überschauen will, durch welche eine Reise in Italien interessant wird.[38]

She invokes the usual experience of travellers who undertake a journey to refresh body and spirit. The exertion for both is such that the traveller rarely finds the opportunity to report on his/her encounters. This first sentence, therefore, is an appeal to universal experience. However, its concluding phrase ("shattered one's peace of mind") points already to von der Recke's more serious intent. The second sentence of this first paragraph forges into the real field of inquiry without breaking ties with the past experience of the potential reader. Even though the purpose of the trip is to rejuvenate enfeebled physical powers (*kränkelnder Körper*) and to learn something useful, the trip proves exhausting for the perceptive traveller who rarely has the energy to write home about his/her experiences. The endeavor to sort out the myriad impressions gained "in this land of contrasts" is what really makes the trip interesting. The *exordium* is thus a balanced and provocative statement which succeeds in engaging the attentive reader.

Von der Recke's ensuing commentary abides by the principle of contrast alluded to in the opening paragraph, a point to which the second paragraph explicitly draws attention by comparing "Eleganz und Bettelhaftigkeit" (elegance versus beggary), "prächtige Paläste und Fensteröffnungen ohne Fenster" (magnificent palaces vs. window openings without windows, *NTM*, 3:40). Those physical contrasts which suggest the differences between the haves and the have-nots are a mere prelude to the dominant thrust of "Blick auf Italien" to spotlight the crass difference in society's treatment of its marginal citizens. Despite its travelogue introduction, therefore, the contrastive technique readily exposes the seven-page piece as a biting critique of social conditions in Italy. Specifically, von der Recke rails against the governmental and ecclesiastical neglect of a whole group of citizens.

That group is comprised of citizens who—through no fault of their own—have been reduced to beggary. Despite the opulence and fertility of their surroundings, thousands of people suffer want. And there seems to be no public will to improve the situation. She writes:

> überhaupt scheint Italien jetzt mit Bettlern, wie ehemals mit Göttern und Halbgöttern bevölkert zu sein. Wohlbekleidete Männer und Frauen strecken den Vorübergehenden flehende Hände entgegen, und eckelhafte, oft scheußliche Bettler tragen ihre offenen Schaden und Wunden zur Schau, und treiben mit diesen einen empörenden Broterwerb, der bei schwangern Frauen nicht selten Aborte bewirkt. Dies moralische Uebel, und die häufigen Mordthaten erfüllen den Fremden, beim Eintritt in dies übrigens herrliche Land, mit Entsetzen.[39]

The contrast between the mythological beings of Rome's past so favored by the Classical and Romantic authors and the widespread penury among ordinary citizens of modern-day Italy is designed to shock the complacent reader (*Schaden und Wunden zur Schau tragen, Aborte, Entsetzen*). The reference to "well-dressed men and women" pleading for alms underscores the fact that many persons have recently joined the ranks of the traditional beggars: the physically and mentally afflicted.

At a time when Italy's landscape and culture were being idealized by the Weimar Classicists, Elisa von der Recke reflects upon the seedy side of Italian life, appealing to her countrymen's social conscience. The social decline of so many citizens she traces to the misplaced values of the Italian Church and to the inept administation of inadequate laws (*NTM*, 1:40). Land and Church reform are a pressing need. A scathing critique follows: the monasteries and a few wealthy families consume a disproportionate amount of the goods, no provision is made for individual ownership of the land by the common people, no public provision for retirement funds has been made. As a result the common man is able to support himself and his family only as long as his health holds up. Once that fails, beggary and misery is the inevitable lot of his family (*NTM*, 3:40f.).

This general indictment of the moral evils of the system is followed up by specific examples. Using the typical scene of the traveller arriving in the center of Naples or Rome by carriage, she reflects upon the Italian's fiery nature. The slightest of provocations causes daggars to be drawn and blood to flow (*NTM*, 3:42). Yet the murderer, who is responsible for his fall from society and sentence of death, is treated with greater kindness than the unfortunate laborer. The first is clearly deserving of his death sentence, while the latter is merely a victim of fate. By contrasting the compassionate, sympathetic treatment of the criminal in his last hours with the benign neglect of the impoverished laborer, who is allowed to sink ever deeper into misery and degradation, von der Recke draws attention to the misplaced societal values (NTM, 3:44f.). The long days and nights of utter hopelessness and pain of so many thousands are more terrible and barbaric than the criminal's speedy execution. The alms which the rich give the mendicant monks do not alleviate the former's plight (*NTM*, 3:41), while the latter is rewarded by sympathetic attention for having savored the sensory delights of life.

The images, language, and style von der Recke uses to paint these scenes are powerful, graphic, and yet classically balanced. Beginning with the general, she moves to the ever more specific only to return to the general in her conclusion. Throughout she makes use of various rhetorical strategies ranging from contrast and comparison to tropes and synecdoche (marked by the frequent use of the hyphen) to engage and retain the reader's interest. In short, she is very conscious of the writing act as a multivalent communicative act. The conclusion of her sketch, "Blick auf Italien"—which we might label a culturally critical essay—makes effective use of an unexpected exhortation (i.e., *sustentio*) in combination with a summarizing rhetorical question. The combination is so effective because it does not allow for a denouement. She laments: "O Regierung und Gesetzgebung!—Welche Verantwortungen laden sie auf sich, wenn sie dem Verbrechen solchen Vorschub leisten" ("O you entrusted with governing and ruling the country! Think of the responsibility you incur by abetting criminal behavior in this way," 3:46). Just as von der Recke had returned from her Italian journey not refreshed but highly stimulated, the reader is supposed to gain a sense of her agitation and concern for the plight of the suffering masses. Into the context of the idealizing tendencies of Weimar Classicism, von der Recke injects a highly charged, socially critical note.

Von der Recke's essay of 1807 is similary concerned with social issues. Yet it too is a poetical gem. Divided into two parts which are apparently only loosely connected, "Ueber die Salzburgischen Tölpel" is nevertheless a unified whole. In the first section von der Recke portrays the unusual natural beauty of the awe-inspiring Schwarzbach, while she focuses in the second on the aberrations of human nature evident in the inhabitants of the Schwarzbach region. It is possible, therefore, to view the contrasting perspectives as complements of a whole; only in combination is the deeper significance of the composition manifest. That is probably the reason why the author printed these two excerpts from her diary of the Salzburg journey together.

At less than six pages the article has the length of an ideal essay. More importantly, its intellectual thrust and poetic style mark it as essayistic. As in the previously discussed contribution, Elisa von der Recke begins with a general observation which lays the groundwork for the body of her commentary. She phrases it in the form of two rhetorical questions:

> Warum machen den tiefsten Eindruck auf unsrer Gefühl diejeni- gen Gegenden, wo aus den sichtbaren Spuren eines großen Um- sturzes neues jüngeres Leben voll Anmuth und reizender Schönheit aufstand? Ist es nicht der Geist der ewig schaffenden und leitenden Huld, der dem Gemüthe begegnet, und ihm selige Ahnungen von der Dauer alles geistigen Lebens zuweht?[40]

Drawing upon the language of Classical Weimar, von der Recke reflects in the first question upon the Schwarzbach with its graceful and powerful beauty. Its impressive cascades and raging torrents sparkling in the sunlight against the dark backdrop of the deep forest make a lasting impression upon her (*NTM*, 3:191). The second question suggests an explanation of those contrasts on a higher, spiritual plane; she sees in nature evidence of "the presence of eternally creating and directing Providence" which lends permanence and meaning to the fleeting moment. Such thoughts guide her ensuing observations of the Swarzbach valley and its inhabitants.

Even as she begins the first section of her meditations with a query, so does she also conclude it on a reflective note: "Why are we fascinated more by the [narrow], raging, wildly twisting Schwarzbach in its gloomy setting than by the tranquil, bright [expansiveness] of the valley?" (*NTM*, 3:192). The answer, of course, is inherent in the opening passage: we are fascinated more by the sight of the raging stream with its wild twists and turns in its dark environment than with the sun-drenched calm of the broad valley because the "rage," "wildness," and "gloom" betray deep lying forces of movement in nature through which change occurs. They stand symbolically for the powers of change imbedded deep inside human nature. Humankind tends toward the sun-drenched calm of the open areas where those "primeval" forces can be channeled into beneficial movement (creation), yet it feels its energizing source to reside in the dark interior. Von der Recke implies this interpretation with her comment at the midpoint of this first part: "Die umher ruhende Waldeinsamkeit dieser Gegend, im Kontraste mit dem lebendig eilenden Wassergetöse laden zum Denken ein, und erinnern an das kreuzende Treiben und Wirken der Welt" (The surrounding sylvan solitude of this region contrasted to the animated, loud turmoil of the water invite reflection, reminding us of the cacophonous hustle and bustle of society, *NTM*, 3:190). The cascading forest stream with its ability to enthrall and intimidate simultaneously (see the description on 191) serves as a symbol of the essence of nature itself.

Part II of these meditations elaborates upon the darker side of natural phenomena. It muses upon the high incidence of poverty and Down's syndrome (*Eretismus*; first mentioned in Part I) among the people who live in the "shadow" of the Schwarzbach. Von der Recke suggests that the arrested human development is caused by the extreme poverty of the area which was created by the expulsion of industrious Protestants by the Catholic Church. Increased poverty led, in turn, to poorer nutrition among the remaining populace (*NTM*, 3:192f., 198f.). She sees the solution to the problem in land reform. By letting out the land for cultivation to the people, the basis for increased health and wealth would be created. The inhabitants would move out of the unhealthy dark recesses of the Schwarzbach into the bright, broad, and fertile valley where they could work the land, developing a sense of self-worth and industry. That is the only way, von der Recke argues, to ensure long-term improvement from generation to generation thus eventually eradicating mongolism (*NTM*, 3:199). The cost of such land reform to the government and the Church would be slight, but the gains for society enormous. Again in very effective fashion, von der Recke concludes her exposé, this time by exhorting the reader to consider the long-term benefits of social reform for the well-being of all humans: "und was gewönne das Ganze! was gewönne die Menschheit!" (What gain for society! What gain for humankind, *NTM*, 3:200).

The two essayistic compositions by von der Recke examined here reveal the progressive nature of her thinking and her accomplished use of language. She expands her personal perspective of experience into the political and social arena. Like Emilia von Berlepsch she uses her pen to advocate change by animating the reader to critical thought. While the writings of Berlepsch and von der Recke are not especially marked by a dynamic sense of the *process* of thinking or experimentation—qualities which have often been cited as distinguishing traits of the essay—they are far from being static. They are, in fact, prime examples of consciousness raising in Iser's or Brodkey's meaning; they are unsettling both in regards to the ideas advanced as well as to the style employed. That style offers a fully rounded rendition of the essence of the phenomenon described (a good wife, the Schwarzbach, the Italian character). In Rasmussen's sense it engages the reader on both an epistemological as well as rhetorical level.[41]

Finally, their compositions bear comparison with those of their male counterparts around 1800. The concerns expressed, the images created, the strategies utilized all have a human rather than a limited gender identification. Berlepsch and von der Recke "did not wish in the least to have their literary activity understood in isolation as a product of their feminine nature."[42] They were obviously as accomplished as prose writers as any of the other authors considered in *Crossing Boundaries*.

The foregoing analyses of texts by two of the many women writers of the late eighteenth and early nineteen centuries represent only the proverbial tip of the iceberg. The obvious gaps in my presentation should be interpreted as a sign that much more work needs to be done. In the spirit of the essayistic writing under investigation in these pages, I wish primarily to "encircle" my topic, to communicate a sense of just having begun the search rather than of having given the final word.

The Romantic Connection

Friedrich Schlegel

Ludwig Rohner considers Friedrich Schlegel (1772–1829) the first German essayist to reflect consciously upon the nature of the essay and of essayism. Schlegel strikes him further as being the first classical essayist in Germany. Rohner defines classical in terms of the quality of a genre and not of a period in literary history.[43] For that reason Schlegel's "Über die Unverständlichkeit" ("On Unintelligibility," 1800) is located in his anthology at the beginning of the volume entitled: "Klassiker des deutschen Essays I" (= Vol. 2). Moreover, Rohner includes Heinrich von Kleist's "Über die allmähliche Verfertigung der Gedanken beim Reden" ("On the Gradual Formation of Thoughts in the Speech Act," 1805/06) and Adam Müller's "Vom Gespräch" ("On Conversation," 1816) because each leads directly to the heart of essayistic writing and thinking (*DE*, 2:7). They could easily be interpreted as elaborations of Schlegel's piece.

These three "classical" essayists from the Romantic period are included at various points in this chapter to demonstrate the continuity of writing and thinking styles from previous epochs. The touchstones of comparison are the same ones cited by Rohner in explaining his selection of classic essays: topic, tone, energetic tropes, and an indeterminancy (*Unwäg-bares*) (*DE*, 2:7). Yet the elegant and virtuoso pieces of these later writers should not blind us to the successes of the eighteenth century. Rohner's statement that fundamental changes in the incidence of essayistic writing occurred in the mid-nineteenth century stands in need of revision. Those changes are already manifest in the mid-eighteenth century.

Schlegel wrote "Über die Unverständlichkeit" in response to the complaints of unintelligibility levelled at his journal, *Athenaeum* (1797–98). The article is, therefore, a defense of the method of his fragments which was to suggest that thoughts are always preliminary, interpretations never finished, and indeterminancy a fundamental aspect of the chaos which envelops us. Truth is paradox, knowledge exegesis, language symbolic signs requiring interpretation, and irony the medium of true understanding. The latter he describes as "consisting in and exciting a feeling for the never-ending conflict between the infinite and the finite, the impossibility and necessity of complete communication."[44] The definition — and the subsequent manner of writing — clearly locate "Über die Unverständlichkeit" in Just's sixth category: the ironic essay.

Without acknowledging his precursors or the source of his notions in Kant and Schiller whose terminology occasionally surfaces here, Schlegel acts as if his approach were novel. He sees it in any event as the wave of the future (*DE*, 2:19f.). Yet like others before him he complains that readers have not learned the true art of reading, that is, discerningly, critically (*DE*, 2:13, 15, 19). He considers the coming age to be tendentious (*das Zeitalter der Tendenzen, DE*, 2:15) in contrast to the current epoch of criticism (which criticizes everthing except itself!). We have seen an awareness on the part of earlier writers such as Lessing, Wieland, and Herder that all dogmatic statements are specious, that truth is pluralistic, and that some truths are even best left unstated. Each of these writers regarded his opinions and works as preliminary sorties, as contributions to a whole. Schlegel takes this skeptical attitude and transforms it into the dominant trait of the intellectual world he envisions.

Although he is not completely accurate in presenting his view of the *necessity* of *Unverständlichkeit* as original, Schlegel does introduce a new note by raising it to the level of a decisive principle. Furthermore, Schlegel writes in a casual, dialogic manner in order to engage the reader in a dialogue by means of which he hopes to "reconstruct" the reader: "Daher hatte ich schon vor langer Zeit den Entschluß gefaßt, mich mit dem Leser in ein Gespräch über diese Materie zu versetzen, und vor seinen eignen Augen, gleichsam ihm ins Gesicht, einen andern neuen Leser nach meinem Sinne zu construiren, ja wenn ich es nöthig finden sollte, denselben sogar zu deduciren."[45] This intention places the Romantic in the tradition of Thomasius and his disciples. And finally, when Schlegel laments the parting of ways between reasonableness and unreasonableness and descries the reduction of science to a spiritless method of rote addition and combination while satirizing traditional intellectuals as shallow and banal (*Die große Scheidung des Verstandes und des Unverstandes wird immer allgemeiner*, DE, 2:20), he reiterates the views of a slew of Enlightenment writers.

In sum, the three major avant-garde tendencies, first published in the *Athenaeum* and cited again in "Über die Unverständlichkeit" are all rooted in the intellectual and literary life of the Age of Reason: the French Revolution, Fichte's *Wissenschaftslehre*, and Goethe's *Wilhelm Meister* (DE, 2:14). Three other maxims from the *Athenaeum* repeated here also point to this "modern" principle of indeterminancy. The first two treat the concept of irony as the "freest of all licenses," poetic or otherwise and culminate in the statement: "Ironie ist die Form des Paradoxen. Paradox ist alles was zugleich gut und groß ist" (Irony is the expression of paradox. Paradox is everything which is good and great, DE, 2:17). Since he later asks rhetorically what is so objectionable about indeterminancy (DE, 2:19), the statement about irony can be seen as representative of a pervasive stance which partakes not only of skepticism but also of syncrasy.

The third fragment from the *Athenaeum* has to do with the quality of classical writing and its effect upon the astute reader: "Eine classische Schrift muß nie ganz verstanden werden können. Aber die welche gebildet sind und sich bilden, müssen immer mehr draus lernen wollen" (A classical work does not even have to be fully grasped. But the educated reader, the one interested in improving him/herself, must desire to learn ever more from it, DE, 2:20). In each case Schlegel writes with a specific kind of reader in mind. In other words, his text is thoroughly informed by audience awareness, a mark of the new, original prose dating from Thomasius. Irony is undoubtedly a major vehicle of communication with that target audience of educated readers willing to exert a little effort in following the author's line of thought. The epithet critical will then be deserved when "mankind rises up *en masse* and learns [really] to read" (DE, 2:13).

While it is true that this essay "defines its object in phenomenological manner," Rohner goes too far in arguing that it is just one large ironic justification of his method.[46] True, the composition is exemplary as ironic writing. Yet not everything Schlegel writes here is meant tongue-in-cheek. Otherwise his vision of a reader capable of understanding his manner of thinking would be deprived of its intended ernestness. We must be careful to understand Schlegel's meaning when he speaks of irony (either to claim or disclaim irony). What he means is closer to Goethe's sense of uninhibited, conscious reflection upon the interconnections of reality.[47] Schlegel takes the concept a step further.

By ironic he signifies thinking that is essentially antidogmatic, antisystematic, and opposed to all attempts to codify it into rigid classifications. Thus, his ironic identification of seven ironic modes exemplifies his disdain of all surface attempts as "para-objectivity." The highest form of irony is the "irony of irony" which is stylistically stressed by the succession of subordinate *wenn*-clauses culminating in the asseveration that the irony of irony arises when the strategy defies all attempts to regulate it (*DE*, 2:17–18).

Objectivity dependent upon some fixed system is not objectivity at all for Schlegel. Rather the nervous energy reflected in the organically contrastive and pluralistic interplay of ideas, structures, texts, authors, readers, and self is the real test of truth. Our existence requires constant redefinition in order to approximate its essence. As in the living organism so too the Romantic world is all preliminary movement on a projectile toward a higher state. Writing and thinking and reading inspired by this kind of muse does not flutter; it soars. And by its velocity and frequent changes of direction it runs the risk of indeterminancy if not of unintelligibility. A writer who composes in this mode engages the willing reader in a dangerous game. Through the play with words, concepts, and systems the reader is forced to reassess and perhaps alter established patterns. Not every reader is capable of playing the game well. The demands Schlegel places on his reader are thus similar to those cited by Harold Brodkey, Stanley Fish, or Wolfgang Iser.

What Schlegel writes about the effect of Georg Forster's essayistic prose can be said about his own "Über die Unverständlichkeit." Forster's writing stimulates reflection by refining our sensitivity and broadening our perspectives. One feels transported to the crest of a hill with an unrestricted view of the surrounding valleys and verdant fields. Every sentence, every thought seems to draw the reader forward.[48] These tendencies were in germination for over a century.

Adam Müller

Adam Müller (1779–1829), a chief representative of the political side of German Romanticism, is a fitting conclusion to our current deliberations on the Classic-Romantic era. Fitting, because the essays by Berlepsch and von der Recke introduced a "political" element into the discussion which was also important for Müller. Fitting too, because his lecture "Vom Gespräch," first published in 1816 but delivered in 1812 as the first of "Twelve Lectures on Rhetoric and its Decline in Germany," is a focused commentary on the integral nexus of ideas first raised in Leibniz's "Ermahnung an die Teutschen, ihren Verstand und Sprache besser zu üben" (1683). Specifically, Müller makes reference to Lessing and Friedrich Schlegel as models of the art of discourse, thereby confirming at least the temporal parameters (1770–1815) of this current chapter. Morcover, Müller's lecture was composed at a turning point from one cultural and political era to another, as was Leibniz's composition.[49]

Loosely divided into three parts, the composition first discusses the nature of true conversation (*DE*, 2:97–100), then locates its origins in the cultured societies of France and England (*DE*, 2:100–105), and finally shifts the focus slightly to a distinction between oratory and art while putting out the call to improve the German situation (*DE*, 2:105–09). However, these subsections are not all that clear. Müller anticipates later parts of his argument, refers back to previous points, and generally acts as if his written discourse were in fact an oral one. During interlocution the participants do not abide by distinctly marked subdivisions.

The argument Müller unravels in "Vom Gespräch" would not have been possible without the momentous changes in the tenor of literary and intellectual life recorded in *Crossing Boundaries*. The evolution of the private and public spheres of intellectual discourse, the radical shift in reading habits and publication practices, the informing of literature by classical rhetoric, and the evolution of a new ideal of aesthetic taste, agreeable writing, and proper social graces are all prerequisite for Müller's point of view. In brief, his approach corresponds nicely to a view of interlocution key to the theory and practice of essayistic writing presented in these pages.

Müller's actual topic is the necessity for reciprocal trust between interlocutors. Without mutual respect genuine communication cannot occur. Furthermore, Müller opines in a manner strongly prefiguring Jürgen Habermas's theory of communicative action that the possibility of communication is enhanced when the two speakers are of differing opinion, but continue to share a common desire for true understanding. In this way a field of dialectical synergy is established which propels both disputants forward in their search for common understanding. Müller writes:

> Zu einem wahren Gespräch gehören gewisse Erfordernisse, die
> sich, zumal in unsrer Zeit, seltner beisammen finden, als man
> denken sollte. Zuvörderst zwei durchaus verschiedene Sprecher,
> die einander geheimnisvoll und unergründlich sind; dann zwi-
> schen beiden eine gewisse gemeinschaftliche Luft, ein gewisser
> Glaube, ein Vertrauen, ein gemeinschaftlicher Boden der Wahr-
> heit und der Gerechtigkeit. Beide Forderungen sollte der
> Mensch eigentlich erfüllen, inwiefern er Mensch ist.[50]

While the intial portion of the quotation contains a foreshadowing of the
requirements of genuine, forward-moving discourse cited by Jürgen Habermas in his *Theorie des kommunikativen Handelns* and incorporated
into our understanding of the essential attitudes of author and reader in
the essayistic stance, the concluding segment makes reference to the *humanitas* belief of the eighteenth century which is predicated on the belief
that all humans share a common bond of "sympathetic feeling." The
passage underscores, then, the proximity of Müller's thinking to the
essayistic mode as well as his intellectual indebtedness to Enlightenment
anthropology. We will recall, for instance, that Thomasius's *Monats-
Gespräche* were premised on the equality and good will of diverse conversation partners. By the same token, the dialogic writing of Klopstock,
Lessing, Wieland, and others was premised on the belief that "sympathetic" souls would respond to their works like a friend or fellow cosmopolite. The prospect of such a reaction was obviously critical for the
success of Emilia von Berlepsch's defense of women's rights.

Moreover, the views on the necessity for a common cultured language
and refined social intercourse modeled on the positive traits of the *galant-
homme* ideal as promulgated by Thomasius are reiterated in Müller's
insistence upon the need for *bon goût*. He praises the natural light touch
and sense of good taste which marked French discourse in its heyday. At
its best it is like the "pulse beat of the nation" (*DE*, 2:102). By contrast
the German nation seems cacophonous because of its linguistic and cultural diversity, so the tones emanating from the German lands are like the
unorchestrated "song of birds in the forest" (*DE*, 2:103). If Müller's
assessment is accurate, it would appear as if the Germans had made no
progress since the late seventeenth century and that Thomasius's, Leibniz's, and Gottsched's reforms had been to no avail. Hopefully, the foregoing textual explications have demonstrated that those efforts were, in
fact, not in vain. In any event, we can see "Vom Gespräch" as a seminal
and summary work within our context.

The tone and the topic are established at the outset of this oration. Müller refers in his opening sentence to his esteemed audience, opining that they will surely agree with the statement that social dialogue is the foremost source of entertainment. (That was in the days before radio and television!). The refined conversationalist is like a gambler, the conversation itself a game with marked elements of chance and mystery (*DE*, 2:97). A series of varied sentiments (*Hoffnungen, Besorgnissen, Täuschungen, Erfüllungen*), it is an exercise involving the total personality of the "players" who experience a sense of superiority because they are somewhat in control of the chance element (*DE*, 2:98). The purpose of the game, however, is not to win or to outwit the other. Instead all players seek a higher goal, one external to themselves individually. That goal might be the recognition of truth or the advocation of fairness. In any event, Müller repeats his conviction that the interlocutors must interact on the basis of mutual trust and harmony: "eine Luft des Vertrauens muß sie beide umfangen, ein Boden der Gesinnung muß sie beide tragen; mindestens muß ein gemeinschaftliches Gesetz des Anstandes und Wohllautes zwischen ihnen obwalten" (They must be surrounded by an air of trust, they must stand on a foundation of mutual conviction; at the very least their exchanges must be regulated by a common sense of decorum and harmony, *DE*, 2:100).

Müller's ideal discourse would seem to combine the distinctive qualities of the three essential dialogic modes identified by Hans-Gerhard Winter in his study of the uses of dialogue in eighteenth-century Germany. Winter associates these modes with the dialogic styles of Wieland, Lessing, and Herder respectively: "the polyperspective, skeptical conversation; the insistently analytical dialogue; and the rhapsodic, associative discourse."[51] We have examples of these variations in Wieland's *Göttergespräche*, Lessing's "Ernst und Falk," and Herder's "Shakespeare." Müller would apparently recommend their individual qualities equally.

The models for these kinds of discourse are provided by France and England. While the brand of British discourse was nurtured by the peculiar conditions of that nation's constitutional government and liberal publishing practices (i.e., the public sphere), the French conversational tone was determined by the literary salon or private sphere. The German situation is dissimilar to either model country. It lacked the coffee houses peopled by parliamentary debaters, on the one hand, and did not possess an extensive network of cultured salons on the other. Instead scholars communicated among themselves in stilted prose. There was a lack of "transcendental" discourse which moved beyond the confines of the erudite halls of academia and of an arcane medium. "Also," Müller concludes, "eine Sprache, die mehr gelesen und entziffert wird als gesprochen, in der viel mehr gelehrt wird als gelernt und gehört" ([It is] a language which is more read and decoded than spoken; a language in which more is taught and learned than heard, *DE*, 2:107).

Rhetoric would be helpful in altering the academic tone of discourse, Müller avers, but the would-be teachers of rhetoric have failed to emphasize those aspects of the art which favor the communicative quality of the discourse he envisions. The genuine orator, he continues, does consciously via such strategies as *contradictio, confirmatio, divisio, confutatio, a exemplo*, etc. what occurs naturally and automatically in a living, pluralistic dialogue (*DE*, 2:105f.). Müller first specifies the characteristic differences between the two discussants and their views, then he demonstrates the common interests of both parties. In a sense, the orator combines in his person three distinct functions. The first two are to reveal the thoughts and feelings of each interlocutor, the third is a superior, sovereign stance not identifiable with the position of either discussant. This third function is the means by which "transcendental" dialogue comes about. Müller laments the absence of any mention in the literature on rhetoric of this third, distinguishing feature of the "genuine" orator (2:106). That sovereign, detached yet affable attitude is the necessary element of true communication. He seals his argument with a quotation from Goethe's *Tasso*, where the Princess replies to Eleonore: "Ich höre gern dem Streit der Klugen zu, / Wenn um die Kräfte, die des Menschen Brust / so freundlich und so fürchterlich bewegen, / Mit Grazie die Rednerlippe spielt" (*DE*, 2:106; *Tasso*, I,i).[52]

This appeal to authority is followed up by examples drawn from the common experience of the audience (the different uses of oratory in the common search for philosophic or religious truth as opposed to the prejudiced view of the lawyer's defense of his client) and then by two examples from history (Macchiavelli, Tacitus) for the use of oratorical skills to defend eternal truths and values (*DE*, 2:106f.).

An appeal to his audience to consider objectively the German situation one last time helps to enhance the contrast between the genuine article and its inferior substitute. Through a series of rhetorical questions he suggests that the time is ripe "to examine the reasons [why rhetoric] is the highest possible form of communication among human beings and to investigate the grounds of that intercourse via written and oral speech in which all questions of war, work, and pleasure are resolved" (*DE*, 2:108). The rhetorical query is topped off by a subsequent wish that the Germans will leave off writing in a pedantic manner and begin instead to engage in discourse as outlined. They must learn to read selectively, not in the widespread indiscriminate manner which has evolved in the wake of the writing and reading revolution but in a manner commensurate with abiding questions. The insertion of the proverb—"was echtes Gold ist, wird bestehen" (genuine gold does not fade)—asserts the preeminence of discourse by practiced interlocutors. A concluding reference to Lessing and Friedrich Schlegel attests to the practicality of the dialogic model of communication. We need now only expand the ranks of the "practiced" readers.

Müller's piece is equally marked by poetic qualities. They are, however, closely linked to rhetorical strategies as in the case of Leibniz's "Ermahnung an die Teutschen." In addition to such deceits already cited as "Pulsschlag der Nation" (pulse beat of the nation) and "Gesang der Vögel im Walde" (song of the birds in the wild), we also find graphic images like: "die großen Räder der europäischen Gesellschaft" (the great wheels of European society) and "wie ein geschmeidiges öl" (like supple oil) as expressions for the smooth operation of society (*DE*, 2:104). Especially successful is the extended metaphor of the flight of the libellula to describe the lauded lightness of French discourse which Müller defends against Goethe's criticism of vacuousness:

> Jener Charakter einer gewissen Nullität, den ihr Goethe
> zuschreibt, jenes libellenartige, farbenspielende Flattern an der
> Oberfläche des Lebens, mit gelegentlichem leichtem Eintauchen
> und Benetzen der Flügel, jene Scheu vor dem Ergründen, und
> vor allem Großen, Überlegenen und Herrschenden,—gilt nur
> von der gegenwärtigen weichlichen, kränklichen Reizbarkeit der
> Gesellschaft.[53]

Goethe's criticism is a faint echo of his assessment of the vacuous state of German literature before 1750, while the distinction between the current and past states of society reminds us of Schneiders's exhortation to separate "false" Enlightenment from its "true" nature. The conclusion of the quoted sentence underscores the point, for Müller states that "the era of Louis XIV is not affected by the criticism." The image of the fluttering dragonfly in the early morning hours exudes a sensation of freshness and naturalness not unlike the effect of Georg Forster's essayism on Friedrich Schlegel. Is it related to Lessing's uncatchable butterfly?

In sum, Müller's "Vom Gespräch" formulates ideas encountered repeatedly in *Crossing Boundaries* and which form the backbone of the Romantic theory of genuine communication as exemplified in Schlegel's "Über die Unverständlichkeit," Kleist's "Von der allmählichen Verfertigung der Gedanken beim Reden," as well as in Müller's own piece. Their perception of discourse evolves from the development of an innovative kind of prose which attained classical proportions by the last third of the eighteenth century and was as common among belletristic writers (men and women) as among philosophers. This prose style has been examined in terms of the concommitant functions of reading (decoding) and writing (encoding) in the process of self-enlightenment.

The views expressed by Schlegel, Kleist, and Müller have a parallel in the Enlightenment allignment of rhetoric and literature in the process of effective communication. Müller, like his contemporaries, expresses those ideas in simultaneously poetic and rhetorical fashion. It is a combination characteristic of essayistic writing in general. As a hybrid of the objective and the subjective, science and poetry, the search for universals and the expression of the self, the essayistic stance is informed by motion. It is never at rest and can always only approximate its ultimate goal in digressive, often playful manner. Essayism thrives on the energy generated by the quest for meaning and is charged by the opposing poles of existence: the self and the other, the subject and the object, the conventional and the avant-garde. When the searcher grows tired of experimenting, the tension of existence eases, and the essayistic stance becomes superfluous. Both the pioneering Enlightener (e.g., Leibniz) and the consummating Romantic (cf. Goethe's *Epimator*) shared these opinions on the discursive nature of valid communication via the printed word. At least in this respect Enlightenment, Classicism, and Romanticism are not diametrically opposed. Other lines of connection would become readily discernible, if we take the syncretic view.

Notes

1. Helmut Rehder, "Reason and Romanticism: On the Beginnings of the German Essay," *Lessing Yearbook* 1 (1969), 162f.
2. Joachim Wohlleben, *Goethe als Journalist und Essayist* (Frankfurt a. M. and Bern: Lang, 1981); first published in *Jahrbuch für internationale Germanistik* 7–10 (1975–78).
3. Wohlleben (1981) devotes a mere page to *Zum Shakespeares-Tag* and does not seem interested in determining its essayistic qualities (62).
4. Hans Joachim Schrimpf, "Anmerkungen—Schriften zur Literatur," in Johann Wolfgang von Goethe, *Werke*, Hamburger Ausgabe in 14 Vols., ed. Eric Trunz (Munich: Beck, 1981), 12:691. Hereafter this edition is cited as HA.
5. Cf. Wohlleben (1981), 159.
6. If the book is to be enjoyable and useful, it must either be actually present or be rendered in lively fashion. "Actually the writer should speak to his audience and make the phenomena come alive like a text, partially by allowing them to present themselves as they appear naturally and partially

by intentionally structuring them according to certain principles made possible by his specific purposes and intents. Only then will a lively presentation not lack explication, clarification, and interpretation" (Goethe, "Farbenlehre," HA, 13:321).

7. Detlef Rasmussen, "Georg Forsters Stil als gegenständliches Denken und Beschreibung der Dinge," *Goethe und Forster. Studien zum gegenständlichen Dichten* (Bonn: Bouvier, 1985), 30–34, discusses Goethe's concept of *Stil* as compared to *einfacher Nachahmung* and *Manier. Stil* represents the highest level of aesthetic production. While "simple imitation" seems static and "mannerism" appears rhetorical (informed by the *Geist des Sprechenden*), only "style" achieves a fully rounded rendition of the essence of the described phenomenon. The gradations are pertinent to the artistic value of essayism. The highest category (*Stil*) combines the characteristically rhetorical and epistemological qualities of the essayistic mode.

8. "We are not helped by merely looking at a thing. Every sense perception leads to reflection, every act of reflecting leads to speculation, every instance of speculation turns into a combining. Thus we can state that we theorize with every attentive gaze into the world. However, to do this freely with consciousness, with self-awareness, and to adopt a bold term—with irony— [is another matter]. Such agility is necessary, if the feared abstraction is to be kept harmless and the hoped-for practical results are to be lively and useful" (Goethe, "Farbenlehre," HA, 13:317). On the role of irony in classical rhetorical traditions, see Ueding and Steinbrink, *Grundriß*, 275f.

9. "Now Shakespeare clearly speaks to our inner sense. In this fashion the metaphorical realm of the imagination is activated which in turn leads to total animation for which we find no explanation" (Goethe, "Shakespeare," HA, 12:288).

10. Wohlleben, "Goethe" (1981), 159: "Letzteres [das Wollen] wird als Signum der Moderne mit abschätzigem Fatalismus beschrieben."

11. "[Shakespeare's] plots are not plots in the normal sense of the word. His plays revolve around a hidden point, as yet unseen and undefined by any philosopher, in which our individual identity, our presumed freedom of determination, clashes with the necessary movement of the whole" (Goethe, HA, 12:226).

12. Friedrich Schiller, *Werke in drei Bänden,* ed. Herbert G. Göpfert (Munich: Hanser, 1966), here 1:701: "Reason has its epochs, its fateful developments just like the heart. However, its history is studied much less. It would seem that people are satisfied to follow the passions in their extreme forms with their aberrations and consequences without considering how exactly they correspond to the belief system of the individual." Hereafter this edition is cited as Hanser.

13. Cf. Helmut Koopmann, *Schiller. Kommentar zu den philosophischen, historischen und vermischten Schriften* (Munich: Winkler, 1969), 2:51.

14. Cf. the similar argument in "Über Anmut und Würde," Hanser, 2:420.

15. "There are four elements from which all beings draw sustenance: the *self, nature, god,* and the *future.* All four are intermingled in countless ways, all

are reproduced in diverse fashion. But there is only *one* truth which is found in common in all religions and all systems [of thought] like an irrepressible axis: 'Grow more like the intuited Divine Being' " (Schiller, "Theosophie," Hanser, 1:718; Schiller's emphasis).

16. "From the great mass of occurrences the historian of the universal fore-grounds those events that have had a fundamental, undeniable, and easily traceable influence on the *present* shape of the world and the condition of its current, living generations" (Schiller, "Universalgeschichte," Hanser, 2:18).

17. Gary Saul Morson, *The Boundaries of Genre* (Austin: University of Texas Press, 1981), 49. See the discussion of these concepts in Chapter II of this study.

18. *Dichter über ihre Dichtungen. Friedrich Schiller*, ed. Bodo Lecke (Munich: Heimeran, 1969), 1:538f.: "so habe ich mich wenigstens auf dem einzigen Wege darum beworben, der meiner Individualität entspricht—nicht das Publikum durch Anschmiegung an seine VorstellungsArt zu gewinnen, sondern es durch die kühne Aufstellung der Meinigen zu überraschen, zu erschüttern, und anzuspannen."

19. Schiller, "Über die notwendigen Grenzen beim Gebrauch schöner Formen," Hanser, 2:521–539. The terminology (*Gesetz der Notwendigkeit, Gesetz der Freiheit, wissenschaftlich, populär, schön, mechanisch, organisch, re-produktiv, and produktiv*) is lifted from this treatise (Hanser, 2:522–526).

20. See my study of Schiller's changing attitude toward the reading public, "Die republikanische Freiheit des Lesers. Zum Lesepublikum von Schillers *Der Verbrecher aus verlorener Ehre*," *Wirkendes Wort* 1 (1979), 28–43. More-over, Quintilian's appeal for a graphic style (*Affektensprache*) was widely noted in the eighteenth century. See, e.g., Johann Jakob Breitinger, *Critische Dichtkunst*, facsimile, ed. Wolfgang Bender (Stuttgart: Metzler, 1966), 1:334–337; also Ueding and Steinbrink, *Grundriß*, 258–63.

21. Barbara Becker-Cantarino, *Der lange Weg zur Mündigkeit. Frau und Lit-eratur (1500–1800)* (Stuttgart: Metzler, 1987), discusses La Roche in some depth as writer and novelist but not specifically as essayist (see especially 278–301).

22. Jean Paul, *Werke*, 12 Vols., ed. Norbert Miller (Munich: Hanser, 1975), 9:55–67, 124–144, 148–54.

23. Kleist's essay is cited according to *Deutsche Essays. Prosa aus zwei Jahr-hunderten*, 6 Vols., ed. Ludwig Rohner (Munich: dtv, 1972), 2:35–41, here 2:36.

24. "I intermingle inarticulate tones, make expansive use of conjunctions, em-ploy an occasional apposition where not necessary, and utilize other strat-egies in an effort to prolong the conversation and to gain the necessary time for fabricating my ideas in the workshop of reason" (Kleist, *DE*, 2:36).

25. For example, there is the "Verzeichniß einiger jetztlebenden Deutschen Schriftstellerinnen und ihrer Schriften" in the *Journal von und für Deutsch-land* (1788. 1:138–142, 2:109–110; 1789. 1:303, 2:466–467; 1790. 1:315–316, 378–382, 2:229–232, 554; 1791. 1:231–232, 2:973–976) and the miniature sketches entitled "Deutschland's Dichterinnen" in *Der Neue*

Teutsche Merkur (1803. 3:258–274). This latter source lists those women writers who had died by the end of the century. If nothing else, these two bibliographies published in two of the major journals of the age attest to the general awareness of the role women had begun to play as writers.

26. "allein seit die vaterländische Poesie die Namen einer *La Roche, Emilie, Elise, Caroline Rudolphi, v. Wohlzogen, v. Imhof, Mereau, Unger, Brun, Pichler, Gabriele, Vieth* [sic], u.s.f. feiert, können sich unsere *Dichterinnen,* sowohl ihrer Zahl als Vortrefflichkeit nach, mit denen aller auswärtigen Nationen vollkommen messen." *NTM* (1803) 3:259.

27. Cf. Barbara Becker-Cantarino's statement about Caroline Pichler: "Dabei darf jedoch nicht übersehen werden, daß diese Frauen ihre literarische Tätigkeit keineswegs isoliert als Produkte ihrer Weiblichkeit verstanden wissen wollten. Caroline Pichler schrieb nicht in erste Linie als Frau für andere Frauen, sondern sie schrieb in geistig reger Anteilnahme an ihrer Zeit als *gebildeter Mensch* für jeden, der sie lesen wollte, Männer wie Frauen." "Caroline Pichler und die 'Frauendichtung'," *Modern Austrian Literature, 12/3-4 (1979)*, 1-23, here 3.

28. *Der Neue Teutsche Merkur* (1791), 2:63–102, 113–134. Berlepsch signed the article simply as: "E. . . . "

29. Ruth P. Dawson, " 'Der Weihrauch, den uns die Männer streuen.' Wieland and the Women Writers in the *Teutscher Merkur,*" *Christoph M. Wieland, North American Scholarly Contributions on the Occasion of the 250th Anniversary of his Birth*, ed. Hansjörg Schelle (Tübingen: Niemeyer, 1984), 242.

30. On the legal status of women in the eighteenth century see Becker-Cantarino, *Der lange Weg zur Mündigkeit. Frau und Literatur (1500–1800)* (Stuttgart: Metzler, 1987), 46–65.

31. See Wieland's explanatory footnote, *NTM* (1791), 2:63f.

32. Dawson, "Weihrauch," 245. Becker-Cantarino makes no mention of Berlepsch's treatise in her study of women and literature (1987).

33. Dawson, "Weihrauch," 243f.; Becker-Cantarino, *Mündigkeit*, 64f.

34. "But natural laws are not to be circumvented. Even as it will remain eternally impossible to transform the soaring eagle into a cooing dove, a rambunctious steed into a meek lamb, the raging storm wind into a gentle breeze, or a loud thunder clap into the soft tones of the flute, so too is it not easy for a woman of fiery spirit, strong conviction and lively imagination to play the quiet sufferer, hanging her head at each unreasoned contradiction and washing away the sense of incurred injustice with a quiet tear" (Berlepsch, "Glück," *NTM* [1971], 2:68).

35. See, for example: "Nein, wir müssen allein stehen lernen! Wir müssen unsere Denkart, unsern Character in unsern eignen Augen so ehrwürdig machen, daß uns das Urtheil andrer in unserem geprüften und gerechten Urtheil über uns selbst nicht irre machen kann" (Berlepsch, *NTM*, 2:90). See also: "Wir die der Menschheit unentweihte Rechte—wenigstens in vielen Stücken—mit den Männern theilen und geniessen: warum sollen wir nicht auch unsre innere, geistige Existenz selbständig und eigenthümlich erhalten?" (Berlespch, *NTM*, 2:91).

36. See footnote 18.

37. von der Recke, "Ueber Naumann, den guten Menschen und großen Künstler" (signed: "E"), *NTM*, 1:107–35, 190–212, 247–89.

38. "Whoever undertakes a trip to intriguing Italy in hopes of healing ailing body and developing the mind, has little opportunity to report to friends from time to time on everything that attracted one's attention, prompted critical reflection, or frequently shatterd one's peace of mind. The reason is that the soul is bombarded with images in this country of contrasts and the body is severly taxed when one makes the least effort to gain an overview of Italian life. However, it is by means of these efforts that an Italian journey really does become interesting" (von der Recke, "Italien," *NTM* [1805], 3:39).

39. "Italy today seems populated with beggars just as it was filled with gods and demigods in ancient times. Well dressed men and women stretch out their hands imploringly to the passersby. Offensive, often repulsive beggars expose openly their injuries and wounds, using them in despicable fashion to earn their bread. The ploy often leads to miscarriages in pregnant women. This moral evil, combined with the frequent murders, fill the visitor to this otherwise wonderful country with horror" (von der Recke, "Italien," *NTM*, 3:40).

40. "Why do those regions where we find visible signs of a great upheaval from which new, more vigorous life full of grace and bewitching beauty emerges affect us so deeply? Is it not the presence of eternally creating and directing Providence which reveals itself to us, imparting a sacred sense of the constancy of all spiritual life?" (von der Recke, "Salzburg," *NTM* [March 1807], 3:187).

41. See footnote 7.

42. Cf. Becker-Cantarino, "Caroline Pichler und die 'Frauendichtung,'" *Modern Austrian Literature* 12:3-4 (1979), 3. Nor did the women wish to be seen as reformist outsiders. See also the concluding comment in Becker-Cantarino's *Mündigkeit*, 352: "So ist der 'Ort' der Frauen in der frühen Neuzeit nicht außerhalb der (patriarchalischen) Gesellschaft, in die sie hineingeboren werden, zu suchen. Mündigkeit ist das selbständige Gehen, Suchen und Infragestellen dieser Gesellschaft."

43. See Rohner's introduction to *Deutsche Essays* (1972), 2:7.

44. Friedrich Schlegel, "Über die Unverständlichkeit," *Deutsche Essays*, 2:16: "Sie enthält und erregt ein Gefühl von dem unauflöslichen Widerstreit des Unbedingten und des Bedingten, der Unmöglichkeit und Nothwendigkeit einer vollständigen Mittheilung."

45. Schlegel, "Unverständlichkeit," 2:11: "Thus quite some time ago I decided to enter into a dialogue with the reader on this topic and to construct—or if necessary, to deduce before his eyes, right under his nose, a different, new kind of reader according to my own ideas."

46. Ludwig Rohner, *Der deutsche Essay* (Neuwied and Berlin: Luchterhand, 1966), 160.

47. Goethe, "Zur Farbenlehre", HA, 13:317.

48. Friedrich Schlegel, "Georg Forster. Fragment einer Karakteristik der deutschen Klassiker," *DE*, 6:221f.

49. Müller's article is cited according to *Deutsche Essays* (1972), 2:97–109.

50. "Certain requirements belong to genuine discourse which are rarer espe-
     cially in our time than one would think. First of all, two thoroughly different
     speakers who are mysterious and unfathomable to each other; then between
     them a certain mutually shared ground, a certain belief, trust, and common
     basis for truth and justice. The human being should meet both of these
     demands by virture of human nature itself" (Müller, "Vom Gespräch," DE,
     2:99).
51. Hans-Gerhard Winter, Dialog und Dialogroman in der Aufklärung. Mit
     einer Analyse von J. J. Engels Gesprächstheorie (Darmstadt: Thesen Verlag,
     1974), 79.
52. "I like to hear the disputes of clever men / When speakers' lips with light
     grace play upon / The forces which so cheerfully and yet / So fearsomely
     bestir the human breast." The translation is cited according to Goethe's
     Plays, translated and introductions by Charles E. Passage (New York: Fr.
     Ungar, 1980), 494.
53. "That character of a certain vacuousness which Goethe ascribes to it, that
     libellula-like, colorful flutter on life's surface with an occasional light alight-
     ing and wetting of the wings, that fear of profound explanations especially
     of the grandiose, superior, and dominant applies only to the current soft,
     sickly irritability of society" (Müller, "Vom Gespräch," DE, 2:104).

CHAPTER 10

Conclusion

Refocusing

Crossing Boundaries uses an interdisciplinary approach and covers a lot of terrain. It is time to draw back and consider what has been accomplished. The ground covered in these pages is normally subdivided into specific parcels belonging to the social historian, the philosopher, the historian of book production and distribution, the chronicler of literary history, and finally also to the literary theorist. The use of a wide-angle lens leads to distortion at the edges, so refocusing at this point is desirable to enhance the overall image. Moreover, I wish to address some unanswered questions about the method, organization, and selected texts of this study.

My method in examining the early theory and practice of essayistic writing is similar to the combinative procedure suggested by Lessing, Goethe, Schiller, and Schlegel in their prose sampled in the foregoing pages. In other words, my method is "ironic" in Goethe's or Schlegel's sense of the term. My purpose was not merely to isolate individual segments (i.e., analysis), but above all to recombine that which had been artificially separated by advancing scholarship (i.e., synthesis). Ultimately it is the approach used by Schiller's "philosophic scholar" as characterized in his inaugural address at the University of Jena in 1789: "Wie ganz anders verhält sich der philosophische Kopf!—Ebenso sorgfältig, als der Brotgelehrte seine Wissenschaft von allen übrigen abgesondert, bestrebt sich jener, ihr Gebiet zu erweitern und ihren Bund mit den übrigen wiederherzustellen—*herzustellen* sage ich, denn nur der abstrahierende Verstand hat jene Grenzen gemacht, hat jene Wissenschaften voneinander geschieden."[1] With his insistence upon an interdisciplinary and unifying method of thinking, Schiller anticipates the thrust of Ralph Waldo Emerson's "American Scholar." Consequently, a quintessential passage from that Harvard lecture stands at the masthead of this inquiry.

"Man Thinking" in Schiller's or Emerson's meaning is creative; her/his writing is creative and the manner in which it must be read in order to be fully appreciated is equally creative. The new scholar/writer is innovative in seeing combinations where others see only divisions. I have endeavored to follow suit in *Crossing Boundaries*. Instead of continuing separations according to received notions, I attempted to join together. I prefer to think of the method as a *re*-membering of what once was.

Isolating details is a necessary step in the process of comprehension. But it was not the ultimate objective of this undertaking. Not the parts, but their context stand at center focus. Thus, an understanding of literature as communicative act was utilized in this study. Most appropriate is the theory of communicative action advocated by Habermas and harking back to the Enlightenment notion of accountability, that is, the giving of reasons. In light of the dominance of that attitude throughout the Age of Enlightenment, it is no accident that the underlying methodology of *Crossing Boundaries* reflects the combinative aspect of essayistic writing which it examines.

Furthermore, this study was premised on the perception that attempts to define the mode of writing known as the "essay" in terms of a genre analogous to the canonical triad were essentially misguided. There are just too many possible formalistic variations for us to delimit a genre labeled essay from related forms such as dialogue, epistle, article, treatise, tract, and feuilleton. The most recent proposal to define the essay in very specific terms (Wardell, 1986) is in the best tradition of *analysis* but ignores the really important question of *synthesis* in assessing the nature of the mode. Wardell is nevertheless wise to be wary of "loose" definitions of the essay and to reject the notion that the form is "undefinable."[2]

Yet any definition that aims to be specific runs the risk of distorting reality or at least of willfully interpreting the world one-dimensionally. Art, it is said, is at its best when it exudes life, not when it is a simple imitation. In the latter capacity the attempt is definable because the parts are foregrounded; in the former it escapes ultimate definition because the totality is front and center. Thus the critic might be advised to rein in the desire to pin down movement and tie up loose ends. S/he might instead make do with a *general* definition, approximating the essence but leaving room for nonessential variations from the norm. If one can determine what is essential about the species fish, for instance, then "formalistic" differences among trout, salmon, guppy, flounder, and so on will not be confusing. But first we must agree on what is fish. After that—to speak metaphorically with Elizabeth Hardwick—it is up to us to hold fast while the creature tries to wriggle away.[3]

In the case of essayistic writing which draws its energy from the principle of the dynamically manifold, I suggested that we consider defining it in terms of the author's and reader's respective postures rather than in a strictly formalistic manner. The form of the essay can be shared by other literary or non-literary types, while essayistic is clearly distinguishable from dramatic, epic, and lyric. In order for the definition to work, we had to presuppose that the reader was "fit," in Stanley Fish's sense, or "ideal," using Wolfgang Iser's terminology. In other words, the reader must *really* read as Harold Brodkey conceived of the act. A "fit" reader consciously enters into a dialogue with the author via the text. S/he endeavors to determine the "accents of meaning" (Ruttkowski), all the while fascinated by the perplexity of the text with its inner sparkle.

The purpose of that engaging dialogue is affective communication; that is, communication that occurs on the basis of mutual respect and between interlocutors interested in understanding the self via the process of understanding the other. This particular craft of communication involves appeals to the heart as well as to the head. What this exchange amounts to is consciousness raising, whether in the manner of Wolfgang Iser's reader-response theory or Jürgen Habermas's theory of communicative action. A communicative theory of essayistic writing was standard in the eighteenth century.[4] Heavily indebted to rhetorical practice, the affective stylistics of essayism represents the best of the rhetorician's art.

In order to reveal the essential unity of essayistic writing despite its ever changing external shell, which makes it so difficult to put one's finger on its true nature, a multilevel strategy seemed most propitious. Since this unity results from the "synergetic interplay" of historical, aesthetic, structural, and epistemic factors, they had to be recounted.[5] An accurate history of essayistic writing seems best achievable only within the framework of these fundamental interdependencies.

Crossing Boundaries is predicated, therefore, on a "dynamic contextual concept of the literary 'work'" which has come to dominate sociohistorical writing.[6] The application of Wolfgang Ruttkowski's category of the artistic and his emphasis on accents of meaning underscored the importance of literature as event. Saul Morson's theory of threshold literature and of boundary works contributed to a better understanding of essayistic compositions as hermeneutically perplexing as well as aesthetically indeterminate.

In order to do justice to the multidimensional approach I had to replace "simple derivative thinking" with "thinking in complex relations."[7] Thus the theory and history of early German essayism became a part of the history of a mentality. Essayism, I suggest, can then be viewed as a semiotic system reflecting the larger framework and simultaneously re-acting to it. It is, in fact, a more reliable barometer of the era than any dogmatic treatise of the time.[8] Not merely a mechanical imitation of those intellectual life forces, essayism is fully imbued with the synergetic energy underlying them. That energy causes creative reproduction. In correlating the new mode of writing and reading with overall changes in society 1680–1815, I hoped to contribute to the rewriting of literary history as part and parcel of social history, since the text of any given essay exists in a larger context which helps define its literariness.[9] The individual textual analyses were designed to serve this larger purpose and were not merely self-indulgent.

Additionally, we saw that the period of Enlightenment experienced a revolutionary writing explosion marked by a dramatic rise in journalistic undertakings. Many aspiring as well as established writers utilized the new medium to reach out to a larger, anonymous audience in order to spread Enlightenment ideals. The periodic literature produced for the journals was frequently marked by the best traits of the new anthropo-philosophic attitude in which literary and non-literary concerns were conjoined. Thus, the era 1680–1815 was analyzed from the unifying perspective of a spirit of innovation and experimentation. The new men-tality was paired with a novel manner of expressing it. That essayistic method of thinking and writing permeated so many levels of literature and society that it deserves a prominent position in our literary histories.

These developments are amply documented by Garve's anecdotal "Das Weihnachtsgeschenk" ("The Christmas Present," 1777), Wieland's pro-grammatic and very influential *Briefe an einen jungen Dichter* (*Epistles to a Young Poet*, 1782 and 1784), Schiller's enthusiastic "Was kann eine gute stehende Schaubühne eigentlich wirken?" ("What Can a Good Standing Theater Actually Accomplish?" 1784), Emilia von Berlepsch's often progressive "Über einige zum Glück der Ehe nothwendige Eigen-schaften und Grundsätze" ("On Some Qualities and Principles Prereq-uisite to Marital Bliss," 1781/1791), Goethe's retrospective "Literarischer Sansculottismus" ("The Literary Left," 1795), and Schle-gel's "Über die Unverständlichkeit" ("On Unintelligibility," 1799). While characteristic of the new literary and cultural atmosphere especially in the waning decades of the eighteenth century, these writings should not blind us to their indebtedness to more distant forerunners. Given the continu-ing debate in the late eighteenth century about the respective preeminence of the ancients or the moderns, it is not surprising that writers such as Horace, Quintilian, and Cicero would be held up for emulation, not mechanical imitation but spiritual symbiosis. Horace's manner of philosophizing in his sermons and epistles, for instance, is so like the essayistic manner of writing that he certainly served as a source of inspiration for German writers along with Montesquieu and Bayle, Fontenelle, Bacon, and Shaftesbury.[10] The seemingly meandering, pointless method of arguing poised in poetic language reemerged in eighteenth-century Germany in a dominant way. The Age of Reason produced so many works of this type that it no longer sounds far fetched to refer to the eighteenth century as "the classical age of essay writing."[11]

Chronological Matters

I argue in *Crossing Boundaries* that the period 1680–1815 reveals an intellectual and literary continuity. In presenting this view I offer a variation of Schönert's contention that the period 1770–1900 be considered a unified segment.[12] In contrast to Schönert's contention that a "prominent dividing line around 1770" exists, I argue that we not overestimate the significance of that decade as a phase in literary history since it does not represent a true break with the preceding movements. While it is true that the *incidence* of poetic prose is much greater in the last third of the century, the *quality* of that writing is inherently linked to preceding efforts. We should not be blinded to the accomplishments of a Thomasius, Pitschel, Abbt, Gellert, Lessing, or Wieland long before 1770.

If we focus on Enlightenment *mentality* in the broader sense of the phenomenon that dominated intellectual circles in the period 1680–1815 and remember that it included sensibility as well as rationality, we would recognize it as an important unifying factor. It was and is a mode of conceiving to which Sensibility, Storm and Stress, Classicism, and Romanticism can all be intimately connected without distorting the historical reality. The most recent literary histories are, in fact, informed by this desire to revise the nineteenth-century canon of literary forms and periods, extending the Enlightenment phase back into the late seventeenth century and forward into the Classic-Romantic era.

But time is relative and we can only estimate beginnings and endings. The uneven cuts are designed to underscore the complexity of any attempt to organize history into neat little packages. The distortion caused by the uneven separations 1680 and 1815 is less of a distortion than the artificially clean lines of 1700–1800 and not as strictly political as 1715–1789. The uneven cuts are designed to underscore the principle of continuity. For instance, Thomasius and Leibniz began writing in the new style after 1680 and Goethe's "Shakespeare und kein Ende" as well as Müller's "Vom Gespräch" both violate the cutoff point of 1815. But their attitudes were nevertheless very similar.

More problematical are the divisions for classifying the genesis of German essayistic style in Chapters VII, VIII, and IX. I would have preferred to discuss all the works in one chapter, for Gellert obviously continued to write after 1750; Herder, Garve, and Wieland long after 1790; Goethe and Schiller before 1790. But that would have been impractical. The titles for Chapters VIII and IX allude to chronological overlappings and the works by individual authors mentioned but not examined are consciously drawn from later periods in an effort to remind the reader of how arbitrary the chronology of literary periods is. That chronology is especially troublesome in the case of writers who have not been assigned to an established school (e.g., Kleist, Berlepsch, von der Recke).

As already noted, my diachronic discussion of the genesis of essayistic writing in German in the eighteenth century is a necessary first attempt at writing the full history of its development. In its current form, the historical sketch is far from complete. Too many essayists had to be excluded (e.g., J. E. Schlegel, Luise Adelgunde Culmus, Liscow, Abbt, Hamann, Lichtenberg, Forster, Marianne Ehrmann, Sturz, Jean Paul, and Hölderlin); even those discussed were dealt with summarily in order to keep the material manageable. But my purpose was not to write an exhaustive account of early German essayism. Instead I wished to sketch its early maturation against a theory of essayistic writing that drew upon germane contemporary ideas in order to stimulate further critical reflection on this complex topic. My diachronic, selective approach must be augmented by synchronic case studies of individual decades or authors. A synchronic view would enable us to ponder the full range of canonical and non-canonical writers by allowing us to delve deeper into a more limited context, for example, the 1740s or 1795–1805. A future focus on depth is thus the necessary correlate to my focus on breadth.

Formal Versus Informal Essay

Critics of the essay have long noted two basic attitudes which they attribute to the diverse "fathers" of the form. The affable, casual stye they trace back to Montaigne, labeling it informal. Bacon's more cerebral manner is called formal. While Montaigne's and Bacon's styles are distinctive, the designations informal and formal are not all that clear. Nevertheless any attempt to dispense with them is not likely to succeed since they are so deeply seated in the critical mind. However, we should interpret the difference between the informal and the formal essay not in terms of influence by the French and English traditions but rather as essential *human* attributes and attitudes. Despite their different tempers both styles mirror the respective author's personal musings, deliberations, thoughts, and inspirations.

Our examination of Thomasius's and Leibniz's work revealed different accents at the beginning of our time frame. Two singular forms had emerged within the first half of the eighteenth century before Montaigne and Bacon had a chance to influence German writing. Neither the rhetorically engaging tone of a Gellert or Pitschel or young Herder nor the philosophic approach of a Gottsched or Kant or older Goethe should be considered inherently better than the other, although we will, of course, have our personal preferences at any given time.

The difference in timbre is no doubt attributable to the larger context of their particular writing and the more or less obvious presence of rhetorical strategies. Yet, beyond mere rhetorical technique, both kinds of text reveal aesthetic characteristics. Wieland's statement of 1782 definitely holds true even in the case of such boundary works: "Each Muse, each Venus, each Grace has her own particular form, her own timbre, cadence and pleasing demeanor, her own rhythm and measure."[13] Yet I would argue that the difference in tonality results from the writer's attitude toward his/her subject and audience. Primary seems to be the *degree* of the author's audience awareness as reflected in the semiotic text itself. Closely related to that consciousness is the author's *perception of an ideal reader* for his/her text. Thus the writer's attitude is decisive in determining the tone adopted. The basic dichotomy is between formal and informal, but there are degrees of formality and informality, such as intimate, solemn, ironic, or titillating.

Because I wished to avoid giving the false impression that the Montaignean brand of essayism is more appealing than the Baconian (especially in light of the German preference for the former, presumably because of a proclivity to Horace), I intermingled the representative samples of both basic styles. In the process I was able to examine essayistic pieces from the same author written in divergent voices. However, the selection of essays from Thomasius to Müller was not totally random. I endeavored to provide a representative sample of both well known and lesser known writers from the Age of Enlightenment. Thus Pitschel appears next to Lessing and Garve beside Goethe. While not wishing to deny verse compositions a claim to inclusion in a history of essayistic writing, I did desire to use the available space economically in judging the intimate relationship between rhetoric and poetic expression. Thus I restricted the survey to prose that bears the strongest imprint of the rhetorician. Additionally, I gravitated to essayistic writing Just labels "culturally critical," "literary critique," and "ironic." They hold the greatest appeal for literary historians who will be the primary readers of *Crossing Boundaries*.

Rhetoric and Essayistic Writing

Rhetoric, as we know, is not poetry. Yet our inquiry into the theory and practice of essayistic writing revealed the fruitful impact of rhetoric on the new style of writing. The *Grundriß der Rhetorik* (1986) by Gert Ueding and Bernd Steinbrink confirmed the ubiquitous nature of rhetorical strategies for our time period.[14] Friedrich Sengle remarked in his *Formenlehre* of 1967 that future studies of literature must be careful to consider the rhetorical element, especially in such periods as the Enlightenment when poets were deeply schooled in Aristotelian poetics and did not, therefore, discriminate as clearly between the two realms as modern writers and critics are wont to do.

Of course we duly noted that theorists, critics, and writers of the essay ranging from Leibniz to Wieland, Friedrich Schlegel, Adorno, and Bense were fond of drawing attention to the affinity between essayist and orator. We saw, in fact, that Leibniz hoped to create a literary language similar to the French gallant style by softening the harsh scholarly mode with the more fluid tones of poetic writing in the vernacular. The result, he foretold, would be a new kind of prose style that would shoot to the fore like a metal tipped, feather-winged arrow released from the bow of experimentation. The metal tip, he explained, was the weight of philosophic reflection, while the feathers connoted the lightly guiding touch of poetic expression. In combination they make mere wood capable of probing the heights. We saw further that rhetorical appeal and aesthetic form were frequently paired, as evidenced by Gellert's activities in Saxony or Wieland's lectures in Switzerland at mid-century. We observed that Goethe's concept of aesthetic style is tantamount to the finest example of rhetorical art, and that Schiller's literary work is unthinkable without the tradition of rhetoric. Because of the "elective affinity" of rhetoric to *belles-lettres*, a dialogic or discursive quality has become a trademark of essayistic writing. Yet not all discourses are alike.

In defining essential traits of essayistic writing, we determined that the author's purpose in writing and his/her attitude toward topic and audience were critical factors. Rhetoric is the art of persuasion. The rhetorician most often sees her/himself as a teacher and the audience as learners.

And the orator's purpose is to bring the listener around to his point of view. The orator is not necessarily interested in truth or in teaching a methodology. The poet may use the same techniques as the orator, but the creative writer—who by the way writes because s/he has something of value to say and wishes to be heard and understood—does not treat his/her audience as objects to be manipulated and cajoled into a preordained position. The poet, moreover, writes from inspiration, writes in order to impart part of himself to the reader. Poetry is always part confession, no matter how masked the process may be. When the poet acts as a preceptor, s/he is not intent upon teaching the *what* but rather the *how*. For the creative writer who uses rhetorical techniques, the decisive factor remains the process of creativity in combining, separating, recombining, drawing near to the point and receding from it like the ebb and flow of the tide as it rises and falls in harmony with its environment.

The rhetorician causes movement toward a definite goal; s/he creates meanings that point in a definite direction. The poet/essayist reflects the motion of creation in his/her writing. S/he varies and changes meanings in the search for ultimate meaning. We can't always define where the motion is headed, but we sense a fulcrum or axis around which the activity takes place. Normally that gravitational center is a far-reaching question like "What is man?" or "What is the purpose of life?" or "What is art?" The orator might feign indeterminacy. When s/he does, it is frequently to gain an emotional or political advantage over the listener in order to achieve a specified, limited objective. But the creative writer often composes in a clear yet indeterminate manner because her/his inspiration is a composite of several impulses which cannot be readily isolated.

Thus the essayistic text is marked by accents of meaning which can be emphasized in different fashion by different readers. To complicate matters further, the essayist's mode of expression is a hybrid of the literary and the didactic, of lively poetry and sober scholarly science. From that hybrid character arises its hermeneutic perplexity as a boundary work between the two realms of specificity and non-specificity. Both the hermeneutic perplexity and literary indeterminacy prevent the essay from controlling the audience to the same degree that the oration exerts coercive influence on an audience. The reader is not supposed to derive *a* meaning from a reading of the text but to learn *how* to read creatively. As Morson pointed out, it is not a question of a reading or readings but of how to read the text.

The essayist invites the reader on a journey of discovery and consequently presents his/her ideas and feelings *as they arise*—that in contrast to the orator who is more often manipulative than not. Yet the essayistic pieces by Kleist and Müller demonstrate that the method of the truly accomplished orator can approximate the phenomenon of poetic inspiration to a very high degree. While Kleist stressed the spontaneity of discourse—the origination of ideas via the thought process itself—Müller accentuated the orator's respect for the listener. Such an orator treats the interlocutor as an equal partner in the communicative act. When the orator sets her/his sights on genuine communication between equal yet different-minded discussants interested in reaching a point outside either one individually, then the art of rhetoric converges with the art of essayistic writing. Then the common purpose is not to dazzle the reader with sparkling virtuosity but to fathom a fathomless truth. Such was the case most especially in the Age of Enlightenment.

The test of the literariness of a text lies in its durability. How often can a reader approach the text and see something not seen before? How often does the meaning seem to shift and vary? How much pleasure is provided by each reading? The pleasure of the aesthetic experience is, of course, primarily cerebral and seldom emotional.[15] The more formal the essay, the less visceral the response. But whether we are dealing with formal or informal qualities of the mode, the critical question is how *engaging* is the text? There is, of course, room for variation in the degree of stimulation to be found in a text even as there are degrees of creativity or responsiveness as reflected, for example, in the Goethean categories of "simple imitation," "mannerism," and "style."[16] Yet the intensity is determined by the writer's abilities as a creative writer and also by the reader's abilities as a creative reader. Goethe's admonition to young poets of 1832 to express "what is alive and active, regardless of what form it might assume" and to create through inner impulse rather than through mere imitation is equally valid for the reader who must be responsive to what is alive and vibrant in her/himself.[17] The work of art will remain as vital as the impulse which first gave rise to it and which figures into its subsequent "revitalization" at the hands of a recipient.

The Ironic Mode: A Most Dangerous Game

"It came into him life; it went out from him truth. It came to him short-lived actions; it went out from him immortal thoughts. It came to him business; it went from him poetry. It was dead fact; now it is quick thought. It can stand, and it can go. It now endures, it now flies, it now inspires. Precisely in proportion to the depth of mind from which it issued, so highly does it soar, so long does it sing." These words from Emerson's "The American Scholar" (1837) are immortal in their own right, rich in both truth and in freshness. They can be read and reread without losing the thrill of the first encounter. What Emerson most concisely describes in the passage is the magic of the literary event seen from the perspective of the creative writer who is capable of lending permanence to the sparkle of life. Juxtaposed to the role of the writer described here is the role of the reader. On that role Emerson also expressed himself: "Undoubtedly there is a right way of reading. There is then creative reading as well as creative writing."[18]

I accorded particular importance to Emerson's words in *Crossing Boundaries* for I saw a similarity between his notion of creative writing (and creative reading) and Klaus Günther Just's sixth category of essays which he labels the "ironic essay." Like Emerson's idea of literature the ironic essay is marked by an unusual method of proceeding. Precise and nimble, it is above all experimental and heuristic. The writer acts as court jester and wise philosopher all rolled into one, enticing the reader on a journey of discovery. The term "ironic" thus designates a playful inventiveness on the part of the author.

We later saw that Goethe recommended a similarly ironic approach to scientific descriptions, calling it "daring." We will never be satisfied, he suggests, with merely looking at an object; we must also "theorize" about what we experience. We must consciously reflect upon the interrelationships of phenomena and upon their significance for our own self-definition. If experience is to be truly useful it must be analyzed in animated fashion. Goethe's conception of the self-conscious thought process presupposes an uncommon freedom of movement. His meaning points to an understanding of irony in the manner of Friedrich Schlegel for whom irony designated a bifocal view of the world. The bifurcation resulted from the observer's awareness that s/he is engaged in an act of observing. The subject is thus conscious both of itself and of the observed object so that subject and object begin to fuse.

Schlegel's sense of irony is even more emphatically informed by a holistic perspective than Goethe's. Schlegel argues that the ironic stance of the writer is designed to illuminate not only the "contextuality" of the writer, but also the "contextuality" of the reader. He thus underscores the notion that neither participant in the literary event has reached a point of stasis. Each exists in a state of flux. Because of the lack of stasis in the universe, the poet/author is highly conscious of the tentativeness of all insights. The structures are not permanent. Thus, the "ironic writer" shies away from dogmatic statements of any kind, except to suggest that making dogmatic statements is imprudent. By analogy this dual perspective extends to a consciousness of the simultaneity of the individual and the universal, the real and the ideal. It takes little to transform Goethe's and Schlegel's concepts of irony into a description of the underlying principle in essayistic writing.

The implied emphasis in the ironic mode on the role of the writer/observer required a balance. That balance is found in the writer's awareness of a fit reader. The reader-role must be played in the same inventive style as the author-role if the text is to be reconstructed as intended, that is, as an heuristic journey. When the reader engages the text like the author would, one human consciousness encounters another and a dangerous game is (re)enacted. The old prescriptive rules are cast aside and reader and writer are set adrift in the realm of first encounters. The reader must map the intellectual and emotional territory him/herself. It is a mapping not only of the other but also a remapping of oneself. Reading, Harold Brodkey tells us, which has the capacity to alter the way we think and feel about ourselves and others, is serious business.[19] Moreover, if it has the forcefulness to alter our perceptions, it possesses an inner truth and logic unbounded by time or space. The text constructed in this way betrays a moral stance; the decoding it requires forces a "reader thinking" into an ethical posture, for s/he is called upon to make choices that have the potential for affecting her/him profoundly.

Crossing boundaries is a dangerous endeavor. The self can lose itself in the object or become fused with the other. If we cross boundaries too often, we begin to lose our sense of orientation, our sense of identity and place. Maybe that is the reason why the essayistic mode has not achieved the status of a canonical category in literary theory and history. With its disregard for lines of demarcation, it is an uncomfortable mode, forcing the reader to question almost all received notions and systems.

Essayism is frequently cited as being a modern phenomenon. Yet, as is the case with so many other modern phenomena, its origins lie in the past. *Crossing Boundaries* has endeavored to cast some light on the early history and theory of a mode of writing and reading that is consciously avant-garde and interdisciplinary. Those tendencies begin to be profiled well before 1750. And so much was written in the course of the eighteenth century in the new mode that we can rightfully admire with Goethe the style of "reviews of works on religious and moral topics as well as on medicinal ones when compared to the critiques of poems and whatever else is related to *belles-lettres*" (HA, 9:277). The Leibnizian arrow of prose composition, fashioned with tip of steel and wings of feather, soared through Goethe's time . . . right into our own.

Notes

1. Friedrich Schiller, *Werke in drei Bänden* (Munich: Hanser, 1966), 2:11: "The philosophic mind acts in a totally different manner. He works to expand his field of study, to rejoin it to other fields of inquiry just as meticulously as the narrow-minded scholar [*Brotgelehrter*] strives to abstract his area of expertise from all others. I say that the philosophic mind endeavors to *rejoin* areas of expertise because the boundaries separating the sciences from one another are not real; they are the product of artificial intellectual vivisection."

2. Wardell, "The Essays of Christoph Martin Wieland," Dissertation, University of Michigan (1986), 33–36.

3. Elizabeth Hardwick, "Its Only Defense: Intelligence and Sparkle," *New York Times Book Review* (Sept. 14, 1986), 1, 44f.

4. The volume, *The Philosopher as Writer: The Eighteenth Century*, ed. Robert Ginsberg (Cranbury, NJ: Associated University Presses, Inc., 1987), contains nine studies of non-fictional work in the Age of Enlightenment. Each attests to the pervasiveness of the "craft of communication" (or affective stylistics) even among philosophical writers. In addition to Koepke's study of "Herder's Craft of Communication" already cited, Lester Crocker's piece on "Rousseau's Two Discourses: The Philosopher as Rhetorician," Harry Solomon's "Reading Philosophical Poetry: A Hermeneutics of Metaphor for Pope's *Essay on Man*," Robert Markley's "Style as Philosophical Structure: The Contexts of Shaftesbury's *Characteristicks*," and Robert Ginsberg's "The Literary Structure and Strategy of Hume's Essay on the Standard of Taste" are all fruitful reading in our present context.

5. Cf. Klaus Weissenberger, "Der Essay," in *Kunstprosa ohne Erzählen* (Tübingen: Niemeyer, 1985), 106.

6. Jörg Schönert, "The Social History of German Literature. On the Present State of Distress in the Social History of German Literature," *Poetics* 14 (1985), 307. My approach, however, was not to seek a simple equation between the literary text and the social conditions of its origination but rather to view essayistic writing as a product of a changing *mentality* that wrought social change and that in turn was seen as a vehicle of further altering the way people interact socially and privately. In this sense, I advocated a communicative version of *Formensoziologie* postulated by Jauss or Iser. Cf. Peter Uwe Hohendahl, "Bürgerlichkeit und Bürgertum als Problem der Literatursoziologie," *German Quarterly* 61/2 (1988), 264–83, especially 278ff. Hohendahl's purpose is to warn against a simple application of sociological categories to the study of literature (his focus is primarily the nineteenth century). He is right also to warn against the "marginalization" of social history, urging that its insights be more closely evaluated and integrated into literary studies (266).

7. Klaus R. Scherpe, "'Beziehung' und nicht 'Ableitung.' Methodische Über-legungen zu einer Literaturgeschichte im sozialen Zusammenhang (am Beispiel der Nachkriegsliteratur)," in *Literatur und Sprache im historischen Prozeß. Vorträge des deutschen Germanistentages Aachen 1982*, Vol. 1, ed. Thomas Cramer (Tübingen: Niemeyer, 1983), 77–90, here 80.

8. Cf. James Van Der Laan, "The German Essay of the 18th Century: Mirror of its Age," *Lessing Yearbook* 18 (1986), 189.

9. Cf. Schönert, 312. On the Question of the coexistence of text and context see Marilyn Randall, "Context and Convention: The Pragmatics of Liter-ariness," *Poetics* 14 (1985), 415–431. She concludes her inquiry with a statement wholly relevant to the situation of essayistic writing as described in *Crossing Boundaries*: "The knowledge presupposed by the literary text is diverse—at once implicit and conventional, explicit and non-conventional, equally discursive and non-discursive. In every case, the text transmits knowledge, signalling a mode of reception with respect to which the text communicates—both the world, and its own literariness" (430). The sta-bility which is a classic characteristic of literariness is provided by the discursive context and quality of essayistic writing and reading.

10. In Wieland's classic translation, that style is succinctly summarized as: "Die Freiheit, ohne Methode, sich bloß von seinen Gedanken führen zu lassen, die dieser Art von Komposition [=Briefen] eigen ist, erlaubte [Horazen] alle die kleinen Episoden und Abschweifungen, auf die ihm seine eigne Laune bringen mochte; seine Hauptabsicht fiel desto weniger in die Augen, und er konnte seinen Discurs auch für andre Leser, als für die, an die er unmittelbar gerichtet war, interessant machen." Christoph Martin Wieland, "Horaz, *Über die Dichtkunst. An L. Calpurnius Piso und seine Söhne*" (1782), in: Christoph M. Wieland, *Werke*, ed. F. Martini and H. W. Seiffert (Munich: Hanser, 1964–1968), 5:592f. See also 5:598.

11. Karl Joel, *Die Wandlungen der Weltanschauung. Eine Philosophiege-schichte als Geschichtsphilosophie* (Tübingen: Niemeyer, 1928–34), 1:714. See also Wardell, ix.

12. Jörg Schönert, "Sozialgeschichte der Literatur," *Poetics*, 14 (1985), 314f.

13. *Horazens Briefe*, transl. from the Latin, ed. with an historical introduction and other necessary commentaries by Christoph M. Wieland, Part 1, new rev. Ed. (Leipzig: Weidmann'sche Buchhandlung, 1790), 291: "Jede Muse, jede Venus und Grazie, hat ihre bestimmte Form, ihren eigenen Ton, Gang und Anstand, ihren Rhythmus und ihre Mensur."

14. Gert Ueding and Bernd Steinbrink, *Grundriß der Rhetorik. Geschichte, Technik, Methode* (Stuttgart: Metzler, 1986), especially 100–140. Ueding takes due note of the impact of rhetoric on the genesis of German literature in his recently published *Klassik und Romantik. Deutsche Literatur im Zeitalter der Französischen Revolution 1789–1815*, Hansers Sozialge-schichte der deutschen Literatur vom 16. Jahrhundert bis zur Gegenwart, 4 (Munich: dtv, 1988), arguing that rhetoric gave rise to "a rhetorical, rhyth-mic prose and essayistic form" (4/2:771). In fact, Ueding makes a first, welcome attempt to address the need for including essayistic writing in our literary histories. He devotes the final forty pages of his 900–page text to what he labels *rhetorische Kunstprosa* (4/2:771–810). While Ueding is not

concerned with essayistic writing in my more precise sense, he does attribute to "rhetorical, rhythmic prose" qualities which essentially describe essayistic writing (see 4/2:779). Yet because he operates on neither a broad historical nor refined theoretical basis, Ueding mistakenly concludes that the writing mode is new and that "its formal characteristics appear so vague and numerous that no clear generic description can be postulated" (4/2:779). Unfortunately, Ueding's work only became available to me after the manuscript of *Crossing Boundaries* had been completed. Thus I was no longer able to respond to his ideas in detail.

15. Wardell (1986), 93, is the most recent critic to express this view.
16. See Rasmussen, "Georg Forsters Stil als gegenständliches Denken und Beschreibung der Dinge" (1985), 33. Rasmussen places his discussion in the tradition of the "creative mirror" (*der schaffende Spiegel*).
17. Johann Wolfgang von Goethe, "Noch ein Wort für junge Dichter," *Werke*, Hamburger Ausgabe in 14 Vols., ed. by Eric Trunz (Munich: Beck, 1981), 12:360.
18. Ralph Waldo Emerson, "The American Scholar," *The Selected Writings of Ralph Waldo Emerson*, ed. Brooks Atkinson (New York: Random House, 1950), 48–51.
19. Harold Brodkey, "Reading, the Most Dangerous Game," *New York Times Book Review* (Nov. 24, 1985), 45, avers: "If the reader is not at risk, he is not reading. And if the writer is not at risk, he is not writing."

Selected Bibliography

Seminal essay collections are listed by title rather than editor for easy identification by the reader.

Primary Sources

Berlepsch, Emilia von. "Ueber einige zum Glück der Ehe nothwendige Eigenschaften und Grundsätze." *Neuer Teutscher Merkur* 2 (April 1791): 63–102, 113–134.

Bodmer, Johann Jakob, and Johann Jakob Breitinger. *Schriften zur Literatur*, ed. Volker Meid. Stuttgart: Reclam, 1980.

Emerson, Ralph Waldo. "The American Scholar." *The Selected Writings of Ralph Waldo Emerson*. Introduction by Brooks Atkinson, foreword by Tremaine McDowell. New York: Random House, 1950.

Engel, Johann Jakob. *Über Handlung, Gespräch und Erzählung*. Facsimile edition, ed. Ernst Theodor Voss. Stuttgart: Metzler, 1964.

Garve, Christian. "Von der Popularität des Vortrags." *Popularphilosophische Schriften über literarische, ästhetische und gesellschaftliche Gegenstände*, Vol. 2, facsimile edition, ed. Kurt Wölfel. Stuttgart: Metzler, 1974.

———. "Über die prosaische Schreibart." *Popularphilosophische Schriften*, Vol. 2, fasimile edition, ed. K. Wölfel. Stuttgart: Metzler, 1974.

Gellert, Christian Fürchtegott. *Die epistographischen Schriften*. Facsimile of the editions of 1742 and 1751. Stuttgart: Metzler, 1971.

———. "Ermahnung an die Studenten der Universität Leipzig." *Deutsche Reden. Part I: Von Berthold von Regensburg bis Ludwig Uhland*, ed. Walter Hinderer. Stuttgart: Reclam, 1973. 258–261.

Goethe, Johann Wolfgang von. "Literarischer Sansculottismus." *Werke*, Hamburg edition in 14 vols., Vol. 12: *Schriften zur Kunst und Literatur*, ed. Eric Trunz, commentary by Herbert von Einem. Munich: Beck and dtv, 1981. 12:239–244. Cited as HA.

———. "Shakespeare und kein Ende." *Werke*, Hamburg edition. Munich: Beck and dtv, 1981. 12:287–298.

———. "Zum Shakespeares-Tag." *Werke*, Hamburg edition. Munich: Beck and dtv, 1981. 12:224–227.

———. "Zur Farbenlehre." *Werke*, Hamburg edition, Vol. 13: *Naturwissenschaftliche Schriften I*, ed. Dorothea Kuhn and Rike Wankmüller. Munich: Beck and dtv, 1981, 13:314–523.

Gottsched, Johann Christoph. *Ausführliche Redekunst. Nach Anleitung der alten Griechen und Römer, wie auch der neuern Ausländer* 1736. Rprt. Hildesheim and New York: Gerstenberg, 1973.

———. ["Furcht und Hoffnung"]. *Der Biedermann. Eine Moralische Wochenschrift*. Facsimile of the Leipzig edition of 1727–1729, ed. Wolfgang Martens with an afterword and notes. Stuttgart: Metzler, 1975. 2:93–98.

———. "Die Lerchenjagd." *Der Biedermann*, Facsimile edition. Stuttgart: Metzler, 1975. 1:109–112. ˙

Hallbauer, Friedrich A. *Anweisung zur Verbesserten Teutschen Oratorie*. Rprt. Kronberg/Ts, 1974.

Herder, Johann Gottfried. *Briefe zur Beförderung der Humanität*. In *Sämmtliche Werke*, in 33 volumes, ed. Bernhard Suphan. Berlin: Weidmannsche Buchhandlung, 1877–1913. Vols. 17–18. Cited as Suphan.

———. "In der Dichtkunst ist Gedanke und Ausdruck wie Seele und Leibe und nie zu Trennen." *Sämmtliche Werke*, ed. B. Suphan. 1:34–400.

———. "Shakespeare." *Sämmtliche Werke*, ed. B. Suphan. 5:208–231. Also in *Der junge Herder*, ed. Wolfdietrich Rasch. Tübingen: Niemeyer, 1969. 74–94.

———. "Wie die Philosophie zum Besten des Volkes allgemeiner und nützlicher werden kann." *Sämmtliche Werke*, ed. B. Suphan. 32:31–33.

Kant, Immanuel. "Beantwortung der Frage: Was ist Aufklärung?" In *Was ist Aufklärung? Aufsätze zur Geschichte und Philosophie*, 2nd edition, ed. Jürgen Zehbe. Göttingen: Vandenhoeck and Ruprecht, 1975. Also in *Kant's Werke*, ed. Königlich Preußische Akademie der Wissenschaften. Berlin: G. Reimer, 1912. 7:35–42. Cited respectively as Zehbe and AA.

Kleist, Heinrich von. "Über die allmähliche Verfertigung der Gedanken beim Reden." In *Deutsche Essays. Prosa aus zwei Jahrhunderten*, in 6 volumes, ed. Ludwig Rohner. Munich: dtv, 1972. 2:35–40.

Klopstock, Friedrich. "Von der Darstellung." *Klopstocks Werke in einem Band*, ed. Karl-Heinz Hahn. Berlin and Weimar: Aufbau, 1973. 272–278.

———. "Gedanken über die Natur der Poesie." *Klopstocks Werke in einem Band*. Berlin and Weimar: Aufbau, 1979. 258–263.

Lessing, Gotthold Ephraim. "Ernst und Falk. Gespräche für Freimaurer." *G. E. Lessings Sämmtliche Schriften*, in 24 volumes, ed. Karl Lachmann, 3rd edition, ed. Franz Muncker. Stuttgart, Leipzig, and Berlin: de Gruyter, 1886–1924. 13:341–406. Cited as LM.

Leibniz, Gottfried Wilhelm. "Ermahnung an die Teutsche, ihren Verstand und Sprache besser zu üben." In *Politische Schriften*, 2 volumes, ed. Hans Heinz Holz. Frankfurt. a. M.: Europäische Verlagsanstalt, 1967. 2:60–80.

Loen, Johann Michael von. "Die Schweitz im Jahr 1719 und 1724." In *Deutsche Essays. Prosa aus zwei Jahrhunderten*, in 6 volumes, ed. Ludwig Rohner. Munich: dtv, 1972. 1:86–92.

Mendelssohn, Moses. *Phädon oder über die Unsterblichkeit der Seele*, ed. Dominique Bourel, with an introduction by Nathan Rotenstreich. Hamburg: Meiner, 1979.

Müller, Adam. "Vom Gespräch." In *Deutsche Essays. Prosa aus zwei Jahrhunderten*, in 6 volumes, ed. Ludwig Rohner. Munich: dtv, 1972. 2:97–109.

Neukirch, Benjamin. *Anweisung zu Teutschen Briefen*. In *Der galante Stil, 1680–1730*, ed. Conrad Wiedemann. Tübingen: Niemeyer, 1969.

Pitschel, Theodor Lebrecht. "Schreiben an einen Freund, bey Uebersendung eines Briefes von einem Freygeiste." *Belustigungen des Verstandes und Witzes*, ed. Johann Joachim Schwabe. Leipzig: Breitkopf, 1741–1745. 2 (1742):393–398.

_____. "Schreiben von der Stärke der einmal angenommenen Meynungen." *Belustigungen des Verstandes und Witzes*, Leipzig: Breitkopf, 1741–1745. 3 (1743):85–93.

von der Recke, Elisa. "Blick auf Italien (Aus der Schreibtafel einer Reisenden)." *Neuer Teutscher Merkur* 3 (Sept. 1805): 39–46.

_____. "Ueber die Salzburgischen Tölpel." *Neuer Teutscher Merkur* 3 (March 1807): 187–200.

Schiller, Friedrich. "Philosophische Briefe." *Werke in drei Bänden*, ed. Herbert G. Göpfert. Munich: Hanser, 1966. 1:701–718. Cited as Hanser.

_____. "Rede über die Frage: Gehört allzuviel Güte, Leutseeligkeit und große Freygebigkeit im engsten Verstande der Tugend?" In *Deutsche Reden. Part I: Von Berthold von Regensburg bis Ludwig Uhland*, ed. Walter Hinderer. Stuttgart: Reclam, 1973. 287–294.

_____. "Über die notwendigen Grenzen beim Gebrauch schöner Formen." *Werke in drei Bänden*, ed. H. G. Göpfert. Munich: Hanser, 1966. 2:521–539.

_____. "Was heißt und zu welchem Ende studiert man Universalgeschichte?" *Werke in drei Bänden*, ed. H. G. Göpfert. Munich: Hanser, 1966. 2:9-22.

Schlegel, Friedrich. "Über die Unverständlichkeit." In *Deutsche Essays. Prosa aus zwei Jahrhunderten*, in 6 volumes, ed. Ludwig Rohner. Munich: dtv, 1972. 2:11–21.

Thomasius, Christian. "Christian Thomasius eröffnet der Studierenden Jugend zu Leipzig in einem Discours Welcher Gestalt man denen Frantzosen in gemeinem Leben und Wandel nachahmen soll? Ein Collegium über des Gratians Grund-Reguln/ Vernünfftig/klug und artig zu leben." In *Deutsche Literaturdenkmale des 18. und 19. Jahrhunderts*, 52/2, new series 2/3, ed. August Sauer. rprt. Nendeln/Liechtenstein: Krauss, 1968.

_____. "Von der Klugheit, sich selbst zu raten." In *Deutsche Literaturdenkmale des 18. und 19. Jahrhunderts*, 52/2, new series 2/3. Nendeln/Liechtenstein: Krauss, 1968.

Wezel, Johann Carl. "Ueber Sprache, Wissenschaften und Geschmack der Teutschen." *Kritische Schriften*, Vol. 3, ed. Albert R. Schmitt. Stuttgart: Metzler, 1975.

Wieland, Christoph Martin. "Sympathien." *Werke*, in 5 volumes, ed. Fritz Martini and Hans Werner Seiffert. Munich: Hanser, 1964–68. Cited as Hanser.

_____. "Theorie und Geschichte der Red-Kunst und der Dicht-Kunst, Anno 1757." *Wielands Gesammelte Schriften*, ed. Deutsche Kommission der Preußischen Akademie der Wissenschaften, Category 1, vol. 4. Berlin: Weidmann, 1916). Cited as AA.

Secondary Sources

Adorno, Theodor W. "Der Essay als Form" (1958). In *Deutsche Essays. Prosa aus zwei Jahrhunderten*, in 6 volumes, ed. Ludwig Rohner. Munich: dtv, 1972. 1:61–83.

Auklärung, Absolutismus und Bürgertum in Deutschland. Zwölf Aufsätze, ed. Frankin Kopitzsch. Hamburg: Nymphenburger Verlagsbuchhandlung, 1976.

Aufklärung. Ein literaturwissenchaftliches Studienbuch, ed. Hans- Friedrich Wessels. Königstein/Ts: Athenäum, 1984.

Aufklärung in Deutschland, ed. Paul Raabe and Wilhelm Schmidt-Biggemann. Bonn: Hohwacht, 1979.

Bachmann, Dieter. *Essay and Essayismus*. Stuttgart: Kohlhammer, 1969.

Barnard, Frederick M. "'Aufklärung' and 'Mündigkeit': Thomasius, Kant, and Herder." *Deutsche Vierteljahresschrift für Literaturwissenschaft und Geistesgeschichte* 57/2 (1983): 278–297.

Brauer, Walter. *Geschichte des Prosabegriffes von Gottsched bis zum Jungen Deutschland*. 1938, rprt. Hildesheim: Gerstenberg, 1974.

Bense, Max. "Über den Essay und seine Prosa" (1947). In *Deutsche Essays. Prosa aus zwei Jahrhunderten*, in 6 volumes, ed. Ludwig Rohner. Munich: dtv, 1972. 1,48–61.

Berger, Bruno. *Der Essay. Form und Geschichte*. Munich and Berne: Francke, 1964.

Berghahn, Klaus. "Das schwierige Geschäft der Aufklärung." In *Aufklärung. Ein literaturwissenschaftliches Studienbuch*, ed. Hans-Friedrich Wessels. Königstein/Ts: Athenäum, 1984. 32–65.

Bergk, Johann Adam. *Die Kunst, Bücher zu esen. Nebst Bemerkungen über Schriften und Schriftsteller*. Jena: Hempel, 1799; rprt. Leipzig: Zentral Antiquariat, 1967.

Biedermann, Karl. *Deutschland im 18. Jahrhundert*, ed. Wolfgang Emmerich. Frankfurt/M: Ullstein, 1979.

Blackall, Eric A. *The Emergence of German as a Literary Language, 1700–1775*. Cambridge: Cambridge University Press, 1959.

Böckmann, Paul. *Formgeschichte der deutschen Dichtung*. Hamburg: Hoffmann and Campe, 1967.

Brodkey, Harold. "Reading, the Most Dangerous Game." *New York Times Book Review* (Nov. 24, 1985): 44ff.

Cassirer, Ernst. *The Philosophy of the Enlightenment*, translated by Fritz C. A. Koelln and James P. Pettegrove. Boston: Beacon Press, 1955.

Culler, Jonathan. "Literary Competence." In *Reader-Response Criticism: From Formalism to Post-Structuralism*, ed. Jane P. Tompkins. Baltimore and London: Johns Hopkins University Press, 1980. 101–117.

Dawson, Ruth P. "Georg Forster, Essayist." *Jahrbuch für internationale Germanistik* 9/2 (1977): 112–125.

―――. "'Der Weihrauch, den uns die Männer streuen': Wieland and Women Writers in *Der Teutsche Merkur*." In *Christoph Martin Wieland 1733–1813. North American Scholarly Contributions on the Occasion of the 250th Anniversary of His Birth*, ed. Hansjörg Schelle. Tübingen: Max Niemeyer, 1984. 225–249.

_____. "Women Communicating: Eighteenth-Century German Journals Edited by Women." *Archives et Bibliothèques de Belgique* 54 (1983):95–111.

Dell' Orto, Vincent J. "Audience and the Tradition of the German Essay in the Eighteenth Century." *Germanic Review* 50 (1975): 111–125.

_____. "Nineteenth-Century Descriptions of the German Essay." *Jahrbuch für Internationale Germanistik* 10/1 (1978):8–22.

Deutsche Essays. Prosa aus zwei Jahrhunderten, in 6 volumes, ed. Ludwig Rohner. Munich: dtv, 1972. Cited as *DE*.

Eisenhut, Werner. *Einführung in die antike Rhetorik und ihre Tradition*. Darmstadt: Wissenschaftliche Buchgesellschaft, 1974.

Erforschung der deutschen Aufklärung, ed. Peter Pütz. Königstein/Ts.: Verlagsgruppe Athenäum, Hain, Scriptor, Hanstein, 1980.

Exner, Richard. "Zum Problem einer Definition und einer Methodik des Essays als dichterische Kunstform." *Neophilologus* 46 (1962): 169–182.

Fish, Stanley. "Literature in the Reader: Affective Stylistics." In *Reader-Response Criticism*, ed. Jane P. Tompkins. Baltimore and London: Johns Hopkins University Press, 1980. 70–100.

Foucault, Michel. "What is Enlightenment." In *The Foucault Reader*, ed. Paul Rabinow. New York: Random House, 1984. 32–50.

Goldfriedrich, Johann. *Geschichte des deutschen Buchhandels*, Vol. 3: *Geschichte des deutschen Buchhandels vom Beginn der klassischen Literaturepoche bis zum Beginn der Fremdherrschaft (1740–1804)*. Leipzig: Börsenverein, 1909.

Grimminger, Rolf. "Aufklärung, Absolutismus und bürgerliche Individuen. Über den notwendigen Zusammenhang von Literatur, Gesellschaft und Staat in der Geschichte des 18. Jahrhunderts." In *Sozialgeschichte der deutschen Literatur*, ed, R. Grimminger, Vol. 3/1: *Deutsche Aufklärung bis zur Französischen Revolution 1680–1789*. Munich: Hanser, 1980. 15–99.

Haas, Gerhard. *Essay*. Stuttgart: Metzler, 1969.

_____. *Studien zur Form des Essays und zu seinen Vorformen im Roman*. Tübingen: Niemeyer, 1966.

_____. "Zur Geschichte und Kunstform des Essays." *Jahrbuch für internationale Germanistik* 7/1 (1975): 11–39.

Habermas, Jürgen. *Strukturwandel der Öffentlichkeit. Untersuchungen zu einer Kategorie der bürgerlichen Gesellschaft*, 16th edition. Darmstadt and Neuwied: Luchterhand, 1986.

_____. *Theorie des kommunikativen Handelns*, 3rd edition, 2 vols. Frankfurt a. M.: Suhrkamp, 1985.

Hardwick, Elizabeth. "Its Only Defense: Intelligence and Sparkle." *New York Times Book Review* (Sept. 14, 1986): 1, 44–45.

Heisenberg, Werner. "Änderungen der Denkstruktur im Fortschritt der Wissenschaft." In *Schritte über Grenzen. Gesammelte Reden und Aufsätze*, 2nd edition. Munich: Piper, 1973. 275–287.

Hennecke, Hans. "Statt eines Vorwortes. Die vierte literarische Gattung. Reflexionen über den Essay." In *Kritik. Gesammelte Essays zur modernen Literatur*. Gütersloh, 1958.

Herrlitz, Hans-Georg. "Lektüre-Kanon und literarische Wertung. Bemerkungen zu einer didaktischen Leitvorstellung und deren wissenschaftlicher Begründung." In *Literarische Bildung und Erziehung*, ed. Harro Müller-Michaelis. Wege der Forschung 333. Darmstadt: Wissenschaftliche Buchgesellschaft, 1976. 243–261.

Herrnstein Smith, Barbara. "Contingencies of Value." *Critical Inquiry* 10/1 (Sept. 1983): 1-35.

Hinderer, Walter. "Über deutsche Rhetorik und Beredsamkeit. Eine Einführung." *Deutsche Reden. Part I: Von Berthold von Regensburg bis Ludwig Uhland*, ed. W. Hinderer. Stuttgart: Reclam, 1973. 15–67.

Horkheimer, Max and Theodor W. Adorno. *Dialektik der Aufklärung. Philosophische Fragmente*, 2nd edition. Frankfurt a. M.: Fischer, 1969.

Immerwahr, Raymond. "Friedrich Schlegels Abhandlung über die Selbständigkeit." *Deutsche Vierteljahresschrift für Geistesgeschichte und Literaturwissenschaft* 60/3 (1986): 426–439.

Iser, Wolfgang. *Der Akt des Lesens. Theorie ästhetischer Wirkung.* Munich: Fink, 1976.

Jacobs, Jürgen. *Prosa der Aufklärung. Kommentar zu einer Epoche.* Munich: Winkler, 1976.

Jauss, Hans Robert. *Literaturgeschichte als Provokation der Literaturwissenschaft.* Konstanz: Universitätsverlag, 1967.

Just, Klaus Günther. "Der Essay." In *Deutsche Philologie im Aufriß*, Vol. 2, ed. Wolfgang Stammler. Berlin and Bielefeld: Schmidt, 1954. Cols. 1897–1948.

Kiesel, Helmuth and Paul Münch. *Gesellschaft und Literatur im 18. Jahrhundert. Voraussetzungen und Entstehung des literarischen Markts in Deutschland.* Munich: Beck, 1977.

Knigge, Adolph Freiherr von. *Über Schriftsteller und Schriftstellerei.* Hannover: Christian Ritscher, 1792.

König, Dominik von. "Lesesucht und Lesewut." In *Buch und Leser,* ed. Herbert G. Göpfert. Hamburg: Hauswedell, 1977. 89–112.

Koepke, Wulf. "Herder's Craft of Communication." In *The Philosopher as Writer: The Eighteenth Century,* ed. Robert Ginsberg. Cranbury, NJ: Associated University Presses, 1987. 94–121.

Kosellek, Reinhart. *Kritik und Krise. Ein Beitrag zur Pathogenese der bürgerlichen Gesellschaft*, 2nd edition. Freiburg and Munich: Karl Alber, 1969.

Küntzel, Heinrich. *Essay und Aufklärung. Zum Ursprung einer originellen deutschen Prosa im 18. Jahrhundert.* Munich: Fink, 1969.

Leventhal, Robert S. "Semiotic Interpretation and Rhetoric in the German Enlightenment 1740—1760." *Deutsche Vierteljahresschrift für Literaturwissenschaft und Geistesgeschichte* 60/2 (1986): 223–248.

Lukács, Georg von. "Über Wesen und Form des Essays. Ein Brief an Leo Popper (1910)." In *Deutsche Essays. Prosa aus zwei Jahrhunderten,* ed. Ludwig Rohner. Munich: dtv, 1972. 1:27–47.

McCarthy, John A. "The Art of Reading and the Goals of the German Enlightenment." *Lessing Yearbook* 16 (1984): 79–94.

———. "Lektüre und Lesertypologie im 18. Jahrhundert (1730–1770). Ein Beitrag zur Lesergeschichte am Beispiel Wolfenbüttels." *Internationales Archiv für Sozialgeschichte der deutschen Literatur* 8 (1983): 35–82.

———. "The Philosopher as Essayist: Leibniz and Kant." In *The Philosopher as Writer*, ed. Robert Ginsberg. Cranbury, NJ: Associated University Presses, 1987. 48–74.

———. "'Plan im Lesen': On the Beginnings of a Literary Canon in the 18th Century (1730–1805)." *Komparatistische Hefte* 13 (1986): 29–45.

———. "The Poet as Journalist and Essayist: Christoph Martin Wieland." Part I: "From Poet to Popularizer: A Descriptive Account." *Jahrbuch für Internationale Germanistik* 12/1 (1980): 104–138. Part II: "Wieland as Essayist: The Cultivation of an Audience." *Jahrbuch für Internationale Germanistik* 13/1 (1981): 74–137.

Manheim, Ernst. *Aufklärung und öffentliche Meinung. Studien zur Soziologie der Öffentlichkeit im 18. Jahrhundert*, ed. Norbert Schindler. Stuttgart-Bad Cannstadt: frommann-holzboog, 1979.

Martens, Lorna. "The Impasses of Genre Criticism." In L. Martens, *The Diary Novel*. Cambridge: Cambridge University Press, 1985. 9-21.

Martens, Wolfgang. *Die Botschaft der Tugend. Die Aufklärung im Spiegel der deutschen Moralischen Wochenschriften*. Stuttgart: Metzler, 1968.

Martini, Fritz. "Essay." *Reallexikon der deutschen Literaturgeschichte*, 2nd edition, ed. Klaus Kanzog. Berlin: de Gruyter, 1958. 1:408–410.

Möller, Horst. *Vernunft und Kritik. Deutsche Aufklärung im 17. und 18. Jahrhundert*. Frankfurt a. M.: Suhrkamp, 1986.

Morson, Gary Saul. *The Boundaries of Genre: Dostoevsky's "Diary of a Writer" and the Traditions of Literary Utopia*. Austin: University of Texas Press, 1981.

Mosenthal, Peter B. "Defining the Expository Discourse Continuum: Towards a Taxonomy of Expository Text Types." *Poetics*, 14 (1985): 387–414.

Mundt, Theodor. *Die Kunst der deutschen Prosa: Ästhetisch, Literaturgeschichtlich, Gesellschaftlich*, Facsimile of the 1837 edition, ed. Hans Düvel. Göttingen: Vandenhoeck and Ruprecht, 1969.

Newman, Charles. *The Post-Modern Aura: The Act of Fiction in an Age of Inflation*. Evanston, IL: Northwestern University Press, 1985.

Nivelle, Armand. *Literaturästhetik der europäischen Aufklärung*. Wiesbaden: Athenaion, 1977.

Perthes, Friedrich Christoph, *Der deutsche Buchhandel als Bedingung des Daseins einer deutschen Literatur*, ed. Gerd Schulz. Leipzig, 1816; rprt. Stuttgart: Reclam, 1967.

The Philosopher as Writer: The Eighteenth Century, ed. Robert Ginsberg. Cranbury, NJ: Associated University Presses, 1987.

Pütz, Peter. *Die deutsche Aufklärung*. Erträge der Forschung 81. Darmstadt: Wissenschaftliche Buchgesellschaft, 1978.

Raabe, Paul. "Aufklärung durch Bücher." In *Aufklärung in Deutschand*, ed. Paul Raabe and Wilhelm Schmitt-Biggemann. Bonn: Hohwacht, 1979. 87–104.

Randall, Marilyn. "Context and Convention: The Pragmatics of Literariness." *Poetics*, 14 (1985): 415–431.

Rasmussen, Detlev. "Georg Forsters Stil als gegenständliches Denken und Beschreibung der Dinge." In *Goethe und Forster. Studien zum gegenständlichen Dichten*, ed. D. Rasmussen. Bonn: Bouvier, 1985.

Ray, William. *Literary Meaning: From Phenomenology to Deconstruction*. Oxford: Basil Blackwell, 1984.

Reader-Response Criticism: From Formalism to Post-Structuralism, ed. Jane P. Tompkins. Baltimore and London: Johns Hopkins University Press, 1980.

Rehder, Helmut. "Die Anfänge des deutschen Essays." *Deutsche Vierteljahresschrft für Geistesgeschichte und Literaturwissenschaft*, 40 (1966): 24–42.

———. "Reason and Romanticism. On the Beginnings of the German Essay." *Lessing Yearbook* 1 (1969): 162–177.

Rohner, Ludwig. *Der deutsche Essay. Materialien zur Geschichte und Ästhetik einer literarischen Gattung.* Berlin: Luchterhand, 1966.

Rößer, Hans-Otto. *Bürgerliche Vergesellschaftung und kulturelle Reform. Studien zur Theorie der Prosa bei Johann Gottfried Herder und Christian Garve.* Frankfurt a.M.: P. Lang, 1986.

Ruttkowski, Wolfgang. *Die literarischen Gattungen. Reflexionen über eine modifizierte Fundamentalpoetik.* Berne and Munich: Francke, 1968.

———. "Gattungs- und Grundbegriffe." In *Das Studium der deutschen Literatur. Eine Einführung für amerikanische Studierende*, ed. Wolfgang Ruttkowski and Eberhard Reichmann. Philadelphia: National Carl Schurz Association, 1974. 1-59.

Sartre, Jean-Paul. "Qu'est-ce que la littérature?" In *Questions de méthode* (Collection Idées, 140). Paris: Gallimard, 1967. 155–171.

Sauder, Gerhard. "Aufklärung des Vorurteils—Vorurteile der Aufklärung." *Deutsche Vierteljahresschrift für Literaturwissenschaft und Geistesgeschichte*, 57/2 (1983): 259–277.

Schenda, Rudolf. *Volk ohne Buch. Studien zur Sozialgeschichte der populären Lesestoffe 1770–1910.* Munich: dtv, 1977.

Scherpe, Klaus R. "'Beziehung' und nicht 'Ableitung.' Methodische Überlegungen zu einer Literaturgeschichte im sozialen Zusammenhang (am Beispiel der Nachkriegsliteratur)." *Literatur und Sprache im historischen Prozeß. Vorträge des deutschen Germanistentages Aachen 1982*, ed. Thomas Cramer. Band 1: *Literatur*. Tübingen: Niemeyer, 1983. 77–90

Schneiders, Werner. *Die wahre Aufklärung. Zum Selbstverständnis der deutschen Aufklärung.* Freiburg and Munich: Karl Alber, 1974.

Schönert, Jörg. "The Social History of German Literature: On the Present State of Distress in the Social History of German Literature." *Poetics* 14 (1985): 303–319.

Sengle, Friedrich. *Vorschläge zur Reform der literarischen Formenlehre, 2nd edition. Dichtung und Erkenntnis 1.* Stuttgart: Metzler, 1969.

Staiger, Emil. *Grundbegriffe der Poetik.* Zurich: Atlantis, 1946.

Steiner, George. "In a Post-Culture." In *Extraterritorial. Papers on Literature & the Language Revolution.* New York: Atheneum, 1976. 155–171.

Todorov, Tzvetan. "Literary Genres." In *The Fantastic: A Structural Approach to a Literary Genre,* trans. by Richard Howard. Ithaca: Cornell University Press, 1975. 3-23.

Der Traum der Vernunft: Vom Elend der Aufklärung. Eine Veranstaltungsreihe der Akademie der Künste Berlin. Darmstadt und Neuwied: Luchterhand, 1985.

Troeltsch, Ernst. "Aufklärung." In *Realencyklopädie für protestantische Theologie und Kirche* 2 (1897): 225–241. Reprinted in *Aufklärung, Absolutismus, und Bürgertum in Deutschand. Zwölf Aufsätze,* ed. Franklin Kopitzsch. Munich: Nymphenburger Verlagsbuchhandlung, 1976. 245–74.

Ueding, Gerd and Bernd Steinbrink. *Grundriß der Rhetorik: Geschichte, Technik, Methode,* 2nd edition. Stuttgart: Metzler, 1986.

Ungern-Sternberg, Wolfgang von. "Schriftsteller und literarischer Markt." In *Hansers Sozialgeschichte der deutschen Literatur,* ed. R. Grimminger. Munich: dtv, 1980. 3/1:133–185.

Van Der Laan, James M. "The German Essay of the 18th Century: Mirror of its Age," *Lessing Yearbook,* 18 (1986): 179–196.

———. "The German *essay* of the 18th Century: An Ecology." Dissertation, University of Illinois at Urbana/Champaign, 1984.

Vierhaus, Rudolf. *Deutschland im Zeitalter des Absolutismus (1648–1763).* Göttingen: Vandenhoeck and Ruprecht, 1978.

Vietta, Silvio. *Literarische Phantasie: Theorie und Geschichte. Barock und Aufklärung.* Stuttgart: Metzler, 1986.

Wardell, James R. "The Essays of Christoph Martin Wieland: A Contribution to the Definition and History of the Genre in its European Context." Dissertation, Universtiy of Michigan, 1986.

Weissenberger, Klaus. "Der Essay." In *Prosakunst ohne Erzählen: Die Gattungen der nicht-fiktionalen Kunstprosa,* ed. K. Weissenberger. Tübingen: Niemeyer, 1985. 105–124.

Wellek, René and Austin Warren. *Theory of Literature.* New York: Harcourt, Brace and Co., 1956

Wilke, Jürgen. *Literarische Zeitschriften des 18. Jahrhunderts 1688–1789),* 2 volumes. Stuttgart: Metzler, 1978.

Wohlleben, Joachim. *Goethe als Journalist und Essayist.* Frankfurt a. M. and Berne: Lang, 1981.

Wolff, Hans M. *Die Weltanschauung der deutschen Aufklärung in geschichtlicher Entwicklung,* 2nd edition, ed. Karl S. Guthke. Berne and Munich, 1963.

Wolffheim, Hans. "Der Essay als Kunstform." *Festgruß für Hans Pyritz.* Special Issue of *Euphorion* (1955), 27–30.

Die Zukunft der Aufklärung. Ed. Jörn Rüsen, Eberhard Lämmert, and Peter Glotz. Frankfurt a. M.: Suhrkamp, 1988.

INDEX

ABBT, THOMAS, 173, 240, 317–18; view of audience, 98

Accountability, 72, 78, 81, 314

Action: communicative, 51–53, 314; extension of self- knowledge, 217; Habermasean categories of, 48–49

ADDISON, JOSEPH, 136, 191

ADORNO, THEODOR W., 144, 320; definition of the essay, 28, 32, 44–47, 53–56, 58–59; interpretation of Enlightenment, 66–70, 75–76, 80, 86–87, 88 n.3. Works: *Dialektik der Aufklärung*, 66–70, 76, 80; *Erziehung zur Mündigkeit*, 75–76

Aesthetic theory: continuity of, 142–64, 165 n.6. *See also* style; stylistics

Age of Reason, 3, 23; is age of essay writing, 317. *See also* Enlightenment

Amaliens Erholungsstunden, 253

AMTHOR, CHRISTOPH HEINRICH, 138

ARNDT, JOHANNES, 108

Ancients and moderns, 267–68, 271

Anthropology, 79–85, 138, 179, 250; and Enlightenment, 303; moral, 85; pragmatic, 83–84; relationship to philosophy, 79. See also *Galant homme*; Gallantry; *Honnête homme*

ARCHENHOLTZ, HEINRICH WILHELM VON, 108

ARISTOTLE, 48, 74, 130–37, 320

Athenaeum, 299–300

Attitude, authorial, 17–21, 30

Audience, 47; active involvement, 279–83, 291; and prose style, 142; awareness of, 19, 31; Leibniz's view of, 185–86; nature of, 112–16; reading public, 98–99; reform of, 184–89; select group, 249; size of, 158, 274

AUER, ANNEMARIE, 37

Author. *See* Writer

BACHMANN, DIETER, 29, 56, 59

BACON, SIR FRANCIS OF VERULAM, 30, 42–43, 66–67, 176–78, 195, 210, 317–19

BARNARD, FREDERICK M., 78

BASEDOW, JOHANN BERNHARD, 151, 240

BAUMGARTEN, ALEXANDER, 183

BAYLE, PIERRE, 8, 175, 177, 183, 317

BECKER, RUDOLPH ZACHARIAS, 103

BECKER-CANTARINO, BARBARA, 289

Belustigungen des Verstandes und Witzes, 190, 200–201, 204, 224

BENSE, MAX, 29, 43–45, 53, 56, 58, 147, 320

BENZEL-STERNAU (also BENTZEL), CHRISTIAN ERNST KARL GRAF VON, 72, 118–19

BERGER, BRUNO, 120–21, 173–75, 223, 230, 238, 257 n.23; definition of essay, 30–31; restrictive view of essay, 61 n.13

BERGHAHN, KLAUS, 124 n.13, 125 n.18

BERGK, JOHANN ADAM, 40, 106–7. Works: *Die Kunst, Bücher zu lesen*, 40

BERLEPSCH, EMILIA VON, 8, 53, 177, 264, 283, 287–92, 303, 316, 318. Works: *Über einige zum Glück der Ehe nothwendige Eigenschaften und Grundgesätze*, 177, 287–92, 316

Berlinische Monatsschrift, 230, 238

Die Berlinische privilegierte Zeitung, 223

BEYER, JOHANN RUDOLPH GOTTLIEB: on reading, 104–5, 123 n.3, 126 n.24. Works: *Über das Bücherlesen*, 104

Der Biedermann, 95, 111, 191

Bildung, 138. *See also* Cultivation; Education

BLACKALL, ERIC A., 130–38, 141–42

BÖCKMANN, PAUL, 201, 204

BODE, JOHANN JOACHIM CHRISTOPH, 176

BODMER, JOHANN JACOB, 130–31,

LINNAEUS, CARL VON, 275–76
LISCOW, CHRISTIAN, 35, 220, 318.
   Works: *Die Vortrefflichkeit der elenden Skribenten*, 35
Literature: as communicative act, 13, 314, 326 n.9; as event, ix, 18, 315, 323; as metaliterature, 2; as speech act, 17–19; communicative theory, 174; boundary literature, 20–24; didactic forms, 22; entails recontextualization as well as conceptualization, 22; expanded view of, 211; hermeneutic perplexity, 56; literary life, 94–101; marked by indeterminacy, 21; threshold works, 21, 280
LOCKE, JOHN, 8, 136
LOEN, JOHANN MICHAEL VON, 45, 195–98. Works: *Der redliche Mann am Hofe*, 195; *Die Schweitz im Jahre 1719 und 1724*, 45, 196–98
Love, 276–77, 291
LUKÁCS, GEORG, 29; definition of the essay, 45–46

Man Thinking, 276
MARTENS, LORNA: impasses of genre, 14, 22; questioning of, 20
MARTENS, WOLFGANG, 107, 191
MARTINI, FRITZ, 38, 214, 220
MATTENKLOTT, GERD, 105
MENDELSSOHN, MOSES, 161, 222, 238–40. Works: *Briefe über die Empfindungen*, 238; *Phädon oder über die Unsterblichkeit der Seele*, 238–40; *Über die Frage: was heißt aufklären?*, 238 *Der Mensch*, 117–18, 200, 210
MERCK, JOHANN HEINRICH, 175
Monats-Gespräche, 96, 139, 178, 303
MONTAIGNE, MICHEL EYQUEM DE, 30, 42–43, 74, 176–78, 191, 195, 215, 221, 250, 318–19
MONTESQUIEU, CHARLES DE SECONDAT, 8, 177, 317
Moral Weeklies, 95–96, 107–8, 111, 137, 141–42, 190–92, 195, 200, 209–10
MORGENSTERN, KARL, 97, 162–63. Works: *Plan im Lesen*, 97, 162
MORITZ, KARL PHILIPP, 175, 286
MÖSER, JUSTUS, 34, 228, 243
MOSER, FRIEDRICH CARL VON, 173
MORSON, GARY SAUL, 273, 280; boundaries of genre, 20–24, 29, 36, 55; threshold literature, 315; writer–text–reader model, 32

MÜLLER, ADAM, 8, 53, 64, 175, 191, 264, 298, 301–7, 318–19, 322. Works: *Vom Gespräch*, 164, 298, 302–7, 318
MÜLLER, JOHANNES, 62
Mündigkeit, 67–69, 72, 78, 231–33, 236. *See also* Accountability
MUNDT, THEODOR: individualistic style, 132–33, 135, 150–51, 163.

Neue Bibliothek der schönen Wissenschaften und der freyen Künste, 247, 249
Neue Beyträge zum Vergnügen des Verstandes und Witzes, 204
NEWMAN, CHARLES, post-modern era, 7–8, 23, 64 n.35
NEUKIRCH, BENJAMIN, gallant attitude and writing style, 139–40, 145–46, 157, 200. Works: *Anweisung zu Teutschen Briefen*, 139–40
NEUMEISTER, ERDMANN, 138
NICOLAI, FRIEDRICH, 99–100, 103, 155, 240. Works: *Das Leben und die Meinungen des Herrn Magisters Sebaldus Nothanker*, 99, 155
NIVELLE, ARMAND, 151, 165 m.6, 169 n.34
Der nordische Aufseher, 102, 120, 210
NEUGEBAUER, WILHELM EHRENFRIED, 131

Objectivity, 301
Olla Potrida, 101
OVERBECK, J. D., 204. Works: *Was ein großer Kopf sey?*, 203; *Yahoonoology*, 204

Paradox, 300
PASCAL, BLAISE, 250
Der Patriot, 111, 141
Perfectibility, 67, 79, 111–12, 116, 127 n.27, 216, 223, 275–76, 303; as human destiny, 74, 82; enlightenment as means of, 79; relationship of gallantry to, 138. *See also* Perfection
Perfection, 117, 216, 223; goal of enlightenment, 72, 74; related to happiness, 81. *See also* Perfectibility *Der Philosoph für die Welt*, 247–48
Philosopher, as essayist, 229–40
Philosophy, nature of, 81
PICHLER, CAROLINE, xi, 264, 283
PITSCHEL, THEODOR LEBRECHT, xi, 7,

fessional, 134; women, xi, 253–54, 264,
283–84, 286–98
Writing: as communicative act, 92 n.34; as
creative process, 2–3, 6, 23, 314; classical, 162–64, 188; complement to thinking and reading, 110–16; epistle, 120–21;
essayistic, 73, 159–60, 174, 176, 222,
248, 286, 315, 321; marked by accents
of meaning, 321. *See also* Prose; Reading

ZACHARIAE, JUST FRIEDRICH WIL-
HELM, 190, 201
ZIMMERMANN, JOHANN GEORG, 173